Indian Cooking

by Monisha Bharadwaj

A Wiley Brand

Indian Cooking For Dummies®

Published by: **John Wiley & Sons, Inc.,** 111 River Street, Hoboken, NJ 07030-5774, www.wiley.com

Copyright © 2021 by John Wiley & Sons, Inc., Hoboken, New Jersey

Published simultaneously in Canada

For general information on our other products and services, please contact our Customer Care Department within the U.S. at 877-762-2974, outside the U.S. at 317-572-3993, or fax 317-572-4002. For technical support, please visit https://hub.wiley.com/community/support/dummies.

Wiley publishes in a variety of print and electronic formats and by print-on-demand. Some material included with standard print versions of this book may not be included in e-books or in print-on-demand. If this book refers to media such as a CD or DVD that is not included in the version you purchased, you may download this material at http://booksupport.wiley.com. For more information about Wiley products, visit www.wiley.com.

Library of Congress Control Number: 2021942647

ISBN 978-1-119-79661-9 (pbk); ISBN 978-1-119-79666-4 (ebk); ISBN 978-1-119-79667-1 (ebk)

SKY10028486_072721

Contents at a Glance

Introduction 1

Part 1: Getting Started with Indian Cooking 7
CHAPTER 1: Exploring India through Food 9
CHAPTER 2: Embracing India's Love of Vegetables 23
CHAPTER 3: Tools of the Trade 33
CHAPTER 4: Shopping for Essential Ingredients 45

Part 2: Getting Comfortable in the Kitchen 65
CHAPTER 5: Common Indian Kitchen Techniques 67
CHAPTER 6: Using Staple Ingredients in Indian Dishes 83
CHAPTER 7: Spices Make Indian Dishes Nice 111
CHAPTER 8: Building a Curry 123
CHAPTER 9: Bringing It All Together in a Deliciously Healthy Meal .. 153

Part 3: Serving Up Indian Specialties 171
CHAPTER 10: Lovely Lamb, Beef, and Pork Dishes 173
CHAPTER 11: Scrumptious Poultry Dishes 189
CHAPTER 12: Delish Fish and Seafood Dishes 203
CHAPTER 13: Vegetables Cooked the Indian Way 217
CHAPTER 14: Rice with a Bit of Anything 235
CHAPTER 15: Can't-Be-Beat Lentils and Beans 249
CHAPTER 16: Exotic Egg Dishes 263

Part 4: Whipping Up Breads, Chutneys, and Tasty Treats 271
CHAPTER 17: Dishes to Start the Day 273
CHAPTER 18: Tasty Snacks and Appetizers 285
CHAPTER 19: No-Bake Breads 301
CHAPTER 20: Chutneys and Salads 311
CHAPTER 21: Desserts and Drinks 323

Part 5: The Part of Tens 335

CHAPTER 22: Ten Time-Saving Tips for the Kitchen 337

CHAPTER 23: Ten Myths about Indian Food 343

CHAPTER 24: Ten Tips on Indian Table Etiquette 349

Appendix: Metric Conversion Guide 355

Index 359

Recipes at a Glance

Basics

↺ Boiled Rice (Chaval), Absorption Method 88
↺ Boiled Rice (Chaval), Draining Method 89
↺ Ginger-Garlic Paste (Adrak Lahsun) 92

Spice Blends

↺ Chaat Masala (Finishing Mix for Sprinkling over Snacks) 121
↺ Garam Masala (North Indian Spice Blend) 118
↺ Sambhar Powder (South Indian Spice Blend) 119
↺ Tandoori Masala (Rub for Grilled Foods) 120

Breakfasts

↺ Aam aur Kaju ki Smoothie (Mango and Cashew Smoothie) 283
↺ Baida Bhurji (Spicy Scrambled Eggs) 277
↺ Batata Bhaji (Spiced Yellow Potatoes) 282
↺ Chile Toast (Cheese Toast with Spices) 276
↺ Dosa (Fermented Rice and Lentil Crêpes) 279
↺ Masala Omelet (Omelet with Spices) 274
↺ Poha (Spiced Flaked Rice) 281
↺ Rava Utappam (Semolina Pancakes) 278
↺ Upma (Savory Semolina Cake) 275

Appetizers

Chicken Tikka (Spicy Chicken Bites) 288
Gosht ke Kebab (Mini Lamb or Beef Skewers with Mint) 289
↺ Onion Bhajia (Savory Onion Fritters) 286
↺ Pakora (Savory Mixed Vegetable Fritters) 287
↺ Vegetable Samosas (Vegetable and Pastry Parcels) 290

Snacks

Amritsari Fish (Spiced Fish Fingers in a Gram-Flour Crust) 300
↺ Bombay Sandwich (Sandwich with Chutney, Vegetables, and Cheese) 297
↺ Chivda (Hot, Savory, and Sweet Mix of Grains, Seeds, and Nuts) 293
↺ Dahi Vada (Lentil Fritters in Yogurt) 294
Macchi ke Cutlet (Spiced Fishcakes) 298
↺ Pav Bhaji (Crushed Vegetable Curry with Bread Rolls) 296
↺ Shakarkand Chaat (Sweet Potatoes with Nuts and Yogurt) 299
↺ Shankarpali (Crisp, Sweet Pastry Diamonds) 292

Chutneys

☙ Aam ki Launji (Sweet-and-Sour Mango Chutney) 318

☙ Haldi Gajar Mirchi ka Achaar (Fresh Carrot, Turmeric, Ginger,
     and Chile Pickle) 162

☙ Hari Chutney (Cilantro and Peanut Chutney) 317

☙ Khajur Imli ki Chutney (Sweet-and-Sour Date and Tamarind Chutney) 313

☙ Lasnechi Chutney (Dry Hot, Sour, Sweet Garlic, Chile, and
     Coconut Chutney) 163

☙ Pudine aur Pyaz ki Chutney (Mint and Onion Chutney) 314

☙ Thengai Chutney (Coconut and Tender Mango Chutney) 315

Salads

☙ Gujarati Sambharo (Cabbage and Carrot Salad) 321

☙ Kachumber (Onion, Cucumber, Tomato, and Carrot Salad) 320

☙ Kheere Tamater ka Raita (Cucumber and Tomato Salad with Yogurt) 319

Main Dishes

☙ Aloo Gobi (North Indian Potatoes with Cauliflower) 220

☙ Aloo Mutter (Pea and Potato Curry) 233

☙ Anda Mutter ki Hari Curry (Egg and Peas Green Curry) 270

☙ Baghara Baingan (Sweet-and-Sour Eggplant Curry) 222

☙ Baida Masala (North Indian Egg Curry) 264

☙ Baingan ka Bharta (Fire-Roasted Eggplant with Spices) 218

Bangda Ghassi (Mackerel Curry with Tamarind) 208

☙ Beans Upkari (French Green Beans with Chile and Coconut) 230

Beef Vindaloo (Sour Hot Goan Curry) 183

Bengali Chicken Korma (Chicken Curry with Cream) 199

☙ Bharvan Bhindi (Okra Stuffed with Spices) 228

Bhuna Gosht (Brown Lamb Curry) 180

☙ Bombay Anda Curry (Smooth Egg and Tomato Curry) 266

☙ Carrot Poriyal (Carrots Cooked with Mustard Seeds an Coconut) 227

☙ Channa Masala (Chickpea Curry) 253

☙ Channa Pulao (Brown Rice with Chickpeas) 246

Chicken 65 (Indo Chinese Chicken) 201

Chicken Biryani (Festive One-Pot Chicken and Rice) 239

Chicken Madras (Chicken Curry with Fennel) 197

Chicken Tikka Masala (Chicken Curry with Spices) 194

Coorgi-Style Pandi Curry (Pork Curry with Vinegar) 178

☙ Dal Dhokli (Lentil Stew with Flour Dumplings) 257

☙ Dal Makhani (Creamy Black Beans with Garlic) 252

Dhabe ka Kheema (Spicy Ground Lamb or Beef) 179

☾ Egg Biryani (South Indian Spiced Rice with Eggs) 243

☾ Egg Kurma (South Indian Egg Curry) 265

☾ Fanshachi Bhaji (Curried Young Jackfruit) 229

Goan Fish Curry (Fish Curry with Coriander Seeds and Coconut) 211

Gosht ka Dalcha (Lamb and Lentil Curry) 177

Hara Gosht (Lamb in a Green Herby Curry) 185

☾ Jeera Pulao (Cumin-Flavored Rice) 237

Jhinga Masala (North Indian Shrimp Curry) 214

Jhinga Pulao (Spiced Rice with Shrimp) 242

☾ Kaddu ki Subzi (Sweet-and-Sour Pumpkin) 231

☾ Kadhi (Chickpea Flour and Yogurt Curry) 260

Karahi Murgh (Chicken Curry with Tomatoes) 193

☾ Kashmiri Pulao (Rice with Mushrooms, Dried Fruit, Nuts, an Spices) 238

Kerala Duck Mappas (Duck Curry with Coconut Milk and Pepper) 198

☾ Kerala Egg Roast (Egg and Curry Leaf Curry) 267

☾ Kerala Vegetable Curry (Mixed Vegetable Curry with Coconu Milk) 223

Kheema Pulao (Spiced Rice with Ground Meat) 244

Khekda Masaledaar (Crab Curry with Pepper) 207

☾ Khichdi (Warming Rice and Lentil Stew) 247

☾ Kobichi Bhaji (Cabbage with Peas and Turmeric) 221

Kofta Curry (Lamb or Beef Meatball Curry) 182

Kolmbi Fry (Fried Spiced Shrimp) 209

Kolmbichi Kadhi (Shrimp Curry with Coconut Milk) 206

Kombdi Batata (Chicken and Potato Curry) 192

Konkani Mutton (Lamb Curry with Cloves, Pepper, and Coconut) 181

Kube Sukke (Clams in a Coconut Crust) 213

Lobster Kalvan (Lobster Curry) 216

Malabar Beef Roast (Deep, Dark Beef with Spices) 187

Malvani Kombdi (Chicken and Coconut Curry) 196

Masala Gosht (North Indian Lamb Curry) 175

☾ Masoor Dal (Brown Lentils with Coconut Milk) 259

Meen Moilee (Salmon Curry with Mustard Seeds) 210

☾ Methi Shakarkand (Fresh Fenugreek with Sweet Potatoes) 226

☾ Mung Usal (Sprouted Mung Beans with Turmeric) 261

Murgh Makhani (Butter Chicken) 191

Murgh Malaiwala (Chicken in a Creamy Cashew Nut and Saffron Curry) 190

☾ Palak Paneer (Spinach with Paneer) 225

☾ Palak Pappu (South Indian Spinach Dal) 256

☺ Paneer Makkai Simla Mirch (Paneer with Corn and Capsicum) 224
☺ Paneer Pulao (Aromatic Rice with Indian Cottage Cheese) 241
☺ Papeta Par Eeda (Egg and Potato Fry) 269
Prawn Patia (Sweet and Sour Shrimp Curry) 215
☺ Rajma Masala (Red Bean Curry) 254
Saag Murgh (Chicken Curry with Spinach) 200
Safed Gosht (Lamb in a Coconut and Cashew Nut Curry) 186
Sali Marghi (Chicken Curry with Apricots) 195
☺ Sambhar (South Indian Lentil Stew) 255
Seyal Teevan (Lamb Chop Curry with Cardamom) 184
☺ Shahi Baida Korma (Egg Curry with Cashew Nuts an Fenugreek) 268
☺ Shepuchi Bhaji (Dill with Mung Lentils) 232
☺ Sunhera Pulao (Golden Turmeric Rice) 245
☺ Tarka Dal (Spiced Lentils) 251
Tilapia Fry (Spicy Fried Fish) 205

Breads
☺ Chapati or Roti (Flatbread) 302
☺ Chilla (Gram-Flour Pancakes) 310
☺ Gobi Paratha (Cauliflower-Stuffed Bread) 306
☺ Naan (Leavened Oven-Baked Bread) 303
☺ Neer Dosa (South Indian Rice Crêpes) 309
☺ Paratha (Layered Bread) 304
☺ Poori (Festive Fried Bread) 305
☺ Thepla (Fenugreek Bread) 308

Desserts
☺ Aam ka Custard (Mango Custard with Tropical Fruit) 327
☺ Badam ke Laddoo (Almond Fudge) 329
☺ Chaval aur Narial ki Kheer (Rice and Coconut Pudding) 324
☺ Chibuda Hashale (Melon and Coconut Milk Pudding) 328
☺ Kesar Kulfi (Rich Saffron Ice Cream) 325
☺ Sooji ka Halva (Warm Semolina and Raisin Pudding) 326

Drinks
☺ Aam ki Lassi (Mango and Yogurt Drink) 330
☺ Elaichi Kapi (Pulled Coffee with Cardamom and Brown Sugar) 333
☺ Masala Chai (Spiced Tea) 331

Table of Contents

INTRODUCTION 1

About This Book 1

Foolish Assumptions 4

Icons Used in This Book 4

Beyond the Book 4

Where to Go from Here 5

PART 1: GETTING STARTED WITH INDIAN COOKING 7

CHAPTER 1: Exploring India through Food 9

The Early Use of Spices 10

How spices traveled outside India 10

The influences that make Indian cooking so diverse 11

The North: Of Conquest, Kings, and Empire 12

Delhi: The Mughals and Islamic influences 12

The foothills of the Himalayas: Basmati rice 13

Punjab and the Partition of India 13

Kashmir and its saffron fields 14

The East: Tea Plantations, Tempting Sweets, and Treasures
of the Sea 15

Tea and the British 15

Kolkata and Bengali sweets 16

Odisha and fish with everything 16

The South: Of Temples, Coconut Groves, and Spice Routes 17

Sacred foods 17

Goa and the Portuguese influence 17

Kerala and its Hindu, Christian, and Muslim cooking 18

Tamil Nadu temples and their fragrant cuisines 19

The West: A Melting Pot 19

Mumbai and the Parsi influence 19

Pune and the Sindhi influence 20

Konkan's golden coastlines 20

Gujarat and its extravagant thalis 20

CHAPTER 2: Embracing India's Love of Vegetables 23

Putting Together Vegetarian and Vegan Meals 24

Bringing Ayurvedic Wisdom to Your Kitchen 26

Following eight easy rules of an Ayurvedic diet 27

Identifying the six tastes and sensations 29

Eating with the seasons 31

CHAPTER 3: **Tools of the Trade** 33

Making Prep Work Easy with the Right Utensils 33
Knives 34
Cutting boards 34
Other utensils. 35
Knowing Which Pots, Pans, and Griddles the Experts Use 37
Karahi 37
Tava 38
Dosa pan. 38
Pressure cookers. 38
Handling Spices like a Pro 40
A spice tin for storing spices 41
Tools for blending and crushing spices .42

CHAPTER 4: **Shopping for Essential Ingredients** 45

Diving into Dry Goods. 45
Spices 46
Grains 48
Nuts 49
Flavorings 49
Beans. 50
Everything else. 50
Yes, We Can!: Stocking Up on Canned Goods 52
Tomatoes 52
Coconut milk and coconut powder. 53
Beans. 53
Mango puree 54
Free-Range Culture: Shopping for Dairy and Eggs 54
Yogurt 54
Cream 55
Paneer. 55
Eggs 56
Knowing Which Fats and Oils You Need 56
To ghee or not to ghee. 56
Must-have oils for an Indian kitchen 57
Drop the Beet: Loading Up on Produce. 58
Aromatics and herbs: Veggies with a punch 58
Eggplants 59
Potatoes 60
Mangoes 61
Shopping for Meat and Poultry. 62

PART 2: GETTING COMFORTABLE IN THE KITCHEN 65

CHAPTER 5: **Common Indian Kitchen Techniques** 67

Chopping Techniques..68

    Chopping, mincing, and dicing 68

    Peeling..69

    Slicing 69

    Butterflying shrimp 71

Marinating Meats and Other Foods 72

    How long to marinate...................................73

    How to build an Indian marinade 74

Sweating Over a Hot Tandoori Oven, er, Stove................76

    Dum: All hot and steamy 77

    Tarka: Don't lose your temper, use it 77

    Bhuna: It's bhuna long time............................79

    Talna: Off to a frying start 80

    Dhungar: A practi-coal solution........................81

CHAPTER 6: **Using Staple Ingredients in Indian Dishes**.......... 83

Focusing on Ingredients.......................................84

    Standardizing recipes..................................84

    Measuring ingredients 85

The Long and Short of Cooking Rice..........................86

Making and Storing Ginger-Garlic Paste 90

    Preparing the ginger...................................90

    Preparing the garlic...................................90

    Making the paste.......................................91

Happy Sour: Using Tamarind...................................93

    Identifying the various forms of tamarind..............93

    Deseeding and making tamarind pulp.....................94

    Trying tamarind in your Indian cooking.................95

You Say To-May-To, I Say To-Mah-To: Using Fresh,
Canned, or Paste 95

    Fresh tomatoes 95

    Canned tomatoes 96

    Tomato paste...97

    Passata 97

Loving Lentils..97

    Cooking lentils 98

    Knowing the correct texture and consistency............99

I'm Not Crying, You're Crying: Working with Onions 100

    Knowing which type to use 100

    Slicing or dicing 100

    Cooking onions for curries.............................102

Drop It Like It's Hot: Cooking with Chilies 103
How to choose the right chile 103
How to use chilies 104
Going Cuckoo for Coconut. 106
Fresh coconut. 106
Desiccated coconut 107
Coconut milk 107
Making and Using Paneer 108
How to make paneer. 108
How to cook with paneer 109

CHAPTER 7: **Spices Make Indian Dishes Nice**. 111
We Seed to Talk: Using Whole Spice Seeds 112
Frying whole spices in oil 112
Toasting whole spices 113
Ground Sterling: Working with Ground Spices 114
Cooking ground spices at the start. 114
At a later stage during the cooking. 115
At the end of cooking 115
Creating a Series of Blends 117

CHAPTER 8: **Building a Curry**. 123
Defining Curry: What It is and What It Isn't .124
Curry sauce. 124
Curry powder 124
Curry leaves 126
First Things First: Choosing a Pan and Using the Right Oil 126
Paying Attention to the Order in Which Ingredients Are
Added to the Pan. 127
Building Different Kinds of Curries. 128
Building a North Indian curry 128
Building a South Indian curry 135
Turning Up the Heat 137
Chilies 138
Pepper. 138
Mustard seeds 139
Adding Depth to Your Curry. 139
Achieving the Right Color and Consistency .141
Color 141
Consistency 144
Jazzing Up the Look with Garnishes 147
Onions. 148
Cilantro 148
Mint 148

Lemon and lime 148
Fresh chilies 149
Ginger 149
Salad vegetables 149
Nuts and dried fruit 149
Spices and dried herbs 150
Boiled eggs 150
Cream, butter and yogurt 150
Banana leaves 151

CHAPTER 9: Bringing It All Together in a Deliciously Healthy Meal 153
Off the Menu: Restaurant versus Home Cooking 154
Classifying foods by heat levels 154
Aiming for the broadest audience 154
Using too much fat 155
Using too much salt 155
Charging an arm and a leg 155
Sticking to a limited list of ingredients 155
Taking the Worry out of Curry 156
Eating the rainbow 156
Talking texture 157
Playing with temperature 159
Heating it up 160
Tickling your palate 164
Putting Together Indian Meals 167
Composing a weeknight dinner 168
Creating an Indian entertaining menu 168
Going all out: Creating a thali 169

PART 3: SERVING UP INDIAN SPECIALTIES 171

CHAPTER 10: Lovely Lamb, Beef, and Pork Dishes 173

CHAPTER 11: Scrumptious Poultry Dishes 189

CHAPTER 12: Delish Fish and Seafood Dishes 203

CHAPTER 13: Vegetables Cooked the Indian Way 217

CHAPTER 14: Rice with a Bit of Anything 235

CHAPTER 15: Can't-Be-Beat Lentils and Beans 249

CHAPTER 16: Exotic Egg Dishes 263

PART 4: WHIPPING UP BREADS, CHUTNEYS, AND TASTY TREATS 271

CHAPTER 17: Dishes to Start the Day 273

CHAPTER 18: Tasty Snacks and Appetizers 285

CHAPTER 19: No-Bake Breads 301

CHAPTER 20: Chutneys and Salads 311

CHAPTER 21: Desserts and Drinks 323

PART 5: THE PART OF TENS 335

CHAPTER 22: Ten Time-Saving Tips for the Kitchen 337
- Prepare Your Ingredients Ahead of Time 338
- Store Your Spices Efficiently 338
- Cook in Batches 338
- Chop Ingredients Evenly 339
- Freeze Basic Curry Sauces 339
- Figure Out the Proper Prep Order 340
- Reduce Food Waste 340
- Keep Your Compost Pail Nearby 341
- Use a Pressure Cooker or Instant Pot 341
- Choose the Right Size Pan and Use a Lid 342

CHAPTER 23: Ten Myths about Indian Food 343
- All Indian Food Is Extremely Hot 344
- Popadams and Dips Are Eaten at the Start of a Meal 344
- All Indian Food Is Curry 345
- Indian Food Is Unhealthy 345
- All Indian Bread Is Naan 346
- Adding Curry Powder Makes a Dish Indian 346
- Eating with Your Fingers Is Unhygienic 347
- Indians Eat Food off Leaves and Not Plates 347
- All Indian Food Is Cooked in Ghee 347
- Indian Food Is Mainly Vegetarian 348

CHAPTER 24: Ten Tips on Indian Table Etiquette 349
- Save Room for Seconds and Thirds 350
- Eat with Your Right Hand 350
- Don't Double-Dip 350
- Show Appreciation to Your Host 351

Wash Your Hands 352
Don't Lick Your Fingers 352
Mix Your Food Intentionally. 353
Clean Your Plate 353
Bring Flowers instead of Food for Your Host 354
Don't Drink Alcohol with Your Dinner Unless You're Offered It 354

APPENDIX: METRIC CONVERSION GUIDE 355

INDEX 359

Introduction

If you've eaten some amazing Indian food and you now want to re-create it in your own kitchen, this is the book for you! You've probably done some research and maybe you don't know where to begin — everything looks so complicated!

Indian cooking *is* complex. After all, the country is not just vast but also very diverse, with numerous languages, religious beliefs, geographical differences, and social and cultural practices. The key to understanding where to begin is to *respect* this diversity — and to begin slowly and simply.

You don't need to create a feast the first time you try to cook an Indian meal. You don't need to pound your own spices every time you cook — store-bought spices, when stored properly, are fine to use. The availability of common ingredients makes Indian cooking easier than ever before!

Cooking Indian food is both a science and an art. You use your senses to smell the spices, your ears to hear them pop, and your eyes to see the colors change. You need the confidence to throw in the ginger and garlic at the right time and to get the consistency of curry pastes just right. In this book, I help you build that confidence so that you'll be up to cooking your Indian dinner, home style, in no time at all.

About This Book

Think of this book as my voice in your kitchen as we create the perfect Indian meal together. I show you how to master the basic techniques, use spices for balance and flavor, and stock your pantry with key ingredients that you may never have cooked with before. I take you on a culinary tour of India, which will help you understand why I talk about regional differences throughout this book.

In this book, you learn to cook rice perfectly and to make Indian breads, even one that takes just 20 minutes from start to finish! With this book by your side, you'll feel confident about how to put the building blocks of a curry together to make one that's full of depth of flavor and not just heat. I also show you how to cook a range of Indian vegetarian dishes that can be served as main meals. I've included recipes that I cook at home — family favorites that will hopefully become favorites of yours, too. These 125 recipes will help you put together various menus — from a weeknight dinner to an extravagant thali meal for your friends, where lots of little dishes make up a feast. I include recipes for breakfasts, chutneys, snacks, and desserts, giving you lots of inspiration to embrace Indian food beyond what you'd expect to see in a restaurant.

This book is a reference, which means you don't have to read it from beginning to end and you don't have to commit it to memory. Instead, you can dip into these pages over and over again to find the information you need.

Here are a few suggestions for getting the most out of the recipes in this book:

>> **Read each recipe from top to bottom before you make your grocery list to ensure you have all the ingredients you need.**

>> **Keep a well-stocked pantry so you don't need to buy every ingredient every time you cook.** You don't need a long list of spices — my recipes call for some key ones that you've probably heard of and just a few that you may not have.

>> **Prepare all the ingredients in the recipe before you begin cooking.** You may find that you need tamarind pulp or chopped herbs and you'll be more efficient and feel more confident if you have got it all ready before you turn on the heat.

>> **Don't be afraid to personalize the recipes and make them your own.** Standardization of recipes is not considered essential in India. There is a good measure of *andaz* (chef's intuition). This intuition comes with confidence, and the more you cook the recipes, the easier you'll find it to tweak them to your taste. I eat and write recipes with a medium level of heat, but if you prefer more or less heat, feel free to increase or decrease the amount of chile in a recipe.

>> **Remember that Indian meals have three to four dishes.** I've written most of the recipes for three to four people, but you may think there isn't enough to make a meal. Even if the quantities in each recipe *look* like they may not be enough, trust me — after you've combined a few items in a menu, you'll have plenty of food to fill the number of people the recipe indicates.

>> **Scale a recipe up if you're cooking for more people than the recipe feeds.** As a guide, if you're doubling a recipe, go double with the spices, too. Anywhere beyond doubling, I recommend adding *half* the quantity of spices for each double up. So, for example, if I were tripling a recipe, I would add 2½ times the amounts of all the spices instead of 3 times. You may need to adjust

the levels a bit to suit your own taste (a pinch more chile powder or aromatic garam masala perhaps).

>> **Don't be afraid to substitute ingredients with what's available in your area.** Some ingredients found in the West are different from those found in India, so in writing the recipes, I adapted them to achieve the flavor I was after. For example, the tomatoes I can get hold of for most of the year where I live, in England, are pale and watery — nothing like the red, juicy ones grown in tropical India. So, I use tomato paste or canned tomatoes for their intense color and flavor. If you can't find an ingredient I mention, you can substitute it — just choose like for like. If the recipe calls for small mung lentils, for example, you could swap them for small red lentils, which are roughly the same size, but don't use large beans because they'll give a different taste and texture. Don't worry, substituting ingredients will become easier with experience.

>> **Make sure you have the right equipment.** Heavy frying pans and sauce-pans (see Chapter 3) will distribute heat evenly and won't burn the food on the bottom.

>> **Pay special attention to your spices.** Spices are pillars of Indian cooking.

>> **Remember that all temperatures are Fahrenheit.** Refer to the Appendix for information about converting temperatures to Celsius.

>> **If you're looking for a vegetarian recipe, look for the tomato icon (🍅).** All vegetarian recipes are marked with the tomato icon in the Recipes in This Chapter lists, as well as in the Recipes in This Book section, after the Table of Contents.

I provide the names of the recipes in the language of the region they come from. I also include rough English translations of the recipe titles, but just keep in mind that it's difficult for these translations to completely reflect the subtle nuances of geography and social practice.

I hope that you'll try some of the unfamiliar recipes and see how it easy it is to prepare them and how delicious they are!

One last thing to note: Within this book, you may note that some web addresses break across two lines of text. If you're reading this book in print and want to visit one of these web pages, simply key in the web address exactly as it's noted in the text, pretending as though the line break doesn't exist. If you're reading this as an e-book, you've got it easy — just click the web address to be taken directly to the web page.

Foolish Assumptions

In writing this book, I made a few assumptions about you, the reader:

>> You've tasted Indian food, and you want to make it yourself.

>> You have basic knowledge of preparing ingredients and cooking.

>> You're adventurous — you're excited to learn some new skills, work with new ingredients, and get to know a cuisine like you've never known it before!

Icons Used in This Book

Throughout the book, you see icons in the margin. Here's what each icon means:

TIP

The Tip icon marks information that can save you time, effort, and money, as well as give you alternative ways of preparing the same recipe.

REMEMBER

I want you to become a confident Indian cook, which means I need you to pay special attention to some techniques that may be new to you. This information is so important that I want you to remember it. When that happens, I flag it with the Remember icon.

WARNING

Think of the Warning icon as a big flashing sign telling you be careful. I use it when I think there's a potential threat of getting something wrong.

CULTURAL WISDOM

So much about Indian food is context. I use the Cultural Wisdom icon when I want to point you to an interesting historical or cultural fact.

Beyond the Book

In addition to what you're reading right now, this product comes with a free access-anywhere Cheat Sheet that includes tips on how to buy key Indian ingredients such as basmati rice, tamarind, and lentils; Indian cooking tools and techniques; and how to build a curry. To get this Cheat Sheet, go to www.dummies.com and type **Indian Cooking For Dummies Cheat Sheet** in the Search box.

Where to Go from Here

If this is your first attempt at cooking Indian food, start simply and read Part 2, which is all about common techniques, how to use Indian ingredients (including spices), how to build a curry, and how to bring a meal together. If you're a bit of a pro at Indian cooking already, head straight for the recipes in Parts 3 and 4. Here, you find everything you need to plan your menu — from curries to rice, breads, sides, and desserts. Regardless of your experience, I suggest you read the bit about how to use spices in Chapter 8 for ideas on how to add more depth and flavor to your cooking.

I hope that this book will be your guide to exploring the many nuances of Indian cooking and will give the confidence to bring all those fabulously aromatic, spicy flavors to your own kitchen. Have fun!

1

Getting Started with Indian Cooking

Embrace India's love of veggies and explore Ayurvedic eating.

Discover the regions that make India's food so diverse.

Use the right tools to make your Indian cooking easy and fun.

Stock your kitchen with well-known Indian ingredients and learn about some new ones.

» **Understanding Islamic influences on North Indian cooking**

» **Exploring how India gave the world chai**

» **Identifying Christian influences that changed South Indian cooking**

» **Delving into the melting pot of Mumbai's cuisine**

Chapter **1**

Exploring India through Food

There is no single Indian cuisine. The more I travel through India in search of new recipes and ways of cooking (I've loved going on food trips for many years now), the more convinced I am that there is no other land as varied. India almost seems like it's several countries in one.

If you've traveled to India, you know what I mean. The food of the North and the South (and I'm bunching vast land masses here) vary hugely and then there are countless more smaller regions to consider, too.

In this chapter, I take you on a journey through India so you can see what influences this diversity.

The Early Use of Spices

Records of excavations of early civilizations suggest that my ancestors were eating grains and spices from as far back as 3000 BCE. Medical texts estimated to be from the first and second centuries mention spices and herbs for healing purposes.

How spices traveled outside India

Early Europeans imported spices from India to use in food and incense. Around 2,500 years ago, the Arabs controlled the trade. Spices could change hands a dozen times between their source and Europe, soaring in value with each transaction, and the Arabs were the greatest of the middlemen. Eager to keep it that way, they did everything possible to confuse consumers about the origins, some stories claiming that spices grew on remote mountains in Arabia!

Pepper was prized and there was even a Guild of Pepperers in London, the records of which date back to 1180. They bought and sold spices and also controlled the quality. Things changed in the 15th century when the Portuguese explorer Vasco da Gama discovered the route to India by navigating around the Cape of Good Hope. Direct trade routes between Europe and the East opened, and spices such as cinnamon, pepper, and cloves became more commonplace in Western markets.

Later, when the British started the East India Company, its officers began sending Indian recipes in letters back home. Slowly, suburban English housewives began to cook curries in their homes. There was of course, a lack of authentic ingredients and cookware: Tender green mangoes were replaced with tart English apples, and curries that were traditionally thickened with onion paste began to be made with a roux of flour and butter. Basically, they started to make a curry and ended up with apple pie.

To compensate for the lack of all the necessary spices, a convenient mix was created and became known as *curry powder*. Even today, curry powder is a generic blend that doesn't even hint at the complexity and variety of India's cooking.

REMEMBER

No self-respecting Indian cook uses curry powder. Instead, there are subtle regional spices blends in every part of the country that make each cuisine distinct.

Soon small Indian restaurants began to be seen in London, and in the last century, Indian sailors who had fled British ships due to terrible working conditions opened Indian takeout restaurants in the East End. Catering mainly to late pub-goers, they created a simplistic curry menu based on pungency. A fiery hot curry was vindaloo (actually a Goan–Portuguese curry), a Madras was medium (you can't find a Madras curry in India, let alone an area called Madras), and a korma was mild (a chile korma can be super spicy in India). Along the way, the popular curry known as chicken tikka masala was invented and caught the fancy of the British public; today it's one of the highest-selling ready meals.

Menus based on heat levels have thrived until present day, and people who have only eaten restaurant food believe it to be the real thing. In this book, I hope to show you how diverse Indian cooking really is and that heat is just *one* of the things to consider when creating your meal.

The influences that make Indian cooking so diverse

With so many regions, it's easy to be perplexed by the variety in Indian cooking. If I tell you that India is a vast country, you may reply that there are many other vast countries in the world. That's completely true, but none has a cuisine that changes every few miles. Here are the reasons Indian cooking is so diverse:

» **Climate:** You may think that all of India is a hot country because it's in a tropical part of the world, but there are many places in the country that are cold enough to experience snowfall. When we're in a hot place, we want to eat cooling foods, like ice cream. But it's India, so we'll talk about spices. Chilies contain a compound called *capsaicin* in their membranes; capsaicin is what makes them hot, but when we eat them, capsaicin also makes our blood vessels dilate and makes us sweat. Have you seen some people mopping their foreheads when eating a hot curry? Sweating helps us cool down, and that's why in hotter parts of India such as the South, which is nearer the equator, recipes have lots of chilies. You'll find milder curries spiced with pepper in the colder regions.

» **Geography:** In such a big country, eating local food and not paying for transport costs is definitely cheaper. Local recipes make the most of ingredients that grow close by, so you'll find coconut-based curries in the South and wheat breads in the North. The desert state of Rajasthan uses few fresh vegetables. The ones that do grow are dried and cooked with fiery spices to combat the searingly hot and dry climate. The availability of water is a big contributor to food diversity. In fertile regions that are fed by rivers and seas, more crops can grow. Similarly, there are a variety of soil conditions all over India — the rich black soil of Western India supports the growth of millet, whereas the alluvial soil of Punjab in the North is good for wheat.

» **Religious beliefs:** India is home to many major religious groups. Growing up in cosmopolitan Bombay (as Mumbai was then called), I had Hindu, Muslim, Jain, Christian, Jewish, and Buddhist friends, and we all celebrated each other's festivals and foods. We knew that some Hindu friends would be vegetarian, whereas others would eat meat but never beef. Our Muslim friends didn't eat pork. The Jains didn't eat root vegetables (their way of life is based on nonviolence, so killing of life forms by uprooting vegetables is prohibited). The cuisine of each community is based on these religious beliefs and meant that I was eating vastly diverse foods from when I was quite little.

>> **Trade, migration, and conquest:** I don't like to use the word *authentic* when speaking about Indian cooking. Although the cuisine is ancient, there are so many foreign influences that make it what it is today. (I explain more about this concept in the sections that follow.) At the heart of the cuisine is the world's need for India's spices and what each of the foreign powers brought with them in exchange. Pepper, the spice that started it all, is said to have changed the history of the world.

The North: Of Conquest, Kings, and Empire

If you travel through North India, you'll be struck by the beautiful Islamic and British architecture in many cities. Over many centuries, parts of this vast region of India have been ruled by the Greeks, the Mughals, and the British. The food you'll eat here is a result of these conquests, and perhaps Mughal cooking was the one that changed the culinary scene the most.

Delhi: The Mughals and Islamic influences

New Delhi is the modern capital of India. It has a cosmopolitan population of politicians, diplomats, and business officials, and the cuisine reflects the diversity of its past history. The streets are lined with stalls selling tandoor cooked foods, crisp samosas, and rich biryanis. As evening turns to dusk, the city's rich and famous dress up in their best silks to attend countless cocktail and dinner parties where tables creak with the best of Mughlai food.

This is a legacy left by the Mughal rulers who reigned over a large part of India from their capital Delhi from 1526, before the British took over. The cuisine was influenced by Persian and Turkish cooking as the rulers had ties with these cultures (the official language of the Mughal rulers was Persian). Today's korma, biryani, kofta, and kebab are a Mughal legacy and have become mainstream North Indian dishes. Traces of Mughlai cooking can be seen in some southern cities such as Hyderabad, where the Mughal Empire extended to.

Because of the Islamic origins of this style of cooking, and in reverence to the many Hindu courtiers that advised the kings, pork and beef dishes were not included. Indian restaurants offering Mughlai food today serve it up as a mild, delicious cuisine based on creamy or nut-based curries laced with dried fruits and rich spices, such as saffron and cardamom. Desserts are flavored with rose water and pistachios, and the recipes are typically richer than those found in other parts of India. This is an indulgent cuisine; in India, it's seen as a treat.

The foothills of the Himalayas: Basmati rice

Although India grows many different varieties of rice, basmati is the best known outside its country of origin. This beautiful, aromatic (the name *basmati* means "fragrant"), long-grained rice finds the climatic and soil conditions at the bases of the Himalayan mountain range ideal.

In India, basmati rice is considered special and is more expensive than other rice varieties. This is because it's a uniquely slender grain that cooks up fluffy, a trait that's valued in Indian cooking. To enhance this quality of cooking into separate grains, it's aged in warehouses where conditions such as light, air, temperature, and humidity are highly controlled. This results in each grain drying and forming a light skin, which can effectively seal the grain and help lock in the starch. The aging process can take anywhere from a year and a half to two years, the longer period yielding a more expensive rice.

When the British divided India at the time of independence in 1947, a part of this basmati-growing territory fell in the newly formed country of Pakistan. The cuisines of both countries celebrate this superlative grain in dishes such as biryani and pulao.

Punjab and the Partition of India

A number of Indians who live outside of India are Punjabi in origin. Around the time of Partition, when the state of Punjab got divided, Hindus living in the newly formed country of Pakistan and Muslims living in the Indian part of Punjab crossed borders, giving rise to one of the world's largest human migrations. The chaos, genocide, and displacement meant that some people fled to postwar Britain where jobs were available along with the opportunity to begin life anew.

They brought with them the unique food of the North — so much so that, today, in many parts of the world, when someone talks of Indian cooking, it's Punjabi food that they're referring to. Rich onion- and tomato-flavored curries, aloo gobi, saag paneer, or the delicious tandoori foods (cooked slowly in a clay oven called the *tandoor*), even the naans and parathas, all came from Punjab.

Ingredients that you would commonly find in a Punjabi kitchen are beans such as chickpeas and red kidney beans; black lentils; vegetables such as cauliflower, potatoes, peas, and turnips; and whole-wheat flour to make many kinds of breads. Punjab grows a lot of wheat and was once known as the granary of India.

There are many stories about how tandoori cooking came to be associated with India. It was already being used in undivided Punjab and, after Partition, found its way to the Indian side of the state. Because a tandoor is quite large and needs to be brought to the right temperature over some time (as you do with a barbecue), it was impractical for every Punjabi home to fire one up every evening. Communal tandoors were set up, with each village having one. People prepared their dough at home and took it to the village tandoor to have their rotis cooked. Eventually, commercial tandoori shops offered cooked breads to take away, and the communal tandoor became less of a ritual; today, only a few villages have one.

Kashmir and its saffron fields

Kashmir is one of the most beautiful states of India, resplendent with green valleys, flowing waterfalls, pine forests, and fruit-filled orchards. Due to its proximity to the Himalayas, Kashmir was the natural passage to India for many invaders. Its cuisine is, therefore, a mix of Indian, Persian, and Afghan styles.

The cooking of Kashmir is best showcased in the Wazawan or traditional Kashmiri feast. Even today, the master chefs of Kashmir are hailed as the descendants of the traditional chefs from Samarkand, the Wazas who came to India with the ruler Timur when he entered India in the 15th century. The royal Wazawan, comprising 36 courses, is a feast that few can get through. The meal begins with the ritual of washing the hands. Then the *tramis* (dishes filled with food) begin to arrive. The entrees are eaten with a sticky, dense variety of rice, which is prized. Much of the Wazawan is meat-based because this is a sign of affluence, but vegetarian dishes with lotus root or potatoes are also served.

Two distinct groups of people live in Kashmir — the Muslims and the Hindus — and their cuisines are also distinct. Spices such as dried ginger, ground fennel, and saffron, which grow in Kashmir, are used. This state is known for its quality saffron. The bright red stigma of the saffron crocus flower produces the spice, which is considered the most expensive one in the world. The cost is due to the labor-intensive harvesting process where around 200,000 stigmas need to be collected to make up a pound of saffron!

Saffron is even used in the tea in Kashmir. Kahwa is green tea flavored with saffron, spices, and nuts.

The East: Tea Plantations, Tempting Sweets, and Treasures of the Sea

The food of East India is also influenced by trade and colonization. Parts of this region share a border with neighboring China and Myanmar, so those influences are evident; you'll find ingredients such as pork, bamboo shoots, and soya beans. Don't be fooled into thinking that all the food here is gentle and mild — this region is also home to one of the world's most fiery chilies, the bhut jolokia, or ghost chile, which is so hot that one little taste and you yourself will become a ghost.

Tea and the British

Have you heard that India is one of the world's largest producers of tea? Much of it is drunk in house, so we have a nation of tea lovers. The industry as we know it today was introduced to India by the British. The Dutch had brought tea back to Europe from the 17th century, and the British considered it to be both a medicinal and a refreshing drink.

China was the only country growing tea at the time, and the British wanted to topple China's monopoly. So, they smuggled opium into China with the aim of exchanging it for tea and even got Bengali farmers to grow opium for them instead of staple crops needed to feed the masses. This did not impress the Chinese.

Early tea plantations were set up in the hilly regions of Assam from 1837. Soon after, tea estates mushroomed in Darjeeling. Both these eastern areas had perfect growing conditions, and even today, driving through the beautiful mountain roads, you can only admire the step plantations carved into every hillside.

In India, everything needs to be spiced with masala, so it isn't surprising that the brew was enhanced with ginger, cardamom, and fennel seeds to make Masala Chai (Spiced Tea; see Chapter 21). The Indian word for tea is *chai*, and I've heard it comes from the Chinese word *cha*. This delicious brew has caught the world's fancy (although strangely called chai tea, which translates as "tea tea," in the West) and seems to be a much-loved flavor in lattes and ice creams.

Kolkata and Bengali sweets

The mere mention of Indian sweets, and I see eyes being rolled and a muttered, "Too sweet for me." Most people not of Indian origin think of all Indian sweets as being cloying. But wait, have you ever had a box of chocolates? It's the same principle: Commercially available sweets have a lot of sugar to increase their shelf life. Indian homemade desserts are subtly flavored confections (see Chapter 21 for some easy and delicious recipes) bursting with fruit, milk, spice, and all things nice.

The eastern state of Bengal is particularly known for its sweet offerings. According to historians, the original name of the area was Gauda, derived from the Sanskrit word for jaggery, the sweet, thickened juice of sugarcane. Because this crop grew here in plenty, and old texts affirm this, it can be safely said that sweets were an important part of the cuisine for several centuries.

But Bengali sweets are unlike those of anywhere else in the country, mainly because many are made with cottage cheese as a base. I've heard that the Portuguese, who were in India before the British, brought the skill of cheese making to Bengal. The Hindus considered the curdling of milk taboo, but that didn't stop them from falling in love with the resulting delicacies. They quickly created recipes using fresh cottage cheese, spices, sugar, and nuts and produced pillowy-soft confections that melted in the mouth and left you wanting more. As these began to be mass produced in factories, the sugar content increased. Today, the gulab jamuns and ras malai you see on Indian restaurant menus have set the stage for everyone thinking that all Indian sweets are syrupy sweet.

Odisha and fish with everything

The state of Odisha enjoys a long coastline along the Bay of Bengal, so it's hardly surprising that fish features regularly on many dinner tables there. Lying on the east coast, Odisha nestles between the South and the North, so the food is inspired by both. The Northern part of Odisha, which borders Bengal, uses mustard paste in curries, whereas southern districts use tamarind, in keeping with South Indian traditions.

I don't hear people around the world talk much about Odia cooking, but this state has produced some of the best cooks of the East. They're known for a simple yet flavorful style, so they're in high demand in other parts of India. Many centuries ago, Odisha built maritime trade ties with Bali in Indonesia, and no doubt they also introduced Indian spices and curry pastes to that land.

The South: Of Temples, Coconut Groves, and Spice Routes

I think of the South as the states of Tamil Nadu, Kerala, Karnataka, Andhra Pradesh, Telangana, and Goa. Each has a unique cuisine, with a few similarities because of what crops grow there and the climate they share.

Sacred foods

All food is considered sacred in India. Nature is worshipped for its generosity, and many ingredients that come from the earth are revered. Wasting food is seen as an insult to the benevolence we are blessed with. Rice, for example, is seen as a staple that can feed countless people and is associated with abundance. Turmeric, the spice, has been valued for its healing properties for centuries and is used in rituals of cleansing and purification.

Invasions through land routes preceded those from sea routes, which were discovered much later. Southern India is surrounded by sea, so it saw relatively fewer foreign invasions, and the ones it did see came later than in the North. It's believed that the native culture of India, both religious and spiritual, is better preserved in the South. Because religion is so pervasive through every aspect of life in India, the food here is also influenced by these beliefs.

South India is well known for its many beautifully sculpted temples. On many of my travels to these temples, I've found, to my great delight, sculptures of ancient foods that were served to devotees who visited or given as offerings to the gods. Some of these carvings are 800 years old and seem like a novel way to preserve the region's culinary heritage!

Goa and the Portuguese influence

Although most people think of Goa as a beach holiday destination, its culinary history is fascinating for what it did to all food in India. As the demand for spices grew in the Western world, Europeans set out in search of the lands that grew them. The Portuguese explorer Vasco da Gama reached the Malabar Coast in Kerala in 1498 and opened the routes for the spice trade.

The Portuguese invaded Goa in 1510 and brought great changes to the cuisine and culture of the region. Many Hindus were converted to Christianity, and people who had earlier not eaten beef and pork began to cook these foods in their homes.

The Portuguese brought to India many ingredients that some people may think are native. Chilies, cashews, potatoes, and tomatoes forever changed the way recipes were prepared. Chilies replaced black pepper, and today, tons of chilies grow all over India, finding their way into almost every savory dish.

Leavened bread called *pao* is another Portuguese food that has endured over the centuries. It's eaten dipped into sweet tea for breakfast or with curries like the vindaloo, another Portuguese-inspired Goan dish. Made up of the Portuguese words for wine and garlic — *vino* and *alho*, respectively — the dish has been interpreted by Indian restaurants around the world as the hottest curry on the menu. People outside India may think of it as being one of the country's best loved curries, so predictable and constant is its presence on menus. In India, it's a tangy, hot curry spiced with chilies, vinegar, and spices that is eaten locally in Goa and is not ubiquitously popular all over the country.

Kerala and its Hindu, Christian, and Muslim cooking

Kerala, which means "land of coconuts," is one of the best places to visit if you love Indian food but want more than the usual tikka and korma. A small state with the hilly Western Ghats on one side and the azure Arabian Sea on the other, its cuisine is inspired by its 560 miles of backwaters. On the banks of these intricate waterways grow coconuts, bananas, and spices such as pepper and cardamom. The backwaters also provide Kerala's best delicacy, a silvery-black fish called *karimeen* or *pearlspot*, which is cooked with hot spices in a banana leaf. Coconut is used in some form (oil, milk, or flesh; grated, roasted, or powdered) in almost every recipe.

Foreign influences are apparent in its cuisine here, too. Judaism and Christianity both came to Kerala many centuries ago, and modern Syrian Christians (the majority Christian population in this state) believe that the Apostle Thomas came here and baptized their ancestors. Later, the Portuguese arrived and continued the conversions, this time to Catholicism.

Early spice routes were controlled by the Arabs. Kerala being the region of India where so many were grown, it's easy to understand how Islam was introduced to this region around the seventh century.

Today, the Kerala Christian table is laden with beef and pork stews, the Muslim one with biryanis and breads such as parottas, and the Hindu kitchen is fragrant with coconut and vegetable or fish curries.

Tamil Nadu temples and their fragrant cuisines

Hindus follow practices that appeal to them from Hinduism's various philosophies and beliefs and build a relationship with a favorite deity chosen from the vast pantheon of gods. One such practice is the offering of special foods to the gods. These foods are cooked in a special way that is considered pure; so, the cook will enter the kitchen only after a cleansing bath, use "allowed" ingredients (disallowed ingredients include foods such as meat, fish, onions, and garlic), and cook with love and devotion. Most Hindu temples of worship have a kitchen attached, and the blessed foods cooked here are distributed to devotees who come from far and wide, free of cost.

Temple foods always seem to taste good and, because they serve the community, their availability means that needy people who live in the vicinity never go hungry. They're available to everyone, so if you do get an opportunity to visit, it's a good idea to sample this truly divine food.

The West: A Melting Pot

I was born and raised in Mumbai, which was then called Bombay. As the commercial capital of India, Mumbai attracts people from all over the country who come to work in finance, business, or films. (India's film industry, which produces the largest number of films every year, is based here.) The cuisine of Western India is a wonderful mix, and I grew up thinking that what I ate was what all of India was eating. Only when I trained as a chef did I realize how privileged I was to have had all of India on my plate in my very own home!

Mumbai and the Parsi influence

India saw two important migrations from Iran. The first were the Zoroastrians, called the Parsis, who arrived around the eighth century as they fled from religious persecution. They arrived on the west coast of India. From here, they moved to other parts of the country, many settling in Mumbai. Their cuisine is a fabulous mix of Indian, Persian, and European styles and is very much a part of the cuisine of modern Mumbai. Signature dishes include dhansak and patia.

The second group of people were migrants from Iran who came to Bombay in the 19th century for economic reasons. They set up Irani cafes, known for their distinctive decor, uncomfortable bentwood chairs (no one is encouraged to linger because trade is brisk), and a unique menu that features dishes like puff-pastry patties, bread pudding, and ground meat curries served with bread. These cafes (very reasonably priced) are popular among students and office workers.

This cuisine is one of my favorites, so I always look forward to being invited to a Parsi wedding. I know the feast will be an extravaganza of fried chicken, meat curries, and delicious desserts served with jewel-colored sodas.

Pune and the Sindhi influence

The Partition of India and Pakistan was a major event that has shaped the history of modern India. Around a million Hindu Sindhis, who lived in the Sindh province, now in Pakistan, are said to have moved to India. Many settled around Bombay and the nearest large town, Pune. They brought a cuisine that was infused with Persian and Arabic flavors but was essentially cooked with a few Indian spices. I've seen a good number of fried foods, such as breads and potatoes, in this meal that are hazardous to my waistline, but there are also recipes for green vegetables, lentils, and chicken that I love for their freshness. My Sindhi friends often serve papads (popadams; the Sindhis are well known for their love of these) with the meal, but never with dips as found in Indian restaurants in the West.

Konkan's golden coastlines

I've never forgotten the short plane trip I made a few years ago from Mumbai to Mangalore on the west coast of India. The plane flew low, and the view was unbroken blue sea bordered by a narrow strip of golden sand merging with lush palm trees. The Arabian Sea along the coast of Konkan provides the perfect ingredients for a cuisine rich in fish and seafood. The trees give coconuts that are grated into curries to make creamy sauces. Tangy fish curries flavored with tamarind or *kokum* (a sour local fruit) are eaten with rice and fried fish or shrimp, dusted with chile powder, salt, and garlic; they make a regular appearance on the Konkani table.

The fish markets on the coast are great for tourists, too, because you can just soak up the atmosphere. At around 7 a.m., the boats come into the dock and, amidst much excitement and shouting, the catch is offloaded into baskets on shore. Fishmongers and restaurants quickly buy what they want, and the rest is sold to home cooks. Never will you find fresher catch available — and often at a very good price!

Gujarat and its extravagant thalis

Gujarat is the mango-shaped state to the west of India. It's famous for its delicate, vegetarian cuisine and especially for the *thali*, a metal plate with several small bowls filled with an array of tempting dishes. The word *thali* means "metal plate," but the term has also come to denote the meal that is served on one. A thali has rice, breads, fried accompaniments called *farsans*, vegetables, lentils, and sweets, all served at once. There are no courses, and you can mix and match dishes as you like.

Because there are so many dishes in this feast, preparing it at home is time-consuming and expensive. Most people go to a specialty restaurant (or a wedding) to enjoy it. It's quite an experience, and best of all, you can eat as much as you want for a fixed price. I think most people grudgingly stop eating because of guilt (what will the waiter say?) or food fatigue (I don't think I'll make it to the door!). You can find more about how to create your own thali meal in Chapter 9.

Chapter **2**

Embracing India's Love of Vegetables

Y ou may have heard that India is the vegetarian capital of the world. It has the largest number of vegetarians, and meat consumption is low. However, Indian cuisine also has a delicious and varied meat, poultry, and fish repertoire.

In India, vegetarian food is the default. If you eat meat, you're referred to as a "nonvegetarian." Most restaurants have both vegetarian and nonvegetarian offerings, and plenty of them cater exclusively to vegetarians. Most religious feasts, such as Hindu weddings, are vegetarian, but to be honest, I've never had a boring one. The vegetarian repertoire of Indian cooking is infinite and delicious!

In this chapter, I tell you how to put together a vegetarian or vegan meal and how to incorporate Ayurveda into your diet.

A BRIEF HISTORY OF VEGETARIANISM IN INDIA

India's association with vegetarianism goes back almost two millennia. Thousands of years ago, animals were hunted for food and meat was eaten regularly. The anti-meat sentiment began to be felt with the rise of Buddhism and Jainism, the founders of which, the Buddha and Lord Mahavira, respectively, taught their followers the doctrines of nonviolence. As more and more people began to convert to these belief systems, Hindu priests, fearing that a great number of their people would convert from Hinduism to these more peaceful ways, also began preaching against the killing of animals. They prescribed a vegetarian diet as being more worthy than the older ideas of animal sacrifice.

Today, almost 85 percent of India follows Hinduism, and some of these people are vegetarian (most of the time for religious reasons). However, not all Hindus are vegetarian — caste and community also affect this choice. Most nonvegetarians eat meat or fish perhaps once or twice a week because it can be expensive. This choice is not seen as a difficult one because of the huge array of vegetables, lentils, beans, and dairy products available.

Modern trade, as well as human migration, has meant that Indian vegetarian food has become more popular and available all over the world.

Putting Together Vegetarian and Vegan Meals

If you've just embarked on a vegetarian or vegan lifestyle, or even if you're just cutting down on your meat consumption, Indian food has lots to offer. You'll want to think not only about stripping your current diet of animal products but also about how to build a sustainable, balanced way of vegetarian or vegan eating that keeps you satisfied and healthy.

Indian meals are a balance of carbohydrates, proteins, fat, and fiber that comes from beans, legumes, and vegetables. There are plenty of options to choose from when planning your vegetarian menu. Leaving out dairy products (such as ghee, yogurt, and milk) and other animal products (like honey) can make it vegan, too. In India, eggs are considered nonvegetarian.

Here are some tips for putting together a vegetarian or vegan meal:

» **Think of your daily nutritional requirements.** It's all too easy to pick carbohydrates such as rice and bread and add vegetables to make up a vegetarian meal, but you'll want to be adding those proteins, too. Getting a balance of nutrients will make it a healthy meal. Here's how to get enough fat and protein in your vegetarian or vegan diet:

- **Eat more beans and legumes.** Introducing beans and legumes into your diet is easy with Indian recipes. Red kidney beans, mung beans, split peas, chickpeas, red lentils, brown lentils, and more are delicious in curries and stir-fries. They pair beautifully with spices and are hearty, too.

- **Combine legumes and grains.** Food professionals have recognized for a long time now that combining legumes (such as lentils) and grains (such as rice) yields a complete protein. It's hardly surprising that in a vegetarian-inclined country like India, the staple meal is rice and dal.

- **Swap meat and poultry with textured vegetable protein.** Textured vegetable protein has been used in Indian vegetarian meals for decades. It's meaty in texture and absorbs flavors of spices easily, transforming it from a rather tasteless ingredient to a delicious one.

- **Add nuts and seeds to your meals.** Many Indian curries have a blended spiced sauce that the main ingredient is cooked in. This base is often thickened with nuts such as cashews, peanuts, and almonds. They also boost the protein and good fat content of the recipe. Also, try sprinkling nuts and seeds over your rice and salads.

- **Include dairy in your meal (if you're not vegan).** Most Indian meals are served with yogurt in some form — either plain or as a raita with vegetables in it. Paneer or Indian cottage cheese is another option, and you'll get some good fats with your dairy, too!

- **Choose the right vegetables.** Avocados are known for their good fats and other wonderful nutrients. Mushrooms and broccoli have not only fiber but also protein.

- **Drizzle over some ghee or coconut oil.** Both *ghee* (clarified butter) and coconut oil have been used in Indian cooking for centuries. Drizzling a spoon of either over your rice or curry (instead of cooking your entire meal in it) means you can keep track of how much you're eating while adding good fats to your diet.

» **Keep it varied.** Many years ago, being vegetarian often meant eating cheese and potatoes every day, but this is no longer the case. The huge variety of ingredients and recipes in Indian cooking means that having a different dinner every night of the year is very possible. Just look at the list of lentils in Chapter 4!

>> **Make a simple meal plan for a few days at a time.** This plan will help you create a menu that is varied and brings in the nutrition you need, too. When you start to cook your meal for the day, instead of cobbling together something easy in a hurry, you'll have control over what you eat. You'll also be able to make the most of your ingredients so there's less food waste. Over the week, a bag of carrots could be used up for a crunchy salad, a vegetable and lentil dal, and a spiced carrot stir-fry.

>> **Stop thinking of a meal as a main with side dishes.** In an Indian meal, everything is served together and is considered a "main." In the meat-based Western diet, people are encouraged to think of the meat as the main dish. Start thinking of your meal in terms of components rather than just one dish that everything else is built around.

>> **Learn about your nutritional needs at different times of the day.** A protein-packed power breakfast will mean less snacking until lunchtime. Add nuts and seeds, nut butters, and milks to stay satiated. Lunch often needs to be quick, so choosing whole carbohydrates, proteins, and unsaturated fats along with fresh vegetables (brown rice with beans or a vegetable dal with an avocado salad) will help you beat that dreaded midafternoon slump.

>> **Have plenty of ingredients to choose from in your fridge and cupboard.** A well-stocked pantry is the vegetarian or vegan chef's joy. If you have cans of beans, bags of dried lentils, rice, flours, spices, and a fridge drawer of colorful vegetables, you can create a vast variety of delicious meals.

REMEMBER

You don't have to make meals that are entirely vegan or vegetarian to add more vegetables into your Indian meal. A fabulous range of lentil and vegetable recipes exist (including in this book), but you can also add nutrition, color, texture, and flavor to any dish by chucking in some frozen peas, corn, carrots, or any other vegetable you like. Don't forget fruit — whip up a fruit salad, spice it with chile and pepper, and serve it with your favorite curry. Try adding some canned beans and herbs to your plain rice and throw some cooked spinach into your bread dough.

Bringing Ayurvedic Wisdom to Your Kitchen

At the heart of all Indian home cooking is the ancient science of Ayurveda. This system of holistic healing is one of the oldest systems of medicine known to man. It was written down thousands of years ago by wise Himalayan sages. *Ayurveda* means "the science of life," and it aims at balancing the body's systems with diet, exercise such as yoga, and meditation.

In this book, we're concerned with the diet aspect and how to incorporate age-old wisdom that encourages wellness through the foods we eat. Every Indian kitchen is considered an apothecary and when someone in the home is feeling sick, spices and herbs are the go-to cures.

But the Ayurvedic way is not only about healing — it's really about eating right to build immunity and not get sick in the first place. This happens in three ways:

>> By eating the correct food

>> By strengthening the digestive system so that it absorbs the nutrients from what we eat

>> By regular elimination to rid the body of toxins

Each of us is said to have one or more of the three constitutions, called *doshas*:

>> **Vata:** Governed by air. If your constitution is Vata, you are lean, restless, and have dry skin.

>> **Pitta:** Governed by fire. If your constitution is Pitta, you anger easily, are frequently thirsty, and can suffer from acidity or heartburn.

>> **Kapha:** Governed by water. If your constitution is Kapha, you suffer from nasal or chest congestion, you're heavily built, and you have a sluggish digestive system.

Ayurveda encourages people to eat the foods that suit their constitution and that keep their bodies and minds well and healthy. You're probably aware of how you react to certain foods already. For example, I know that very spicy foods don't agree with me — I get heartburn, so I've learned to steer clear of them.

Following eight easy rules of an Ayurvedic diet

TIP

If Ayurveda sounds a bit complicated, here are some practical rules you can follow:

>> **Choose a combination of heavy and light foods.** Processed and fried foods are examples of heavy foods. Vegetables and fruit are light. Ayurveda says that if you choose all heavy ingredients in a single meal, you may feel bloated and the food may take longer to digest.

FINDING MORE INFORMATION ON YOGA AND MEDITATION

If you'd like to incorporate more of Ayurveda into your lifestyle, beyond just diet, you'll enjoy trying yoga and meditation. Never tried either before and not sure where to start? Here are some tips:

- **Yoga:** *Yoga For Dummies,* 3rd Edition, by Larry Payne and Georg Feuerstein (Wiley), is a great place to start. You can find yoga studios in big cities and small towns and everywhere in between, but if you'd like to try yoga from the comfort of your own home, one popular place to turn is Yoga with Adrienne on YouTube: www.youtube. com/user/yogawithadriene. Adriene Mishler has yoga routines for all levels of yoga practitioners, and she has a gentle and encouraging tone.

- **Meditation:** *Meditation For Dummies,* 4th Edition, by Stephan Bodian (Wiley), explains how you can put meditation to practice in your life. If you're looking for someone to guide you through meditation practices, a popular choice is Headspace (www.headspace.com), which you can use from the web or as an app on your smartphone.

These are just a few resources — many more are out there. Find what works for you, and set aside what doesn't.

>> **Choose more cooked foods than raw.** Raw foods are harder for the body to digest. In Indian cooking, raw salads are never the main meal; instead, they're included in a meal to add a bit of flavor, texture, and color. Also, stir-frying foods keeps them lighter than deep-frying.

>> **Pay attention to effect that various foods have on your body.** Certain foods or food combinations can give you gas or constipation or cause improper digestion. Ayurveda suggests antidotes such as adding herbs and spices or limiting your portions.

>> **Control the quantity of food you eat.** Ayurveda says that eating large meals could put pressure on the digestive system. Eat smaller meals more frequently.

>> **Eat seasonal and local.** Foods are their best when they're in season and fresh. They also taste better.

>> **Eat when you're hungry.** Let a meal be properly digested before you eat again. This practice helps your body do its job properly. Boredom snacking, eating just because it's lunchtime, or nibbling on something because everyone else is eating may cause you to overeat.

>> **Don't be distracted while eating.** No eating in front of the TV or reading while you're eating! According to Ayurveda, being distracted from eating means that we chew less and gulp our food more.

>> **Go with your instinct.** Don't force yourself to eat what you don't feel like eating. Your body and its needs are unique, so there's no rule that you have to love a certain food just because everyone else around you does. As a chef, I'm surrounded by other chefs who love garlic is all its forms, but I don't really love whole garlic. Indian cooking uses garlic in almost all savory dishes, but I prefer it pureed so that I don't have to bite into it — that's why all my recipes call for garlic paste rather than chunks of garlic!

Identifying the six tastes and sensations

Ayurveda recognizes six tastes and sensations, called *rasa* in Sanskrit:

>> **Sweet:** Sweet taste is also called neutral taste. It includes grains, dairy, some fruits, vegetables, and lentils. Sweet is not simply the taste of sugar or desserts — it's said to make us feel good, and you'll probably find that your favorite comfort food falls into the sweet category.

>> **Sour:** Sour taste includes all foods that are aged, ripened, fermented, or naturally acidic, such as citrus fruit, yogurt, and wine. Sour foods are said to help stimulate the appetite (thinking of something sour often makes the mouth water) and can be digestive aids. Eating too much sour food can lead to heartburn or acidity.

>> **Salty:** Salty taste, found in salt and sea plants, stimulates the flow of saliva and, thus, helps digestion. Too much salt can lead to inflammation or fluid retention and overwhelms all the other senses. If you accidentally put too much salt in your food, you'll most likely notice just the salt. However, it's also what brings a rounded, solid completeness to your food, like in the saying, "salt of the earth."

>> **Pungent:** Pungent taste includes foods and spices that are spicy, hot, and sharp, such as chilies, garlic, ginger, black pepper, and cloves. Their warming quality stimulates the digestion, but too much of this taste could lead to heartburn, acidity, and irritability. The pungent flavor is experienced as an irritation of the tissues and nerve endings rather than receptors on the tongue. Pungency can help to dry excess moisture, so these ingredients often find their way into home remedies for cold (such as ginger tea).

>> **Bitter:** You've heard of "bitter medicine." Bitter is considered a healing taste and is found in spices such as turmeric, in leafy vegetables, and in eggplant. Many cuisines try to get rid of bitterness in foods by salting them, but this

taste is considered valuable in Indian cooking for its ability to cleanse the body. Eating too much of this taste is thought to bring feelings of anxiety, so be careful how much you eat!

>> **Astringent:** Astringent is the dry taste left in the mouth after a sip of black tea or dry white wine, when the inside of your mouth feels like it's contracting. Just try biting into an unripe banana or pomegranate! According to Ayurveda, the astringent taste does have benefits and helps when there is excess fluid or swelling in the body.

CULTURAL WISDOM

Incidentally, the word *rasa* also means emotion, which tells you how closely the two are linked. You've heard phrases like "That's a sweet thing to say" or "He has turned into a bitter old man." Clearly, we often use taste to express our emotions.

An Indian meal should have a balance of the tastes so that it not only tastes good but also contributes to physical and emotional well-being.

INTRODUCING CHILDREN TO INDIAN FOOD

With so many of us having access to international cuisine, it's only natural that our children will be eating more and more world cuisines earlier in their lives. Still, you may not know how to introduce Indian food to children. In the West, babies are weaned on what's appropriate for their age, so you wouldn't feed a baby steak, for example. Similarly, with Indian food, think of Indian baby food and not curry. Indian babies are introduced to gentle spices quite early. Warm teas are made with fennel (it helps to keep colic away) and ajowan or carom seeds (to help the digestion).

Soft, slightly overcooked white rice is the traditional weaning food all over India. By the time babies are a year old, many are ready for a little lick of a mild curry.

Here are some tips for introducing your kids to Indian food:

- **Start them early.** If you're keen to get your kids to eat a variety of foods, it's a good idea to begin early when their tastes and habits are forming. They'll probably get used to variety if they're introduced to it as soon as they're ready to be weaned.

- **Start babies with a gently spiced drink.** Even before weaning begins, you can gently teach babies to enjoy spices. Boil 1 cup of water with ¼ teaspoon of fennel seeds. Cool the drink to a safe, drinkable temperature, and offer it to your baby once every few days.

- **Cook a chile-free curry for toddlers.** There are plenty of flavors that children can enjoy in an Indian meal, but chile is not at the top of that list! Instead, you can let them enjoy the tastes and aromas of cumin, ground coriander, cinnamon, and nutmeg, none of which is pungent.

- **Feed young children yogurt and rice.** Lots of Indian children love this creamy combination. Add a spoonful of a mild curry or even a mild mango chutney on the side, and you may find that it becomes a much-loved dinner. If your little one accepts and appreciates yogurt and rice, try adding some vegetables to the rice — I added cooked peas and finely diced cucumber and tomatoes to my children's meals.

- **Get older children to help with the cooking.** Rolling out naans, pounding spice seeds in a mortar and pestle, whisking a batter, and sprinkling in spices can all be fun! If you get your kids involved in the kitchen and give them tasks that are safe and playful, they may want to eat the fruits of their labor!

- **Eat together and eat the same meal.** With my children, I found that they accepted whatever was on the table because we were all eating the same thing, together. The meal was full of flavor, and they were encouraged to try everything. I don't ever remember making separate meals when they were old enough to eat at the table.

Eating with the seasons

With the way food stores now work, we can buy almost any food year-round. We've somewhat lost the joy of looking forward to certain foods at only certain times of the year and having to wait for our favorite foods to come into season.

One food that comes to mind is the Indian mango, the Alphonso variety in particular. Considered to be one of the best in the world, it's sweet, very fragrant, saffron colored, smooth, and very seasonal. Around the middle of April, markets in western India see the arrival of boxes of Alphonso mangoes. Always highly priced, they still sell very well because buyers know that the season is short. The arrival of the first monsoon in June marks the end, and Alphonso mangoes disappear from the markets as suddenly as they first appeared.

Ayurveda even has a name for this kind of healthy eating: ritucharya (*ritu* means "season"). Mankind has known about the benefits of seasonal eating for a very long time! I find seasonal eating quite exciting because it connects me to my surroundings and makes me look forward to different foods at various times of the year. Berries and nectarines only taste good to me in the summer, and winters are for Brussels sprouts!

Here are some benefits of eating seasonally:

>> **It's great for your health.** Fruits and vegetables are more nutritious when they're in season. Strawberries ripen well in the summer sun, and they struggle when they don't have optimum growing and ripening conditions. Winter tomatoes are often watery and dull. Nutrient-rich foods hold the promise of good health, so why *wouldn't* we choose them?

>> **It tastes great.** This is why farmer's markets are so popular — seasonal food tastes like it should! If you've ever grown your own vegetables, you don't need me to tell you any more. Fruits and vegetables are seasonal for a reason. Keep in harmony with the balance of nature, and you'll give yourself the best chance of good health.

>> **It's great for the environment.** You may argue that a food is in season somewhere in the world year-round. But transporting it to your local store means fuel emissions and a relatively long delay between harvesting and being on your table. You're probably thinking that so many Indian ingredients are flown into our markets when they're in season in faraway countries like India and Kenya. True, but in some recipes, you can swap some of those with what's growing near you.

>> **It's great for your budget.** When foods are in season, markets are flooded with them, so naturally, prices go down. You'll know this if you've ever tried to buy apricots in the winter. As for Alphonso mangoes, thankfully, you can't buy them out of season, for love or money.

Chapter **3**

Tools of the Trade

For many people, setting up their first kitchen involves getting essential cook-ware as hand-me-downs from family or friends. Then as you expand your cooking skills and possibly have a little more disposable income, your tools become more sophisticated. You may hold on to a few of those original pieces for emotional reasons — I still own (and use) a bright orange plastic colander a dear friend gave me many years ago. Or you may add a nifty gadget that helps save time or do the job better. Buying the right tools and looking after them means that they'll last.

In this chapter, I walk you through the tools you'll need for Indian cooking. Many of these tools you'll likely already have; others may be new to you. Either way, if you're looking for an excuse to shop, this chapter is for you!

Making Prep Work Easy with the Right Utensils

You've decided to cook a curry. Devoting some time to do all the prep work before you even turn on the stove will make it easy and fun to prepare. And for this, you need the right tools.

If your kitchen is small, look for tools that are multifunctional. A food processor that can chop, slice, mince, and more is far more practical than several relatively cheaper implements that perform just one function.

Knives

Professional chefs choose and care for their knives like some people do with jewelry. They're possessive about them, too — most chefs bring their own knives to any kitchen they work in and make sure to sharpen their knives themselves. (Many chefs believe that each person uses a sharpener differently, so the blade may be ruined if it's sharpened by many hands.) Here are the knives you need to prepare the recipes in this book:

>> **Chef's knife:** This all-purpose knife is good for all your chopping needs. A 10-inch chef's knife that is balanced in weight (meaning that the handle and blade weigh about the same) is best for home cooks. Invest in a good-quality chef's knife, because you'll be using it every day!

>> **Serrated knife:** A serrated knife is used to cut breads such as naans. You can also use a serrated knife on thin-skinned vegetables and fruits such as tomatoes without the knife slipping.

>> **Fillet knife:** Although a fillet knife isn't absolutely essential, after you've use one, you'll wonder how you ever managed without. The blade of a fillet knife is thin and flexible, so it can get between the fish and the skin to bend and remove it without much waste.

Cutting boards

In addition to knives, you need a good cutting board. I use a plastic cutting board because it can go in the dishwasher; plus, plastic is nonporous, so it doesn't hold onto smells such as onion or garlic. Wooden cutting boards are long-lasting, but they need regular sanitizing with a kitchen-safe cleaner and proper drying so they don't become moldy.

Another advantage of plastic cutting boards is the ability to use different colored boards to prevent cross-contamination of foods. In my kitchen, I have white, green, and brown cutting boards for vegetables and foods that won't be cooked before serving (like bread), a red cutting board for raw meat, and a blue cutting board for raw fish.

Place a piece of moist paper towel or a nonslip mat under your cutting board to prevent it from sliding around as you work.

KEEPING YOUR KNIVES IN TIP-TOP SHAPE

After you've bought that lovely, expensive knife, you'll want to look after it to make sure it does its job for a long time to come. Here are my best tips for caring for your knives:

- **Use knives only for the purpose they were intended.** I know it probably happens in every home, but it makes me mad when someone in my family (I'm not naming names) uses one of my kitchen knives to rip open a cardboard box. It dulls the blade, and the knife isn't meant for that job. If you have someone who does that in your house, hide your knives — or threaten them.

- **Store your knives separately.** Don't just throw your knives in with everything else in your cutlery drawer. Keep them in a separate compartment, in a knife block, or attached to a magnetic strip on the kitchen wall. (Just make sure if they're attached to a magnetic strip, they can't be knocked off and fall to the ground where they could harm your feet, pets, or children underneath.)

- **Use soap, warm water, and a soft sponge to clean your knives immediately after using them.** If you leave them caked with food to be washed later, you'll be tempted to use steel wool on them, but steel wool may scratch or dull the blade. I never put my knives in the dishwasher and don't ever soak them either. Dry them with a soft tea towel and put them back into storage after use. A knife is like a child: Neglect it and it won't turn out well.

- **Keep your knives sharp.** A sharp knife is possibly the most essential tool in any kitchen. Just try using a blunt knife, and you'll know the meaning of frustration. Plus, a dull blade requires more pressure, which increases the risk of the knife slipping and injuring you. Invest in a good knife sharpener that you can use each month to keep that blade sharp. A knife steel can give you an uneven edge if you use different strokes each time, and they hone more than they sharpen. Sharpening involves the removal of a tiny amount of metal, so for a home cook, it's probably a good idea to let a sharpener with a constant angle do the job. Always wipe the blade with some paper towel after you've sharpened it, holding the knife with the sharp end facing away from you. Your local butcher or kitchen store may be able to help you with professional sharpening if you prefer.

Other utensils

The following utensils are especially useful when making Indian recipes:

- » **Rolling pin:** Not all rolling pins are created equal. In fact, you can buy different rolling pins for different tasks. I've been to a kitchen shop in London that had a whole wall of rolling pins in various shapes and sizes! A traditional Indian rolling pin (see Figure 3-1) is slimmer than a Western one and comes with a round rolling board, which acts as a template to get the chapattis round as you roll them. The pin itself is tapered and light, which allows you to apply just the right amount of pressure to push the dough into a thin circle.

>> **Grater:** A stainless-steel box grater is easy to clean, has various-sized holes on each face, and is safe to hold and use.

>> **Garlic crusher:** I can't stand garlic presses — they're too fiddly to clean, and you lose half the garlic in the pressing compartment. Instead, I use a plastic twist garlic crusher. You'll be able to mince fresh ginger in it, too. Best of all, it's easy to clean under running water, and there's no waste either.

>> **Peeler:** If you've tried peeling your vegetables with a paring knife, you'll know how much safer it feels to do the job with a peeler. Look for a Y-shaped, fixed-blade peeler with a good grip. Choose a functional but inexpensive one that you can replace when it gets dull.

>> **Ladles:** You don't need special ladles for Indian cooking, but my advice is to have a couple of ladles you use just for this purpose. If you use wooden or silicone ladles, the turmeric in curries will turn them yellow, and some even hold on to the aroma of spices.

>> **Tea infuser:** A round, mesh snap ball tea infuser is great to fill with spices and immerse into rice or curries while they're cooking. Just lift out the infuser at the end of cooking and discard the spices.

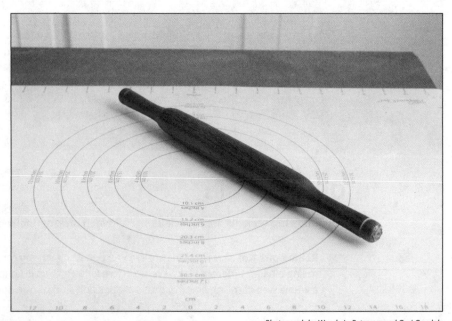

FIGURE 3-1:
An Indian
rolling pin.

Photograph by Wendy Jo Peterson and Geri Goodale

>> **Sieve:** You'll need a sieve for washing rice and lentils and for rinsing beans from a can.

>> **Colander:** A colander is used for draining cooked rice in the sink or for washing larger vegetables such as cauliflower florets and potatoes.

Knowing Which Pots, Pans, and Griddles the Experts Use

You can cook your curry in a standard cooking pot or frying pan, so don't rush out to buy any specialty equipment just yet. That said, having some Indian cookware makes the experience more fun and authentic. After you've tried the recipes and found the ones you love (and made some space in your kitchen), you may want to buy some of the items in this section.

Karahi

You may have seen small decorative versions of karahis — they're often used as serving dishes in Indian restaurants. You can't use decorative karahis for cooking. Instead, what you're looking for are the larger cooking karahis (see Figure 3-2), which are somewhat similar to a wok in shape but are made of a thicker material. Some karahis have two small ear-shaped handles; others have none. Karahis are sold with a pair of tongs because the handles are made of metal and get as hot as the karahi itself! You can also buy a matching lid with your karahi — the lid has a lip that allows it to sit snug over the top, sealing in the steam.

WARNING

You can't use a wok instead of a karahi — your curry might stick to the bottom. Although woks have a similar shape, a wok is much thinner because it's used for stir-frying on a high heat. A karahi is used for longer cooking processes and is much thicker.

I use a 14-inch (diameter) karahi for a curry for four people, but I also have a huge set of karahis in varying sizes all stacked up in my kitchen drawer. I also use them for frying, because the convex shape allows the oil to pool at the bottom, which means you can use much less oil than you would need in a frying pan. You can cook curries, dals, and dry vegetable dishes in karahis. And best of all, they're dishwasher safe!

FIGURE 3-2:
Karahis.

Photograph by Wendy Jo Peterson and Geri Goodale

Tava

A tava (see Figure 3-3) is a flat or slightly convex griddle for cooking chapattis, rotis, or other stovetop flatbreads on. You can choose between an iron tava that gets seasoned when used regularly or a nonstick one.

TIP

A Western substitute for a tava is a 10-inch nonstick frying pan that can comfortably hold a roti.

Dosa pan

Dosas are South Indian rice and lentil crêpes (see Chapter 17). They need to be spread thinly so they go a bit crisp while cooking. A dosa pan (see Figure 3-4) is flat and large (around 13 inches), and it doesn't have sides, so you can spread the batter right up to the edge. The lack of sides also makes it easy to get under the dosa and flip it.

Pressure cookers

I don't know of a single Indian kitchen that doesn't have at least one pressure cooker. Typically, these are traditional pressure cookers that seal the food in and time the cooking process with a series of whistles. You may find recipes (though not in this book) that ask you to cook a curry for "three or four whistles." Some modern pressure cookers, such as the Instant Pot, are electric.

FIGURE 3-3:
A tava.

FIGURE 3-4:
A dosa pan.

I love using pressure cookers! They cut down on cooking times and are very fuel efficient. The tight lid has a release vent and helps keep the steam locked in. Pressure cookers cook food using moisture, unlike ovens, which use dry heat. Many Western cooks have told me they're frightened of pressure cookers blowing up, but honestly, modern ones are much safer than the ones that were used years ago.

You can buy pressure cookers in various sizes. I have about five in my kitchen — small ones for everyday cooking and the largest one for entertaining. I use them to cook meats, lentils, potatoes, and even rice. I've seen a large pressure cooker being used to cook three things at once, to make a quick meal — a stack of shallow dishes with a lid on top can contain rice, dal, and vegetables. These are placed in the cooker with some water at the bottom and in each individual dish. The cooked lentils and vegetables can later be spiced up in a separate pot.

REMEMBER

Whichever pressure cooker you buy, follow the manufacturer's instructions, because they vary.

An Instant Pot is more than a pressure cooker. You can use it to build curries by adding various building blocks to the pot and then cooking everything together. Some ingredients that are popular in the Indian kitchen (such as beans, lentils, and meats) can take a long time to cook, but the Instant Pot, which is a combination of a pressure cooker and a slow cooker, can take the pressure off and cook them to perfection without your needing to stand by stirring the pot. Put your ingredients into the pot in the correct sequence, adjust the settings, and walk away to finish other chores. You'll have a fuss-free dinner waiting for you when you return.

Because the Instant Pot has temperature settings you can adjust, they're also great for fermenting foods. Getting your dosa batter to go all bubbly is easy in an Instant Pot, as is making soft, set yogurt.

Handling Spices like a Pro

After you've bought your spices, store them correctly to keep them fresh for as long as possible. Spices contain volatile oils that can dissipate with time and improper storage. I have a three-way system at my cookery school (I buy large bags to decant into jars and then into my spice tin), where we cook with spices every day.

A spice tin for storing spices

To make your cooking really easy and to feel like an expert Indian cook, treat yourself to a spice tin (or *masala dabba*). They're usually round, made of stainless steel, with seven small bowls that fit snugly inside (see Figure 3-5). Some have a double lid to seal in the freshness. With a proper spice tin, you'll have your favorite spices on hand just with the opening of one lid.

FIGURE 3-5:
A spice tin.

You'll find lots of different spice tins on the market, made of metal or plastic. You can even find fancy wooden ones. I prefer a steel spice tin, because they're easy to wash, won't get stained, and don't absorb the flavors of the spices. Choose a size that fits your kitchen and needs, but don't worry too much about the size — you'll be refilling your tin from time to time anyway.

REMEMBER

Don't overlook the lid when you're choosing a spice tin. Lids vary, and the wrong lid, made of glass or clear plastic, could mean the slow demise of your spices, which like to live in dark, dry conditions. Choose an opaque lid instead.

Most spice tins come with a small spice spoon, but if yours doesn't, buy one. A regular teaspoon won't fit easily into the small bowls. You can use the same spoon for all the spices, but if you're fussy, sets of small, stainless-steel spice spoons are also available.

TIP

Here are some tips on using your new friend in the kitchen:

>> **Choose your spices.** Spice tins around India contain a varying mix of spices depending on the regional cuisine. Fill your tin with whatever you use most. My essential spices are black mustard seeds, cumin seeds, ground cumin, ground coriander, turmeric, medium-hot chile powder, and garam masala.

>> **Fill your tin.** Buy small packs of spices and use them up quickly so your stock remains fresh. Decant the spices into your spice tin, and seal and store the remainder in a dark, dry cupboard. Refill your tin as and when necessary, but fill each bowl only three-quarters full, or you'll end up with a mess.

>> **Keep your spices fresh.** Spices like to stay dry. When adding them into your pan while cooking, just tip a spoonful in and resist the temptation to do an artistic sprinkle. The longer you hold your spice spoon over a steaming pot, the more the moisture it will bring back to the tin, making your spices clumpy.

>> **Bring your tin to the stovetop, and hold it in one hand as you add spices with the other.** This will reduce spillage (think of those little mustard seeds that might escape), and you'll have the next spice on hand, if they're going into the pan in a sequence. If you think you need to practice spooning out your spices neatly, mix them in a small bowl before you begin cooking. Remember to only mix those that go into the pan at the same time, so seeds and powders will have to be kept separate (see Chapter 8).

>> **Clean your tin regularly.** You'll notice that the tin gets a bit grungy after a few uses. Lift out the little bowls and give the tin a good wipe with clean paper towel. Once in a while, you can tip the spices into other bowls and give the whole tin a good wash. Dry it completely before reintroducing the spices.

Tools for blending and crushing spices

A blender is the secret to many curries. You'll want a blender for pureeing curry base sauces and smaller appliances or utensils for crushing small amounts of spices. Here's what to look for:

>> **Blender:** A blender is a must-have in the Indian kitchen. In the days before blenders, people used grinding stones that produced concentrated curry pastes, but they required a lot of elbow grease. Choose a blender that can puree rather than a food processor that chops very finely. You'll want a powerful one with a high wattage, so it gets everything smooth. Some blenders have attachments for wet and dry blending or compact jars for smaller quantities. Washing your blender thoroughly is important. Check to see if the base comes apart from the jar and undo it each time you clean it.

>> **Spice mill or grinder:** You may think that spices need to be crushed every time you begin cooking a curry, but that isn't true. It's perfectly acceptable to use ready-bought spices, although some, such as ground coriander or garam masala, lose their flavor very quickly so either use them up soon or grind them at home. Investing in a small electric spice or coffee grinder will make crushing those seeds, bark, and nuts feel like child's play, and your kitchen will smell heavenly, too! I suggest not blitzing coffee and spices in the same mill (excuse me waiter, there's a coriander seed in my coffee). And remember to wipe out the mill after each use.

>> **Mortar and pestle:** A good mortar and pestle is essential in your Indian kitchen because you'll use it a lot. Look for a heavy one (for example, one made of granite) that's hard enough to crush tough spice seeds. I find that a ceramic mortar and pestle is too delicate for robust spice crushing. Wash your mortar and pestle after each use to keep the flavors of different blends distinct.

>> **Peppermill:** You've probably already got a peppermill at home that you use for crushing peppercorns. Buy another one and fill it with toasted spice seeds (try cumin). A few turns over curry will give an instant top note of fresh spice flavor.

Chapter **4**

Shopping for Essential Ingredients

I f this is the first time you're trying your hand at Indian cooking, you may be wondering where to begin with ingredients. The good news is that you don't need a lot of specialty ingredients to prepare your Indian feast. But having some well-chosen ones will definitely up your game.

When you feel like cooking an Indian dinner, your well-stocked pantry can give you lots of inspiration and save time and money, too. No last-minute dash to the corner shop to buy expensive spices or lentils. A well-planned pantry and fridge can work hard for you, leaving you to enjoy the preparation and the eating of your meal.

Diving into Dry Goods

Every good pantry has a stock of dry goods that can be bought in bulk because they have a long shelf life. This saves money and means you don't have to add those items to your weekly shopping list.

TIP

Make sure your pantry is dry and packets are stored in airtight containers to keep pests away. You want to feed yourself, not the mice!

Spices

You need to need to get them right in order for your Indian cooking to work well. I'm always excited to see rows and rows of colorful spices at my local Indian shop. The aromas that hint of faraway lands are no less tantalizing. However, I'm aware of how overwhelming all this can seem to a novice. Spice names written in various Indian languages and scripts, as well as whole, crushed, and powdered forms of the same spice can be too much to handle. Plus, there are all those variations — for example, chile powder sold in various strengths of pungency, as well as from different regions of India.

Don't worry, I won't be going to ask you to go buy out your local Indian market. A few key spices and spice blends are all you need. After you've tested a few different brands and found the ones you love, you'll be shopping like a pro!

TIP

When buying and storing spices and herbs, here are some useful tips.

>> **Buy from a shop that does a brisk business.** When lots of other shoppers go there to buy spices, shelves will be restocked more frequently and spices will be fresher. Typically, this means shopping at an Indian grocery store.

>> **Buy small quantities.** Often, buying in bulk is cost-effective, but in the case of spices, it isn't. Ground spices last for around six months; the seeds last for a year. Even if a big bag is cheaper than several smaller ones, you may end up needing to throw it out. Better to buy two or three smaller bags and open one only after you've used up the previous one.

>> **Store them in airtight containers in a dry, dark cupboard.** Spices and herbs can deteriorate with light and air.

>> **Use spices in other cuisines, too.** That way, you'll use them up faster and keep your stock fresh. Try adding a pinch of turmeric to rice and pasta, or add a bit of garam masala to your roast meat.

>> **Depending on what your go-to recipes will be, buy a few key spices first and then build up your collection.** The spices I can't live without are:

- Black mustard seeds
- Chile powder
- Cumin seeds
- Garam masala

- Ground coriander
- Ground cumin
- Turmeric

Table 4-1 can help you decide which spices to buy and suggests which dishes they compliment. When you become familiar with their flavors, you'll feel confident to use them in other recipes too.

TABLE 4-1   **Buying Spices**

Spice	Description
Ajowan	Also called *ajwain*, these small, sharp-tasting seeds give Indian fritters like onion bhajia and snacks their distinctive taste.
Amchur	Sometimes spelled *amchoor*, this is a dried green mango powder used to add a fruity sour note to samosa and stuffed bread fillings where moisture needs to be restricted. It's also used in North Indian chutneys and salads.
Asafetida	This very strong-smelling powder comes from the root of a plant species of ferula. It's used in small quantities for its digestive properties in recipes with lentils, beans, and certain vegetables. If you just can't find it and a recipe calls for it, you can just leave it out.
Cardamom	Green cardamom is used in both savory and sweet recipes. It has a strong citrusy aroma. Black cardamom is bigger and has a smoky aroma. Look for plump pods when buying both.
Chaat masala	Chaat masala is a spicy, sour, salty blend of spices such as mango powder and chile. It's sprinkled over snacks as a finishing spice. It's sometimes sold as "chunky chaat masala."
Chile powder	Varying heat levels are available, from mild to extra hot. I suggest a medium-hot variety, such as Kashmiri chile powder, which also gives dishes a lovely deep red color.
Cinnamon	The quills are crumbly, sweet, and aromatic. You can substitute cinnamon with cassia, which is cheaper, coarser, and slightly bitter but still aromatic. Both cinnamon and cassia are used in rice dishes and some curries.
Coriander	Coriander is available as seeds and ground — you'll need both. Buy smaller packs of ground coriander because it loses its aroma quite quickly when opened. (**Note:** The leaves and stem of this plant are referred to as cilantro, but coriander is the term used for the dried seeds.)
Cumin	These small, long seeds are highly aromatic. You'll need both the seeds and ground cumin.
Garam masala	Garam masala is an aromatic blend of spices such as cardamom, cinnamon, cloves, coriander, cumin, nutmeg, and pepper. Recipes vary so find a blend you like.
Fenugreek	Fenugreek is available as seeds and dried leaves, which are essential in dishes like butter chicken. The seeds are used in lentil and vegetable dishes. You can't swap leaves with seeds, or vice versa, so pay attention to what the recipe calls for.

(continued)

TABLE 4-1 *(continued)*

Spice	Description
Mustard seeds	Mustard seeds are used a lot in South Indian cooking. Look for black or brown ones. Yellow mustard seeds are not commonly used.
Pepper	Pepper is used in spice blends and for seasoning. Buy black peppercorns and crush them at home in a peppermill for the freshest flavor.
Saffron	Saffron is the world's most expensive spice. Look for Spanish or Kashmiri saffron. It's used in small quantities in sweets and rice dishes.
Turmeric	This bright yellow-orange powder has an earthy aroma. Look for a vibrant hue. Fresh turmeric root is also available, but you can't use it instead of the powder in Indian recipes. (I tried, so you don't have to.)
Whole dried chilies	You'll need chilies to add color and flavor to some curries such as rich lamb curries or South Indian dishes. Choose a dark red, mild variety such as Kashmiri chilies.

Grains

Your Indian meal will always have grains as a part of it. The grains could be in the form of rice or breads made with wheat or lentil flours. Although the variety of Indian ingredients in supermarkets keeps growing, you'll probably find a larger variety at an Indian grocery store. It's worth a trip just for the wonderful aromas and unusual ingredients you'll see — you won't need to buy them all! Table 4-2 lists the ones you'll want to stock up on.

TABLE 4-2 **Buying Grains**

Grain	Description
Atta	A stoneground (called *chakki* on Indian packaging) whole-wheat flour used for making rotis, parathas, and other breads. You can't use whole-meal flour instead, so if the recipe calls for atta, use atta.
Besan	A kind of chickpea flour used for batters for fritters like pakora, to make gluten-free breads, or for thickening curries
Poha	A dried flaked rice that rehydrates easily to make a quick, hearty snack when cooked with spices. It's available as "fine" or "medium"; I always buy the medium because it holds its shape better.
Rice	Indian basmati rice is available in most stores. Look for aged, mature, or old basmati (you'll often see these terms on the packaging) because it'll fluff up better. Or if you can't bother to read labels, just buy the most expensive one because it's likely to be the best aged. Cheaper basmati is good for rice pudding and for blending into a batter for rice and lentil pancakes called dosa.
Semolina	Wheat broken down into various-sized grains. Coarse semolina is used in puddings and pancakes, and fine semolina is used as a crust for fried shrimp and fish.

Nuts

During Diwali, the grandest festival celebrated in India, people send boxes of nut selections across the country as gifts. All these nuts are plump and glossy, and they're meant to be enjoyed during the holiday season. An Indian kitchen, however, requires a variety of nuts that need to blended to a paste, and it would be sacrilege to use those fat beauties in a curry base! Instead, you'll want to visit an Indian grocery store for cheaper versions of nuts that will add texture and thickness.

TIP

Because nuts kept for too long can go stale, it's a good idea to buy small quantities. Also, unless you're specifically buying them to blend, buy whole nuts — they'll keep longer, and you can slice or chop them for garnishes as you need.

Here are the nuts you'll want to have on hand:

>> **Almonds:** Buy whole almonds to slice as a garnish for desserts and rice dishes. You can use ground almonds to thicken some curries.

>> **Cashews:** Look for packs of broken cashews that can be blended to a paste and added to curry bases. Halved cashews are good for adding texture to vegetable dishes or chopped up as a garnish over curries and desserts.

>> **Peanuts:** Although technically not nuts (they're legume), peanuts are the most popular nut in western Indian kitchens. Roasted, salted peanuts are good lightly crushed as a garnish for salads and curries. You can also blend them to a paste to thicken curry sauces.

>> **Pistachios:** You'll need a few of these, shelled, to garnish Indian desserts. The green color is a beautiful pop over cream and fruit.

>> **Walnuts:** Walnuts aren't often used in curry sauces because they can add a bitter note. Use them chopped for garnishes or in salads.

Flavorings

Salt is a very important ingredient in the Indian kitchen, and your food just won't taste right without it. It won't taste good without sour ingredients either. You've probably tasted tamarind already (just check the ingredient list on your bottle of Worcestershire sauce) or in Asian and Mexican foods. Sweet tamarind is different from the sour pods needed in Indian curries.

Table 4-3 lists the flavorings you should have on hand.

TABLE 4-3   **Buying Flavorings**

Flavoring	Description
Salt	Choose fine sea salt if you want additive-free or you can use regular table salt.
Sugar	Granulated sugar is used for sweets or to balance flavors in a curry without changing its color.
Jaggery	Jaggery is a block of cooked sugarcane juice. It's used in some Indian desserts and curries to add an earthy sweetness. The block can be grated or cut. Jaggery melts like sugar when heated. It can be stored in an airtight box for up to a year. Brown sugar can be used as a substitute for jaggery.
Tamarind	The sausage-shaped fruit of a large tree, tamarind is sold in blocks that can be stored for up to a year. Look for wet tamarind, which feels softer than hard blocks. It's rehydrated in hot water (see Chapter 6). Tamarind concentrate can be too intense and can change the color of the final dish, so avoid it. Jars of ready-made paste are available, but they're more expensive than buying the blocks and making the paste yourself.
Vinegar	White or brown vinegar is used in some Indian curries to add a sour note. Specially flavored vinegars aren't essential because the subtle notes will be lost among the stronger-smelling spices.

Beans

I don't know of a single Indian kitchen that doesn't have an assortment of lentils and legumes. The word *dal* is used to mean raw legumes, as well as the cooked dish. All lentils have a fairly similar taste, but some are slightly earthier or sweeter than others. They also have varying textures.

Although you don't need to stock a huge variety if you're not eating lentils every day, you may want to vary what you buy so that you can pick your favorite ones. I choose mine based on how long they'll take to cook, so bear in mind that the smaller the lentil, the faster it will cook, especially if it's had the skin removed. If you want to swap, try like for like sizes to keep textures and cooking times similar.

Indian packaging companies are notorious for calling pulses and legumes by various names; I've suggested a few in Table 4-4.

Everything else

Eat in an Indian home, and you'll most likely find that a selection of store-bought foods like *achaar* (pickles) and *chaats* (called *popadams* in the West) are also brought to the table. These add another layer of flavor and texture to the meal and help to personalize heat levels for each person.

TABLE 4-4   **Buying Lentils, Beans, and Legumes**

Pulse	Description
Black gram	Available as whole black beans, split in half with the skin on, and split without the skin. You can't swap them in most recipes, so pay attention to what's called for. The sticky texture of the split ones is important in pancake batters (dosa), and the whole beans make a black dal creamy. Also called urad or urid.
Brown, red, or orange lentils	Available whole as brown lentils or split and skinned as red or orange ones. The split ones cook faster. Also called masoor.
Gram lentils	The largest of the yellow lentils, these take the longest to cook and can be soaked before-hand to hasten cooking time. Also called chana dal or Bengal gram.
Mung	Available as whole green beans called (mung beans), split in half with the skin on, and split without the skin (which are called mung lentils). Each has a different texture. The whole beans can be sprouted. Also called moong.
Pigeon peas	Yellow in color, they're slightly larger than mung lentils. They take much longer to cook, so they can be soaked in boiling water for 30 minutes or so prior to cooking. Also called tur, toor, or arhar.

Pickles

Just have a look in this aisle in your local Indian shop, and you'll be blown away by the variety of pickles on offer. Indian pickles are nothing like Western ones, which are mostly vegetables preserved in brine, vinegar, and a few herbs and spices. Achaars are always intensely flavored, come in a variety of consistencies and heat levels, and are always eaten in small quantities. A good Indian pantry always has a few of these. After you open the jar, refrigerate them and they'll last up to a year.

Here are two varieties to look for:

>> **Sweet pickles:** The most popular one in the West is mango chutney (an Indian chutney is usually fresh or dried, so this preserve is called a pickle!). You'll also find sweet lime, eggplant, or even shrimp pickle. Some may be hot as well.

>> **Hot pickles:** You'll see many of these with varying degrees of heat. It's hard to tell from the packaging exactly how hot they are, so you'll just have to try a few. The obvious one if you're a heat lover is chile pickle. Other varieties include green mangoes, lime, garlic, and mixed vegetables.

Popadams

Your Indian shop will have these in a range of flavors, like plain, garlic, and green chile. Dry-roast these on an open flame or in a microwave, or fry them in oil if you prefer. In some places in India, popadams are made at home by kneading a dough with lentil flour and rolling them out into thin discs. These are typically dried in the summer sun to be stored for use during the rest of the year. Many people, especially those with time, space, or motivation constraints, buy them commercially.

Dried fruits

Raisins and sultanas are sometimes added to rice dishes and desserts. Dried apricots and dates can add a sweet garnish to salads and some curries, too.

Chai

You'll need black tea to make Indian chai and instant coffee granules for Indian flavored coffee. If you're a coffee aficionado, forget I just said that and use your bespoke brand of coffee beans.

Yes, We Can! Stocking Up on Canned Goods

Some ingredients are just easier in cans. Either they taste better or save you time and effort. They're versatile, too, and you may already have some of these in your pantry.

Tomatoes

Tomatoes make an appearance in so many Indian recipes that it's a good idea to always have some on hand. A can of Italian chopped tomatoes goes a long way toward creating an instant base for a delicious curry. Look for the following:

>> **Canned tomatoes:** Blend these to a puree to make a curry base sauce or tip the can into the pot if you want texture.

If you're replacing fresh tomatoes (especially if they're pale and tasteless) with canned, bear in mind that there's more liquid in canned tomatoes, so you'll need to add less water to the curry or cook it for longer to get some of it to evaporate off.

>> **Tomato paste:** Tomato paste, which is available in cans or tubes, helps to thicken curries and give them a beautiful color, too. Refrigerate opened tubes and decant spare paste from cans into tubs that can go into the freezer for up to two months.

>> **Passata:** Pureed, strained uncooked tomatoes are easy to use — you can just pour them into your curry sauce without needing to blend them. Passata can thin down your curry sauce so adjust the amount of water or other liquid you add.

Coconut milk and coconut powder

Many kitchens in southern and western India begin with the cracking open of a coconut to be used in the day's cooking, either shredded or made into milk. You don't need to do that, though, because coconut milk is so readily available in cans and cartons.

WARNING

Read the ingredients and choose a brand that has at least 50 percent coconut extract, better if it's higher. The rest will be water and stabilizers.

Partly used cans of milk can be decanted into tubs and frozen for later use.

I prefer to buy the full-fat version rather than the reduced-fat or "light" ones, which I find don't give the consistency and richness needed for an Indian curry.

TIP

If you just need a small amount of coconut milk, don't bother opening a tin. I just use coconut powder or creamed coconut, both of which are available in Indian grocery shops. Mix 3 tablespoons coconut powder or creamed coconut (or more, depending on how thick you want the milk to be) with 1 cup warm water; whisk until smooth.

Beans

I'd like to give whoever canned the first beans, a big prize. They've shortened prep time and taken the guesswork out of cooking beans correctly. I know some cooks prefer soaking dried beans and cooking them for hours, but I'm not one of them. Some say that the dried beans taste better, and maybe they do. I soak beans and chickpeas when I have the will, but more often, I take a quick trip to my pantry to pull out a can.

Black beans, red kidney beans, garbanzo beans, black-eyed beans, and white beans all can go into curries and are handy when you want one in minutes. All you'll need is a few spices and a can of tomatoes to create the base, and you'll find that you've got comfort in a bowl. Make sure to wash them first in a sieve under running water to get rid of excess salt and canning liquid.

You may have heard that not cooking red beans for long enough may not destroy a toxin they contain. The good news is, canned red beans are safe to use straightaway.

Mango puree

Very little beats the taste and aroma of a ripe Indian mango. They're seasonal, though, so some companies have captured their sweetness and fragrance in cans. Look for Alphonso or Kesar varieties to make into smoothies, ice cream, or desserts, or just to eat on their own. Try drizzling some on your breakfast cereal, too.

TIP

You can easily freeze mango puree, either in a tub or in ice cube trays for more convenient portioning.

Free-Range Culture: Shopping for Dairy and Eggs

Choosing the right yogurt, cream, and paneer can be the difference between a successful curry and a flop. With such a range of fat contents to choose from, this section looks at what you need for Indian recipes.

Yogurt

If you make your own yogurt at home (which is easy to do in an Instant Pot), you can skip this section. If you have yogurt on your shopping list when you go to the supermarket, however, here are your options:

>> **Whole-milk yogurt:** Great for making lassi or for adding to curries, whole-milk yogurt has 6 to 8 grams of fat per cup.

>> **Low-fat yogurt:** With 2 to 5 grams of fat per cup, low-fat yogurt is great if you're looking to reduce the fat in your diet. Use it for cold dishes like dips and raitas, though — high temperatures could make low-fat yogurt split.

>> **Greek yogurt:** Greek yogurt has had the whey strained off, so it's thicker and better for cooking because it's less likely to split. I like using Greek yogurt in raitas, too, because it makes them creamy and delicious!

TIP

If you're vegan, you can use coconut yogurt (for cooking with) or soy yogurt (in uncooked preparations like raitas).

Cream

Some indulgent Indian recipes such as Murgh Makhani (Butter Chicken; see Chapter 11) taste nice with a bit of cream, but it's not the norm in an Indian kitchen and can often be substituted with coconut milk. I buy two kinds:

>> **Single cream, light cream, or pouring cream:** With a fat content of less than 20 percent, this cream is thin enough to pour easily. It's good for adding to curries after they've finished cooking. Adding 3 to 4 tablespoons gives a silky finish and smooth taste and consistency. Cooking it on a high heat may cause it to split.

>> **Double cream or heavy cream:** The fat content is higher, even up to 50 percent, so this thick cream can be added to curries while they're cooking or still very hot. The high fat content helps this cream to remain stable.

Paneer

Paneer is Indian cottage cheese. Paneer doesn't melt upon cooking and takes on the flavor of the spices its cooked in, so it's great in curries or baked as an appetizer. You can choose from plenty of brands, so you may have to try a few to pick a favorite. Here are your options:

>> **Blocks of paneer:** Available in 7-ounce packs (enough to add to a mixed curry for three to four people) or larger packs (for curries where paneer is the star ingredient).

>> **Cubed paneer:** If you want to save even more time, cubed paneer is for you. It can stick together, though, so you'll need to separate the cubes before adding them to the pan.

>> **Tofu:** If you prefer a vegan alternative, try firm tofu, which has a similar texture to paneer and a neutral taste.

TIP

You can make your own paneer at home, if you want. It's easy and requires very little effort, but it is time-consuming. You need just two ingredients: whole milk and lemon juice. Boil the milk and split it by adding lemon. Strain to remove the whey, and then hang it up for a few hours to make a dense, mild-tasting, cuttable cheese. If you don't want to wait, head to your local Indian grocery to buy the prepackaged stuff.

Eggs

Although duck eggs are eaten in some parts of India, the most widely available ones are from chickens. I always go for large, free-range organic eggs, but in Indian curries, size doesn't matter, so choose medium ones if you prefer. Color doesn't matter either — you won't be able to tell the difference between a white egg and a brown one after they're cooked.

TIP

Pay attention to the expiration date. You can also check for freshness by immersing the egg into a bowl of cold water. If it sinks to the bottom of the bowl and lies on its side, it's very fresh. If it sinks but stands on one end, it's still fresh enough to eat. If the egg floats, it isn't a good idea to eat it. When you crack open an egg, a firm, bright yolk indicates freshness, whereas a flabby pale one means the egg is stale.

Knowing Which Fats and Oils You Need

Fat is essential to making curries taste good. The frying of onions adds an unmistakable sweetness, and hot oil is essential to draw out the aromatic oils in spices. You don't need much oil — I get grossed out at the sight of restaurant curries floating in fat. But cooking at home means you can choose which fat to use and how much oil to put into the pan to elevate the flavor and not widen your waistline.

To ghee or not to ghee

Ghee has been around in India for a few thousand years. It's essentially butter that is clarified by heating it to evaporate any moisture and caramelize the milk solids that are then strained off. The clarifying process helps to increase the shelf life and keeps it fresher longer. In the Indian kitchen, ghee is used for shallow-and deep-frying and for drizzling on top of some dishes to make them taste all buttery and delicious.

Many people outside India believe that all good Indian cooking must begin with ghee, but this is a myth. Most Indian cooks use plant oils for everyday cooking and use small amounts of ghee for savory or sweet dishes. A biryani also tastes divine when cooked in ghee. Remember that although ghee is a great fat to cook with and tastes lovely, it has more calories than butter, so you need to be careful how much you eat. You don't want your entire daily calorie intake to be used up by ghee!

Why not just use butter, you may be wondering. Ghee has a higher smoke point than butter, which means it won't burn when you're cooking those onions or spices over high heat.

When you look in the ghee aisle in your Indian store, you may see cans or cartons of two kinds of ghee:

» **Butter ghee:** This is the kind I describe earlier. The best ones are made with butter from grass-fed cows. They have higher levels of omega-3 fatty acids, which are good for us. It's also called "pure ghee" or "desi ghee."

» **Vegetable ghee:** This kind of ghee is made by hydrogenating vegetable oil and has a higher proportion of trans fats (which are bad for you). Vegetable ghee is much cheaper than butter ghee, which is why it's the fat of choice for many Indian restaurants, which can claim that their food is "cooked in ghee." The fine print written in invisible ink at the bottom of the menu says "vegetable ghee," which really isn't ghee at all. The word *ghee* has come to be loosely applied to any saturated fat, so it's quite easy for people to be misled. Don't buy vegetable ghee — go for butter ghee every time.

REMEMBER

After you open ghee, store it in the fridge unless you plan to use it every day.

Must-have oils for an Indian kitchen

Various regions of India use different cooking oils based on what crops grow there. The West grows peanuts, whereas coconut trees abound in parts of the South. Local cuisines have come to be distinguished by the aroma of the cooking oil they use. In my kitchen, I have a few kinds of oil because I love cooking all kinds of regional Indian food.

You may not want to invest in several bottles of infrequently used oils, however, so I suggest stocking up on two or three that remain stable at high temperatures.

Many curries begin with the frying of spices, which need heat to split and release their aromatic oils. A *stable* oil, which is one that doesn't easily react with oxygen to form free radicals, has a high smoke point. If an oil is heated beyond its smoke point, it decomposes and releases toxic fumes and can also get close to the point of catching fire.

Table 4-5 lists some common types of oil you may want to buy.

TABLE 4-5　**Buying Cooking Oils**

Oil	Description
Canola	Called rapeseed oil in some countries, canola oil has a high smoke point. It can be used for frying and pan-frying and for everyday Indian cooking.
Coconut	In recent years, coconut oil has been hailed as a superfood in the West, but it has been used for centuries in South India. It's high in saturated fat, though, so limit your use of it.
Corn	The high smoke point of corn oil makes it a good one for deep-frying with, and its neutral taste is good in curries.
Sunflower	Neutral tasting, sunflower oil will not add another layer of flavor to your curry. It also has a high smoke point, so it's good for Indian cooking. It can be used for shallow or deep-frying.

Drop the Beet: Loading Up on Produce

I've heard people in my cooking classes say they're nervous about going into an Indian grocery store because of the unfamiliar ingredients and produce. They're probably seeing many vegetables never found on the Western table, with names that mean nothing to someone who doesn't speak fluent Hindi. In this section, I take the mystery out of some of those fresh ingredients.

Aromatics and herbs: Veggies with a punch

Fresh aromatics and herbs are as important as spices. Here's what to look for when choosing them and how best to store them:

» **Fresh chilies:** You'll want to use the same variety of chile every time, so you know how hot it is whenever you use it and not have to play chile roulette. I prefer the bird's eye or thin green chilies. The smaller the chile, the hotter it is, so these are pretty powerful. You can control the heat by the way you chop them (see Chapter 6). Most recipes ask for fresh green chilies, although you can use red ones as well. Red chilies are just green chilies that have ripened, so they have a shorter shelf life. You can freeze fresh chilies, but use them from frozen because they go limp when defrosted.

» **Cilantro and mint:** An Indian store will have big, fresh bunches tied together as opposed to a few stalks you see wrapped in plastic bags in bigger supermarkets. To store, line a large, airtight plastic box with paper towel and place the herbs in. Store in the fridge for a couple of weeks, replacing the paper towel every few days.

>> **Curry leaves:** You'll find the freshest ones in the Indian market. The stalks are sold in small plastic bags. It's easy to dry them at home, and they taste much better than the dried ones you can buy commercially. Just take them off the stalks and dry them on a tray on your kitchen counter for three to four days. Put the dehydrated leaves into an airtight box in the fridge up to two months. If you can't find fresh curry leaves, the store-bought dried ones will do.

>> **Fenugreek:** Fenugreek leaves are available as a fresh bunch and are used in vegetable dishes the way spinach is used. They're also dried to use as a herb called kasuri methi, which is available in packs and will last up to a year if stored in a cool, dark place. Fenugreek is the essential flavor in dishes such as Murgh Makhani (Butter Chicken; see Chapter 11). Fenugreek seeds are the spice and can't be used in place of kasuri methi.

>> **Garlic:** Much of what you see in the produce aisles is Chinese garlic. You can tell by the fact that it's sold rootless, which reduces shipping weight and costs. Garlic grown domestically mostly has roots. You can use either type. Choose fat bulbs that don't collapse when you press them and look for mold around the root end, which is a sign that they're going bad. Store garlic in your onion basket or in the fridge.

>> **Ginger:** Most of the ginger you see in your grocery store probably comes from China, but you may also find organic ginger from Peru. Look for firm, shiny-skinned ginger with as little discoloration as possible. A crinkly skin means that it's getting a bit old and dehydrated, so the flesh will most likely be very stringy.

The best thing you can do with ginger and garlic is make your own paste, a lovely homemade ingredient that will speed up your Indian cooking. (You can find out how to make and store your own ginger-garlic paste in Chapter 6.)

If you want to leave some ginger whole, store it wrapped in paper in the fridge or freezer and grate from frozen into curries.

Eggplants

Eggplants are enjoyed in every regional cuisine of India. This shiny purple vegetable can be prepared in so many ways — combined with spices, yogurt, onions, or tomatoes, or thrown into curries to make them meatier and delicious. You've probably seen a variety of eggplants. Table 4-6 explains how to pick the right one.

TABLE 4-6   Buying Eggplant

Variety	Description
Globe, American, or Dutch	These varieties are large with dark-purple skin. They're good in many Indian recipes, such as curries, and for fire roasting (see Chapter 13) to mash with spices. Because they're fat and meaty, they slice well for fritters, too.
Graffiti	Graffiti eggplant is pretty to look at, with purple and white stripes. They're as versatile as the globe eggplant. The stripes aren't retained during cooking, and they have fewer seeds than the globe eggplant.
Indian or Kenyan	These varieties are smaller and rounder, so they taste delicious stuffed. Slit it into quarters, leaving the stalk on, so you can fill with your favorite spice masala and cook whole. They can have lots of seeds, so if you're looking for a smoother texture, choose the Chinese eggplant.
Chinese or Japanese	Long and thin, they're meaty enough to be diced up for curries and can be stuffed.
White	There's no difference in taste. They just look very pretty.

Potatoes

Although potatoes were introduced to India relatively recently, in the early 17th century (remember that India's culinary history goes back thousands of years), they're a much-loved ingredient in the Indian kitchen. Potatoes are added to curries to make them go further, cooked with spices to be eaten with Indian breads, battered and fried as snacks, and mashed to make spiced cakes.

I often get asked whether to use waxy or floury/starchy potatoes in curries. The good news is that it's not always that important. Potatoes don't need to hold their shape in all curries and some actually taste better when the potatoes crumble and add thickness to the sauce.

>> **Floury:** These are high in starch and have less moisture than the other kinds, which causes them to lose their shape easily. Stirring them constantly while cooking breaks them up and releases the starch, resulting in a gloopy curry. This is fine in some dishes that have potato as a main ingredient, such as the breakfast Batata Bhaji (Spiced Yellow Potatoes; see Chapter 17). They're best used in recipes that need mashed potatoes such as Vegetable Samosas (Vegetable and Pastry Parcels; see Chapter 18). Examples of starchy potatoes include russet and red potatoes.

>> **Waxy:** On the opposite end of the spectrum are potatoes with a higher moisture content and lower starch content. These potatoes hold their shape better when cooked, and they taste buttery. They're great in curries where

they share the stage with other ingredients such as Aloo Gobi (North Indian Potatoes with Cauliflower; see Chapter 13) and for boiling. Varieties include new or baby potatoes and red fingerlings.

» **All-rounders:** These fall somewhere in between the other two in terms of their starch and moisture content. They do all jobs well, so if you don't want to buy a variety of potatoes, a bag of all-purpose white or yellow potatoes will be perfect for all your Indian recipes. Some cooks deliberately crush a few of the potatoes after they're cooked to add to curry sauce to thicken it up.

Mangoes

The concept of eating seasonally is still very popular in India. Farmers markets in the winter are filled with dark orange carrots and gleaming white cauliflowers. But it's the summer markets that excite me the most. Every year, around April (start of the summer in India), all of a sudden you see stalls filled with mangoes start to pop up in these markets. These aren't just any mangoes either — they're the most fragrant, sweetest, firmly fleshed mangoes in the world. The mighty Alphonso mango is arguably India's best loved variety, and shoppers are willing to pay any price for those first few boxes. The price never really comes down because the season is short and demand is high. It's no wonder that the mango is the national fruit of India. Alphonso mangoes are grown in a small region of India in the western state of Maharashtra. Other mangoes, such as the not nearly as good Kesar mango from Gujarat, start to appear a few weeks later.

Then as suddenly as they appeared, the Alphonso and Kesar disappear with the first rains of the monsoon season in June. It's astonishing to me that the end of the season is so final — you see them in the market one day and they're gone the next.

Then arrive the monsoon varieties, which are also delicious but don't seem to have the glamour of the Alphonso. These varieties also quietly leave the market as the monsoons fade away in September.

You'll find fresh Alphonso mangoes in some Indian stores during the season, although I've heard that each year availability could be affected due to import bans. Happily, there is an alternative: Cans of Alphonso and Kesar mango puree are available year-round, so you can easily whip it into ice creams and drinks like smoothies and Aam ki Lassi (Mango and Yogurt Drink; see Chapter 21). You may find cans of sliced Alphonso mangoes in syrup, but I find them too soggy for my liking.

Shopping for Meat and Poultry

When buying meat and poultry for an Indian recipe, you'll want to manage your time by buying cuts that cook quickly but without going tough or by using the right cookware such as a pressure cooker or Instant Pot (see Chapter 3).

Chapter 5 tells you which cuts of meat and poultry are best for Indian curries. *Red meat* often means lamb or goat in a country where beef is not popular due to religious reasons. However, it's certainly okay to replace lamb with beef if you prefer. The cooking times may change depending on the cut you use.

TIP

Here's what I'd consider when buying meat and poultry.

>> **Lamb and beef:** The most common way these will be put to use in an Indian kitchen is in a curry. The relatively long cooking time could toughen the meat, so I look for some marbling of fat that will keep the meat moist and tender. Lamb shoulder or chuck steak both have a good proportion of lean meat and collagen without a great deal of external fat. Because both these meats can take a bit of time to soften, I cube them into smaller ¾-inch pieces.

The more tender cuts such as sirloin and lamb chops are used for "drier" cooking methods such as pan-frying and grilling when making kebabs.

When buying meat, make sure it's bright red and not brown or gray, which may mean that it's getting to its use by date.

>> **Chicken:** The quality of the meat varies from one commercial producer to another, so you'll need to try out a few before you decide on a favorite. I look for texture and size, because I don't want the meat to toughen when I cook, especially in dry-cooking recipes like kebabs and tikkas.

The cut is a matter of preference. Some people like boneless chicken breast; others enjoy thighs on the bone. Generally speaking, Indian curries benefit from having some bone because it adds to the flavor of the sauce.

You won't see skin-on chicken in curries because it can slip off during the cooking. If you've bought skin-on chicken, hold the skin with some paper towel and rip it off. The paper towel will give you a better grip.

To prevent salmonella poisoning, wash your hands and all surfaces with hot soapy water after preparing raw poultry. Food safety organizations recommend that raw chicken not be washed at all. Use a separate cutting board, and never place a cooked food on a surface that had raw chicken on it.

TIP

After you've chosen the right cut of meat or poultry for your Indian recipe, you'll want to bring it home and store it safely until you're ready to use it. Start by checking the expiration date — use raw meat or poultry by that date or freeze it.

To store it in the fridge, wrap your meat or poultry and put it in the fridge as soon as you get home from the store. For a whole chicken, save time later by cutting it up into curry cut (see Chapter 5) before refrigerating it.

To freeze it, put it into freezer bags, pushing out as much air as possible before you seal them. (If you've bought in bulk, divide it up into smaller portions before freezing.) Label each bag with the date and what the bag contains. (Frozen poultry can be deceptive — you may inadvertently thaw chicken thighs when what you really need is chicken breast.)

Defrost meat or chicken in the fridge or microwave (on low). Make sure to put a tray in the fridge under the defrosting chicken to collect and discard any dripping juices. Never defrost your chicken at room temperature on the kitchen counter. Cook your meat or poultry as soon as it has thawed.

2

Getting Comfortable in the Kitchen

Master Indian kitchen techniques, like chopping and marinating, and be able to tell the difference between a tikka and a curry cut.

Learn to prepare ingredients such as chilies, tamarind, and the world's best homemade Ginger-Garlic paste.

Play with spices and figure out when to add them to the pan.

Identify the building blocks that add depth and flavor to any curry.

Put an Indian meal together and personalize it to make it hotter or milder.

Chapter **5**

Common Indian Kitchen Techniques

You're probably familiar with some of these techniques already because they're used to some extent in many cuisines. You've fried an egg and sautéed an onion, but are you able to recognize that split second when a spice goes from beautiful to burned? Have you ever tried to cook an onion bhajia only to discover that a soft, gooey center was *not* what you were after?

Replicating some of the food made popular by Indian restaurants at home (and bettering it) means that you need to master the techniques used by Indian cooks to get it right every time.

In this chapter, I explain why chopping evenly not only makes food cook uniformly but also makes it look prettier. I show you how to marinate meat and fish like a pro, so the spices permeate to give you depth of flavor. I explain why aromatics and spices are often fried and added at the end to finish dishes and why meat doesn't need to be browned at the start of making a curry. I also show you how to get that smoky, tandoori flavor into your kabobs without firing up a tandoor or a barbecue — prepare to have your mind blown!

In my cookery classes, I talk about inappropriate stirring. Sometimes we even have a "stir jar" (sort of like a "swear jar") — students who stir way too much have to put a few coins in. In this chapter, I give you some tips so that you'll become a pro at understanding when stirring is appropriate (and not have to fill that jar!) and how it cuts down massively on cooking time.

Chopping Techniques

How big each piece of meat or vegetable is cut dramatically impacts the way it cooks and contributes to the final flavor. Evenly cut ingredients mean even cooking, so you won't get a few hard bits of vegetable while others turn to mush.

Chopping, mincing, and dicing

Different dishes need different cuts because the cuts affect the final texture or consistency of the dish. (So guess what? Size *does* matter, at least when it comes to cooking!) You want to chop vegetables fairly small so that they absorb the spices as they cook. If you have large cuts of cauliflower or eggplant, for example, the spices will coat the outside and never quite get into the heart of the vegetable.

When you want a vegetable to disintegrate and make a sauce, such as onions in some curries, you need to mince it finely. I always mince my green chilies and garlic as finely as I can because I don't like biting into them (and most likely you don't either).

I find that dicing to a ¼-inch cube is useful when cutting main ingredients such as meat, fish, or vegetables, so they'll all cook the same way at the same time.

TIP

Chop a couple of pieces of your vegetable, and leave them on your chopping board to create a template as you cut the rest, which will go into a bowl. You can be your very own quality control!

The most common fresh herbs you'll use in your Indian kitchen are cilantro, mint, and curry leaf:

>> **Cilantro:** When cilantro is really fresh, the stalks are juicy and tender, so it's perfectly okay to use them for curries, although I prefer to use just the leaves for garnish.

>> **Mint:** The stems of mint are often woody so I pull off the leaves and discard the stems.

>> **Curry leaf:** Curry leaves need to be pulled off the hard stalks.

When chopping cilantro and mint, fold the bunch into a small bundle, hold it down tightly with one hand, and chop with a sharp knife, using a rocking motion to get a *chiffonade,* or very fine ribbons of the leaves. I'd try not to put too much pressure on the knife — if your chopping board turns green, you'll know you've bruised the herb too much and lost some of the flavor. If your cutting board turns red, however, something has gone very wrong! Keep it light and keep it sharp — that's the trick.

Most Indian recipes call for curry leaves to be added whole, but they're quite tough and chewy to eat, so people pick them out of a curry and put them to one side of their plate, losing out on all the health benefits they bring. In my cookery classes, we almost always chop curry leaves like we do cilantro — that way, they seem to release more flavor and get eaten!

If you don't need your herbs to be super fine — say, if you're folding them into a curry and they'll cook down — you can use a pair of scissors to chop them directly into the pan.

Peeling

Peeling or *paring* means removing the skin of fruits and vegetables. I tend to use a sharp peeler rather than a paring knife, because it's quicker, safer, and easier. I very rarely peel vegetables because I try to minimize food waste in my kitchen. If the skin is edible, I add it to the pan. Some vegetable skins are notoriously hard to cut — try butternut squash! Luckily, the curry-making process where ingredients are braised in a spiced, seasoned liquid is very forgiving of these tough-skinned vegetables, and you'll find that the curry is enhanced by that extra bit of texture. With very thin-skinned vegetables like ginger, you'll be safer scraping just the top skin off with a teaspoon, and there'll be less waste, too!

REMEMBER

Many peels are said to be rich in nutrients and fiber, so leave them on if they're edible and not disgustingly bitter or chewy.

Slicing

With slicing, as well as with all other chopping, aim to get everything even. The most common vegetable you'll slice is an onion (I know, you're going to cry, but you'll do plenty of that for Indian cooking!), but more about that technique in

CUTS OF MEAT USED IN INDIAN COOKING

CULTURAL WISDOM

Indian Muslims eat only halal meat. *Halal* is an Arabic word for "permissible," and the meat is cut according to religious laws that make it acceptable to eat. Here are the various cuts of meat you'll see called for in Indian recipes:

- **Tikka:** This term loosely refers to a boneless piece of meat, usually chicken, that's about a 1-inch cube. The term is also used with paneer or firm Indian cottage cheese. Chicken tikka usually refers to breast meat that is even in color and texture. Through Indian restaurant menus, the word *tikka* has come to mean a grilled chicken or paneer dish that has spiced cubes of meat or cottage cheese on skewers and sometimes interspersed with onions and colorful bell peppers. You'll want to use tikkas for recipes that use quick cooking methods — otherwise, there's a danger that the meat will overcook and toughen.

- **Boti:** Diced, boneless leg of lamb, goat, or beef is often referred to as *boti.* These are also -1-inch cubes. Indians prefer their meat to be lean, so most of the fat is trimmed off. You'll find that these terms are used loosely so sometimes, a boneless cut of chicken thigh may also be called *boti.* Restaurants have popularized the word by offering boti kabobs — grilled chunks of lamb, mutton, or beef that are spiced and cooked in the tandoor oven. If you're cutting meat yourself, be sure to cut against the grain — this breaks the muscle fibers and shortens them so you'll end up with a tender, melt-in-the-mouth dish.

- **Curry or karahi:** This is essentially a whole chicken or piece of lamb or beef cut into manageable pieces that will fit into the pan and on your plate with rice and a few sides on it. Karahi refers to the wok-shaped Indian pan that many curries are cooked in. Offal and gizzards are not included in the curry cut, but you can ask the butcher to throw those in for a few more bucks. Indians usually prefer skinless chicken (to keep it lean), so make sure to pull the skin off if you've bought it skin on. (To take the skin off chicken easily, hold it with a paper towel, which gives you a firmer grip, and yank it off.)

  The idea of the curry or karahi cut is to create an interesting mix of both white and dark, boneless and bone-in meat that gives a contrasting experience of soft and slighter tougher meat all in one dish. Curry cut is used for recipes with longer cooking techniques, which let the meat simmer slowly until it almost falls off the bone.

- **Biryani cut:** You'd be forgiven for thinking that the curry cut and the biryani cut are one and the same. The only difference is that in a biryani cut, you have a higher proportion of meat-on-the-bone pieces that create a meatier bone stock to add flavor to the dish. Biryanis are rich one-pot dishes where rice and meat (or vegetables for a vegetarian version) are cooked to together in water or stock. The word *biryani* comes from the Persian *birian,* which means "fried before cooking." There are several different recipes all over India — versions exist everywhere that the Mughal Empire spread.

Chapter 6. Slicing everything else is less emotional, and as long as your knife is sharp and your chopping board is secure and doesn't slide around (put a damp kitchen towel under it to prevent it from sliding), it's easy.

Butterflying shrimp

Shrimp is popular in India — both the salty, sweet marine variety and the slightly muddy river shrimp. Most people, including me, are queasy about the digestive tract and its gritty contents, so I'm quite grossed out when I see that offending dark vein in restaurant curries. If you've bought head-on, shell-on shrimp, you'll want to shell and devein them so that the flavor of the spices permeates and doesn't get discarded when you shell them at the table.

Cleaning and deveining shrimp can make some people queasy, but trust me, after you've done it a few times, you'll find it to be just another kitchen activity that promotes mindfulness! Turn on some soothing music for company. Here's how to clean and devein shrimp:

1. **Put your shrimp into a large bowl, wash them in cold water, and drain them.**

   You can put them into a colander to drain away all the water, which will make them easier to handle when you shell them.

2. **Lay a couple of paper towels on your kitchen counter, place a food compost pail or recyclable food bag nearby, and get a small, sharp kitchen knife.**

   Some people use a pair of kitchen scissors, instead of a knife, to cut through the shell — use whatever tool you're most comfortable with. If you use a knife, just make sure your knife isn't serrated, or you'll get a jagged edge.

3. **Holding one shrimp, snap off the head and discard it.**

   Wipe the cut end of the body on the paper towel to get rid of the gunk.

4. **Shell the shrimp, starting from the underside, removing the legs as well.**

   You may need to do this in two or three parts, because the legs sometimes break away from the shell.

5. **Hold the tail and twist it from side to side to loosen it, and then gently pull it off.**

   This helps to loosen the tail and stops the tail meat from being pulled off as well. Such a waste!

6. **Now run the tip of a sharp knife down the outer curve of the shrimp's back and cut through until you can see the dark digestive tract.**

   You can also cut through the shell with a pair of kitchen scissors, if you prefer.

   Sometimes this tract will be colorless or there may not be one, but it's always worth checking, so cut roughly halfway into the body. This is called *butterflying shrimp.* It makes them more succulent and bigger because they open up during cooking.

7. **Lift the tract out with your knife and discard.**

   Put the discarded tract on the paper towel. (It's easier to toss than wash it off your compost pail.)

REMEMBER

   Go all the way to the end of the tail. There always seems to be a bit of tract at the very end of the shrimp.

8. **Carry on for all the shrimp similarly and then rinse in cold water to clean thoroughly.**

   Using hot water will start to cook them, and you'll end up with rubbery shrimp in the final dish.

WARNING

There's another dark vein on the underside of the shrimp, but this doesn't have anything to do with digestion and can be left in.

TIP

Marinating Meats and Other Foods

I'm not a big fan of marinating meats for curries because the relatively long cooking process helps to soften and flavor it anyway. One way of stopping your meat from getting as tough as old boots during grilling or baking, however, is to marinate it. Most Indian marinades have spices for flavor, oil or yogurt to carry the flavor into the meat, and acid in the form of lemon, lime, or vinegar, as well as salt to soften it. Most of us don't have a *tandoor* (a clay oven heated by coals to a whopping 900 degrees) in our backyards (the closest thing I have is a plant pot!), so we need to get those flavors as close to the real thing in our kitchen ovens as we can.

Table 5-1 walks you through the ingredients in a marinade and how each ingredient works.

REMEMBER

Acidic foods can over-tenderize some foods by loosening the muscle fibers and making them lose their texture while cooking, so be sure to check the marinating time in the recipe.

TABLE 5-1   **How Marinating Works**

Ingredient	What It Does
Spices	Adds flavor and color to marinades. The various combinations of spices sometimes give a kabob its name, such as kali mirch tikka, prepared using a top note of black pepper.
Salt	Helps to take water-soluble flavors, such as mint and cilantro, deep into the meat and seasons the food.
Acids	Denatures protein and loosens the muscle fiber for better absorption, in addition to adding flavor.
Seasoning	Builds on flavor. Indian marinades almost always have ginger and garlic. Sugar is not common in Indian marinades because the accompanying dip is usually a combination of sweet, spicy, and sour flavors.
Fats	Slightly dilute the acids, which can oversoften the meat. Yogurt and oil are widely used in Indian marinades because they carry the fat-soluble flavors of spices well.
Herbs	Bring flavor and liven up a marinade.
Enzymes	Help to break down the protein and tenderize meat. Indian marinades sometime use fresh raw papaya or its enzyme papain, sold in powdered form in Indian shops.

How long to marinate

Here's a guide to how long to marinate meats and other foods:

» **Chicken:** Removing the skin and cutting the chicken into bite-size pieces will improve absorption of the marinade. Choose an oil-based marinade for short cooking times on a high heat (as for tikka) and a yogurt marinade for longer cooking times at a lower heat (as for biryani). Marinate chicken for up to 24 hours in the fridge. I don't really marinate foods for curries because the long, slow cooking time will carry the flavor into the meat, but if you want to, half an hour should be plenty.

» **Meat:** You can marinate diced or ground meat for up to 24 hours (in the fridge) for kabobs. Then you can cook it on a baking tray or thread it onto skewers (shape the ground meat into sausage shapes on the skewers). Because meat is tougher than chicken, the tenderness of cooked meat is enhanced by tenderizers so a yogurt-based marinade, which will help soften the meat, is preferable. If you're using a strong tenderizer, like papaya or papain (roughly 1 tablespoon of raw papaya or ½ teaspoon of papain powder for 1 pound of meat), the marinating time should be around 2 hours, but no more than 6 hours.

» **Fish and seafood:** These should be marinated in the refrigerator for 24 hours, but skip the acid because it can start to "cook" fish and make it mushy when cooked. Add the acid, usually some lemon or lime, up to 30 minutes before cooking.

» **Vegetables:** Hard vegetables, such as carrots and potatoes, need just an hour or so of marinating so that there is some absorption of flavor. They'll absorb more during the cooking process when heat softens them and allows flavor-carrying moisture to permeate. Soft vegetables such as eggplant don't need to be marinated at all because the salt can oversoften them, making them soggy. No need to refrigerate either.

» **Paneer:** A cube of Indian cottage cheese can be marinated because it will absorb flavor. I'd leave it for up to 24 hours in the fridge.

REMEMBER

Take your refrigerated, marinated food out of the fridge half an hour before cooking, and bring it to room temperature so that it cooks more evenly and remains juicy during cooking.

How to build an Indian marinade

This is a good basic technique that can be applied to kabobs, curries, and biryanis. Some recipes have variations on this technique, based on which cut of meat is used, what flavor top note is required, or what texture the final dish should have.

1. **Choose a bowl big enough to hold the main ingredient you're going to marinate.**

    You'll need a size that allows you mix the marinade with the ingredient comfortably without any spillage and then fit in the fridge.

2. **Tip in your spices and salt.**

    The marinade must be high in taste and seasoning because it's going to flavor the main ingredient. You'll probably need more salt than you think you will —it may look like a lot, but you won't be eating it all yourself!

3. **Add the seasonings and herbs.**

    I use ginger and garlic in paste form rather than chopped because I don't like biting into whole chunks of garlic. The paste coats the food more evenly, too. Use fresh or dried herbs, but keep in mind that cilantro and mint always taste better fresh.

4. **Mix in the papaya or papain, if using.**

    Add this sensibly — too much for too long, and you'll have cooked shreds rather than cubes.

5. **Drizzle in the lemon or lime juice (except for fish and seafood).**

Use lots of it, too. It'll help the food absorb the flavors.

6. **If making a yogurt marinade, add the yogurt now and finish like this:**

a. Choose a high-fat yogurt for cooking — low-fat ones tend to split and become watery.

b. Taste the marinade now. You've got it right if the spices, salt, and lemon/lime make your eyes water and your face crinkle.

c. If you think it's perfect and you can easily eat the whole bowl, it'll be underwhelming when you add the main ingredient in, so crank up those flavors — add more spice, salt, and lemon/lime.

d. Taste again and add the main ingredient.

e. Mix well to coat, cover, and leave for the desired time.

If making an oil marinade, proceed like this:

a. Taste the mixture in the bowl — it should be very high in taste, just like for the yogurt marinade.

b. Mix in the main ingredient before you add any oil.

c. Rub with your fingers if you're not squeamish.

d. Finish off by drizzling in the oil. Adding the oil to the marinade before the main ingredient may create a barrier and prevent the flavors from permeating. Adding it at the end allows it to bind the spices to the food.

TIP

Make the marinade and then add the raw meat, chicken, or fish to it rather than putting the marinade ingredients into a bowl of meat. That way, you can taste and adjust seasoning and flavoring safely.

TRICKS OF THE TRADE: WHAT THEY DON'T TELL YOU

If you've enjoyed chicken tikka and tandoori chicken in a restaurant, you'll no doubt have tried to guess what makes the food so intensely flavorful. What would bring those flavors alive at home without a tandoor or without using that dreaded red food coloring that makes tikka look like something from Mars?

First, remember that tandoori foods do *not* need to be blazing red. Yes, you do want color, but there are ways to keep it natural and healthy.

(continued)

(continued)

Here are some tricks to do it restaurant-style:

- **You want those flavors to penetrate, so make gashes through the chicken legs or breasts.** If you're using smaller cuts, prick them evenly with a cocktail stick before marinating.

- **For color, use turmeric, that lovely golden spice, and when adding chili powder, make sure it's Kashmiri chili.** Kashmiri chili is a natural, crimson spice with a medium heat — I like to think of it as all bark and some bite. That way you can forget about the food coloring that makes many of us see red.

- **Use mustard oil.** The oil used in a marinade makes a big difference — who'd have thought? With so much going on with the spices and aromatics, you might have thought the fat was just a carrier. But apparently not. Restaurants swear by mustard oil! This pungent, sharp-tasting fat adds drama and pizazz to everything else in the bowl and adds a depth of flavor like no other. Try it!

- **Go for Greek yogurt.** The yogurt used in marinades will add texture and hold the spices together. Restaurants often use hung yogurt — this is the full-fat kind, put into a muslin cloth, and hung to drain away the liquid. I can't be bothered with all that so I use Greek yogurt. It's just as good!

- **For tikkas and larger cuts of meat and poultry used for kabobs (not for ground meat or for meat going into curries), you want to marinate twice!** You'll break the process into two steps. For the first round of marinating, rub the meat with salt, lemon or lime, and ginger-garlic paste. Cover and refrigerate for two to three hours. This allows the moisture in the meat to be drawn out and the seasoning to seep in. Then, for the second round of marinating, add everything else, including the yogurt or oil. Sometimes yogurt and mustard oil are *both* added in this second round.

Sweating Over a Hot Tandoori Oven, er, Stove

Getting up to speed with some of the essential Indian cooking techniques means fewer accidents in the kitchen (no more overcooked vegetables or underdone meat) and certainly better results when using spices, which can be notoriously fragile to cook and yet super-robust in flavor.

Heat regulation is critical because most curries are built in a sequence, with ingredients going into the same pot one after another, with enough time given to each one to cook to the correct level before adding the next one.

Typically, the ingredient that takes the longest time to cook or needs the highest level of heat goes in first. This ingredient is brought to a certain stage in its cooking — say, when onions start to brown or spice seeds begin to splutter — and then the heat is lowered allowing these ingredients to proceed to the next stage of cooking without burning. Then when the next ingredient in the sequence is added, the heat is turned up to maintain the temperature of the pan and keep the food cooking evenly and at the right pace. When this second ingredient has cooked to a certain level, the third one is added, regulating the heat so that the food doesn't burn and yet keeps cooking.

REMEMBER

Stirring helps to mix the food and cook it evenly but constant stirring will only make the food take longer to cook — much longer because it doesn't allow the ingredients to absorb the heat of the pan because the contact with the pan is lost every few seconds. You want to become confident enough to leave ingredients be and to stir only occasionally. The best way to do this is to stand by the pan and keep an eye on what's going on but resist the urge to keep stirring.

TIP

Spread your ingredients in the pan in a single layer rather than piling them up — that way, they'll all absorb heat and cook evenly.

CULTURAL WISDOM

Considering that India has hundreds of languages the culinary terms I mention in this section could be endless! I use Hindi terms for the most part, because it's the most widely spoken language in India.

Dum: All hot and steamy

Dum means to breathe in or to steam. It's a technique in which a pot is sealed with dough made from wheat flour and water. A tight-fitting lid ensures that no steam can escape and all the flavor is retained in the dish. The dish is cooked slowly, retaining all the flavor and making the food tender and moist.

This technique is used mostly in rich biryanis and some meat curries, but quite a lot of Indian cookery depends on this method of covering the pot tightly and letting the steam cook the food. When vegetables are prepared as side dishes, they're often cooked with spices and herbs and just enough water that will turn to steam and leave the dish dry and perfectly textured.

Tarka: Don't lose your temper, use it

Also called *tadka* or *chownk,* this technique (commonly known in English as *tempering* or *blooming*) is what makes Indian food so aromatic and heady. It's done to bring out the flavors in the aromatic ingredients through frying and give the dish they're added to extra depth. Spices or flavorings such as onions, garlic, ginger, or chilies are cooked in hot oil to extract and develop their flavor.

CULTURAL WISDOM

Different regions of India use different ingredients in the tarka. The North may have cumin seeds and garlic, whereas southern kitchens may use mustard seeds and curry leaves.

Tempering can be done at two stages of cooking:

>> **At the start of the cooking process:** Most Indian dishes begin with the frying of spices or aromatics such as onions in oil. That mix of aromatics is called *tarka,* but the word also means something that is added at the end! You'll find that start of cooking tarka is used in dishes such as Tarka Dal (Spiced Lentils; see Chapter 15). The oil used varies from region to region all over India and contributes to the final flavor of the dish.

>> **At the end of the cooking process:** Used as a final finishing step when, for example, cumin seeds or chopped garlic may be fried in oil and poured over a curry along with the oil. The oil gets infused with the aromatic oils extracted from the spices or garlic and helps to disperse them throughout the dish. Finishing tarka is applied to dishes like chutneys or some vegetable curries. I love to use ghee in the finishing tarka — ghee makes the dish all buttery and rich — but it's equally okay to use oil. Make sure to use an oil with a high smoking point, such as coconut or canola, because it will get pretty hot! Spices bloomed in oil or ghee become the top note of the dish. Ingredients used in the finishing tarka vary from mustard and cumin seeds to curry leaves and lentils.

So, when do you use a starting tarka and when do you want a finishing one? Generally speaking, I'd go for a starting one for a one-pot dish I'm building in a sequence. And I'd finish with a tarka for added top notes. Some dishes have *both* a starting and a finishing tarka. I promise you, it's not as complex as it sounds!

TIP

A finishing tarka is done in a small frying pan or a special tarka bowl, a heavy ladle with a heatproof handle. A starting tarka will go into the cooking pot you're using to make the curry.

To get your finishing tarka right, follow these steps:

1. **Warm the oil or ghee.**

You don't want to heat the fat too much, because the spices will burn as soon as they go in. Put them into fairly cool oil or ghee and wait for them to bloom. (More about this in Chapter 7.)

Also, you shouldn't need to stir the spices — give the pan a few shakes and let them get on with blooming. Shaken not stirred.

2. **Add the ingredient that needs the highest temperature first.**

   Among spices, mustard seeds go in before the other spice seeds and must start to pop before the next lot of spices go in.

3. **Keep all the ingredients for the tarka ready before you turn the heat on.**

   Measure out spices and keep them separate because they may go into the pan at different times. Chop ginger or garlic. Wash, dry, and chop curry leaves. When the oil is hot, you'll be adding the sequence of ingredients in very quickly and it'll all be done in a few seconds. Also, have close by the curry you want to pour your tarka into.

4. **Cook the ingredients until just done.**

   The high heat in the oil will continue to cook the food, so take the pan off the heat when the ingredients have changed color — always a good indication of doneness. Garlic, for example, will need to be just turning a light golden. A few extra minutes will burn the spices and aromatics like garlic. If the tarka burns, very annoyingly, you'll have to get rid of it and start all over again.

WARNING

Don't add water or other liquid to a tarka. The oil will be very hot and you may start a fire. Make sure to wipe any washed ingredients like curry leaves or lentils dry on a paper towel, or else the oil will spit and splutter all over your stove. More cleaning, less joy.

REMEMBER

If the oil gets too hot, the spices will burn so after the first spice has gone in and popped or changed color, turn the heat down before adding the next ingredients. You can always turn the heat back up if things slow down too much.

Bhuna: It's bhuna long time

The process of sautéing or stir-frying in some fat, over a high heat that is reduced to medium when the ingredient has started to soften or brown is called *bhunana*, *bhunao*, or colloquially, *bhuna*. Don't confuse this with the French technique of sautéing. Bhuna is done at several stages of the cooking process and sometimes a little liquid — water, yogurt or tomato, for instance — is added to prevent ingredients such as spices from sticking.

You'll probably start by frying the seed spices in oil as you begin making the tarka (see "Tarka: Don't lose your temper, use it," earlier in this chapter). Then a moist ingredient such as onions will be added and cooked until it's brown. When it just about starts to stick to the pan, the heat is lowered and the next ingredient is added — but only after the pan is scraped to get all the flavors back into the sauce. A little water or other liquid such as light broth may be added to deglaze the pan. This liquid is cooked on a high heat and allowed to evaporate so that the controlled sticking and deglazing can happen all over again.

The process of stir-frying, stirring intermittently, deglazing the pan, and cooking the ingredients to a desired level of doneness is what most people mean by *bhuna*. The French word sauté means "to jump," because foods cook quickly and almost jump out of the pan — but you won't be jumping for the Indian version of it. Bhunao needs patience, so take joy in the fact that you're creating a masterpiece to be admired and enjoyed.

Now, how can you tell that you're a pro at the bhuna technique? When you've added water to deglaze the pan and let it evaporate, you'll be looking for the oil to separate. This is a major Indian recipe instruction, and what it means is that the fat that went in at the beginning starts to rise to the surface or gathers around the edges of the sauce. You'll need to have started with a reasonable amount of fat — skimping will mean that this essential visual clue will be lost. If the fat doesn't separate, add another splash of water and let it evaporate again, stirring intermittently. The separation of oil is a good indication that this bhunao is complete, and you can add the next ingredient.

TIP

In Indian curries, meat bhunao or sautéing stops before it gets brown. Unlike in Western food, where browned meat is visually appealing, this doesn't matter in a curry. Also, you don't want to create a hard layer on the outside because it won't let the flavors in the sauce permeate.

Talna: Off to a frying start

I know, I know, you're probably thinking, here we go — everyone knows that Indian food is oily and unhealthy. Well, no. Some foods are shallow fried and some are deep fried and this technique is called *talna*. Deep-frying is usually done in a *karahi* (a heavy, wok-shaped metallic pan used in Indian kitchens). Fried foods are always well drained, so they have a crisp texture but are not greasy.

To deep-fry evenly, begin with hot but not smoking oil. You'll know it's ready when a slice of what you're going to fry, dipped slightly into the oil, begins to sizzle. Or drop a little batter into the oil — it should rise in 3 to 4 seconds. Any quicker, and the oil is too hot, so reduce the heat and wait for it to cool down a bit. Any later and the oil is too cold — wait for it to heat up a bit more.

Heat regulation is critical during frying, because foods need to cook evenly, especially in the middle, without burning or turning too dark on the surface. How many times have you fried a pakora until it's golden brown and then discovered that the center is floury and raw? This is because the heat was too high and the outside cooked too quickly.

Start off at a high heat and when the food has sealed and started to change color, reduce the heat to medium and cook it slowly until the right color has been achieved.

REMEMBER

Make sure to have a plate lined with paper towel ready to put your fried food on because you'll want to drain off any excess oil as soon as you've finished frying it. Letting it sit in a pool of oil can make it soggy.

Dhungar: A practi-coal solution

That smoky flavor we all associate with restaurant-style kabobs comes from the tandoor. Even if you were a tandoor fan and enthusiastically built one in your backyard, imagine inserting your hand into that inferno-like cavity to place skewers in or slap naans onto the inner walls! It takes a *lot* to be a tandoori chef, and those who work long hours in restaurants have all my respect.

TIP

To bring those smoky flavors into your homemade kabobs, here's a neat little trick that not only feels and looks impressive but also adds that barbecue dazzle to your food. It's called *dhungar*, and it's a stovetop method that can be done easily in a home kitchen:

1. **Place a small metal bowl on top of your marinated food.**

   You can use this technique to smoke cooked foods like curries and kabobs, but it can be an overwhelming taste. Smoking raw marinated food gives a mellow effect.

2. **Hold a piece of coal with a pair of tongs, and light it outdoors or near an open window.**

   You can light it on your gas stove if you're feeling confident, but make sure that the extractor hood is on.

3. **When the initial thick smoke has died away and the coal has turned gray, place the coal in the bowl.**

   Make sure that the coal is gray — if it's burning, it'll scorch the food.

4. **Pour 1 tablespoon of ghee over the coal.**

It'll start to smoke furiously.

5. **Quickly cover the pan with a tight-fitting lid and seal for 2 to 3 minutes.**

The longer you leave it, the smokier your food will be, but I suggest a maximum of 10 minutes.

6. **Lift the lid, remove the bowl of coal, and discard the burning coal safely.**

You're ready to cook your tandoori-style kabobs!

IN THIS CHAPTER

» **Understanding Indian ingredients**

» **Cooking perfect rice every time**

» **Preparing your own ginger-garlic paste**

» **Working with tamarind**

» **Using tomatoes in all their forms**

» **Making just-right lentils**

» **Slicing and dicing onions like a pro**

» **Chopping chilies safely**

» **Adding coconut to your routine**

» **Making homemade paneer**

Chapter **6**

Using Staple Ingredients in Indian Dishes

RECIPES IN THIS CHAPTER

🍲 **Boiled Rice (Chaval), Absorption Method**

🍲 **Boiled Rice (Chaval), Draining Method**

🍲 **Ginger-Garlic Paste (Adrak Lahsun)**

O n one of my trips to India, I was invited to a friend's house for dinner, and I enjoyed the curry so much that I headed to the kitchen to chat with the cook in the hopes of coming out with a new recipe. He was generous and happily shared the information, delighted that I'd loved his food so much. At the end of his explanation, I asked about the cardamom. He hadn't mentioned any, and I'd definitely tasted it. "Of course," he said, "that goes without saying — just throw a bit in." I wasn't surprised or annoyed — that's how everyone in India cooks, using judgment, common sense, and a good helping of gut instinct.

In this chapter, I help you build that instinct and get the basics right so that, in time, you won't have to refer to a recipe for every how-to step. You'll gain confidence in knowing two methods that produce fluffy rice and how to save time by making a batch of ginger-garlic paste and freezing it. I explain why canned tomatoes work better than fresh in some dishes and tell you when to dice and when to slice onions. If you've ever chopped a chile and rubbed your eyes, you'll know why conquering these beasts is crucial to your well-being — with the tips in this chapter, you'll never have dangerous chili on your hands again.

Focusing on Ingredients

There is no concept of standardization in everyday Indian cookery. The word *andaz* features in any discussion about a recipe; it means an intuitive approximation or just knowing how to put it all together. Indian cooks know that cooking isn't a precise science and that using your judgment is key. In this section, I show you how to use your nose, ears, and eyes before you even *taste* the food to check the flavors. Cool or what?

Standardizing recipes

One of the big reasons why standardization is so elusive is that names of recipes are very general and open to interpretation. Take the case of *aloo gobi* (literally "potato cauliflower"). With such a vast array of ingredients to choose from, a cook can make up the recipe any which way, as long as it contains potatoes and cauliflower.

But it isn't as simple as that. Nothing in India is. With hundreds of languages spoken, various religions practiced, and countless cuisines enjoyed, diversity is key. The language in which the name of the recipe is written holds clues as to what should go into the cooking pan. *Aloo* and *gobi* are North Indian words from the Hindi or Punjabi language, so the style of cooking will be North Indian, with ingredients such as onions and tomatoes forming the base sauce. In the western part of India, you'd find *fulawar batata* ("cauliflower potato"), but in this region, you'll probably find curry leaves, cloves, and coconut, too.

Personal preferences also count. I'm not a great lover of very spicy, hot foods, so I often decrease the heat level when I'm cooking. When you're confident with creating balance and depth of flavor, you can add more or less of an ingredient to personalize the recipe. There isn't a hard and fast rule about how a dish should be prepared, but keeping true to regional, cultural, and historical influences is vital.

Measuring ingredients

When you're cooking a recipe for, say, four people, you may wonder why the yield appears as though it may not be enough or that you could eat the whole thing yourself.

An Indian meal is made up of several dishes, so you'll be cooking two or three recipes, which will make enough for everyone.

Then there are the extras — perhaps some yogurt, a few slices of tomato or cucumber, and a store-bought pickle to add some zing.

When using spices, you can't really wing it when you're new to Indian cooking. Table 6-1 is a list of some common spices and how much you'll need for a recipe. A set of measuring spoons is a must, and all measures are level, not heaped.

TABLE 6-1

Spice Measurements

Spice	How Much to Use for Four Servings
Asafetida	¼ teaspoon
Bay leaves	2 fresh or 3 dried
Cardamom	4 to 5 pods
Chile powder, medium-hot	1 teaspoon for a low-to medium-hot dish (but use more or less depending on your preferences, making sure not to exceed 2 teaspoons)
Cinnamon	1-inch stick
Cloves	4 to 5
Coriander, ground	1 to 2 teaspoons
Coriander, seeds	2 tablespoons
Cumin, ground	1 to 2 teaspoons
Cumin, seeds	1 teaspoon
Curry leaves	10 fresh or 15 dried
Garam masala	1 to 2 teaspoons
Mustard seeds	1 teaspoon
Turmeric	½ teaspoon to mildly color rice

1 teaspoon for curries |

The Long and Short of Cooking Rice

Raise your hand if you've ever cooked rice expecting a fluffy result, but it's gone all stodgy. I hope you can see my hand raised very high. There could be several reasons for this — from choosing the correct rice to getting the ratio of rice to water absolutely perfect.

With Indian cooking, you almost always want to cook your rice fluffy, with the grains separate and lustrous. Although many varieties of rice are grown and eaten all over India, in the West, what you'll find most easily is basmati rice, a slender, long-grained, fragrant variety.

CULTURAL WISDOM

The word *basmati* means "queen of fragrance." Basmati rice is grown in the foot-hills of the Himalayas. Because it's expensive in India, it's reserved for special dishes on festive days.

Becoming a confident rice cook is a wonderful thing because you'll find yourself reaching for the bag of rice every time you think of preparing an Indian meal. When you get the basics down pat, you'll be sure to have a plate of fluffy rice with separate grains, every time.

TIP

Here are my tips for making the perfect rice:

>> **Start by choosing the right kind of rice.** All basmati is not equal. You want to buy *aged* basmati, which means that the rice has been matured over one or two years in very controlled conditions. Each grain dries a bit and develops a skin that seals the starch in. Not much gets out during cooking, giving you a higher chance of fluffiness.

>> **Rinse the rice before using it.** Rinsing removes any loose starch that may detract from the final fluffiness. To rinse it, put the raw rice in a sieve and hold it under a cold running tap. Resist the urge to run your fingers through the wet rice — if you agitate the grains in this way, they may break, which will make the final dish starchy. (Or put the rice in a bowl, cover the rice with cold water, and swirl your fingers through it gently. Then drain it through a sieve.) Rinse the rice in the sieve until the water runs clear.

Some people like to soak their rice before using it. If you have the time and the will, you can soak the rice in cold water for 15 minutes to an hour. The rice will absorb the moisture, expand, and can take less time to cook. White basmati doesn't take long to cook anyway, though (only 10 to 15 minutes at the most), so soaking really isn't necessary. Brown basmati is a different matter — I soak brown basmati because it takes longer to cook and soaking helps to hydrate it and start the softening process.

Don't forget to drain off the soaking water and cook the rice in fresh water. If you soak the rice, there's no need to rinse it.

>> **If you're frying the washed and drained rice, say for a pulao, do so in a few drops of oil.** This helps to seal the rice slightly. But remember not to stir too much — excessive stirring can break the grains and release the starch, putting to waste that beautiful aging process.

>> **Add the correct amount of water.** If you're using the absorption method (see the following recipe), you'll need to measure the water exactly as the recipe states. For the draining method (see the recipe later in this chapter), you want enough water in the pan so that the rice can be submerged even when it's boiling — the movement of the water helps to separate the grains.

>> **Choose the right pan.** Rice cooks better in a saucepan than it does in a frying pan for two reasons:

  • A deep pan provides more room for the rice to move around when it's simmering.

  • There's less evaporation than from a wider frying pan, so there's less chance of the rice drying out while cooking.

  For the absorption method, you'll need a pan with a tight-fitting lid, too.

>> **Add a few pinches of salt.** Salt gives a rounded flavor, but don't add too much because rice will always be eaten with a seasoned side.

Boiled Rice (Chaval), Absorption Method

PREP TIME: ABOUT 5 MIN	COOK TIME: 15–18 MINUTES	YIELD: 3–4 SERVINGS

INGREDIENTS

2 cups white basmati rice, washed and drained

4 cups warm water

¼ teaspoon salt

DIRECTIONS

1 In a saucepan, combine the ingredients. Bring to a boil over high heat. Then reduce the heat to the lowest setting, cover with a tight-fitting lid so that no steam escapes, and cook for 10 minutes without lifting the lid.

2 Turn the heat off and leave to rest, still covered, for 5 minutes.

3 Remove the lid, fluff the rice with a fork, and serve hot.

TIP: For brown basmati rice, use 2 cups of warm water instead. After it has come to a boil, simmer for 20 minutes, covered, on a low setting.

TIP: If you have leftover rice, cool it completely and refrigerate for up to 1 day. To make it safe to eat, reheat until it's steaming, either in a microwave or a steamer. Don't reheat rice more than once.

Boiled Rice (Chaval), Draining Method

PREP TIME: ABOUT 5 MIN	COOK TIME: 12–15 MINUTES	YIELD: 3–4 SERVINGS

INGREDIENTS

2 cups white basmati rice, washed and drained

8 cups boiling hot water

¼ teaspoon salt

DIRECTIONS

1 In a saucepan, combine the ingredients. Bring to a boil. Then reduce the heat to low and simmer for 10 minutes, making sure that the water has some movement to keep the grains separated.

2 Check if it's done by squashing a few grains between your fingers or simply taste it! Turn the heat off and drain the rice in a colander in the sink.

3 Serve hot.

TIP: You can use this method for brown or whole-grain basmati, too. Just allow 35 to 40 minutes of cooking time.

TIP: If you have leftover rice, cool it completely and refrigerate for up to 1 day. To make it safe to eat, reheat until it's steaming, either in a microwave or a steamer. Don't reheat rice more than once.

Making and Storing Ginger-Garlic Paste

If you've cooked Indian food before or eaten at an Indian restaurant, you know how important the ginger-and-garlic flavor combination is. Ginger-garlic paste is not only a key ingredient in the Indian kitchen but also a healthy powerhouse that can help soothe colds and reduce blood cholesterol.

People seem to either love or hate ginger and garlic, and the lingering aromas in the kitchen can sometimes be off-putting. Make sure to open a window or have the fan on! Although you can buy it ready-made in Indian shops, making your own is best — that way, you know what's in it.

Preparing the ginger

Start by choosing the freshest ginger you can find. Look for firm, shiny, skinned "hands" that are not wrinkled or rough to the touch.

The next step is to prepare the ginger. You want to remove the topmost skin — that light golden layer — but not the flesh underneath it. (The fine layer just under the skin is full of immunity-boosting compounds.) To do this, hold the ginger firmly and, using a teaspoon, scrape the top skin off. (You can use a small sharp knife if you prefer, but a spoon is safer.)

TIP

It's perfectly okay to leave the skin on and eat it, but it can sometimes be woody in texture and leave hard bits in the paste.

Preparing the garlic

Choose garlic bulbs that are firm to touch and free from any mold. To prepare the garlic, you need to peel it. Peeling garlic can be fiddly and, often, as you chop, it starts to stick to your fingers and the knife. To prevent this from happening, follow these steps:

1. **Cut off the woody top bit of the clove.**

2. **Lay the broadest part of your knife flat on the clove, and give it a good whack with your other hand.**

   This loosens the skin, which you can now easily pull off.

3. **Now you can just chop it roughly, because it'll just be going into the blender.**

   You don't need to discard the green soul from the center of the garlic — it's edible and any bitterness it has will add to the balance of flavors in the dish the paste is used in.

TIP To get rid of the smell of garlic from your fingers, wash them in cold water and rub them on a bar of steel soap (you can find it in kitchen stores), or just run your hands over your steel kitchen sink.

Making the paste

The following recipe makes a batch of ginger-garlic paste. I always have some in my freezer — it cuts down massively on the time it takes to prepare a curry, and it's my favorite cheat ingredient! I'm sure it'll be yours, too.

Ginger-Garlic Paste (Adrak Lahsun)

PREP TIME: ABOUT 20 MIN	COOK TIME: NONE	YIELD: ABOUT 2 CUPS

INGREDIENTS

½ cup fresh ginger, skin scraped off and chopped

1 cup garlic, peeled and chopped

DIRECTIONS

Put the peeled and chopped ginger and garlic in a blender along with enough cold water to just cover the mixture. Blend to a fine puree. Use as much as you need right away and then store the rest in the refrigerator or freezer (see the tips below).

TIP: If you just need a small amount, you can grate (or crush in a mortar and pestle) 1 part ginger and 2 parts garlic. (For example, if you need 1 tablespoon of ginger-garlic paste, use 1 teaspoon ginger and 2 teaspoons garlic. *Remember:* 1 tablespoon equals 3 teaspoons.)

TIP: To store in the refrigerator, transfer to a clean jar, pour in enough oil to just cover the ginger-garlic paste (any cooking oil will do), and put it in the fridge for up to 3 weeks. You may find that the oil layer decreases with each scoop of paste used — just add more oil as necessary. The oil seals it from the air and stops it from oxidizing so it stays fresh longer.

TIP: To freeze the paste, pour it into a freezer bag, lay the bag on a metal tray, pat it flat, and freeze it as a sheet of ginger-garlic paste (you don't need to add oil while freezing the paste). It will store for up to 3 months in the freezer. The paste becomes quite brittle when it freezes, so you can snap off as much as you need for each recipe, adding it directly to the pan. If you prefer, you can put the paste into an ice cube tray and freeze it that way. The downside to this technique is that you have to thaw ginger-garlic cubes when you remove them from the freezer (whereas the bits broken off from a flat sheet can be added directly to the pan).

Happy Sour: Using Tamarind

Tamarind is a sausage-shaped fruit that grows on large trees. The pods ripen in the summer — the flesh becomes soft, and the shell becomes brittle. Within the flesh are squarish, dark brown, shiny seeds and fibers that hold it all together. The pulp is the part you use; the seeds and fibers are discarded.

You may think you've never tasted tamarind, but you probably have. It's used in Thai and Mexican cuisines, as well as Indian, and you can find it in sodas in parts of Latin America. Its fruity sour taste has probably made you pucker up, but you've still reached for more — the taste is addictive! Growing up in India, it was something we looked forward to eating every summer.

CULTURAL WISDOM

The story goes that an English officer returning from India in the 1800s, brought back some tamarind and asked his local chemists, John Wheeley Lea and William Henry Perrins, to replicate a recipe for a sauce he'd enjoyed there. After a few trials and some luck, a winning formula was discovered, and Lea & Perrins Worcestershire Sauce was born!

Identifying the various forms of tamarind

Tamarind is available in the following forms:

» **Blocks:** You'll find compressed blocks of tamarind in Indian grocery shops. They're sold in two forms: a hard brick and a softer, "wet" tamarind. Don't bother with the hard brick — it doesn't have much pulp, so you'll be doing a lot of work for very little result. The wet version is a joy to work with, though, and I find it to be a mindful kitchen activity, and I hope you will, too. (Think of soaking your fingers in a pool of warm softness!)

» **Pulp:** If soaking your fingers in a pool of warm softness isn't for you, you can buy tamarind pulp in jars as ready-made paste, which is fine to use.

You may also be able to get ahold of frozen unsweetened pulp. Break it up and freeze it in individual pouches of 3 to 4 tablespoons so it's easy to grab and use.

» **Concentrate:** You'll see tamarind concentrate in stores, but I recommend staying away from it — I find it too intense, too dark in color (enough to spoil the appearance of some dishes), and slightly bitter.

» **Pods:** The pods are usually Thai sweet tamarind that's eaten as a snack or dessert. You don't want to use tamarind pods in Indian cooking because it doesn't have the required tang.

Deseeding and making tamarind pulp

If you want to buy a block of tamarind and extract the pulp yourself, follow these steps:

1. Gather your ingredients and equipment.

For a recipe meant for 4 people, you'll need the following:

- About 2 tablespoons of wet tamarind block
- About ½ cup warm water (cool enough to handle)
- 2 bowls
- A sieve

This should make roughly ¾ cup of pulp.

2. Soak the tamarind in enough warm water to just cover it (roughly 4 tablespoons).

Soaking helps to soften the tamarind and makes the next step easy.

3. Mash the tamarind with your fingers, holding the bowl firmly with the other hand.

You'll find that the liquid turns a chocolate brown color as the pulp separates from the fiber and seeds. Keep going until the liquid is thick.

4. Place a strainer over an empty bowl and pour the mashed tamarind and liquid into the strainer.

5. Use your fingers to push the liquid through the strainer and press down to get as much through as possible.

6. Put the contents of the strainer back into the first bowl and do a second pressing, adding a little less water.

You'll find that there's quite a bit of pulp to be extracted. You may be able to get a third pressing. Don't use too much water, though, or else the result will be too thin.

7. Discard the contents of the strainer.

Most of what's left in the strainer will be the fibers and seeds.

8. Place whatever you don't need in an airtight container in the refrigerator or freezer.

It will keep in the fridge for up to 1 week or in the freezer for up to 3 months.

Trying tamarind in your Indian cooking

To give tamarind a go in your foray into Indian cooking, try these tips:

TIP

» Add a couple of tablespoons to a curry for an acidic top note.

» Use tamarind in a marinade for pan-fried fish. (Just don't leave the fish in the marinade for more than 30 minutes — the acid will start the cooking process.)

» Stir tamarind into some oil, season with salt and pepper, and drizzle over your salads.

» Make a summer drink: tamarind pulp, sparkling water, salt, sugar, fresh mint, and lots of ice. Yum!

You Say To-May-To, I Say To-Mah-To: Using Fresh, Canned, or Paste

Looking at Indian recipes today, it's difficult to imagine that tomatoes were introduced to India by the Portuguese less than 500 years ago. In a culinary history that goes back a few thousand years, that's practically modern!

Tomatoes are now a staple ingredient in curries from almost all over India. They provide color, tanginess, and volume to sauces, but they're also used in salads and chutneys for their tomatoey goodness. There are so many ways to use tomatoes — fresh, canned, as a paste, or even *passata* (those fabulous Italian sieved tomatoes) — so how do you choose which one to use and when? Read on!

Fresh tomatoes

Tomatoes can be added at two stages in a curry: toward the beginning when they're cooked down to form the base sauce (along with onions and aromatics) or toward the end to add texture and a fresher flavor. If you're after the latter, you'll want to use fresh tomatoes. You'll be pleased to hear that, most often, the entire tomato is used, seeds and all. Some recipes do call for a smoother, skinless, fresh tomato puree. There's a really easy way to do peeling and pureeing (rather than blanching and blending) in one simple step, and it's called grating!

To grate a tomato, follow these steps:

1. **Cut the tomato in half.**

   Cutting it vertically makes it easier to grate because the tough core holds it together, giving you a firmer grip. Choose ripe tomatoes for maximum grated flesh.

2. **Using a grater with large holes, grate the flesh and discard the skin.**

   The large holes will give you a coarse result but will be easier to get the tomato through.

   Grate the cut side of the tomato (as shown in Figure 6-1), and you'll have a bowl of puree within seconds. Don't worry about the seeds — it's only the skin you're trying to get off.

FIGURE 6-1:
How to grate a tomato.

Illustration by Elizabeth Kurtzman

Canned tomatoes

To make a thick, red base for your curry, especially if you live in a place where fresh tomatoes can be pale and watery, I recommend using canned ones. Canned chopped tomatoes save time and effort, so I hardly ever buy whole canned tomatoes. Bear in mind that the cans have more juice, so you'll have to adjust the amount of water or other liquid you add to the pan to loosen the sauce or put into the blender to create a fine curry base.

If you're preparing a salad or a cold side dish — like the Kheere Tamater ka Raita (Cucumber and Tomato Salad with Yogurt; see Chapter 20) — you'll need the best fresh tomatoes you can find. But when a curry needs a rich red color, I find myself partial to canned tomatoes. I often add a pinch of sugar while cooking them to balance out the acidity, but I think they bring a depth of flavor that weak fresh tomatoes simply don't have.

MAKING LENTILS LESS GASSY

It's a sensitive topic, but one that many people are aware of. Lentils and beans can make you feel bloated because they have such high amounts of fiber. Some tricks may help because you don't want to be missing out on this superfood:

- **Wash them well and soak them before cooking for four to five hours.** This helps soften them and is said to make them easier to digest.
- **Skim off the scum that rises to the top while they're cooking.** This is unwanted starch and also looks unsightly.
- **Add a spice called asafetida to dal.** Indians believe it helps in the digestion of fiber and can help stop you from you know what. (More about this spice in Chapter 4.)

Tomato paste

I use tomato paste (called puree in some places) from a can or tube in recipes that benefit from its color or consistency. So, if I'm making a bright red base for a curry like Channa Masala (Chickpea Curry; see Chapter 15) or I want to add depth to a tomato-flavored dish like Papeta Par Eeda (Egg and Potato Fry; see Chapter 16), I'll choose paste.

Bear in mind that paste is concentrated and sometimes salted, so you'll need less than fresh tomatoes and you may have to adjust seasoning. Cook it for a few minutes to get rid of a slight metallic taste, and add a bit of water after it's hot so it blends into the sauce easily.

Passata

For a more liquidy but equally flavorful and bright ingredient, you can use passata. Cook it with some coconut milk, and you have a curry base in minutes!

Loving Lentils

If you've been to India, you know that lentils are a staple food, eaten almost daily almost everywhere. They're easy to buy, store, and cook, and a little goes a long way. Lentils are good for you and super-delicious, too!

Now, I have some good news and some not-so-good news about lentils. The good news is, when you've got some basics right, it's really difficult to go wrong while cooking lentils. For Indian cooking, you generally want them to fall apart and soften completely. The not-so-good news is that lentils can make you feel bloated because of a complex sugar they contain that isn't easy for everyone to digest. (Think: gas.) There are some things you can do to help with this issue, though (see the nearby sidebar). The following sections have you covered for the rest.

Cooking lentils

To cook dry lentils, follow these steps:

1. **Wash the lentils in a sieve under a cold running tap.**

    This helps remove any loose starch and dust. Continue doing this until the water runs clear.

2. **Transfer the lentils to a large pan with double the amount of water by volume. Don't add salt.**

    The lentils will swell and triple or more in volume. Adding salt makes them take longer to cook.

REMEMBER

3. **Bring to a boil; then lower the heat to medium and simmer.**

    Keep an eye on them because they can easily boil over. One way to prevent them from boiling over is to place a wooden spoon horizontally over the mouth of the pan. When the bubbles hit the spoon, they'll break and fall back into the pan.

4. **As the water is absorbed, top off the pan with hot water.**

    The lentils need to be submerged in order to cook evenly. Gauging the exact amount of water isn't always easy. The final consistency can vary depending on what you're eating the lentils with. Only add enough water to cover the lentils because you don't want to drain away any flavor if you add too much.

5. **Check if they're done.**

    Smaller lentils should take around 30 minutes of simmering; bigger ones can take up to 45 minutes. The lentils should lose their shape and resemble oatmeal. If you think they're cooked, taste a spoonful. There should be no crunch.

REMEMBER

    It's hard to overcook lentils, because you want them mushy, but they're also easy to scorch at the bottom if they dry out, so keep the pan topped up with water.

6. **Season the lentils after cooking and add any other flavoring according to the recipe.**

Some recipes start with the cooking of the lentils in this way. The flavored base sauce is prepared separately, and the two are combined as in the case of Tarka Dal (Spiced Lentils; see Chapter 15).

TIP

For cooking in a pressure cooker or Instant Pot, follow the manufacturer's instructions.

Knowing the correct texture and consistency

Whoever said that there's only one way to cook an Indian recipe? So much depends on who's cooking, who's eating, and what it's going to be eaten with. Dal made with lentils is no exception. The good thing is that you can't overcook it. Phew! But you can certainly design the consistency according to your preference. To make a decision, look at your menu. If you're eating it with bread, the consistency should be thick so it's easy to scoop up with a piece of roti or naan. If you're eating it with rice, the consistency should be a bit soupier to act as a sauce that moistens and binds the rice on your fork.

CULTURAL
WISDOM

The most popular South Indian lentil dish is called *sambhar.* It's sometimes eaten at every meal. A breakfast sambhar is thick because it goes with rice cakes and pancakes. It's diluted slightly to be served with rice at lunch.

Lentils are also used for texture, so in some recipes, they're fried or toasted to add a crunch. They cook quickly, so keep the heat medium and don't take your eye off the pan.

You'll find that lentil dishes thicken up as they get cold because the lentils keep absorbing liquid. Just add water to loosen them up, and don't forget to adjust the seasoning. You'll find that a few lentils go a very long way, but they're also easy to freeze, so nothing should get wasted. When you defrost lentils, you may find them a bit watery because the liquid seems to separate out. Give them a good whisk, a good boil, and they'll be good to go.

I'm Not Crying, You're Crying: Working with Onions

If you've shopped in an Indian grocery store, you've probably noticed huge bags of onions and wondered how anyone could get through all of them. Well, the answer is, easily. Many curries start off with the frying of onions, and they form the flavor and bulk base that will receive the next ingredient.

Knowing which type to use

Onions grow all over the world, but the easiest way to tell them apart is by color, taste, and shape. India uses a medium-size (think: golf ball) pink onion; it's not the same as the Western red onion, which has a sweeter flavor profile. If you can lay your hands on these pink ones, which are sometimes available in Indian markets, use them. Otherwise, the brown-skinned onions, which are also called yellow onions, are suitable for everything.

I find Western red onions — the ones with the deep purple skin — cook too sweet and too dark, so they often change the flavor and appearance of the final dish in ways you didn't want them to. The elongated shallots aren't the best either, but if that's all you've got, they'll do.

REMEMBER

Use red onions in raw salads and raitas, but if you're cooking them, don't take your attention away from the pan. They turn from a lovely purple to almost black in a very short time.

Slicing or dicing

You'll find that some Indian recipes call for slicing and others for dicing. So, when do you do which? My simple rule is that when you're going to puree onions in a blender, you can save time and effort by slicing. If you're going to leave them unblended, for texture and bulk, dice them. A few recipes in this book call for sliced onions to be left unblended because they provide a texture or appearance that matches other ingredients used. Whichever cut you choose, chopping everything evenly is key.

TIP

Chilling onions in the fridge for an hour before you chop them may make your eyes water less. Or just stand a step away from the chopping board so that the fumes don't rise up into your eyes. You can also work near an open window or wear goggles if all else fails!

How to slice an onion

To slice an onion, follow these steps:

1. **Cut off the top off and then slice down through the root vertically, cutting the onion in half.**

   The root end is fibrous and the top is pointed. Cutting this off gives you a firm base to place on your chopping board when you cut the onion in half.

2. **Holding the edge of the peel, take it off on both halves.**

   If there's a dry layer just beneath the skin, take that off, too. It won't cook well and will leave hard bits in the curry.

3. **Place the cut side of the onion on the board and cut off the root at a slight angle.**

   This ensures that you take off the entire root — it's what holds the onion together — and you'll get slices that fall apart and you won't have to pry them apart in the pan.

4. **Slice along the grain, in the direction of the fine lines on the onion.**

   The onion will bruise less and cook more evenly. Try to slice as finely as you can — it'll save on cooking time.

How to dice an onion

To dice an onion, follow these steps (see Figure 6-2):

1. **Cut off the top off and then slice down through the root vertically, cutting the onion in half.**

   The root end is fibrous and the top is pointed. Cutting this off gives you a firm base to place on your chopping board when you cut the onion in half.

2. **Holding the edge of the peel, take it off on both halves.**

   If there's a dry layer just beneath the skin, take that off, too. It won't cook well and will leave hard bits in the curry.

3. **Place both halves on the cutting board, with the cut side down.**

4. **Leaving the root on, slice them with the tip of your knife lengthwise into fine slices.**

5. **If the onion is large, make a couple of horizontal cuts, holding the onion on top so that you don't slice through your fingers!**

6. **Cut the onion crosswise, as finely as you can, and discard the root.**

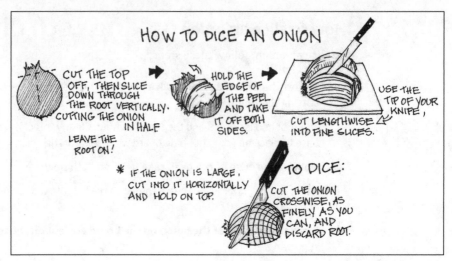

FIGURE 6-2:
How to dice
an onion.

Illustration by Elizabeth Kurtzman

Cooking onions for curries

Depending on the consistency and color you want, onions can be fried, stir-fried, or boiled:

>> **Frying:** If you're frying onions for a biryani or for a curry where you want a rich, dark color, add enough oil to cover the base of the pan and fry them over high heat until they begin to color. Then cook them slowly over low heat until they're dark but not burned.

>> **Stir-frying:** You'll probably use this technique the most while making a base curry sauce. Start with enough oil to coat the base of the pan and cook the onions over high heat. When they start to color, turn the heat to low and continue cooking for 8 to 10 minutes until you can insert a knife into a piece and there's no resistance. This is essential when you're going to blend the cooked onions in a blender; otherwise, you'll have the taste of partially raw onions in the sauce.

>> **Boiling:** When you don't want any color, you can boil onions in enough water to cover them. Again, cook them until very soft because you'll always be blending them to a fine puree.

Drop It Like It's Hot: Cooking with Chilies

You may be thinking this section is one of the most important ones in the book, considering that most people talk of Indian food and the word *spicy* in the same breath, right? Not really. Heat is a relative thing, and some Indian food doesn't have any. It's an important taste sensation no doubt, because it contributes to the balance and depth of flavor, but you can personalize your recipe to suit your chile tolerance.

TIP

Contrary to what's done in the West, people in India don't deseed chilies — if you want less heat, use fewer chilies. The heat comes from the capsaicin in the membranes and not the seeds. Some capsaicin transfers to the seeds that are touching the membranes, but mostly, deseeding a chile is a waste of time.

How to choose the right chile

When you're shopping for chilies, look for the following:

>> **Fresh green chilies:** I use these when I want a pale or green curry and a fresh, vegetal flavor profile. Fresh red chilies are just ripened green ones and have a shorter shelf life. If the green ones ripen in your fridge, you can certainly use them in dishes where the color isn't green. Generally speaking, the smaller the chile, the hotter it is. A good variety for Indian cooking is the Thai green or bird's-eye chile, which is fine skinned and reliably hot without being searing.

>> **Dried red chilies:** Some recipes use these for their smoky flavor and deep ruby color. I like the dark red dried Kashmiri chile — colder regions grow milder chilies, so this one won't blow your head off. Happily, it has more drama than fire, so it'll add a beautifully natural, crimson glow to curries. Some dried chilies are super-hot — they're usually quite small, so I'd stay away from small dried chilies if you're nervous about heat.

>> **Red chile powder:** I use Kashmiri chile powder. It's brightly colored and medium in heat, so it won't overpower your cooking.

TIP

I'm often asked if it's better to use fresh green chilies or red chile powder in Indian recipes. The answer: It depends whether you want a green herby flavor or a smoky one, or if you want a red sauce or a pale one. I like the freshness of green chilies and the fact that you can use them to personalize the heat in your recipe.

How to use chilies

If you've got a pair of gloves in your kitchen that you use to handle those dangerous little chilies, throw them away now. I'll show you a nifty trick so you'll never have burning fingers or have those fiery flavors creep up on you again. Follow these steps:

1. **Place your chile on the chopping board, and hold it by the stalk.**

   Neither the outside of the chile nor the stalk have any of the capsaicin that can make your hands and mouth sting, so holding it by the stalk is perfectly safe.

2. **Using the tip of a sharp knife, slit or slice the chile lengthwise down the center.**

   Don't remove the stalk.

   TIP

   Adding slit chilies to your pan is a great way of adjusting the heat. You can lift them out by the stalk at any point during the cooking process, but if you've cut off the stalks, there's a good chance the chilies will disintegrate into the sauce.

   Don't scrape the seeds and membranes out — that's where the heat is, so there's little point in adding chilies to your Indian cooking if you take the best part out. If you really don't like heat, leave out the chilies.

3. **Wash your hands with soap and water.**

Some recipes require chilies to be diced. This may be so that they blend into the sauce or provide a stronger kick (because they can't be fished out midway through cooking). To dice chilies, follow the first two steps for slicing, and then proceed as follows:

1. **Holding the stalk, dice the chile finely, seeds and all.**

   Chop as finely as you can, using a sharp knife and rocking movements so that the seeds don't fly around. I don't enjoy the sensation of biting into a big bit of chile, so I always dice mine very, very finely. Take your time.

2. **Scrape them off the cutting board with a spoon or the back of the blade of your knife.**

   WARNING

   Too many times, I see people in my classes follow all the rules of safe chopping and then lift the bits with their fingers. Don't make this mistake! Continue safe practice right until the end.

3. **Wash your hands with soap and water.**

Figure 6-3 shows you how to slice *and* dice a chile.

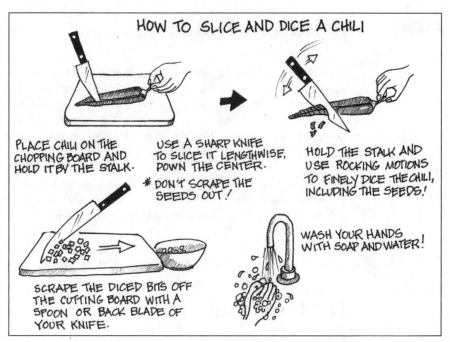

FIGURE 6-3:
How to slice and dice a chile.

Illustration by Elizabeth Kurtzman

TIP

Capsaicin dilates blood vessels to increase circulation and promotes perspiration. However, if the heat gets to be too much, water won't help — capsaicin is insoluble in water (like oil). Dairy products have the power to neutralize capsaicin, so try yogurt or milk to put out the blaze.

TIP

The seeds in dried chilies are harder and more bitter than they are in fresh ones, so if you're going to chop or blend the chilies, it's a good idea to get rid of them. Just break each chile in half and shake out the seeds (you may not get every one, but most should fall out). Chop the chilies into bits, using a pair of kitchen scissors. Steep them in hot water for 30 minutes or so to soften, and then blend them to a fine puree along with the soaking water. If you're cooking chilies whole, more for flavor than for heat, leave the seeds in. You can also toast dried chilies in a dry pan along with other spices until they blister and then crush them into a spice blend.

REMEMBER

Heat can vary from chile to chile, so it's a good idea to add less to begin with and build up later by adding more after you've had a taste.

Going Cuckoo for Coconut

Does the thought of breaking a coconut sound like a daunting task? For most people, it is. I grew up in a largely South Indian home, and a fresh coconut was broken and processed almost every day. I watched and took it to be a normal part of kitchen life until I had to do it myself! Negotiating the hard exterior and then getting the white flesh off (without any of the thin but hard brown layer) was a job for a coconut pro, not a novice like myself.

Happily, I've broken a few coconuts since then and now enjoy the laborious process as much as anyone can but there are so many other forms that it's available in. In this section, I walk you through your options.

TIP

I don't use coconut cream at all because I find that fresh coconut, desiccated coconut, or coconut milk works perfectly in my recipes.

Fresh coconut

Here's how to process a fresh coconut:

1. **Pull off the fibrous husk and discard it.**

   Do this over the kitchen sink or outdoors — it's messy.

2. **Holding the coconut over a bowl, pierce the "eyes" on one end with a screwdriver or corkscrew.**

3. **Invert the coconut and pour out the fresh water into the bowl.**

4. **Strain this water, and enjoy one of nature's tastiest drinks!**

   If it's cloudy or smells off, discard it along with the coconut.

5. **Hold the coconut in one hand with a tea towel, and carefully use a hammer to thump the coconut along its equator line.**

   This loosens the flesh inside and will help to crack the coconut open in two neat halves. When you see the crack forming, hit a bit harder so that the coconut splits open.

6. **Insert a firm knife between the meat and the shell and pry it away.**

   You'll find that the brown bit of the skin also comes away. You can either peel this part with a peeler or cut it away with a small knife. You don't want to grate it with the white meat — it'll spoil the appearance and leave hard flecks.

7. **Shred or slice the meat.**

   Use a large grater for a coarser result or a fine one for small bits. You can also do this in a food processer or simply slice it.

You can buy frozen fresh coconut shreds in Indian grocery shops. Thaw as much as you need and steep in hot water to loosen. If you blend frozen or very cold coconut for a chutney or curry, the oil in it can separate and make the mix sticky or gummy, so toast it in a frying pan with no oil until it just starts to turn golden before blending.

Desiccated coconut

If you don't want to go through all that bother, you'll be happy to know that you don't always have to use fresh coconut. Dried and shredded or desiccated coconut often works just as well. You can buy it both sweetened and unsweetened; because you'll be using it in savory dishes, I'd go for the latter.

It's worth knowing that coconut flour is not a good substitute for desiccated coconut in Indian cooking — it doesn't have the texture needed and won't bulk out curries enough.

Here's where you can use desiccated coconut:

» **In curry sauces:** You can add it to the base sauce ingredients in the correct sequence (see Chapter 8) and cook it until it's toasted to a light golden brown. I find this makes the curry sauce more coconutty because those wonderful oils get released.

» **As a garnish:** If you want to more or less replicate fresh coconut, soak the desiccated coconut in hot but not boiling water, pouring in enough to cover it up to ½ inch. Mix it well so that it's even, and then cover it and leave it for 45 minutes to absorb the liquid. Drain through a strainer and squeeze out the excess moisture so that it resembles fresh coconut rather than a sludge.

Coconut milk

I could tell you to soak fresh, shredded coconut in warm water, blend it in the blender, and squeeze out the thick coconut milk, but there is a much simpler way to get your hands on it: Buy a can. Test some different brands, because they differ in consistency. Also, look at the ingredients and watch out for a high proportion of sneaky thickeners and stabilizers.

Making and Using Paneer

Paneer is Indian cottage cheese, made by splitting milk with an acid. If you're vegetarian, you've probably eaten paneer in many dishes in an Indian restaurant. It looks nothing like the lumpy, moist cheese available in tubs in the West. It's more like cheddar in appearance, and it has a texture similar to halloumi. It's an unsalted, unaged cheese M. Commercially available paneer is very dense because it's pressed under commercial weights. At home, you'll get a softer, more delicious cheese.

How to make paneer

Follow these steps to make your own paneer:

1. **Place a sieve over a bowl and line the sieve with a big piece of muslin.**

2. **Have a tall bucket ready and a wooden spoon that will sit horizontally across the top of it.**

3. **Pour ½ gallon of whole milk into a saucepan and bring to a boil.**

   Choose milk with the highest fat content possible. The higher the fat content is, the more paneer you'll get.

4. **Turn down the heat and squeeze in the juice of 1 lemon, making sure to avoid adding the pips.**

   Adding an acid such as lemon, lime, or vinegar will start to split the milk. You may need to add a bit more juice if this process is too slow. What you're looking for is a separation of the curds and whey. The curds will form small cloudlike balls, and the whey will be cloudy but not milky.

5. **Carefully pour the contents of the saucepan into the muslin.**

   Hold the corners of the cloth together and lift gently so the whey starts to drain into the bowl.

6. **Working over the sink, tie the ends of the muslin into a knot, and push the handle of the wooden spoon through the knot.**

   Some cooks like to wash the paneer under cold water and then squeeze out the excess water. I prefer to place it over the tall bucket, making sure it doesn't touch the bottom and there's enough room for the whey to drain.

7. **Leave it for 4 hours in a cool place and then place the paneer in the fridge.**

In an hour or so, you should have a firm but soft paneer that's easy to cut. If you want it firmer, place the heaviest weight in your kitchen (mine is a large granite mortar and pestle) on top of it for 30 minutes or so. Fresh paneer will last in the fridge for up to 3 days.

TIP

If you'd like a crumbly paneer that you can cook as you would scrambled eggs, drain it over a bucket for a couple of hours and use right away.

How to cook with paneer

Paneer won't melt and doesn't take long to soften and absorb all the flavors in the sauce. You can use it as a vegetarian substitute in many meat and chicken dishes by adding it in directly (heat it long enough to make it spongy-soft) or mixing it with some salt and oil and baking it at 400 degrees for 10 minutes. I find this a great alternative to frying paneer, which just makes it spit and results in a messy stovetop. If you're still keen to fry it, cover the pan so you're safe.

TIP

Frying or baking paneer until it's golden can help it to keep its shape and look pretty. It can also harden up a bit, so a good trick to soften it is to submerge it in a bowl of water as soon as it's cooked. Leave it for two or three minutes; then squeeze the water out and add it to your curry.

Chapter **7**

Spices Make Indian Dishes Nice

RECIPES IN THIS CHAPTER

☼ **Garam Masala (North Indian Spice Blend)**

☼ **Sambhar Powder (South Indian Spice Blend)**

☼ **Tandoori Masala (Rub for Grilled Foods)**

☼ **Chaat Masala (Finishing Mix for Sprinkling over Snacks)**

D on't let anyone ever fool you into thinking that it's spice that makes an Indian dish. Well, that's partially correct, but it's truer to say that it's a *balance* of spices. You can't just throw in any amount of spices at any time and expect a fabulous result. A curry, for example, is a carefully orchestrated dish with the spices acting as a dazzling supporting cast with the main ingredient shining through on center stage.

The question I most frequently get asked at my cookery school is about how to cook spices just right. No burning, no flying out of the pan, no underdone or overdone bitterness and no underwhelming flavors. Get this right and I promise you, it'll be the eureka moment when everything else starts to make perfect sense.

Why do we need both whole and ground spices? Because they bring different flavors, colors, and textures to the final dish. Some recipes may have whole, others ground, and often, they'll have both, added at different stages of the cooking.

We Seed to Talk: Using Whole Spice Seeds

Spice seeds such as mustard, cumin, or fenugreek can go into the oil at the start or end of cooking, or they can be powdered to make a ground spice. Spice seeds contain aromatic oils, which are released either by heating the spice or by crushing it. Think of the time you fried a spice and the kitchen filled with fragrance, or when you turned a peppermill and the fragrance of fresh pepper wafted up.

Frying whole spices in oil

There are some basic rules to cooking whole spices in oil. You may find my advice contrary to what you've heard or seen before, but trust me, the following steps work, and you may start thinking it's too simple to be true.

1. **Put the required amount of oil or fat in the pan.**

   Do this before you turn the heat on, and make sure to choose an oil or fat that has a high smoke point and won't burn. Try corn oil, canola oil, sunflower oil, coconut oil, or ghee.

2. **Add the spice seeds to the oil, and then turn the heat on high.**

   Spices seeds need to cook at a certain temperature so that they split open and release their aromatic oils into the cooking oil. You don't need to introduce them into hot oil, though. You can bring the heat up to the required temperature slowly so that you're in control and the spices don't burn as soon as they go into the pan. Harder or bigger spices such as cinnamon sticks are more robust and won't burn that easily.

3. **Observe these changes that tell you the spices are cooking.**

   As soon as the oil achieves the right temperature, you'll notice three stages happen in quick succession:

   a. The seeds will sizzle, pop, or move, perhaps even slightly. Resist the urge to stir the seeds, or you may miss this.

   b. The color will begin to change. Darker spices go slightly lighter, and pale seeds go darker.

   c. You'll smell the aroma of the seeds as the volatile oils release.

4. **Have your next ingredient or finished dish ready.**

   The three stages happen quickly when the fat is hot, so have the next thing that goes into the pan chopped and close by to add to the pan quickly and to avoid burning the spices.

Sometimes, a recipe will call for a top note of spices. The seeds can be cooked in oil or ghee and poured on top of a cooked dish to give a finishing flourish or tarka (see Chapter 6).

If you do burn spices, there's nothing you can do to salvage them. Get rid of the lot and begin again. Burned spices will overpower the dish with an acrid, bitter taste and sometimes, a gritty texture.

Mustard seeds take longer to cook than other seeds, so put them into the oil first. The next spice that goes into the pan will take less time to cook because the oil will already be hot by now.

Toasting whole spices

Seeds can be toasted and crushed for a fresh flavor, but it is *not* necessary to do this every time you start to cook a curry. I toast and crush spice seeds when I want a single top note of flavor, as in cumin seeds for a raita (see Chapter 20), or to make spice blends that are crushed to a fine or coarse powder depending on the recipe. Toasting takes away any moisture and makes the spices brittle or crisp enough to crush easily. Whole spices are mildly aromatic in their dormant state. Heat releases their flavors making them nutty and aromatic rather than raw and acrid. Some spices that can be toasted successfully are cumin, fenugreek, coriander, fennel and mustard seeds, cinnamon, dried red chilies, cloves, peppercorns, star anise, and cardamom. Follow these steps:

1. **Put the whole spices into a small frying pan and then turn the heat to high.**

    Some recipes that use a combination of spices ask for all of them to go in at the same time if they're all roughly the same size and will need about the same time to cook. Other recipes will suggest you put the spices into the pan one by one, especially if they're all different shapes and sizes, giving each spice the correct time to get to the perfect stage. Read the recipe before you begin.

2. **Look for the changes that will begin as soon as the pan is hot.**

    When frying whole spices in oil, you'll notice the following three stages: physical movement (some spices such as cloves spit and jump, so stand back and be careful!), change of color, and a developing aroma. Shake the pan from time to time to stop the spices from burning. You want them to cook a just shade or two darker.

3. **Have a small bowl nearby to decant the spices into.**

    Spices can burn in the time it takes to go get a bowl from the kitchen cupboard, so have one ready before you start toasting. Unless you're using them immediately, let the spices cool in the bowl. This lets any steam evaporate off (whole spices can have some moisture, which turns to steam in the toasting process). Cooling the spices before crushing them is essential if you're making a blend to store — any residual moisture can make the ground spices powder sticky or gummy and reduce its shelf life.

4. **When they're cool, crush or powder them.**

Depending on the recipe, you can now do one of the following:

- Leave them whole. They'll add a nutty crunch to some recipes such as rice or breads. Make sure not to use the woody ones like coriander and fenugreek seeds in this way because they remain hard even after toasting, but do try cumin seeds.

- Crush them roughly, using a mortar and pestle or a rolling pin (put the spices into a tea towel or a heavy-duty freezer bag first), for a Vegetable Samosa (see Chapter 18). You can do this with cumin and coriander seeds.

- Grind them to a powder in a mortar and pestle or a small spice mill reserved just for spices if you have one. Hard spices such as cinnamon sticks can be broken up to help crush them easily. Make sure to crush the spices to a fine powder. You want them to blend into a sauce and provide thickening and flavor but not texture.

REMEMBER

If the whole spices begin to smoke in the pan, they're about to burn or they're already burning. Tip them into a bowl quickly to stop them from cooking any further.

Ground Sterling: Working with Ground Spices

Conjure up the dazzling colors and aromas of an Indian market — those tall heaps of golden turmeric and cherry red chile powder, the fragrance of crushed cardamom and star anise — and imagine bringing that excitement to your own kitchen as you create the magic of a curry!

Ground spices add color, body, and flavor to Indian dishes, but adding the right amount and cooking them correctly is what makes a good curry great. For how much to add, turn to Chapter 8. In the following sections, I show you how to cook ground spices in three ways.

Cooking ground spices at the start

If you're using a cooked main ingredient such as canned chickpeas or roast chicken to make a curry, you'll want to cook the raw ground spices first. As with the whole spices, put these into cold oil and then bring them up to heat. Look for the three stages — the sizzle, the darkening of color, and the aroma developing. These happen as soon as the oil has heated to the correct temperature.

With ground spices, it's not always easy to tell when the perfect aroma has been achieved and that the spices have bloomed enough. Partially cooked spices can be harsh, and eating them will carry that rawness into the body, making them aggravating rather than healing. To make them soft and subtle, add a splash of cold water — about 4 to 5 tablespoons for a dish for four people — to the pan after the three stages have been reached. Keep cooking them on a high heat; the water cools the pan and allows the spices to cook for longer. You'll notice the aroma changing from being a back-of-the-nose harsh one to a soft, floral, almost-not-there kind of one.

When the water has evaporated, the spices will be left in oil and will have formed a kind pf paste. Now it's time to add your cooked ingredient.

At a later stage during the cooking

If you're cooking a curry from scratch and building up the layers (see Chapter 8), the ground spices in that sequence can go in after the raw main ingredient. This will stop them from burning, and they'll cook for long enough along with all the other ingredients in the pan. Again, if you find that the spices are sticking to the bottom of the pan or not evenly distributed through the food, add 3 to 4 tablespoons of cold water. This will deglaze the pan and stop the spices from burning, as well as distribute them evenly through the pan. Keep everything cooking on a high heat because you'll want some of the liquid to evaporate.

If you want to be safe with the spices, mix them into a few tablespoons of water in a bowl, creating a wet sludge. This will stop them from burning when you add them to the pan.

At the end of cooking

Some ground spices can be added at the end of cooking, as finishing spices, to add a top note or to adjust the color or flavor. These don't need long cooking. Spices in this category include pepper, chile powder, Garam Masala (see the recipe later in this chapter), and a unique spice blend called Chaat Masala (see the recipe later in this chapter), which you sprinkle over snacks.

Some recipes get a mighty punch of flavor and color by pouring a ground spice tarka (see Chapter 5) on top, as in the yogurt and flour Kadhi (see Chapter 15). The cooking oil gets infused and distributes the flavor through the dish.

When cooking ground spices in oil, make sure you add enough to make a liquid paste. If there's too little oil, the spices will look clumpy and can scorch quickly.

If you're a beginner to cooking Indian food, you may want to combine your ground spices in a ramekin before you begin cooking. This will save you from struggling with finding the right spice and the correct quantity when the pan gets hot.

SPICE STAR: UPPING YOUR SPICE GAME

Cooking like an Indian chef means learning to respect spices in order to bring out their best. Here are some of the tips we follow in my cooking classes — the little things we don't often give a thought to, but that can add that extra something to your cooking experience.

- **Don't toast ground spices.** They're too delicate and will burn very easily.

- **Store your spices in a dry place.** Moisture and spices are sworn enemies, so you want to keep them as dry as possible. A sneaky way moisture can get into your spice tin or jar is if you sprinkle the powders over your food slowly. The spoon catches the steam and carries it back to the jar, reducing the shelf life and making spice powders lumpy. Tip the powders in with a flick of the wrist, and mix in with your ladle to distribute the flavors.

- **Check that your spices haven't expired.** Spices lose their volatile oils with time, so you may find that using old spices makes your curry underwhelming even after you've followed a good recipe. They may also have dulled in color. Adding more could make the curry gritty.

- **Shop for a heavy mortar and pestle, as well as a small spice/coffee mill.** You'll use both for different things, and you'll certainly enjoy a mortar and pestle if you're a tactile cook, but my life changed when I bought a spice mill years ago and got spices blitzed to a fine powder in a matter of seconds. Make sure to use the mill on a pulse mode instead of going full throttle, and follow the manufacturer's instructions.

- **Amp up the flavor with freshly crushed spices.** I sometimes put my toasted spices (mainly for Garam Masala [see the recipe later in this chapter], which I use regularly) into a peppermill. That way, I can aromatize up a curry at the last minute with a just few quick turns.

- **Scale up when necessary.** You can double up some spices such as coriander, cumin and garam masala, but I'd only go one and a half times up on the stronger ones like turmeric and chile when doubling a recipe. If you're scaling up further, taste before you add too much heat and adjust as necessary.

- **Understand the truth about cardamom.** The aromatic oils in cardamom are present in the seeds and not the husk. I always take the seeds out and crush them to get the best flavor and aroma (and discard the husk). Try it! I find it quite inelegant to pull whole cardamom out of my mouth when I inadvertently bite into it in a pulao or curry. So annoying! And I'd fish those bay leaves and sticks of cinnamon out before serving, too.

- **Get acquainted with chilies.** You may want to experiment with heat levels, so try a variety of chilies in your cooking. I like a medium heat and have found Kashmiri chile to be my go to.

Creating a Series of Blends

Forgive me for my little rant here, but curry powder is *not* an Indian thing — at least not the curry powder that can be supposedly added to anything to make it Indian. The stuff you see in the West was historically a convenience food created and popularized by those who colonized India. Because spices were not easily available in the West, a generic blend was marketed as being the real thing. We're still, as Indian chefs, shouting from the rooftops that it's not true.

REMEMBER

The "real thing" is an array of carefully orchestrated blends that reflect regional differences and secret family recipes carefully passed down from one generation to the next. If you're using commercial curry powder, you'll know how vexing it is to make your curries all taste different — they won't. But with these bespoke blends, each with a distinct name, you'll have a palette of flavors and colors to play with as you move from one gastronomic region of India to the next

TIP

A spice blend or a combination of spices or even a spiced curry base sauce can be referred to as a *masala*. Indian restaurants apply this term to curries to mean a dish that is cooked with a blend of spices. Spice blends are unique blends, and they often add a regional note to a dish. For example, a dal made with lentils may have garam masala from the North or a sambhar powder from the South. The base ingredient remains the same, but the spicing makes it distinct.

CULTURAL
WISDOM

In some Indian languages, the word *masala* is used colloquially when referring to a movie that has a mix of many genres — Bollywood masala films often have action, drama, romance, tragedy, and music all thrown in.

You can buy many of these spice blends commercially. But just be aware that they vary from brand to brand, so you may have to experiment to find your favorite. Or you can make your own in batches and use them over the next three months or so. They take minutes to make after you've gathered your ingredients. Following are four that I use a lot of in my recipes.

Garam Masala (North Indian Spice Blend)

PREP TIME: ABOUT 10 MIN	COOK TIME: 10 MIN	YIELD: ABOUT ⅓ CUP

INGREDIENTS

1 teaspoon black peppercorns

2 teaspoons coriander seeds

2 teaspoons cumin seeds

One 2-inch stick of cinnamon, broken up

10 large green cardamom, deseeded and husks discarded

5 black cardamom, deseeded and husks discarded

10 cloves

3 dried bay leaves, crumbled

3 blades mace

1 teaspoon fennel seeds

4 shavings nutmeg

DIRECTIONS

1   Put the spices in a small frying pan and heat on high. Shake the pan from time to time so the spices don't burn.

2   When the spices begin to turn slightly dark, turn the heat down and continue cooking until an aroma develops. Don't let them get too hot and smoky.

3   Tip them into a bowl and let them cool completely.

4   Blitz in a spice mill to a fine powder. Store in a clean, airtight jar up to 3 months.

NOTE: The word *garam* means "warming," so this is an aromatic blend made with spices that warm the palate rather than heat it like a chile would do.

NOTE: Green and black cardamom are two different spices. The black ones are larger and have a smoky, savory aroma, whereas the green ones are smaller and have a sweet, citrusy one.

Sambhar Powder (South Indian Spice Blend)

PREP TIME: ABOUT 10 MIN	COOK TIME: 10 MIN	YIELD: ABOUT ⅓ CUP

INGREDIENTS

½ teaspoon black mustard seeds

½ teaspoon black peppercorns

1 teaspoon coriander seeds

½ teaspoon cumin seeds

½ teaspoon fenugreek seeds

2 dried red Kashmiri chilies, stalks removed, halved, and seeds shaken out, then crumbled

2 teaspoons white urad dal (split matpe beans)

½ teaspoon turmeric

¼ teaspoon asafetida

DIRECTIONS

1 Warm a small frying pan over high heat, and add the mustard seeds. When they start to pop and jump, pour them into a bowl, and turn the heat down to medium.

2 Repeat Step 1 with the peppercorns, coriander seeds, cumin seeds, fenugreeks seeds, Kashmiri chilies, and urad dal, one by one. They will each cook in 2 to 3 seconds because the pan will be hot. If they get too smoky, turn down the heat. Keep shaking the pan to cook them evenly.

3 Cool them completely in the bowl. Then blitz them to a fine powder in a spice mill or mortar and pestle. Add the turmeric and asafetida. Store in a clean, airtight jar up to 3 months.

NOTE: Asafetida is often used in Indian vegetarian cooking but only in very small quantities because it's very strong and pungent.

Tandoori Masala (Rub for Grilled Foods)

PREP TIME: ABOUT 10 MIN | YIELD: ABOUT ¼ CUP

INGREDIENTS

6 green cardamom, seeds crushed to a powder and husks discarded

1 teaspoon finely crushed black peppercorns

1 teaspoon ground coriander

1 teaspoon ground cumin

1 teaspoon ground fenugreek

1 teaspoon ground ginger

1 teaspoon garlic powder

½ teaspoon ground cloves

½ teaspoon ground cinnamon

1 teaspoon Kashmiri chile powder

½ teaspoon turmeric

DIRECTIONS

Combine the spices in a bowl and mix well. Store in a clean, airtight jar up to 3 months.

TIP: Tandoori foods in Indian restaurants are often glowing red because of added food coloring. If you want a brighter rub, add a couple teaspoons of sweet paprika to the mix.

Chaat Masala (Finishing Mix for Sprinkling over Snacks)

INGREDIENTS

2 teaspoons coriander seeds

2 teaspoons cumin seeds

1 teaspoon fennel seeds

2 teaspoons finely crushed black peppercorns

2 teaspoons amchur (dried mango powder)

Salt to taste

1 teaspoon Kashmiri chile powder

DIRECTIONS

1 Warm a small frying pan over high heat and add the coriander, cumin, and fennel seeds. Shake the pan frequently. When they start to darken and jump, tip them into a bowl.

2 Cool them completely and crush to a fine powder in a mortar and pestle.

3 Stir in the peppercorns, amchur, salt, and chile powder. Store in a clean, airtight jar up to 3 months.

TIP: You can buy amchur in Indian grocery stores. It's made of dried, tender green mangoes and has a fruity, tangy flavor. The salt most used in chaat masala is black salt, a sulfuric variety that some people find too strong. If you'd like to use it in this recipe, add ½ teaspoon to begin with or more if you like it.

» **Understanding the importance of oil**

» **Focusing on the order of the ingredients**

» **Getting your curry just right**

» **Prettying your plate with garnishes**

Chapter **8**

Building a Curry

Although curry, in its various forms, is popular throughout most of the world, people associate all cooking from the Indian subcontinent with curry and nothing else. So, is all Indian food curry? Of course not. But curry is certainly the dish (or group of dishes) that makes Indian cuisine stand apart from the rest.

CULTURAL WISDOM

The word *curry* is said to come from the South Indian word *kari,* which means sauce or vegetable dish. Its use was popularized during the British rule in India as a dish with spices. Letters sent back home carried recipes, and housewives in cold, gray England began conjuring up mulligatawny soup and hot sauce. Without authentic ingredients such as spices, tamarind, and sour mango, British curries became lesser versions that used curry powder, cooking apples, and vinegar instead. I've also heard that the word *curry* comes from the French word *cuire,* meaning to cook, but I'm not convinced of that. Anglicized recipes were a curious combination of European and Indian techniques and ingredients, and without the relevant experience or information, they became popular in this new form. Even today, you'll find recipes that ask you to brown meat or add flour to thicken curries — techniques that you won't really find in an Indian kitchen.

CULTURAL WISDOM

British writer Hannah Glasse wrote her book *The Art of Cookery Made Plain and Easy* in 1747. It was the first time a recipe for curry was seen in a British cookbook.

In this chapter, I explain what a curry is and what the basic types of curries are. I show you how to achieve depth of flavor so that each mouthful sings on your palate and doesn't just sear it with heat. I believe anyone can make a hot curry, but it takes a superstar to make a flavorful one. If you've been let down by the consistency of your curries, where the solid and liquid parts stay obstinately apart, read on and discover my easy remedies that will help you attain master chef status.

Defining Curry: What It is and What It Isn't

Curry is a savory dish that has a spiced sauce (called "gravy" in India) and a main ingredient like meat, poultry, fish, vegetables, or paneer. The word *curry* is used far more outside of India, and often in a way that refers to a foreign cuisine rather than a particular dish. In India, you'd use the word *curry* when speaking in English, but in the 800 or so Indian languages that are spoken, each dish has a unique name. Impressed? Wait, there's more: Each region has an extensive repertoire of curries, and no one person has cooked or even heard of them all, so don't worry — there isn't a pop quiz at the end of this chapter!

In the following sections, I explain how the word *curry* is used to mean different things.

CULTURAL WISDOM

Curry night is a colloquial British way of saying Friday night, because so many British people have curry every Friday night.

Curry sauce

Ready-made curry sauce that some people pour out of a jar to make what they call Indian food will make every Indian dish you cook with it taste the same. The stores have shelves and shelves of the stuff. I know, I know, time is short, you don't have the ingredients or the equipment, you're hungry now, and so on. But I can't imagine anyone who truly loves Indian food enjoying that over-spiced, pasty sauce that passes off as a true masala sauce. I don't even go down that aisle in the supermarket.

In my cooking classes, I sometimes meet people who have only ever cooked out of jars. I suggest to them that they make their own base sauces and freeze them for the same ease and comfort. The added advantage is knowing what's gone into them and using the best ingredients they can afford. The taste difference is remarkable.

Curry powder

Curry powder, a general spice blend that supposedly makes all stews into curries, doesn't exist in India. In India, people use a the grinding stone that produces fresh ground spices and curry pastes. When Indian food was introduced to England more than two centuries ago, curry powder was a quick and necessary substitute. Curry powder also reached other areas, such as Japan and the Caribbean, through colonization, indentured labor, and travel. Most curry powders have spices such as turmeric, cumin, coriander, and cardamom. In India, each region has its own unique spice blend with a distinct name, and there's not a curry powder in sight.

TIP

STARTING TO COOK

Indian cooking is no different from any other kind of cooking, but if you're new to it and it all looks complex (which it sometimes is), some things will help you be more organized and allow you to enjoy the process:

- **Read the recipe in full.** Sometimes a recipe may ask you to soak an ingredient such as lentils or to have hot water ready to pour in at a precise stage later on. Prepare everything before you turn on the heat.

- **Wash fresh ingredients if you possibly can.** I wash fruits and vegetables to make sure they're clean and don't have any grit on them. I also wash fish and shelled shrimp, but I don't wash meat or chicken. Washing meat can increase the risk of food poisoning through the spread of bacteria that can get splashed onto work surfaces.

- **Have a compost pail or bowl nearby.** In all my classes, we have a compost bowl at each station so that there are fewer trips around the kitchen and recycling at the end of cooking becomes manageable.

- **Prepare your ingredients.** If you're just getting the hang of Indian cooking, it's a good idea to do all your prep work before you begin. When you're more confident, it'll be easier to prep as you go along, but in my experience, having everything ready makes cooking so much more relaxed and fun.

- **Place your prepared ingredients near your stovetop in order of appearance.** This is a key step that will save you many a disaster in the kitchen. Having everything in an assembly line means all you have to concentrate on is timing.

- **Have your equipment ready.** Many curries require ingredients to be blitzed in a blender, so it's useful to have the blender plugged in and ready. Maybe you need a grater? Or a mortar and pestle? If so, have them ready to go, so you're not digging around in cupboards or drawers trying to find what you need.

- **Cook with confidence.** I think this is the key to a lot of skills including cooking. Equip yourself with everything and then go for it knowing that you're creating a masterpiece of culinary perfection.

Curry leaves

Confusing as it may sound, *curry leaves* are not a part of curry powder. And they're not the same as the curry plant, which to some, smells of curry, but is inedible. Curry leaves are woody and immensely fragrant. Their slightly bitter yet citrusy aroma is the distinct top note in southern and western Indian, as well as some North Indian cooking, but if you ask me to describe it, I'll probably tell you that they smell of curry leaves. It's like asking what chicken tastes like.

First Things First: Choosing a Pan and Using the Right Oil

When you start cooking a curry, the first step is to choose the correct pan. How many people are you cooking for? Is the pan big enough? Is it a curry that can be made in a saucepan, or is it a sautéed dish that will be better made in a frying pan? (The recipes in this book tell you which kind of pan to use, so you don't have to worry you've chosen the wrong one.)

After you've got the pan sorted, it's all about the oil.

CULTURAL WISDOM

India is huge, and the kind of oil that hits the pan first depends on the region of the country where the recipe originates. In southern Kerala, for example, it'll be coconut oil, whereas in the West, it'll most likely be peanut oil. If you're in Bengal, you'll taste the unique depth of mustard oil.

TIP

So, do you need to buy a range of cooking oils for various regional dishes? The simple answer is: No. Most Indian cooking can be done using just two or three oils and fats.

The main factor to consider when choosing an oil is the *smoke point* (the point at which a fat begins to smoke and changes its composition, which is not good news). Indian cooking is based on techniques of heat regulation. Some ingredients (such as whole spices) need to be bloomed at high temperatures to release their aromatic oils. This means that choosing an oil with a high smoke point is key. In my kitchen, I use sunflower, coconut, corn, or canola oil, all of which can take high temperatures without changing in flavor or in nutritional value. (Turn to Chapter 4 for more information on which oil to buy.)

The exception is mustard oil, which is heated to remove the acridity and improve the flavor.

HOW MUCH IS TOO MUCH?

I've often heard people in the West say that Indian food is oily. That's generally true of restaurant food, but home cooking is far less greasy. Fat certainly makes things taste nice, but you don't want a layer of oil floating on top of your food.

How much oil you need depends on what you're going to cook in the oil: Is it one onion, two onions, or more? The quantity of what you're cooking directly impacts the amount of oil you need, so that the ingredient is properly coated. Not having enough oil may make the ingredients burn and scorch because they'll come in direct contact with the pan instead of having a buffer of oil. Roughly speaking, for a curry for four people, you're looking at 2 tablespoons of oil. If you're just blooming 1 teaspoon of spice seeds, you'll need just 2 teaspoons of oil.

A good way of judging how much you'll need is to coat the base of your pan with a thin film of oil, As your first main ingredient goes in and starts to cook, you can add a bit more oil if necessary.

For deep-frying something like fritters, which will go into your curry you're going to need much more. Fill your frying pan with enough oil to submerge what's being fried so it cooks evenly. The food will also need to be turned in the oil — if it sits on the bottom of the pan, it can burn on the underside. Don't use too much oil, though — it's just a waste of oil, heat, and most important, your time!

TIP

A high smoke point is one of the reasons why ghee or clarified butter is popular in Indian cooking.

Paying Attention to the Order in Which Ingredients Are Added to the Pan

When you understand the order in which ingredients go into the pan, how long they stay there, and why, you'll experience that eureka moment when all Indian cooking begins to make sense! Indian cookery is a set of orchestrated processes that result in the right flavor, color, texture, and aroma. The sequence is decided by how each ingredient influences the cooking of the other. Adding salt too early while cooking lentils increases the cooking time and cooks the dal unevenly.

If you've had a go at cooking Indian food and it hasn't turned out as you hoped, technique is probably what's missing. Don't take shortcuts while cooking — I've written the recipes in this book with a particular sequence in mind (although if you talk to other Indian chefs, you'll see that some variations exist depending on who's cooking). A great friend of mine, a chef himself, adds garlic before the onions, but I'm happier doing it the other way around. Spices are what make Indian dishes nice, so getting them into the pan at the right time is essential. Put whole spices at the middle of the sequence and you'll end up with a dish with barely any flavor. Color is another consideration — each ingredient must be cooked for long enough so that it develops the right shade.

Building Different Kinds of Curries

Indian curries vary from place to place, and there are too many to list here. In this section, I show you two curries from opposite ends of the country — the North and the South — so you can see how similar they are in some respects and also how they differ.

Building a North Indian curry

In this section, I group huge swathes of land into one culinary region, the North, because a basic simple curry from this region progresses more or less the same, even though there are thousands of variations.

The following sections walk you through what you need to make a basic North Indian curry, in order.

Whole spices

Of all the ingredients you need for the curry, whole spices require the highest temperature to split open and release their aromatic oils into the cooking oil, so you'll want to add these first.

Think about it like this: There are two levels of heat at which whole spices cook. Here's what happens at each level:

>> **Level 1:** You put cold oil into the pan and add the whole spices (this is level 1). *Then* you turn the heat on high.

>> **Level 2:** This is the heat level at which the spices will bloom. You have enough time to calmly wait and watch as the temperature gradually rises to this level. You're in control.

If you put the spices in here, after the heat has already hit the level at which the spice will bloom, you'll most likely see them fly out of the pan wildly or go dark and burn too quickly. I don't know about you, but I've never enjoyed sweeping mustard seeds off my kitchen floor.

At level 2, you'll notice three major physical changes happen so look out for them:

- A sizzle, pop, or movement
- A change of color
- A developing aroma

TIP

These stages happen quickly at heat level 2 (an eagle eye is key), so you don't want to leave them at this level for too long. If the heat level rises beyond level 2, the spices will burn, so turn down the heat if they cook too quickly.

Make sure to have your next ingredient prepared and close at hand.

REMEMBER

Most recipes and chefs will ask you to put whole spices into hot oil, but I've done it this way for years. It works and I've found that as long as you let the spices get to Level 2, you'll be okay. Don't undercook them or overcook them and you're off to a great start.

Onions

After the whole spices, the first of the aromatics, the onions, go into the pan. Onions take the longest to cook, and they help decide the color of the final dish. You can play with time and temperature here. A golden rule to curry making is that you need to cook the onions really well, which means to the correct degree of softness. Onions are often blended to a puree to add body and texture to a curry, so you have to cook all the rawness out before you do that. Partially cooked onions will give you bits in the puree. If the recipe doesn't involve any blending, dice the onions as finely as you can — you'll want them to melt into the sauce, giving it some volume and thickness.

Most people in my cooking classes who are new to curry making are astonished at how long we cook the onions. Starting over a high heat, we cook them for 3 to 4 minutes, until they start to turn golden. Then we turn down the heat and cook the onions long and low for 8 to 10 minutes, until they're soft enough to cut with a spoon and there's no resistance. This also makes them sweet, adding a beautiful depth to the final curry. When all those chefs go on about "caramelization," this is what they're talking about.

If you're worried about burning your onions or you just want to cook them more evenly, add a pinch of salt to the pan. This helps to draw out the moisture from the onions, and it takes less time to cook them. They begin to sweat a little and won't dry out and scorch easily.

I don't add water to the onions when I cook them at this stage because I want to fry them for color and sweetness rather than poach them. If you find that they're turning too dark too quickly, lower the heat.

Some curries may have main ingredients that take a long time to cook but are added at a later stage in the sequence, such as beef or lamb. The onions still benefit from some cooking at the start, because they begin to caramelize in the oil.

REMEMBER

This is your first opportunity to start building volume. Don't skimp on the onions — choose medium to large ones.

Ginger and garlic

If you've got that fabulous life-changing ingredient, Ginger-Garlic Paste (see Chapter 6), on hand, add it after the onions have cooked to perfection. The paste doesn't take long to cook, but keep an eye on it — burnt garlic is not a desirable flavor, at least in Indian cooking. If you're concerned about the consistency of the paste and you find it too liquidy, don't worry — it will evaporate off and the solids will blend seamlessly with the onion.

If you've diced the ginger and garlic, add them halfway into the cooking of the onions — they'll need longer to soften and develop their flavor. Ginger is harder than garlic, so you may want to grate it in rather than chop it so that it blends to a fine puree more easily.

Aromatics need time to become, well, aromatic. You'll notice a distinct change in perfume. I don't like raw garlic, so I wait for the mellowing of the harshness. This stage is like magic to me. The aroma of fried onions, which brings memories of hot dogs and fairground food, fills the kitchen, and the sweetening of the ginger-garlic transforms the pan into a chalice of tropical allure and excitement.

TIP

The amount of ginger and garlic you add is crucial. Too much, and the curry will become overpowering. I recommend 2 to 3 teaspoons for four people.

WARNING

Be careful not to get it all over your hands. The smell clings worse than a cheap perfume!

Fresh chilies

Ginger will already have added some heat, but here you can build on that heat and start to personalize the curry. You can increase or decrease the heat level to your preference by adding more or fewer chilies. Simply slit them so you can lift them out at any stage (see Chapter 6) or dice them finely to get them to disintegrate into the masala sauce. Leave the seeds in. Select a variety that you're familiar with or, if you're adventurous, experiment. I'm not a great one for hot curries, so I'm cautious.

Curries don't have to be hot. You can adjust the heat level with condiments that will make the meal complete.

Ground spices

In some recipes, ground spices can go in at this stage, after the ginger and garlic. In other recipes, they go in after the main ingredient. Why? Because it depends on how long and at what temperature that ingredient needs to cook.

Say, for example, you have meat — it'll need a high temperature and a certain amount of time to seal and lose its pinkness. Ground spices can burn if they're cooked too long or at too high a heat without timely intervention. So, if they go in *before* the meat, there's a chance that they'll stick to the pan.

However, if your main ingredient doesn't need this flash of heat, your ground spices will go in after the aromatics and start blooming from the heat in the pan. As they cook through the three stages of sizzle, color, and aroma (very quickly, because the pan is hot now), you'll want to add a splash of cold water as a precaution (see Chapter 7). Why? Because uncooked spices can make your curry bitter, and you'll find it really hard to remove that bitterness at the end. The spices won't get that intensity of oily heat at a later stage of cooking after the liquid ingredients have gone in.

Uncooked spices can also make the sauce gritty. I'm skeptical of Indian ready meals for this reason. Having trained chefs from some of the biggest food companies in the United Kingdom, I've found that factory processes sometimes supersede common practice and the spices are either not cooked long enough or go in too late.

Cook off that splash of water, and the aroma in your kitchen should be spiced but light. The water will take away any acridity, and the spices should be left in oil (not swimming in oil, because you didn't add too much at the start, but gathering around the edges of the mixture).

Another way to be sure you don't burn the spices is to mix them into some cold water before you add them to the pan. Make a slurry (not a paste and not too thin a mixture). As the spices cook, the water will evaporate off and, again, you'll see the oil start to separate. If you're using this technique, it helps to mix the spices in water before you begin cooking. They'll rehydrate in that time and be less likely to burn.

This is the second time in the sequence at which you'll be able to add thickness to the curry (the onions started that process). Some ground spices are mild in flavor but are great bodybuilders. Take ground coriander, for example, which isn't over-powering in either flavor or color, so adding an extra teaspoonful won't hurt.

Having said that, when cooking with ground spices, less is more. Putting in ladles of spices won't make the curry tasty. Let them be the sidekick and allow the main ingredient to be the hero. You may watch the film to see Batman, but it's not as good without Robin.

A main ingredient that needs searing

Red meat goes in *before* the ground spices. Anything that needs quick searing (such as chicken or fish) goes in after the ground spices. They don't take too long to be seared, so they won't interfere with the cooking of the ground spices. Make sure to chop everything evenly. Not only do big chunks not look pretty, but they don't absorb flavors well.

Tomatoes

If you're cooking with an ingredient that doesn't need to be seared (vegetables, for example), the next building block you'll need is tomatoes. You could use them fresh, canned, or as a paste or passata. They add body, so choose which one to use accordingly (see Chapter 4).

REMEMBER

If you're using canned tomatoes, they'll have more liquid than fresh ones, so you'll need less water later in the sequence. If you're using tomato paste, cook it off a little to help it lose its slight bitter notes. It's a good idea to add some water to the paste to dilute it — it blends in better and cooks without sticking to the pan.

TIP

Adding a pinch of salt will break down the tomatoes faster. Also, chopping them up as small as you can will help. Should you keep the skin on and seeds in? Yes. Be sure to cook the tomatoes down to a mush — this will add body and flavor to the sauce.

Liquid

Here, you decide how thick or thin you want the sauce to be and, based on this, how much liquid to add. The liquid is usually water. Stock is a Western or restaurant concept where staff and the necessary equipment are available to dedicate a corner of the kitchen to stock making. In homemade curries, the stock builds up in the pan as part of the one-pot, layering technique.

TIP

If you have liquid left from, say, boiling lentils or vegetables, it's perfectly okay to add it in. It'll enhance the flavor and prevent food waste.

Heat regulation is vital at this point — too many cooks have complained that curry making takes too long or that everything in the pan has overcooked. Give this step time and patience because it can make or break your curry. After the liquid sauce is boiling, reduce the heat, cover the pan, and let it all simmer to perfection.

Some recipes call for yogurt to be added at this stage. If so, choose a full-fat yogurt that won't split when heated. Stir it in a bowl before adding it, to remove any lumps and ensure even blending into the masala sauce. Bringing the yogurt to room temperature also seems to help. Don't add too much — 3 to 4 tablespoons for four people should be enough. Too much yogurt may make the curry sour because you already have another acid (tomatoes) in there.

TIP

Some of the ingredients will release their juices with the addition of salt (later in the sequence), so bear that in mind when adding liquid. You can always add more (and probably will), if the sauce becomes too dry or thick.

A main ingredient that doesn't need searing

Vegetables, paneer, boiled eggs, and beans can all go directly into the sauce without the need for searing first. From here on, the time taken to cook the curry will depend on how long this ingredient takes. Carrots and potatoes take longer than green peas.

TIP

Covering the pan will keep the steam and flavors in and reduce the time it takes to cook the curry. Some recipes may need the sauce to thicken at this stage; if that's the case, leave the pan uncovered.

Salt

Salt is that key ingredient that makes a good curry great. Many people are nervous about adding salt to their food, but if you cook your own (and have no health issues that restrict you from eating salt), you're not likely to go over the limit prescribed by health agencies. I find that it's the hidden salt in processed foods (and also the salt people sprinkle over food at the table) that's the danger. One good pinch per person and one for the pot is my philosophy. You can always adjust the amount of salt, but food shouldn't taste "salty" — it should just taste well balanced when you eat it.

TIP

I like using fine sea salt because it's supposedly better for you than table salt. Coarser salts have air between the flakes, so it feels like I'm adding a lot even if it's the same amount as finer salts.

Different chefs add salt at different stages of cooking. On most occasions, I add it when everything else has gone into the pan so I can judge the quantity of volume and season accordingly. Bear in mind that you've probably already added some salt during the sequence — while cooking onions or tomatoes perhaps, or in a marinade for meat — so be careful when adding it here. If you've oversalted the curry, you may be able to add a few spoonsful of yogurt to balance it, but it's better to get it right the first time and not have to spend time adjusting.

Finishing spices

A finishing spice doesn't need much cooking, if any at all. A pinch will give your curry a wonderful top note. Finishing spices include garam masala, red chile powder, or crushed *kasuri methi* (the dried fenugreek leaves that give such a wonderful depth of flavor with so little).

You don't want to use spices that definitely need to be cooked, such as turmeric or ground coriander, as a finishing spice. They won't blend in easily and can give the sauce a raw taste. If you want to adjust the color or balance, give the curry a good boil after adding them (see "Achieving the Right Color and Consistency," later in this chapter, for tips on how to correct your curry).

Tasting

To taste as you go along or not? There are numerous opinions on this one. My answer is based on logic and hygiene, and it's what I do in my kitchen: I taste it at the end, when I think it's ready.

While cooking, I would only want to taste my curry for flavor and to make sure that the balance and depth are what I'm trying to achieve. I don't need to cook the onions and check if they're done by tasting or cook rice and check for doneness by tasting. Why? I can easily poke a knife through a piece of onion or squash a cooked grain of rice between my fingers to make sure they're ready.

In my opinion, tasting everything as you go along can be unhygienic, especially if there's double-dipping going on. Your guests don't want to eat your saliva, and you don't want to eat the chef's in a restaurant. In India, people are very particular about this sort of thing. In fact, when a famous British chef went to India to film a TV series, he cooked a curry and tasted it several times, using the same spoon to double-dip. When he offered the finished dish to his audience, all made up of Indian people, no one stepped forward to have a taste. The chef looked at the camera and said that perhaps they didn't trust his curry-making skills, but all the Indian people who watched knew what the *real* reason was.

If you must taste, have a few tasting spoons on hand. But take it from me: Building the confidence to go through the cooking sequence without tasting at every stage will make you feel like a pro and keep the magic of the dish alive when you finally sit down to enjoy it. I'm sometimes asked to cook for large numbers — 200 people or so — and I find that I have to check the seasoning and adjust it several times, all at the end of the sequence. By the time the curry is cooked, and I'm satisfied with the flavor, I've lost all interest in eating it. I'm known to go away and enjoy a cheese sandwich (yum!) while the other chefs dig into the curry.

REMEMBER

Because curries are built up in a sequence, you'll know if you've got the balance and flavor right only at the end after everything has gone into the pan. That's when it's best to taste.

Garnish

All food looks better when it has been garnished. With Indian cooking, the rich colors and aromas of finishing ingredients adds to that. Imaginative garnishes can make your dish into a work of art, and they don't take much effort or time to rustle up. You'll probably have everything in your kitchen already. Maybe you've even used some of the ingredients in your curry.

Your garnish could be just a sprig of cilantro or a full flourish of a tarka where spices are bloomed in oil and poured over the final dish. The eye has to be drawn to the hero dish and not just to the accoutrements.

TIP

A little goes a long way when it comes to garnishing. You want the curry to have an interesting pop, not a smother. A leaf or two is elegant; the entire bush is overkill.

Building a South Indian curry

In this section, I make generalizations about a huge area, South India, for ease of explanation. In actual fact, there are five big states in the South, and each has a distinct and delicious cuisine.

The following sections walk you through what you need to make a basic South Indian curry, in order.

Whole spices

Just as with North Indian curries, whole spices go into the oil first; the oil should be cold or just warm to begin. Many curries in this region start with the popping of mustard seeds; to know that they're ready, you'll need to listen for this sound. They'll begin with a couple of pops and then become more furious, like raindrops on a window. You don't want to wait for the popping to subside — if you do, you may burn them. When you're satisfied that they're all popping, add the next ingredient, which may be other whole spices (such as cumin seeds, which take less time to cook than mustard seeds).

Onions, aromatics, and ground spices

You'll cook the onions as you would for the northern curries (see "Onions," earlier in this chapter). When you add the aromatics, such as garlic and ginger, you'll often use an extra one: curry leaves. Curry leaves bring a wonderful bittersweet note to the dish, but they're too woody to be chewed. That's why they're discarded to the side of the plate — such a waste! I often chop them finely and then add them to the curry. They give a deeper flavor note because they've been bruised, and you can eat them up!

Your recipe may also ask for a couple of dried red chilies here. These add color, smokiness, and heat (the level of which you can personalize). If you want no heat, leave the chilies whole. If you'd like a bit of heat, break the chilies in half and shake out the seeds (not because they're hot, but because they're woody). If you'd like a big kick in your curry, chop the chilies or use chili flakes (but be warned — undoing this kind of heat at the end of cooking isn't easy!).

Fresh, shredded, or desiccated coconut goes in after the onions and other aromatics have softened. It gives body, sweetness, and texture to the final dish and is used in recipes where blending this mixture into a puree follows.

Acidic ingredients

Tamarind pulp, which gives a fruity tanginess to South Indian curries is added at this point. Although it can be eaten raw, it loses its sharpness on cooking while retaining its sour notes. Tomatoes are sometimes added, too, more for their acidic flavor than for bulk, which can come from onions, coconut, and spices.

Sweet ingredients

Acidity needs counterbalance in order for it to shine, so some recipes call for a bit of sugar or jaggery. Jaggery is raw, unrefined block sugar produced when sugarcane juice is boiled at the start of the sugar-making process. It's similar to panela and can be substituted with soft brown sugar if you have trouble finding it.

You don't want to add much sugar or jaggery. South Indian cooking isn't sweet like some other regional cuisines.

Cooking liquid

After the main ingredient has gone into the pan (as in North Indian curries), you add liquid to create the masala sauce (or "gravy" as it's referred to in India). Coconut milk is popular — after all, South India grows masses of them — but long cooking times can make coconut milk split. For this reason, two types of coconut milk are used for many recipes: A thin milk with a low fat content that won't split is used for the cooking process and added in at this point, and a thicker coconut milk is added at the end to finish, fatten up, and smoothen the curry.

Getting a thinner and thicker coconut milk is easy to do when you're breaking open a fresh coconut yourself and extracting the milk. But if you're like me, more often than not, you'll use a can of coconut milk. You can dilute half the can with some water, and use the other half to finish. I prefer full-fat coconut milk over the lighter canned ones for this reason. I don't use coconut milk very often, but when I do, I want to enjoy the rich coconut taste.

I've seen some vegetable curries being cooked in milk to add a certain richness. Again, whole milk won't split, but low-fat milk might.

After you've added the liquid, you'll finish with a top spice and garnish as you would with North Indian curries (earlier in this chapter).

Turning Up the Heat

There's a huge difference between *hot* and *spicy,* and yet, so often, these terms are used to mean the same thing when people talk about Indian curries. All over the West, curries are classified by their heat level ("How hot do you like your curry?"). In India, you're more likely to be asked whether you enjoy Punjabi food.

REMEMBER

You don't need to eat a ridiculously hot curry to prove that you're macho, brave, or better than everyone else.

A couple of years ago, I went to a chile shop in New Orleans and decided to try the hottest sauce there (I must have been feeling macho). To tell you the truth, although I had just a tiny drop (I swear), I had to be put into a corner and had to embarrassingly wait for those singing birds to stop flying around my head. So, when I hear people boast about their exploits with chilies, I'm not impressed.

I've heard people refer to Indian food as having a slow burn as opposed to a sharp, swift strike of heat. Curries seem to linger and create different effects in the mouth. Some have an after-kick — just when you think you can manage it, a powerful whack makes you stop in your tracks and reach for something to put out the fire. The fat in curries coats your mouth and disperses the heat, which is why it seems to linger long after you've swallowed your food.

Spiced curries have a host of health benefits, but hot ones can lead to bowel irritation in some people. Spices contain compounds that are good for you in moderation. According to *Ayurvedic* wisdom (the system of holistic healing that is practiced in Indian and that includes yoga), there is such a thing as "millennia of body conditioning." What our ancestors ate caused their bodies to adapt to the diet, and experts claim that gut size and brain size adjusted accordingly.

That's all a whole other subject, but I *can* say for sure that someone who's been used to eating spices from a very early age, and whose cultural diet has included them, is more likely to be able to digest them better, in moderation. I'm certainly able to eat spices comfortably every day, but my body doesn't tolerate cheese as easily.

You may find, depending on your heritage, that your relationship with spice and heat is different from someone else's. So, what brings heat to a curry? Read on.

Chilies

There are so many varieties of chilies to choose from, all over the world. Find what you can tolerate, and use those. The capsaicin will combine with the fat in the curry and get distributed. That fat sticks to your mouth, and you feel the heat as an afterburn.

TIP

There is no difference in heat level between green and red chilies of the same variety — it's only a matter of ripeness. Dried chilies can be searingly hot, especially as flakes, when the membranes and the seeds get finely mixed and you can't separate them out from the mild skin. I never use chili flakes in Indian cooking.

Pepper

Many of my friends not from India will happily crush pepper over their food but are nervous about eating a curry. I'm always fascinated by this. Peppercorns also give you a heat sensation, but the compound they contain is different from chilies.

Pepper has piperine, and chilies have capsaicin. Both act as irritants to humans, which contributes to that stinging, almost throbbing sensation as they hit the pain receptors on the tongue. That sensation is the "taste" we associate with hot foods.

Spice blends such as garam masala have some pepper, too.

Mustard seeds

You'll find white, yellow, black, and brown mustard seeds in the shops, but your Indian pantry won't need the paler ones. The heat in yellow mustard seeds stays on the tongue, whereas in the darker seeds, it travels up to the nose and beyond, and lingers longer with a deeper intensity, which is desirable in Indian cooking.

The compound sinigrin in mustard seeds is responsible for the particular kind of heat shared with ingredients such as horseradish. Eating certain kinds of mustard makes my eyes water and gives me a kick at the back of my nose. But in Indian curries, it's mostly seeds that are fried at the start of a curry (although Bengali cooking from eastern India makes use of fresh mustard paste to cook fish and shrimp).

A recipe for four people will usually have 1 teaspoon of black or brown mustard seeds. To get them to impart their heat without burning, turn to Chapter 7.

Adding Depth to Your Curry

Curries need time to develop their true potential and allow all the ingredients to be in synchrony. Balancing the six tastes or sensations — sweet, sour, salty, pungent, bitter, and astringent (see Chapter 2) — is at the heart of achieving depth. When you understand that concept, it's easy to replicate over and over again. Each ingredient has one or more of these tastes or sensations; making them work together in harmony is what Indian cooking is all about.

One of the main reasons that you may find that your curry doesn't have depth is because it has been under-salted. Health agencies are always telling us that we shouldn't eat too much salt — and it's true. But saltiness is one those six essential tastes, and unless we've added it in, everything else will taste out of balance.

Think of a horizontal line. If all the tastes are under that line, you have to bring them all up to the line. How deep each one taste goes will vary — you don't want each taste to be present in the curry in equal measure (imagine putting in equal quantities of bitter and salt!) — but they all have to be present. All these tastes come from putting various ingredients into the pan. Sweetness, for example, can come from cooked onions, sugar, or browned garlic. Sourness can be introduced with tomatoes, tamarind, or lemon. But saltiness comes with salt, so getting that right will be a major contributor to the overall depth of your curry. I'm not advocating turning your curry into seawater, of course, but use your best judgment (and your own taste buds) to determine how much to put in.

I'm not a great fan of complicated, time-consuming recipes with long lists of ingredients and processes, but I have found that when you give curries enough time to cook, they taste better. That's why understanding the sequence of cooking is essential. Don't let anyone fool you into thinking that you throw everything into the pot and it comes up smelling like roses. Each ingredient needs a different cooking time and temperature, and layering them in the right order will give you depth. My golden rule: Taste every dish before you send it to the dinner table; otherwise, it'll come straight back. (My children certainly don't have a problem critiquing my cooking!)

TIP

Here are some common issues people experience with depth of flavor, and how to correct these problems:

>> **Too underwhelming:** If there's not enough oomph, try adding a pinch of salt to lift the curry. Acidity can also improve flavor, so squeeze in some lemon or lime after you've turned off the heat — cooking lemon or lime juice can sometimes make it bitter. Tamarind pulp tastes better when cooked, so if you're adding it at the end, give the curry another boil. I've also found that adding 1 teaspoon of Ginger-Garlic Paste (see Chapter 6) will lift it. Again, give it a boil.

>> **Too bland:** Amp up the heat by adding a little red chile powder (only a little — it's impossible to take it out if you add too much) or throw in a very finely diced chile. Give the curry a boil — you don't want too much heat as a top note.

>> **Too rich:** Perhaps you've added too much coconut milk or cream and now the curry tastes only of those ingredients. Adding an acid, such as lemon juice, will cut through the richness, as will stirring in a finely diced tomato. Bring in some freshness with herbs like cilantro or mint; a little sprinkle of sugar will also help.

>> **Too hot:** This problem is a common one, and learning to adjust the heat of a curry will improve your Indian cooking like nothing else. First, try adding more of the main ingredient (cooked, of course) — cook it separately and add it in, or add another one that doesn't take time to cook. For example, you can add frozen peas to a chicken curry or boiled eggs to a vegetable one.

Adding lemon or lime juice will help to cut the heat, too. If the recipe allows it, add a bit of cream, milk, or coconut milk without changing the consistency greatly. Serve the curry with a few neutral side dishes like plain boiled rice (see Chapter 6), Greek yogurt, and an undressed green salad with lettuce and cucumber.

» **Too sour:** If your curry is making you pucker, add something sweet like raisins, sugar, or honey. Make sure there's enough salt, too — if it's under-salted, the sourness can become the top note.

» **Too sweet:** Balance the sweetness with some lemon or lime juice and salt. Bitter notes help complete the balance in Indian food, so throw in some herbs like chopped cilantro and perhaps a fresh, sliced green chile.

» **Too bitter:** This problem has probably occurred because the spices weren't cooked long enough or the heat was too high and they burned. Correcting this problem at the end of the curry is difficult, so make sure to cook your spices right the first time (see Chapter 7). If you have a slight bitterness, you can add some richness in the form of cream or coconut milk to help sweeten the curry.

Achieving the Right Color and Consistency

Have you ever been to a buffet with what seems like hundreds of dishes that all look like they could've come out of the same pot? All a similar color and consistency? At home, some curries won't fall off the serving spoon, while others swim about on your plate. So, what's the perfect color and consistency for a curry? I explore both of these factors in the following sections.

Color

A pale-colored korma, like Bengali Chicken Korma (Chicken Curry with Cream; see Chapter 11), and a bright orange Channa Masala (Chickpea Curry; see Chapter 15) look and taste different, and their base masala curry sauce can be combined with any number of other main ingredients to form a feast of curries. Choosing a different colored curry can help design a new plate each time you cook.

Here are some possibilities:

» **White masala sauce:** You probably won't see too many of these on your average restaurant menu in the West, because so many are regional and most Indian restaurants in the West feature a particular kind of repertoire. In this curry base, pale ingredients are used to keep the color creamy white. You'll find coconut, white poppy seeds, white sesame seeds, cashew nut or almond puree, yogurt, and milk in the list, but also onions that are used to thicken and flavor many curries.

TIP

Frying onions at the start will most likely make them start to color and turn golden, unless you carefully sweat them. To be absolutely sure that they don't get any color at all and yet cook them to the softness needed for blending them to a smooth puree, boil onions in water.

Sometimes nuts such as cashews are added as in the Safed Gosht (Lamb in a Coconut and Cashew Nut Curry; see Chapter 10), so they soften along with the onions and get blended, resulting in a velvety white puree. Don't be fooled by the creaminess of these curries, though — some can be extremely hot if they also contain lots of green chilies that are boiled with the onions to neutralize their color. You're never safe!

>> **Yellow masala sauce:** What makes a curry yellow? Turmeric! That beautiful golden spice that changes everything it touches, including kitchen counters and white clothes. Most Indian curries have turmeric (except the white ones), but the quantity varies so it may or may not become the top hue. These curries often need a pale base as a backdrop so the turmeric can shine through. Coconut milk or cashew puree are perfect partners in dishes such as Meen Moilee (Salmon Curry with Mustard Seeds; see Chapter 12) or Murgh Malaiwala (Chicken in a Creamy Cashew Nut and Saffron Curry; see Chapter 11).

TIP

Curries cooked on festive occasions may use saffron for that deep golden color, but because it's an expensive spice and has a flavor that may overpower a dish, it's used carefully.

>> **Green masala sauce:** Plenty of fresh herbs (such as cilantro, mint, dill, curry leaves, and green chilies) are included in a green masala sauce. You'll need big handfuls, because herbs cook down or blend to very little.

TIP

If you've got a big bunch of cilantro in the fridge that's wilting and you've used as much as you can for garnishing, toss it into a blender and you'll have a perfectly fragrant base for your next curry. You'll need to add something to add texture — possibly onions, poppy seeds, or nuts. If you'd like a brighter sauce, throw in a few handfuls of spinach or kale.

For most herbs, I use the stalks as well. There's lots of flavor in the stalks, and a bit of fiber, too, which helps the body of the curry. Skip the stalks with mint, though; they can be woody (which is the wrong kind of body).

>> **Red or orange masala sauce:** You'll find lots of red, purple, or orange ingredients in the Indian kitchen — tomatoes, chili powder, and dried red chilies, of course, but also saffron, mace, oranges, beetroot, pomegranate, and the more obscure ones like cockscomb flowers and ratanjot or alkanet root, both of which are used in some Kashmiri cooking. You'll also find kokum petals from the *Garcinia indica,* which gives food a deep purple hue.

Tomato- and chile-based curries are the easiest to re-create because the ingredients are widely available. Cayenne and paprika are not Indian spices, but a huge number of chile powders are available in various shades of red and in a range of heat levels.

>> **Brown masala sauce:** It's hard to imagine a rich, dark curry with your favorite ingredient, whether meat or vegetables, and not salivate. There's something enticing about these dishes — whether it's the depth of flavor or the rich color. The browning in many dishes comes from frying the onions until they achieve that chocolate color, but remember to stop cooking them before they go too far and get dark and taste burnt.

Interestingly, meat doesn't need to be browned to lock the moisture in as you would for a Western stew. Browning meat may create a barrier and not let the flavors through, so searing lightly is usually enough.

Some spices, such as cloves, cinnamon, cumin, coriander, and garam masala, also add color. In some regional recipes, a spoonful of sugar is caramelized at the start of cooking.

Here are some common color issues and how to correct them:

>> **Too pale:** Did you toast your spices until they darkened? A rich brown toast gives your curry a depth, so be patient during that process. Blackened spices aren't what you want, so be aware of that moment when they've cooked just right.

Add a pinch of turmeric and red chile powder. Remember to give the curry a final boil to cook the spices and blend in the colors. Use a mild chile powder like Kashmiri or a sweet paprika if you absolutely don't want any more heat.

>> **Need more red:** If you need lots more color, consider soaking whole dried Kashmiri chilies in boiling water for 30 minutes after deseeding them. Then blend them in a small blender to make a red chile paste to add to the curry, which you'll need to boil. Or add in a couple of spoonsful of pomegranate or beet juice.

>> **Not brown enough:** If the curry isn't brown enough try one of the following:

- Fry a couple of onions long and slow for 20 to 25 minutes; then blend to a puree in the blender and add to the curry.

- Fry 1 teaspoon of garam masala in 1 tablespoon of oil and pour it in.

- Pour in a few tablespoons of black tea — just the most ordinary blend, with no flavors added. If you want more color, put some loose tea in a small infuser, dip it into the curry, and boil it. Remove the infuser when you get enough color from the tea leaves. (Some recipes involve cooking the main ingredient in a tea infusion right from the start.)

Consistency

Consistency largely depends on what's being eaten with the curry. If your carbohydrate is rice, the masala sauce should be soupier so when it's poured over the top and mixed with the rice, it makes everything easier to lift onto a fork, a spoon, or your fingers (see Chapter 24). If you're eating a bread with the curry, it'll have to be thicker to be scooped up with a piece of roti or naan. There are a few dishes in the repertoire that are soupy, like some South Indian lentil dishes, but curries need to be thick enough to coat the back of your spoon.

Some curry masala sauces are blended to give a creamy richness or smoothness, whereas others are left unblended to benefit from the texture of ingredients such as onions and tomatoes. Whichever method you choose, the ingredients must meld together and not stand apart. The slow simmering process helps to cook off any excess liquid and thicken up masalas. Keep the heat low and decide whether you want to cover the pan, depending on how much liquid there is.

REMEMBER

If you've added an ingredient that has liquid, such as yogurt, make sure to adjust the amount of water that goes in. Vegetables and meats release their juices when you add salt, so don't pour in water before this happens or you may get a watery sauce.

TIP

Curry making involves adding liquid to the pan at various stages. Add a little at a time. You can always add more, but if you have to evaporate the excess out, you could overcook the rest of the ingredients.

TIP

Here are some common consistency issues and how to correct them:

>> **Too watery:** The easiest way to correct this problem is to simmer the curry until it thickens. If you're worried about overcooking the other ingredients, pour the liquid into another pan and reduce it by boiling it. When it's thick enough, add it back to the curry.

If you've added too much liquid to the masala, cook it for longer before you add the main ingredient. Masalas often benefit from this long, slow cooking and develop better flavors.

Be careful when you blend masala base sauces in a blender. Add only enough water to cover the ingredients and turn the blades.

>> **Too thick:** You can thin your masala sauce by adding a liquid such as water, coconut milk, or stock from cooking something else (such as lentils, rice, vegetables, or meat). Remember to add a little liquid at a time.

» **Too lumpy:** This problem could happen in a blended masala sauce if any of the following occurs:

- *You didn't have enough liquid in the blender to turn the blades smoothly.* Add a bit more water and blend again. (To prevent the problem in the future, add enough liquid to just cover the ingredients.)

- *You didn't blend the mixture long enough.* Different ingredients in the same mix need less or more time to be blended. For example, cooked onions turn to puree quicker than cooked nuts do. Check the blended puree for any bits or lumps before you pour the masala into the curry. Blend for a bit longer if you see lumps.

- *You didn't whisk the flour you added until it was smooth.* Make sure to combine the flour with some water and then add it in. To disperse flour lumps in the curry, try whisking them or breaking them up with the back of a spoon.

» **Too thin:** This problem could happen if you've used too few base ingredients (for example, onions or tomatoes), low-fat yogurt that may split, or a can of cheap coconut milk that's watery to begin with. When faced with this problem, you can boil off the excess or you can add in thickening ingredients such as:

- Fried onions, blended to a puree

- Cashew nut or almond puree

- Almond flour

- Thick cream

- Desiccated coconut, toasted and blended to a puree

- The thick part of good-quality coconut milk that rises to the top of the can (open it without shaking the can and scoop off the top bit)

- Canned chickpeas or beans, pureed

- A few tablespoons of full-fat yogurt

- Tomato paste or pureed canned tomatoes

- Cooked lentils from a previous meal or from a can

- Some of the ingredients in the curry (such as potatoes, beans, or carrots) mashed up

- A bit of gram flour (which is made with a kind of chickpea) in a roux (see the nearby sidebar for instructions)

MAKING A GRAM FLOUR ROUX

To make a gram flour roux for a recipe for four people, follow these steps:

1. **Toast 2 tablespoons of gram flour in a dry frying pan, over medium heat, stirring constantly until it turns slightly golden and gets a nutty aroma.**

2. **Tip the flour into a bowl, and whisk in 4 tablespoons of cold water to make a slurry.**

3. **Mix the slurry into the curry when it's off the heat, stir well, and then bring to a boil.**

4. **Cook until the curry thickens and there is no raw flour taste left in the sauce, about 6 to 8 minutes.**

IMPROVISING LIKE A PRO

I'm a great fan of improvisation, but I find that I'm more confident at doing it when I know some of the basic rules. Put me into a kitchen in a country where I've never tasted the cuisine, and I definitely need a recipe and some guidance.

I've traveled all over the world with my family, and one of the things we love to do is to taste the local cuisine, buy specialist ingredients, and try to re-create the flavor in our kitchen in London. It doesn't always work (my children can tell you all about that!), but we've made some really wonderful dishes, especially after our many trips to the heartland of India.

If you're a confident cook, take the time to understand the cultural and social nuances that make the cuisine unique. In Indian cooking, understanding the regions is crucial because it's easy to create a mishmash of flavors that don't work well together. Then it's just about getting the ingredients and knowing which ones you can do without or substitute.

At this stage, the kitchen becomes a playroom or a laboratory, depending on how you want to approach it. Every time you cook an Indian meal, your muscle memory improves and, one day, creating a feast without once looking at your recipes will be easy.

Here are my tips for improvising:

- **Get familiar with the flavor combinations you enjoy.** For example, I don't enjoy too much heat in a curry, so I'm not likely to experiment with that. Discover which ingredients bring in your favorite flavors. My kitchen always has a lemon or two, cardamom, and cinnamon. So clearly, my choice is sweet and sour. What's yours?

- **Learn the techniques unique to the cuisine.** To wing it in your Indian kitchen, you'll need to know the basics of how to bloom spices, blend curry pastes, cook lentils, roll naans, and more.

- **Swap ingredients mindfully.** You could use a can of red beans instead of chickpeas, fresh tomatoes instead of canned ones, fish instead of shrimp, chicken instead of turkey. . . . You get my point. Remember to swap like for like as much as you can, both in terms of size and in terms of how long something takes to cook. Or adjust quantities and cooking times. If you're using beef instead of chicken in a curry, you'll need more cooking liquid and more flavoring (because chicken has a lighter flavor than beef) and you'll need give it longer to cook.

- **Throw away those jars and experiment with masala curry bases.** When you've mastered the basics, you'll no doubt create some bespoke blends for yourself. Very little in Indian cookery is really authentic, depending how far back in history you want to go. If you can't find an Indian chile, use a local one. After all, chilies were brought to India only around 500 years ago. What were they using before then? Black pepper.

- **Don't worry about goofing up.** At worst you'll throw it away; at best, you'll learn how to salvage it. Every chef has had disasters in the kitchen. Many acclaimed recipes are the result of "failures." Keep calm and curry on!

Jazzing Up the Look with Garnishes

Many Indian curries look pretty similar — a main ingredient immersed in a spiced masala sauce that's often red, brown, or yellow. This is when things can be smartened up using two things: garnishes and creativity.

Indian garnishes aren't often fancy. You don't see too many carrots carved into flowers or a compote of raspberries poured over a creamy dessert. Mostly, it'll be a bit of an ingredient used in the cooking of the dish that's also sprinkled on top, or a bit of spice or dried herb that's in the kitchen and needs no delicate preparation. Easy, isn't it?

You don't have to stick to just one garnish per curry. Try a sprinkle of ground spices along with a few chopped cilantro leaves and some drops of cream. Or a twist of lime with a couple of slices of red chile. A good rule to work with: Use dark garnishes on paler curries, and vice versa.

In the following sections, I walk you through some options for garnishes.

Onions

Onions are used in many savory dishes, so they won't mess with the flavor profile. I use the yellow (or brown) ones for frying and the red ones raw. Fry sliced onions until they're a deep golden color, and sprinkle over rice and curries.

Onion rings or slices work well, too, but remember to keep the bits really thin and delicate. Less is more. Nobody wants to chomp on half an undercooked onion during dinner!

Cilantro

Cilantro is possibly the most commonly used garnish. I use just the leaves. There are two schools of thought here: Some chefs like to use a whole leaf or a sprig, and others prefer to chop them fine. I do both, depending on the situation. When I want the freshness, but I don't need the herb to impart much flavor to the dish, I'm happy to place a small, well-shaped leaf on top. When the flavor contribution is important, I'm more likely to chop it up.

What I *don't* do is a rough chop. It looks messy, and biting into bits of cilantro isn't pleasant. Bear in mind that some people don't like cilantro at all — it's a love-it-or-hate-it thing — so ask before you garnish with cilantro. If you have cilantro haters on your guest list, you can keep it separate in a little bowl on the side.

Mint

Mint leaves look prettier when they're left whole. Chop them, and they seem to disintegrate into a limp mess. Stick in a single pert sprig, and it'll liven and freshen the dish instantly.

Lemon and lime

Lemons and limes are easy to find in Indian kitchens, because they're squeezed into so many dishes as a top note. Slice them finely, cut through the radius, and twist them into a spiral to place on top of rice or grilled foods. Or cut them into wedges to go with snacks.

I sometimes dip the cut edge of a lime wedge into red chile powder for a dramatic effect. Play with color — the yellow of lemon, green of lime, and red of chile powder can liven up a plate of brown fritters. As the saying goes, food is art!

Fresh chilies

Green and red chilies both work well, but choose the freshest ones in your collection. You can use them in several ways:

» **As small slices:** Get them as thin as possible and scrape out the seeds to get tiny rings of color. Make sure to warn your guests!

» **As long slices:** Take the stalk off and cut the chile lengthwise in half. You can remove the seeds or leave them in if removing them is too much of a hassle.

» **Chile flowers:** Hold the chile at the stalk and make several lengthwise cuts with the tip of a sharp knife. Put the chile into a bowl of iced water for 30 minutes or until it has opened up into a flower.

Ginger

Juliennes or matchsticks of skinned fresh ginger are a great way of adding texture, as well as a burst of flavor. You want the ginger to be juicy and not fibrous so that it cuts cleanly.

Salad vegetables

You can add instant color and texture with shredded carrots, finely diced cucumber, and cherry tomatoes. I love slices of colored bell peppers — what an easy way to prettify a plate! I also use small, pink-skinned radishes — slice them finely, and you'll get a bright pop of color on yellow or white foods.

Nuts and dried fruit

You can use the following to create a layer of richness, flavor, and crunch:

» **Almonds and pistachios:** Toasted or untoasted flakes, roughly crushed, peeled (blanched) or left in their skins, powdered . . . you can do any of it.

>> **Raisins and sultanas:** You have a few colors to play with here, ranging from green and golden to black, but keep in mind that their sweetness may not complement all dishes. Use them for a creamy chicken or vegetable curry.

>> **Peanuts:** Used in Indian recipes, peanuts can be used roasted and salted, crushed, or powdered. (If you have any dinner guests, just be sure no one has a peanut allergy.)

>> **Dried and fresh fruit:** You can choose red, brown, orange, or gold to get a pop of color. Orange segments or peel or a scatter of cranberries or pomegranate seeds can make curries look festive.

Spices and dried herbs

A tarka (see Chapter 5) is a common yet effective garnish, and you can cook some pretty ingredients (such as star anise, black mustard seeds, cumin seeds, dried red chilies, or curry leaves) in the oil before pouring it on top before serving.

Crush cardamom seeds for a dark sprinkle on light curries or dust with other finishing spices like a red chile powder, toasted crushed cumin (see Chapter 7), and garam masala.

Kasuri methi (dried fenugreek leaves) can be crumbled on top, but use just a few — they're powerful in aroma and bitter in taste. They'll go well on a curry that has them in its masala, but be careful with other curries because it may create too stark a contrast of flavor.

I've seen some chefs use dried rose petals. I find them overpowering in Indian dishes, so I'm not a fan, but if it's your thing, go for it.

Boiled eggs

Eggs are always dramatic looking. Just make sure they're fresh and the yolks are deep golden in color. Hard-boil them and then either halve them horizontally so you get two ovals or chop them finely and scatter over curries along with some cilantro.

Cream, butter and yogurt

Draw in a swirl of cream or drizzle in a few dots. Too much, and you'll create a white layer on top, which is difficult to erase unless you stir it in. Build it up slowly!

Add 1 teaspoon of butter or ghee to steaming hot curries. It'll give a lovely glaze and a beautifully rich flavor.

A dollop of full-fat yogurt can provide contrast to dark masala sauces, but again, just a spoonful, or it could look messy. Top it with cilantro or mint for an even better contrast.

Banana leaves

If you want to be *really* fancy, head to an Indian, Thai, or Sri Lankan market, and see if they have fresh banana leaves. They can be 6 feet long, so if you do find them, you may not use them all in one go (but you can freeze them). Sometimes they're sold frozen. The leaves are thin and tear easily. Cut off rectangular bits with your kitchen scissors, wash, dry, and use the leaves to line serving bowls or platters.

KITCHEN CUPBOARD CURRY: COOKING WITH FEWER INGREDIENTS

If I told you that it was possible to make an Indian meal in less than 15 minutes, would you believe me? Well, my family didn't either. When my daughter was leaving for college after a few days at home, she gave me her usual "I'm so hungry look," so I said I'd make her favorite curry and rice. "I don't have time — it'll take too long," she said. "Time me," I replied.

It took me 14 minutes.

With a well-stocked pantry, a few spices, and a good deal of confidence, cooking with few ingredients to produce flavorful Indian food is not rocket science.

You want to whip up something with both less prep time, as well as less cooking time, like a weeknight dinner. So, where do you begin?

- **Keep it simple.** The whole premise of a quick curry is that it's simple. Don't attempt a showstopper. Choose one or two dishes that are delicious and fuss-free. When you've aced your routine, you'll go back to those same curries over and over again.
- **Stock your pantry so your ingredients are ready when you are.** You'll be able to create quick meals and, best of all, the hard work's all been done for you. Keep a few spices handy — too many and you'll be overwhelmed choosing which ones to use.

(continued)

(continued)

- **Replenish what you've used.** Building a kitchen cupboard curry isn't easy if the cupboard's empty. Think about your budget and whether you like following specific recipes or enjoy winging it. Are you catering to different dietary needs?

- **Flaunt your flavor.** Few ingredients with lots of flavor? It's got to be spices. Use the heat of chilies and pepper, the tang of lemon or amchur powder (see Chapter 4), enough salt, and perhaps a pinch of sugar. Getting a balance of flavor is important, so don't skimp. Use aromatics like ginger and garlic, which don't take ages to cook, especially if you've cleverly created your own paste and frozen it ahead of time. (see Chapter 6). Swap prep work with pre-prepared (for example, use canned tomatoes instead of fresh, red chile powder instead of fresh green chilies, lemon juice instead of tamarind, which needs to be pulped).

- **Pay attention to color.** Tomato paste adds a bright burst to many quick curries so I always have some on hand. I buy cans of the stuff, put it into freezable bags or containers, and freeze it for up to three months. It cuts like hard butter with a sharp knife and disintegrates into a hot masala sauce within seconds. Turmeric and red chile powder can make the dullest masala brighten up in seconds, so keep a fresh stock (anything older than eight months has to go).

- **Make it an event.** Even if you've prepared it in minutes, you'll want to enjoy it like a proper feast. Add quick glamor to your meal with a few sliced salad vegetables like tomatoes, cucumber, and lettuce on the side. Serve up a bowl of plain yogurt sprinkled with a bit of garam masala and red chile powder, and put out a few store-bought condiments like lime pickle and mango chutney. No one will notice that your curry was made with just a few ingredients in a matter of minutes.

between restaurant and home cooking

» Destressing your curry-making experience

» Serving up a balanced plate of components

Chapter **9**

Bringing It All Together in a Deliciously Healthy Meal

RECIPES IN THIS CHAPTER

- ⏱ **Haldi Gajar Mirchi ka Achaar (Fresh Carrot, Turmeric, Ginger, and Chile Pickle)**

- ⏱ **Lasnechi Chutney (Dry Hot, Sour, Sweet Garlic, Chile, and Coconut Chutney)**

In this chapter, I show you how to eat like an Indian! But I mean eating the way you would in an Indian home, not in a restaurant. If you dropped in on your Indian friend unannounced at dinnertime, this is what you'd find. (You'd also be invited to join the family for dinner — feeding a guest is a big thing in India.)

Indian restaurant food and home cooking could really be two separate cuisines. Many people who haven't traveled to India have perhaps only experienced Indian food in a restaurant, so the way it's enjoyed in a home may come as a bit of a surprise. I urge you to eat the home-cooking way — it's tastier and more balanced and you'll soon be convinced that it's also healthy and not crazy hot.

At home, various dishes are served together, so you'll want to make the plate as interesting as possible in terms of texture, taste, color, and temperature. In this chapter, I show you why a popadam is eaten *with* the meal rather than before and why a bowl of raw, sliced veggies is always brought to the table at a restaurant.

Because food is cooked for the entire family, which may include grandparents as well as young children, food in an Indian home isn't as intense as it is in a restaurant. It's all about personalizing your plate to suit your taste.

Off the Menu: Restaurant versus Home Cooking

Outside of India, restaurant food has largely come to mean North Indian food that can be described easily and served quickly. This means that a restaurant patron can order their food based on familiar parameters (mainly, heat levels) and the chef can send out the order within a prescribed time (because so much of the work has been done in advance).

In this section, I explain some of the key ways that restaurant foods aren't as good as home cooking.

Classifying foods by heat levels

When Indian, Bangladeshi, and Pakistani restaurants mushroomed in England, the easiest way to make ordering simple was to base the menu on heat levels. A korma was mild, a madras was medium, and a vindaloo was fiery. This labeling probably gave rise to the myth that all Indian food is about chilies. In reality, these recipes have nothing to do with heat; instead, they're regional dishes that reflect social history and local ingredients.

In an Indian home, food is never classified by the heat level. In fact, even in most restaurants in India, classifying food simply by heat would be considered ludicrous. Homemade food is subtle, fresher, and more nuanced — something people can eat every day, unlike restaurant fare, which is only an occasional meal.

Aiming for the broadest audience

Restaurant meals are cooked to suit a majority of customers, so they can't be personalized. Customized dishes are integral to home cooking. Family recipes passed down through the generations, or ones created in your own kitchen, will be suited to *your* taste rather than what a chef thinks you should be eating.

Using too much fat

All curries need some fat or oil so the spices cook properly. A fat-free curry won't taste or smell right. But many restaurants use way too much fat. Of course, fat makes things taste good, but the long cooking process and the reheating of curries brings it all to the surface. (If you've ever had Indian takeout food, you'll have a picture of this in your head right now.)

Plus, the fat most restaurants use isn't the high-quality oil you'd use in your own kitchen. Homestyle recipes don't call for a lot of oil either.

Using too much salt

Most restaurant food — of any cuisine — is too salty. Salt makes things taste nice, but if you find yourself waking up through the night to have a glass of water after you've eaten out, your dinner has definitely been over-seasoned. When you're hungry and expecting a treat in the form of a restaurant meal, that salt, fat, and spice hits all the right spots. It's only later — when you're unusually thirsty or feeling lethargic — that you realize the chef went a little overboard.

Home cooking is based on principles of well-being and good health, so there is more balance and softness of flavor.

Charging an arm and a leg

Indian ingredients aren't expensive, but you can end up paying quite a bit for food that can be hit or miss in terms of heat levels and flavor. Buying a bag of rice, lentils, or flour is a cost-effective way of sticking to your food budget. I'm not exaggerating when I say that the price of a restaurant meal could feed the family for several days. My family goes out to eat on special occasions or if I'm completely fed up with my own cooking, but it's not part of our weekly routine.

Sticking to a limited list of ingredients

Most restaurant food has come to mean a limited menu familiar to diners. Think about the vast cuisine that lies unexplored out there! Home cooking makes the best use of a vast range of vegetables, lentils, and beans never seen on restaurant menus. You only have to go to an Indian grocery store to see the range of ingredients available, and they're all truly delicious. Restaurant eating is like opening a random chapter of a book and never reading the rest (and then going back a hundred times and rereading the same pages).

Most Indian dishes never make it to a restaurant menu because they're regional and there's such a great repertoire. Eat in an Indian home, or several if you're lucky, and you'll know what I mean. On my trips to India, when friends suggest a new restaurant, I'm likely to ask if we can eat at home instead. That way, I'm sure to get a healthy, regional meal, prepared with care and consideration. And best of all, I know I'll get a chance to chat with the cook about the recipes — that's much more fun than sitting in a restaurant eating what everyone else is having!

Taking the Worry out of Curry

One of the nicest things about Indian cooking is that, when you have the ingredients, understand key techniques, and have some experience and confidence, the kitchen is your oyster. So much of the process of creating a meal is about personalizing it to your taste and making it your own. But to do this like a boss, you need to know which components you can play with and which instructions are best followed to the letter.

Eating the rainbow

An Indian meal is usually eaten as a single course, so creating a visually exciting plate is essential. Creating a meal that includes all shades of one color (usually brown or yellow with Indian cooking) is easy, so think about ways to add some variety. Your spice tin will give you some vibrant colors, but fresh herbs, fried onions, tomatoes, and various beans and lentils will add energy to the palette as well.

TIP

Here are some tips for adding more color to your meal:

>> **Plan a menu by color.** Start by choosing a recipe that has a carbohydrate (rice or bread) and a protein (meat, poultry, fish, eggs, beans, nuts, lentils, or dairy), as well as a good source of fiber (vegetables or fruit). Choose a recipe of a different color for each group. For example, you may have a white rice, a green protein curry, and a side dish of orange or red vegetables.

>> **Add a bright garnish.** Cilantro and mint are easy garnishes to use because the flavors blend with lots of Indian dishes. You'll add a fresh, green pop with very little effort. Colorful vegetables, a spoonful of yogurt or nuts, and dried fruit can add visual contrast and interest as well.

>> **Change an ingredient.** If your recipe calls for green bell pepper and there's already a lot of green in your menu, consider using red, orange, or yellow bell

peppers instead. Adding spinach puree to a curry sauce adds not just color but nutrients, too.

>> **Vary the base masala sauce.** Base sauces for curries can be anything from white to yellow to green (see Chapter 8). Cook your favorite ingredient in a different masala base each time.

>> **Add a fresh salad.** Fresh vegetables may inspire your work of art. Choose red tomatoes, green cucumbers, yellow corn, purple cabbage, and orange citrus fruit (among many others) to give color, health benefits, and texture.

>> **Jazz up your carbs.** White rice is a great candidate for creativity. Add a pinch or two of turmeric to create a golden hue, or throw in some frozen green peas or sweet corn. A tablespoon of tomato paste will quickly give white rice an orange touch, and a few slices of beetroot can add a natural pink tone. Also, try creating contrast by adding a diced carrot or some fresh spinach into a yellow dal.

Talking texture

A popadam is generally a wafer-thin disc of lentil or rice flour that has been dried and is cooked by roasting over an open fire or frying in hot oil. Popadams come in a variety of flavors, but they're all crisp and add a certain texture to an Indian meal.

TIP

Introducing texture into an Indian meal is crucial. Everything is served together in one course, so you want to make it an exciting sensory experience! Plus, crunchiness elevates the experience of eating because the noise denotes freshness. Apparently, it also draws people's attention to the food in their mouths, making them more mindful of what they're eating.

So, if noise and crunch excite people so much, how do you amplify it on your Indian plates? Read on.

Popadams

I'll call them papads for simplicity's sake. I buy mine at the local Indian shop, and I particularly enjoy pepper and garlic ones. In an Indian home, you'd eat these cracker-like discs with your meal, breaking off a bite-size piece to eat with each mouthful, mainly to add crunch and some flavor.

I'm sometimes asked if I make my own papad. The answer is no. They're typically sundried on terraces during Indian summers and then stored in a cool, dry container to be used during the rest of the year. I live in London and, beautiful as it is, the weather is never predictable. I'd have to wait a long time for a hot sunny day, and it might be interrupted by the odd rain shower. Not perfect conditions for papad-making.

If you visit your local Indian grocery store and look at the papad aisles, you'll probably see a wide range — some made of lentil or rice flours and even tapioca. Some are colored, so they add a visual pop to your plate.

When you buy papad, they're still raw and need to be cooked. Be gentle — they shatter easily and you'll often find little bits that have fallen off in the pack. Here's how to cook papads:

>> **Toasting over an open flame:** I hold the papad with a pair of tongs and toast it over an open flame on my stovetop. I look for the papad to go opaque and start to curl. It also blackens a bit, so you have to flip it constantly to get it evenly opaque all over before it catches fire (it can easily do so if left too long on the flame). This technique does take some time to get used to, and it requires some amount of skill, judgment, and confidence.

You'll find that even after it goes opaque, the papad still seems a bit floppy and not crisp as it should be. It'll turn crisp when you take it off the heat and it cools. The slight charring adds to the smoky flavor. You'll see bubbles on the surface — these form as the little moisture in the papads expands into steam.

>> **Microwaving:** You can cook your papads in a microwave if you like. Place one papad on a plate and cook them one at a time, for 1 minute each. They'll curl up a bit and go crisp. If they cook unevenly (as things sometimes do in a microwave), just reposition the papad and cook it in 5-second bursts until it's cooked all over.

If you have cooked papads as leftovers, store them in an airtight container and eat them as soon as you can. The crispness goes flat in no time if they're kept out in the open. Cook only as many as you'll eat, and store the rest of the uncooked pack in a cool, dry place. Cooked papads are also incredibly brittle. Be gentle, or you'll be left with shards (not unlike what's at the bottom of a potato chip bag).

>> **Frying:** To fry a papad, heat enough oil in a frying pan big enough to hold the papad flat in a single layer. The oil should come up about ½ inch in the pan. Immerse one end of the papad in the oil to check if it's hot enough; it should sizzle. When the oil is ready, gently slip the papad in, and you'll see it quickly rise to the surface. It'll go opaque and bubbly, so flip it over with a pair of tongs to make sure it cooks on the other side, too, and then it's time to take it out of the oil and drain it. Put it on paper towel and, as it cools, it'll get crisp. Fry one papad at a time. Serve them in a stack for people to help themselves.

Papads cook in seconds at the right heat. Don't get busy with doing anything else while you're cooking them because they could easily burn. You want them crisp, but not *burned* to a crisp.

Salads

The word *salad* often conjures up a medley of interesting ingredients tossed with a delicious dressing. Indian salads are often much simpler and could be just a few slices of onion, cucumber, and tomato placed on a plate with a light dusting of salt and lemon juice. If you want to jazz it up a bit, add some pepper and chile powder. If you dice your vegetables finely, it's called *kachumber* or *koshimbir* (depending where you are in India). Sometimes, nuts such as cashews or peanuts are added for a crunchier oomph.

You just scoop a bit of kachumber along with every bite to add crunch. If like me, you don't like raw onions, try slices of carrot, raw beetroot, or radishes. Leaves are not often added because they're not always crisp enough.

There are a few hero salads, too — those regional gems that use local ingredients and bring a new dimension to a meal. Salads are not generally eaten as a main meal in India — they always accompany one.

In some Indian restaurants, the waiter may bring out a plate of complimentary fresh salad with your meal to provide an extra crunch. I've sometimes seen a few green chilies in there, looking all fresh and juicy. Beware, though — these are stingingly hot and not for the fainthearted. I've seen some people crunch them up along with their dinner, and I've had to look away.

Chips

If you don't have papads, you can add instant crunch by serving up a bit of any crisp snack you have in your store cupboard, with your meal. I've seen it done in South India. I love banana chips, potato chips, vegetable or tortilla chips, and even rice crackers.

Playing with temperature

Playing with temperature — serving foods hot or cold — can give an interesting twist to your Indian plate. But when I say "cold," it's actually food served at room temperature or just lightly chilled. According to the Indian holistic healing system *Ayurveda* (see Chapter 2), very cold foods are said to dull the digestion. Indians like curries to be piping hot and salads to be, well, tepid. The heat of tropical India means that nothing stays very cold for very long anyway. Drinking very cold water is said to dampen the digestion, so even in the blazing summers, we're encouraged to drink tepid water.

I've heard lots of people say that yogurt is served with Indian food to cool the palate because everything is so spicy. That's not completely true. A good meal shouldn't be so hot and spicy that you need to keep cooling your mouth. But small amounts of yogurt mixed into your bite of curry and rice can temper any excessive heat and help you personalize your plate.

Here are some ways you can add a cool side dish to your hot meal:

>> **Raita:** You'll often find a *raita* (a mix of raw or cooked vegetables, fruits, or herbs mixed into seasoned yogurt) served with a meal. Because most Indian meals are served hot, this gives a contrasting sensation of coolness. Raita is tempered with spices like smoky cumin that can add a flavor note, too.

>> **Yogurt:** Many Indian meals finish with a spoonful of yogurt, either served plain or seasoned with salt and pepper. If you're invited to a South Indian home, the last bit of rice on your plate will be meant for mixing with yogurt. This cools the mouth, and the probiotics help with digestion.

>> **Salad:** A cool salad bitten into from time to time gives a delightful contrast of temperature, as well as texture.

>> **Chutneys:** A fresh chutney made of vegetables and fruit (like carrot or coconut) and herbs (such as cilantro and mint) will add a cool note to your plate.

The word *chutney* comes from the Hindi *chatna,* which means "to have a lick." Indian chutneys and Western ones are not the same. In the West, you'd probably think of a chutney as a preserve of some kind, made with vinegar and sugar to increase its shelf life. An Indian chutney can be dry or wet; some can be preserved, while others have to be eaten within a day or two. They're all mostly served cool.

>> **Snacks:** The concept of serving a snack with a main meal may come as something of a surprise. Often an Indian feast has a couple of snacks as side dishes, to add texture and taste and change the temperature. It could be a small rice cake or a gram flour roll that has been made in advance and can be served cold.

Heating it up

If you think meat and two veg should really be heat and two veg, this section will show you how to heat up your plate.

Being the alpha person in the room, the one who can eat the hottest chile, is not something to boast about. You may find yourself seriously uncomfortable. Plus, you won't enjoy all the other flavors in your food.

In an Indian home, you'll find a selection of condiments placed on the table at meal times that are used to personalize the heat level of your own plate. Not everyone has to eat hot food. Someone may enjoy a bigger kick than the rest of the family. It's all about adjusting the food to what gives you the most satisfaction. The easiest way to add heat to your plate is with pickles and chutneys that have varying levels of heat to suit everyone.

Achaar is a general term for pickled condiments and relishes, and although some people make it at home, it's more common to buy a selection of ready-made ones from an Indian market. That way, you can keep trying new achaars in small quantities until you find the one you love!

You may have tried an achaar in an Indian restaurant, although it's often served as part of the selection of dips that arrives with your popadams at the start of the meal. The hot lime or mango pickle and even the sweet mango chutney are all called *achaar*, and they're served with the meal!

TIP You can always tell when someone is new to the Indian way of eating: They'll help themselves to the same amount of achaar or chutney as they would a side dish. But pickles and chutneys are served and eaten in small quantities. You only serve yourself ½ to 1 teaspoonful, and then you just dab it on your rice or bread before mixing in or scooping up a curry. That way, you create a mini explosion of flavor rather than a volcano of heat that you didn't expect.

Indian pickles and chutneys can be hot, sweet, sour, salty, bitter, or a combination. This variety gives you the choice of what flavor you want as a top note in your food. If you enjoy heat, a hot chile pickle or mango and chile chutney will add a powerful kick. If you want just a little pop, a mild mango one may be for you. Pickles are either made with oil (usually mustard oil) — enough to submerge the achaar and stop it from spoiling — or with brine and lemon or vinegar.

Although many achaars are traditionally matured in the hot Indian sun, some can be made in small quantities in the West and consumed within a few days.

Here's a quick and easy, hot and sour homemade vegetable pickle to try. I also show you how to make a dry garlic and coconut chutney that works well sprinkled over rice and curry.

Haldi Gajar Mirchi ka Achaar (Fresh Carrot, Turmeric, Ginger, and Chile Pickle)

PREP TIME: ABOUT 20 MIN	COOK TIME: NONE	YIELD: 3 TO 4 SERVINGS

INGREDIENTS

1 small carrot, peeled and very finely diced

2 inches fresh turmeric root

2 inches fresh root ginger

2 to 3 small fresh green chilies, finely diced, seeds and all, stalks removed

Enough lemon juice to cover the mixture

½ teaspoon salt

DIRECTIONS

1 Fill a small saucepan with water and add the carrot. Boil until it just begins to soften, about 3 to 4 minutes. Drain and dry completely on a tea towel.

2 Wearing gloves, scrape the skin off the turmeric and ginger, and dice both very finely.

3 In a glass bowl, mix the carrot, turmeric root, ginger, and chilies using a metal spoon (so the turmeric doesn't stain your wooden utensils).

4 Add the lemon juice and season with salt.

5 Transfer to a sterilized, airtight container; seal tightly; and shake well to blend. You can use it right away or store it up to 1 week in the refrigerator.

Lasnechi Chutney (Dry Hot, Sour, Sweet Garlic, Chile, and Coconut Chutney)

PREP TIME: ABOUT 15 MIN	COOK TIME: NONE	YIELD: 6 TO 7 SERVINGS

INGREDIENTS

½ cup desiccated unsweetened coconut

5 large cloves fresh garlic, peeled and finely grated

2 tablespoons Kashmiri chile powder

2 teaspoons sugar

1 tablespoon mango powder (amchur)

Salt to taste

DIRECTIONS

1 In a bowl, mix the coconut, garlic, chile powder, sugar, amchur, and salt.

2 Wearing gloves, rub together with your fingers until well combined.

3 Taste the mixture. It should be salty, sweet, hot, and sour. If it isn't, add a bit more salt, sugar, chile, or amchur.

4 Tip into a clean glass jar and store in the refrigerator for up to 1 month.

NOTE: Amchur is a dry beige powder made from drying and grinding raw green mangoes. It has a lovely, fruity tang and can be sprinkled on many dishes as a finishing spice.

TIP: This chutney goes well with lots of Indian dishes, but it's also excellent on a piece of buttered toast!

Tickling your palate

You just know that some foods go together — for example, ginger and garlic, salt and pepper, milk and sugar. Culinary traditions guide us when we're making these choices, so tried-and-tested recipes are a real friend. If you read up on classic flavor combinations in world cuisines, Indian food will stand out like the proverbial bad boy, not following any rules, and yet it manages to get all the flavors just right. The Europeans have their rules down to a T, even pairing wines perfectly with their foods. When it comes to Indian cooking, it's "Rules, what rules?"

In this section, I walk you through how to introduce flavor into your meal in both subtle and bold ways with a few neutral tasting dishes and others that are intense. I list the various tastes you can play with to create your own combinations and choose a top note such as sweet or hot that you enjoy. Until you build that confidence, I also give you some tried-and-tested spice pairings that you can rely on.

Offer contrasts of flavor

Indian cooking has big bold flavors, but you don't want to overwhelm the palate throughout the meal. That's why having a very spicy main dish isn't really my thing. A bit of heat brought to the plate with a little pickle is so much more interesting than one continuous whack.

Having a neutral food to provide contrast is another key. I'm sometimes asked about what spices can be added to rice or breads to add more oomph. Carbs are the base of your meal, and they're best kept neutral — so think plain rice or roti, so the flavors of the other dishes shine in comparison. If you choose a flavored rice, like a biryani or bread, eat it with a more neutral side, like plain Greek yogurt.

TIP

Let the flavors build. Have a few uncomplicated dishes and don't be afraid to keep things simple. A plain rice with a barely spiced dal, accompanied by some hot pickle and a tangy Kachumber (Onion, Cucumber, Tomato, and Carrot Salad; see Chapter 20) is the stuff of dreams for many people, myself included!

TASTE VERSUS FLAVOR

Taste and flavor are linked but different. *Taste* is what your tongue tells you about sweet, salty, sour, bitter, and umami. *Flavor* is linked to smell and texture. When both are combined, it gives you a great plate of pleasurable food. I've often heard people use the two words to mean the same thing — the sensation of how eating a food makes them feel. This connection of food and feeling is intrinsic to Indian eating.

Think of the top note

Your Indian meal will have several small components. Traditional recipes are written to create a balance of taste and flavor, so you may be thinking, "Wait, if my curry has all the tastes, how do I put a menu together that has variations?"

TIP

Think of the *predominant* flavor and taste. Is the curry savory, sour, or hot? A curry with dried fruit will have a sweet note. Lemon and tamarind will bring tang. If you have a tamarind curry, a slightly sweet side like a mango chutney will be perfect. Remember that you're working with extremely vibrant tastes here — bringing it all together harmoniously is the key, and adding the bolder ones with the help of condiments rather than drowning your entire meal with them is wise. The dairy, fat, and herbs will provide contrast, cut richness, and carry flavor, so try not to be stingy with those.

In the following sections, I suggest some ways to bring top notes of flavor to your meal.

SWEET

In the Indian taste wheel, sweetness is also a neutral taste, so it could include sugar, fats, rice, and wheat. It's a big group of quiet ingredients that will be the base of the meal.

Bold sweetness isn't always welcome in an Indian recipe. Most people don't enjoy an overly sweet main course — we have an amazing repertoire of desserts for that. A subtle sweet note is added by cooking the onions slowly until they caramelize, adding spices such as cardamom and cinnamon, and introducing nuts such as cashews into a curry masala base sauce.

When planning your menu, start with sweetness, so choose a neutral base. You'll want to add accents, too:

>> Plain rice or subtly favored rice (with a single note, such as turmeric or cumin)

>> Unflavored bread, such as roti or paratha

>> A lentil dish such as Tarka Dal (Spiced Lentils; see Chapter 15)

>> Sweet mango chutney

>> Gujarati Sambharo (Cabbage and Carrot Salad; see Chapter 20)

SOUR

I love this taste because it reminds me of forbidden childhood treats like tamarind and raw mangoes eaten away from the stern eyes of adults that told us they would make us sick if we ate too many. Fast-forward to my adult kitchen, and these same ingredients are used to add bright tangy notes in curries, chutneys, and salads.

The mere thought of sour makes the mouth water, so it's not surprising that sour ingredients are found in street foods to entice passersby. Foods like lemons and limes that make us pucker balance out sweet foods.

Here are some ways you can add a sour note:

» Tamarind/vinegar-based curry, such as Beef Vindaloo (Sour Hot Goan Curry; see Chapter 10), Bangda Ghassi (Mackerel Curry with Tamarind; see Chapter 12), Prawn Patia (Sweet and Sour Shrimp Curry; see Chapter 12), or Baghara Baingan (Sweet-and-Sour Eggplant Curry; see Chapter 13)

» Chutneys, such as Khajur Imli ki Chutney (Sweet-and-Sour Date and Tamarind Chutney; see Chapter 20)

» Some lemon or lime juice squeezed over a curry

HOT

Hot is more a sensation than a taste. Our taste buds recognize the feeling of heat and pain, which causes the sting on our tongues. Although it's not necessary to have crazy amounts of heat in your meal, a bit of a kick does jazz it up. I'd go for the following:

» Store-bought hot pickle

» A hot curry (**Note:** The recipes in this book are mostly for medium-hot ones so add a couple more chilies if you like yours hot!)

SALTY

This taste comes with, well, salt. Many people in my classes are nervous when they see me add salt to my cooking, but trust me, it's important. Indian cooking needs salt to intensify the other tastes; otherwise, the whole plate will be underwhelming.

PERFECT COMBINATIONS TO RELY ON

If you're nervous about trying too many new variations, here are a few ingredient pairs that are used by every Indian cook

- Ginger and garlic, for depth of flavor
- Ground cumin and coriander, for sweet and bitter notes in savory dishes
- Saffron and green cardamom, for sweet and bitter notes in desserts

TIP

I prefer to salt my cooking and not have a salt shaker on the table. I find it easy to oversalt if I'm just sprinkling it on top of my food. I also find that adding salt during the cooking process allows it to permeate more deeply into the other ingredients. I love using good-quality sea salt and have a couple of options in my kitchen — fine salt for cooking with and coarse flakes for sprinkling over salads (they add a lovely texture as well).

BITTER

This is an important taste in the Indian scheme of things. Some spices like turmeric and fenugreek will add a note of bitterness, but they do need to be cooked properly (see Chapter 7) so they're not unpleasant in the final dish.

In Indian cooking, we don't peel away the bitter skins of vegetables, take the green shoot out of garlic (considered bitter by some European chefs), or salt and drain away bitter juices from vegetables like eggplants. We leave all that in so it brings balance in an unobtrusive way.

Putting Together Indian Meals

European cuisines serve various courses to tease and excite the palate, but in Indian menu planning, the skill lies in creating that same interest in a single plate, without overwhelming you. Think about flavors, textures, colors, and temperatures when putting together various dishes. When you're confident about creating an exciting Indian meal, you can put those skills to good use whether you're whipping up a quick midweek dinner or going full out with an Indian feast.

Composing a weeknight dinner

If you ask a friend in India what they had for dinner, you'll probably be impressed that there were so many parts to their meal. You'll possibly learn that there was rice or bread (or both), dal, a couple of vegetable sides, a curry, salad, and condiments. Remember that in many parts of India, families have kitchen staff or a member of the family (usually the lady of the house), whose responsibility it is to cook several meals a day. Dinner is when the family eats together so a full, proper meal is expected. Lunch may be a slightly simpler version of dinner, but only just, and it's often carried to work in the morning or delivered at lunchtime by a member of the household staff.

In India, extended families often live together, bringing several generations under one roof. But I've lived away from India since my twenties, and I have a smaller family and no kitchen staff, so dinners in my home in London are much simpler. We usually have rice or roti (more often rice because our food heritage is South Indian, where rice is preferred), a curry, and a side salad. Our pantry has a variety of hot, sweet, and sour pickles and we always have plain Greek yogurt in the fridge. If I'm feeling indulgent, I'll cook one more thing — a dal or a vegetable side dish.

Bring your weeknight dinner together with a carbohydrate, such as a rice or bread dish; a protein such as a meat, fish, egg, bean, or paneer curry; and a vegetable side that could also be a salad. Embellish it with store-bought condiments and perhaps a popadam. A midweek dinner should take no more than 40 minutes from kitchen to table, so keep it simple.

Creating an Indian entertaining menu

I believe that Indian food is perfect for entertaining in the West because so much can be prepared in advance, leaving the hosts to enjoy the evening, too. Indian feasts don't involve expensive ingredients. Instead, the number of dishes served goes up from an average family meal. You want the table to be more or less creaking with food, but it need not take hours to cook and some of it may not be a cooked dish at all.

I add in a few salads and raitas to plump up the menu; then I add curries and sides, depending on how much time I have. There's always one rice dish. And don't forget to cater to the vegetarians and vegans on your guest list! Indian recipes are great for those with allergies because there are so many substitutes — coconut milk for cream, gram flour pancakes instead of wheat breads, and lentils instead of nuts in some recipes.

Because of the number of dishes served, Indian parties for many guests end up being a buffet where all the food is on the dining table and guests help themselves and settle on various couches and chairs around the room. A sit-down dinner is possible only where passing dishes around the table is easy, which means for small numbers.

Plan your menu by choosing some starters and appetizers to pass around with drinks. Some may be served cold so you can prepare them in advance, and a couple may need to be cooked or assembled at the last minute. I like serving Onion Bhajia (Savory Onion Fritters; see Chapter 18) or Amritsari Fish (Spiced Fish Fingers in a Gram-Flour Crust; see Chapter 18). I also have some bowls of Chivda (Hot, Savory, and Sweet Mix of Grains, Seeds, and Nuts; see Chapter 18) scattered around the room for guests to munch on as soon as they arrive. This mix of grains, nuts, and dried fruit can be made ahead of time — you'll just need to hide it from yourself so you have some left for the party! You can also buy some at the Indian market.

Parties mean desserts, so pick one that complements the rest of the menu and the season. Fruit puddings are lovely in the spring (when seasonal Indian mangoes come to the markets) and summer, and rich, milky puddings are delicious in the winter. There's a misconception that Indian desserts are overly sweet, but these are just the commercially available ones. They have to be sweet to increase their shelf life, just as a box of chocolates does. Homemade desserts are less sweet and fresher, so don't be afraid to try some of the recipes in this book.

Going all out: Creating a thali

A *thali* generally means a plate, usually made of metal, that your food is served on. When Indian meals become celebratory, a large thali is filled with numerous little bowls (called *katoris* in Hindi and not to be confused with *kachori*, a fried dumpling) containing sweet, sour, hot, and salty foods that complement each other visually and texturally. Like many other words in India, the word *thali* doubles up to also mean the array of foods served on such a metal plate.

Some regions of India, such as Gujarat in the West and much of the South, where the food is served on a banana leaf rather than on a metal plate, are famous for their thalis — plates of endless food that never stop giving. The more dishes in the thali, the more pampered your guest will feel. Presenting a thali was historically a show of prosperity and indulgence.

Dessert is also served along with this meal, so there are no courses. You're encouraged to combine contrasting tastes — perhaps having a bite of dessert in the middle of your savory meal. It's similar to having a sorbet in the middle of a

French feast, to cleanse the palate. Many thalis are vegetarian but some restaurants also serve a fish, chicken, or mutton thali, all of which have fewer dishes than the vegetarian ones, possibly for monetary reasons.

You can re-create a thali by placing lots of ramekins around each plate, although you'll need a few sets. When planning a thali menu, you'll need to think of some wet curries and some dry ones. There'll always be some crisp sides — a pakora or a bhajia and chutneys to accompany them. You'll find small servings of many dishes in a thali, so it's quite a lot of work creating one, but so worth it.

Even today, on every trip back to Mumbai, I seek out my favorite thali restaurant and go there for a meal — just one, mind you, because eating a thali is like pigging out until you get food fatigue. It's almost like you're not supposed to eat until you're full — you're supposed to eat until you disgust yourself. Because of the complexity of the thali (mainly, the number of dishes served), it's best had at a restaurant devoted to this kind of meal, but it's quite good fun to create a mini thali that takes less effort, at home.

A typical restaurant thali may contain up to 25 items. Here are some suggestions of what to include in a simpler one at home:

- Flavored rice
- Bread, roti, or poori
- Dal
- A wet curry or two
- Two dry vegetable side dishes
- Raita
- Salad with a wedge of lime or lemon
- Popadams and store-bought pickle
- Dessert
- A drink to wash it all down — usually a light lassi or masala chai (tea)

3

Serving Up Indian Specialties

Add slow-cooked meat curries to your international repertoire.

Re-create restaurant-style chicken curries in your home kitchen.

Bring India's sunshine coast to your table with fish and seafood curries.

Discover the repertoire of vegetable dishes that give India the distinction of being the vegetarian capital of the world.

Impress your family with hero rice dishes like pulao and biryani.

Prepare a range of plant-based lentil and bean dishes.

Create easy egg curries for a quick weeknight dinner.

Chapter **10**

Lovely Lamb, Beef, and Pork Dishes

RECIPES IN THIS CHAPTER

* Masala Gosht (North Indian Lamb Curry)

* Gosht ka Dalcha (Lamb and Lentil Curry)

* Coorgi-Style Pandi Curry (Pork Curry with Vinegar)

* Dhabe ka Kheema (Spicy Ground Lamb or Beef)

* Bhuna Gosht (Brown Lamb Curry)

* Konkani Mutton (Lamb Curry with Cloves, Pepper, and Coconut)

* Kofta Curry (Lamb or Beef Meatball Curry)

* Beef Vindaloo (Sour Hot Goan Curry)

* Seyal Teevan (Lamb Chop Curry with Cardamom)

* Hara Gosht (Lamb in a Green Herby Curry)

* Safed Gosht (Lamb in a Coconut and Cashew Nut Curry)

* Malabar Beef Roast (Deep, Dark Beef with Spices)

I n India, meat is complicated — Muslims and Hindus eat different kinds of meat (see the nearby sidebar for more information) — but none of that matters in this chapter, where I offer a variety of recipes for you to choose from.

Most Indian homes have pressure cookers. If you have one, you'll save a lot of time and effort (listening out for a timer to go off rather than keeping a constant eye on the frying pan). You can use an Instant Pot or a slow cooker — just follow the manufacturer's instructions for cooking times. Bear in mind that red meat benefits from slow, long cooking so be prepared to put in over an hour to make a rich, deep curry.

Having said that, one of the best things about meat curries is that they can be made ahead of time and that they only develop their flavor and become better in the process. The spices and aromatics seem to penetrate the meat better, and every note seems to sing a song in perfect unison. They also freeze well for up to three months, so consider cooking up a batch when you have the time.

Finally, you can substitute the meat in many of these recipes. I've used lamb because it best replicates the goat eaten in India (see the nearby sidebar), but you can use beef if you prefer, or even chicken or vegetables. Experiment, adjust cooking times, and enjoy the dishes you create by using my recipes as a template to guide you.

Masala Gosht (North Indian Lamb Curry)

INGREDIENTS

3 tablespoons vegetable oil, divided

3 cloves

1-inch stick of cinnamon, broken up

4 dried red Kashmiri chilies, deseeded and broken up

5 green cardamom (seeds only, husks discarded)

2 black cardamom (seeds only, husks discarded)

2 yellow onions, finely sliced

3 teaspoons Ginger-Garlic Paste (see Chapter 6)

2 tablespoons tomato paste

2 fresh or dried bay leaves

1.25 pounds lamb shoulder on the bone (or boneless, if you prefer, cubed)

2 teaspoons garam masala

1 teaspoon turmeric

1 teaspoon Kashmiri chile powder

2 teaspoons ground coriander

2 teaspoons ground fennel

Salt to taste

Several stalks fresh cilantro, finely chopped, for garnish

DIRECTIONS

1 In a heavy saucepan, warm 1½ tablespoons of the oil over high heat. Add the cloves, cinnamon, chilies, and the seeds of both types of cardamom. Fry until an aroma develops, about 2 minutes, and then add the onions. Fry until the onions begin to turn golden; then lower the heat to medium and cook, stirring occasionally, until very soft, about 8 to 10 minutes.

2 Turn up the heat, add the Ginger-Garlic Paste, fry for 30 seconds, and then add the tomato paste. Stir a few times, and remove from the heat.

3 Transfer the mixture to a blender, add enough water to just cover the mixture, and blend. Set aside. (This is the masala base sauce.)

(continued)

4 In a pan, warm the remaining 1½ tablespoons of oil over high heat, and fry the bay leaves until they darken slightly, about 1 minute. Then add the lamb. Sear on medium heat until the lamb is no longer pink, about 3 to 4 minutes. Then add the garam masala, turmeric, chili powder, coriander, and fennel, and fry for 2 minutes. Add the masala base sauce from the blender. Rinse out the blender with about 1 cup of water and add the water to the pan.

5 Season with salt and bring to a boil. Reduce the heat to low, cover, and simmer for about 1 hour or until the lamb is done (you should be able to break up a bit of meat with a spoon). Add more water as necessary to create a thick sauce.

6 Sprinkle with fresh cilantro and serve hot.

TIP: If you prefer, in Step 5, you can cook the curry in an Instant Pot, pressure cooker, or slow cooker. Just follow the manufacturer's instructions.

TIP: A bit of plain Greek yogurt or Kheere Tamater ka Raita (Cucumber and Tomato Salad with Yogurt; see Chapter 20) and a few slices of cucumber added to the plate with this curry makes a great meal.

TIP: Serve this curry with rice or bread.

MEAT AND INDIAN RELIGIOUS PRACTICES

Most Hindus, who form the majority of the population of India, don't eat beef. The Muslim minority don't eat pork — they eat only *halal meat* (meat that's been butchered to religious specifications), and there are bespoke butchers who specialize in this practice. So, goat is what's served in most restaurants. The Christians, in places like Goa and Kerala, eat goat, beef, and pork, and their cuisines have some wonderful recipes that showcase the bold flavors that red meat can take.

In India, the red meat most consumed is *mutton,* which most Westerners would think of as an older sheep but in India is actually goat. Goat is leaner than sheep and has a subtler aroma. In the West, where goat isn't as easily available, Indian mutton recipes are best re-created with tender lamb so that the meat softens and absorbs the flavors of the spices.

Murgh Malaiwala (Chicken in a Creamy Cashew Nut and Saffron Curry; Chapter 11)

Murgh Makhani (Butter Chicken; Chapter 11)

Sali Marg ... hapter 11)

Fanshachi Bhaji (Curried Young Jackfruit; Chapter 13)

Kashmiri Pulao (Rice with Mushrooms, Dried Fruit, Nuts, and Spices; Chapter 14)

Egg Biryani (South Indian Spiced Rice with Eggs; Chapter 14)

Masala Omelet (Omelet with Spices; Chapter 17)

Kachumber (Onion, Cucumber, Tomato, and Carrot Salad; Chapter 20)

Chapati or Roti (Flatbread; Chapter 19)

Lobster Kalvan (Lobster Curry; Chapter 12)

Masala Chai (Spiced Tea; Chapter 21)

Badam ke Laddoo (Almond Fudge; Chapter 21)

Gosht ka Dalcha (Lamb and Lentil Curry)

PREP TIME: 15 MIN PLUS 30 MIN SOAKING TIME	COOK TIME: 1 HR 30 MIN	YIELD: 3–4 SERVINGS

INGREDIENTS

⅔ cup chana dal (yellow split gram lentils), washed and drained

1.25 pounds lamb shoulder on the bone (or boneless, if you prefer, cubed)

1 teaspoon turmeric

2 teaspoons Kashmiri chile powder

2 teaspoons garam masala

2 teaspoons ground coriander

2 teaspoons ground cumin

2 tablespoons vegetable oil

2 fresh or dried bay leaves

2 yellow onions, finely diced

3 teaspoons Ginger-Garlic Paste (see Chapter 6)

1 tablespoon tomato paste

Salt to taste

2 tablespoons tamarind block made into pulp (see Chapter 6)

Several stalks fresh cilantro, finely chopped, for garnish

DIRECTIONS

1 Fill a stockpot with water and bring to a boil. Turn off the heat, add the lentils to the water, and soak 30 minutes to soften.

2 In a bowl, combine the lamb with the turmeric, chile powder, garam masala, coriander, and cumin; set aside.

3 In a heavy saucepan, warm the oil over high heat, and add the bay leaves. Fry until the bay leaves turn slightly dark, about 2 minutes, and then add the onions. Fry until the onions begin to turn golden, about 3 to 4 minutes; then lower the heat to medium and cook, stirring intermittently, for 3 to 4 minutes.

4 Turn up the heat, add the Ginger-Garlic Paste, and fry for 30 seconds; then tip in the lamb. Stir-fry or bhunao (see Chapter 5) until the meat sears, adding 2 tablespoons of water to allow for easy stirring.

5 Drain the lentils and add them to the pan with the meat. Pour in enough boiling water to cover the mixture, and bring to a boil. Lower the heat and simmer for 45 minutes, adding more hot water when the curry thickens.

6 Add the tomato paste, salt, and tamarind pulp, and continue cooking until the lentils are falling apart and the lamb is tender, about 1 hour and 20 minutes. The curry should look thick and creamy.

7 Top with the chopped cilantro and serve.

TIP: Serve this curry with rice or bread and a fresh green salad.

NOTE: You'll find plenty of regional recipes where meat and lentils are combined. This one is from the southern city of Hyderabad — a clue lies in the use of tamarind, which is popular in South Indian cooking.

Coorgi-Style Pandi Curry (Pork Curry with Vinegar)

PREP TIME: 20 MIN	COOK TIME: 1 HR 15 MIN	YIELD: 3-4 SERVINGS

INGREDIENTS

1.25 pounds pork loin (or pork belly, if you prefer), cubed

1 teaspoon turmeric

1 teaspoon Kashmiri chile powder

Salt to taste

1 teaspoon cumin seeds

1 teaspoon coriander seeds

10 black peppercorns

5 cloves

1-inch stick of cinnamon, broken up

2 yellow onions, sliced

2 teaspoons Ginger-Garlic Paste (see Chapter 6) or 6 cloves of garlic and a 1-inch piece of ginger, peeled and diced

2 fresh green chilies, diced

15 fresh curry leaves or 2 big pinches of dried curry leaves

1 large handful cilantro, chopped, stalks and all

2 tablespoons vegetable oil

1 tablespoon Kachampuli vinegar or substitute with balsamic vinegar

DIRECTIONS

1 In a bowl, combine the pork, turmeric, chile powder, and salt; set aside.

2 To make the dry spice masala, warm a small frying pan on high heat and add the cumin seeds, coriander seeds, peppercorns, cloves, and cinnamon. Shake the pan frequently until they develop an aroma. Then tip them into a spice mill and blitz, or pound them in a mortar and pestle until fine.

3 To make the wet masala base, place the onions, Ginger-Garlic Paste (or garlic cloves and ginger), green chilies, curry leaves, and cilantro in a blender with enough water to cover the mixture, and blend until pureed.

4 In a heavy frying pan, warm the oil over high heat. Then add the pork and cook until it's seared. Add half of the dry spice masala. Mix well and add ½ cup water. Bring to a boil.

5 Add the wet masala base to the frying pan, rinse the blender with 1 cup of water, and add this water to the pan. Stir in the vinegar. Add more salt to adjust the seasoning. Reduce the heat to low, cover, and simmer for 30 minutes. Add the remaining dry spice masala and continue cooking until the pork is tender and the sauce is thick, about 25 minutes.

TIP: Kachampuli is a blackish vinegar unique to the town of Coorg in South India. It gives the curry its deep color, so if you're using balsamic vinegar, you may need to add an extra teaspoon to achieve the same depth.

Dhabe ka Kheema (Spicy Ground Lamb or Beef)

PREP TIME: 15 MIN	COOK TIME: 35 MIN	YIELD: 3-4 SERVINGS

INGREDIENTS

2 tablespoons vegetable oil

2 fresh or dried bay leaves

3 green cardamom, seeds crushed (discard husks)

1 medium onion, diced finely

2 teaspoons Ginger-Garlic Paste (see Chapter 6)

2 fresh green chilies, diced

1.25 pounds lean ground lamb or beef

½ cup frozen peas

1 teaspoon turmeric

2 teaspoons garam masala

1 teaspoon dried fenugreek leaves (kasuri methi), crumbled between your fingers

Salt to taste

½ can chopped tomatoes or 2 large fresh tomatoes, diced, seeds and all

Several stalks fresh cilantro, chopped finely, for garnish

DIRECTIONS

1 In a frying pan, warm the oil over high heat. Add the bay leaves and cardamom, and fry for a few seconds, until the leaves begin to darken. Add the onions, and fry until they start to turn light golden. Add the Ginger-Garlic paste and chilies, and continue frying for 1 minute.

2 Add the ground meat, breaking it up and stirring until it turns brown. Keep the heat high. If the meat catches, scrape it back into the mix to make the most of the bhunao technique (see Chapter 5).

3 Add the peas. Stir in the turmeric, garam masala, fenugreek, and salt. Mix in the tomatoes and cook until sizzling, about 3 to 4 minutes. Turn down the heat, cover, and cook until the lamb and peas are done, about 15 minutes.

4 Garnish with the chopped cilantro, and serve hot.

TIP: Serve with Chapati or Roti (Flatbread; see Chapter 19) and Kheere Tamater ka Raita (Cucumber and Tomato Salad with Yogurt; see Chapter 20).

TIP: This dish is a versatile one. It can be folded into a roti to make a wrap, fried in pastry for samosas, or even eaten with pasta as a spicy dinner.

Bhuna Gosht (Brown Lamb Curry)

PREP TIME: 15 MIN	COOK TIME: 1 HR 30 MIN	YIELD: 3–4 SERVINGS

INGREDIENTS

2 tablespoons vegetable oil

2 fresh or dried bay leaves

5 cloves

2 medium onions, diced finely

1 tablespoon Ginger-Garlic Paste (see Chapter 6)

1.25 pounds boned lamb loin, cubed

1 teaspoon turmeric

1 teaspoon Kashmiri chile powder

2 teaspoons ground coriander

2 teaspoons garam masala

1 teaspoon dried fenugreek leaves (kasuri methi)

Salt to taste

½ can chopped tomatoes or 2 large fresh tomatoes, diced, seeds and all

3 tablespoons plain full-fat Greek yogurt

One ¾-inch knob of fresh ginger, skin scraped off, flesh cut into matchsticks, for garnish

DIRECTIONS

1 In a frying pan, warm the oil over high heat. Add the bay leaves and cloves, and fry for a few seconds. Add the onions, and fry until they turn light golden, about 3 to 4 minutes. Add the Ginger-Garlic Paste, and continue frying for 1 minute.

2 Add the lamb, stirring it intermittently until it changes color, about 3 to 4 minutes.

3 Mix in the turmeric, chile powder, coriander, garam masala, and fenugreek. Season with salt.

4 Keep the heat high, and when the meat starts to stick, add ½ cup water and deglaze the pan, scraping all the flavor back into the sauce. Bring the curry to a boil. Then lower the heat and continue cooking until the meat begins to stick again. Add another ½ cup of water and repeat the bhunao process (see Chapter 5). You'll need to increase the heat every time you add water and decrease it when the curry boils. You can use hot water to speed this up.

5 When the meat has started to soften, after about 10 minutes, add the tomatoes and yogurt. Mix well and cook over high heat. Lower the heat and cook until the lamb is tender, adding a bit of water whenever the sauce dries up as in Step 4. The curry should stick to the meat.

6 Garnish with the fresh ginger, and serve hot.

TIP: This dish goes well with an Indian bread such as Chapati or Roti (Flatbread; see Chapter 19) or Naan (Leavened Oven-Baked Bread; see Chapter 19). Or, if you're feeling indulgent, serve it with Poori (Festive Fried Bread; see Chapter 19). Scoop up those flavors!

VARY IT! You can use beef for this recipe, too. Because this curry benefits from long, slow cooking, use a cut such as tenderloin, which won't toughen.

Konkani Mutton (Lamb Curry with Cloves, Pepper, and Coconut)

PREP TIME: 20 MIN	COOK TIME: 1 HR 30 MIN	YIELD: 3–4 SERVINGS

INGREDIENTS

3 tablespoons vegetable oil, divided

6 cloves

1 teaspoon black peppercorns

2 medium onions, finely sliced

1 tablespoon Ginger-Garlic Paste (see Chapter 6)

½ cup desiccated coconut (unsweetened)

4 or 5 stalks of cilantro, roughly chopped

1.25 pounds lamb shoulder, on the bone (or boneless, if you prefer, cubed)

1 teaspoon turmeric

1 or 2 teaspoons Kashmiri chile powder

2 teaspoons ground coriander

2 teaspoons garam masala

Salt to taste

1½ tablespoons tamarind, made into a pulp, roughly ½ cup (see Chapter 6)

DIRECTIONS

1 In a frying pan, warm 1½ tablespoons of the oil over high heat. Add the cloves and peppercorns. As soon as they start to sizzle (cloves can burst and pop so be careful!), add the onions, and fry until they turn light golden, about 3 to 4 minutes. Turn down the heat and cook for 7 to 8 minutes, stirring intermittently until they're very soft. Add the Ginger-Garlic Paste, and continue frying for 1 minute.

2 Tip in the coconut and cook over high heat, stirring frequently, until it starts to turn brown, about 3 to 4 minutes. Turn off the heat and add the cilantro.

3 Transfer this mixture to a blender, add just enough cold water to cover it, and puree.

4 Wipe the pan clean and heat the remaining 1½ tablespoons of oil over high heat. Add the lamb, and sauté until seared.

5 Sprinkle in the turmeric, chile powder, ground coriander, and garam masala, and fry until an aroma develops, about 2 to 3 minutes.

6 Pour the curry base from the blender into the pan with the lamb, season with salt, and add the tamarind.

7 Rinse the blender out with 1 cup of water and add to the pan. Bring to a boil, and then reduce the heat, cover, and simmer until the lamb is tender, about 45 to 60 minutes, stirring occasionally. Add a bit more water during the cooking if the sauce becomes too dry. You should end up with a curry of pouring consistency.

TIP: For any easy wow factor, serve with Sunhera Pulao (Golden Turmeric Rice; see Chapter 14). This dish also goes well with Chapati or Roti (Flatbread; see Chapter 19) or Chilla (Gram Flour Pancakes; see Chapter 19).

Kofta Curry (Lamb or Beef Meatball Curry)

PREP TIME: 20 MIN	COOK TIME: 45 MIN	YIELD: 3-4 SERVINGS

INGREDIENTS

1 pound ground lamb or beef

4 teaspoons Ginger-Garlic Paste (see Chapter 6), divided

2 fresh green chilies, very finely diced

Salt to taste

2 tablespoons vegetable oil

2 fresh or dried bay leaves

2 large onions, diced finely

1 teaspoon turmeric

1 teaspoon Kashmiri chile powder

1 teaspoon ground cumin

2 teaspoons ground coriander

2 teaspoons garam masala

One 15-ounce can chopped tomatoes or 3 large fresh ones

Small handful of cilantro, finely chopped (reserve a bit for garnish)

Pepper to taste

4 tablespoons plain full-fat Greek yogurt (reserve a bit for garnish)

DIRECTIONS

1 Preheat the oven to 425 degrees.

2 Knead the meat, 1 teaspoon of the Ginger-Garlic Paste, the chilies, and the salt together into a smooth ball. Pull off a couple teaspoonfuls of the mixture and roll between your palms to make a smooth, tight, large cherry-size ball. You should get around 35 balls. Place the balls on a lined baking tray.

3 In a frying pan, warm the oil over high heat. Add the bay leaves and sizzle. Add the onions, and fry until they turn light golden, 3 to 4 minutes. Lower the heat and soften the onions for 7 to 8 minutes. Add the remaining 3 teaspoons of Ginger-Garlic Paste, and fry for 1 minute.

4 To the frying pan, add the turmeric, chile powder, cumin, coriander, and garam masala, and fry until an aroma develops, about 2 to 3 minutes. If the spices stick to the bottom of the pan, add a splash of water, deglaze the pan, and let it evaporate. Add the tomatoes and cook over high heat until they bubble.

5 Bake the meatballs for 10 minutes.

6 Lower the heat on the curry, add the chopped cilantro (reserving some for the garnish), salt, and pepper, and simmer until the tomatoes have collapsed into the curry sauce. Fold in the Greek yogurt, adjust the seasoning, and warm through. Turn off the heat.

7 When the meatballs are brown, cut open one to make sure they're cooked through and are still moist and spongy. Then gently mix them into the curry.Top with cilantro and a drizzle of yogurt.

TIP: You'll love this with Chapati or Roti (Flatbread; see Chapter 19) or Naan (Leavened Oven-Baked Bread; see Chapter 19).

Beef Vindaloo (Sour Hot Goan Curry)

PREP TIME: 20 MIN	COOK TIME: 1 HR 30 MIN	YIELD: 3–4 SERVINGS

INGREDIENTS

10 dried red Kashmiri chilies, broken in half and seeds shaken out

8 garlic cloves, chopped

One 1-inch piece of fresh root ginger, scraped and chopped

½ teaspoon salt

¼ cup dark malt vinegar

3 cloves

2 teaspoons cumin seeds

One 1½-inch stick of cinnamon

½ teaspoon freshly ground black pepper

2 onions, sliced finely

2 tablespoons vegetable oil

1.25 pounds boneless, trimmed beef shoulder, cubed

Salt to taste

DIRECTIONS

1 Place the dried chilies, garlic, ginger, salt, and vinegar in a small bowl, cover, and steep for 20 minutes.

2 In the meantime, warm a frying pan over a high heat. Add the cloves, cumin seeds, cinnamon, and pepper, and dry-toast for 40 seconds, shaking the pan frequently, until the spices are fragrant. Then tip them into the chile vinegar mixture.

3 Put the onions and the chile vinegar mixture into a blender, add a little water, and blitz to a puree. This is the vindaloo masala base.

4 Heat the oil in a saucepan over high heat. Add the beef and fry for 3 to 4 minutes to sear, but not brown, the meat. Stir in the vindaloo masala from the blender. Rinse the blender with 1 cup of water, and add the water to the pan. Season with salt.

5 Bring to a boil. Then reduce the heat to medium, cover, and cook until the beef is tender, about 1½ hours, adding a bit more water if the curry dries out.

NOTE: Outside of India, vindaloo has come to mean one of the hottest restaurant curries you can eat. In India, a vindaloo is a regional pork curry, not always searing hot, from the coastal state of Goa, which was for several years a stronghold of the Portuguese. The name is believed to be a derivation of the Portuguese words for wine and garlic — *vinho* and *alhos,* respectively — but in India, because people prefer to drink wine over cooking with it, the wine got replaced with vinegar.

Seyal Teevan (Lamb Chop Curry with Cardamom)

PREP TIME: 20 MIN	COOK TIME: 1 HR 30 MIN	YIELD: 3–4 SERVINGS

INGREDIENTS

2 tablespoons vegetable oil

5 green cardamom, seeds crushed (discard husks)

2 black cardamom, seeds crushed (discard husks)

3 onions, finely diced

3 teaspoons Ginger-Garlic Paste (see Chapter 6)

1.25 pounds lamb chops, trimmed

1 teaspoon turmeric

1 teaspoon Kashmiri chile powder

2 teaspoons ground coriander

2 teaspoons garam masala plus a large pinch more for finishing

4 tablespoons plain full-fat Greek yogurt

3 large tomatoes, diced, seeds and all

Salt to taste

DIRECTIONS

1 In a heavy frying pan, warm the oil and add the green and black cardamom. When they sizzle, add the onions, and sauté on high heat for 3 to 4 minutes. When the onions turn golden, add the Ginger-Garlic Paste, and cook for 1 minute.

2 Add the lamb chops, turmeric, chile powder, coriander, and garam masala. Stir in the yogurt and 3 tablespoons of water. Continue to sauté, turning down the heat when the curry starts bubbling. Cover and cook for 10 minutes or so.

3 Raise the heat, add the tomatoes, and season with salt. Keep sautéing or bhunao (see Chapter 5) — you want the juices from the onions and tomatoes to keep the meat moist. When the tomatoes have collapsed, add 1 cup of water and bring the curry to a boil. Reduce the heat to medium, cover, and simmer for 30 to 45 minutes or until the lamb is tender, adding a bit of water as necessary to make a thick curry sauce.

4 Sprinkle with a large pinch of garam masala and serve.

TIP: Serve this curry with rice and a popadam.

NOTE: The Sindhis, who moved to India during the Partition from Pakistan, brought a simple but delicious cuisine with them. Many recipes, such as this one, require time but not too much in the way of processes such as blending.

Hara Gosht (Lamb in a Green Herby Curry)

PREP TIME: 15 MIN	COOK TIME: 1 HR 30 MIN	YIELD: 3–4 SERVINGS

INGREDIENTS

1.25 pounds lamb shoulder on the bone (or boneless if you prefer, cubed)

2 teaspoons garam masala

1 teaspoon ground turmeric

Salt to taste

2 large handfuls fresh cilantro leaves and stems, washed and chopped

2 large handfuls fresh mint leaves, washed and chopped (stems discarded)

2 fresh green chilies, stalks removed

8 fresh curry leaves or 15 dried curry leaves

2 tablespoons Ginger-Garlic Paste (see Chapter 6)

1 large onion, chopped into large chunks

3 spring onions, chopped

One 13.5-ounce can of coconut milk, divided

¼ cup water

2 tablespoons vegetable oil

½ lemon

DIRECTIONS

1 In a large bowl, mix the lamb with the garam masala, turmeric, and salt; set aside.

2 In a blender, place the cilantro, mint, chilies, curry leaves, Ginger-Garlic Paste, onion, spring onions, 7 ounces of the coconut milk, and water, and blitz until smooth.

3 In a heavy-bottomed pan, heat the oil, add the lamb, and fry the meat to sear, about 3 to 4 minutes. Pour in the green curry paste from the blender and adjust the seasoning. Rinse out the blender with 2 to 3 tablespoons of water, and add the water to the pan.

4 Cook over high heat until the curry starts to bubble. Then lower the heat, cover, and cook until the lamb is tender, about 1 hour or a bit longer, adding more coconut milk and water as necessary to create a thick masala sauce.

5 Remove from the heat and squeeze in the lemon.

TIP: Serve with rice or Chapati or Roti (Flatbread; see Chapter 19).

VARY IT! Throw any bits of green vegetables, such as spinach, kale, or broccoli, that are lurking in the fridge into the blender while you're making the masala base. It'll amp up the flavor and put this dish higher on the veg-o-meter.

Safed Gosht (Lamb in a Coconut and Cashew Nut Curry)

PREP TIME: 15 MIN	COOK TIME: 1 HR 30 MIN	YIELD: 3–4 SERVINGS

INGREDIENTS

2 tablespoons white sesame seeds

2 onions, sliced

3 tablespoons unsalted cashew nuts

2 green chilies, chopped roughly with the seeds

2 tablespoons vegetable oil

2 teaspoons Ginger-Garlic Paste (see Chapter 6)

1.25 pounds lamb shoulder on the bone (or boneless, if you prefer), cubed

2 teaspoons garam masala

Salt to taste

One 13.5-ounce can coconut milk

3 tablespoons heavy cream

DIRECTIONS

1 In a small bowl, place the sesame seeds. Add enough boiling hot water to cover them, and allow to steep for 10 minutes.

2 Put the onions, cashew nuts, and chilies in a saucepan. Add just enough boiling hot water to cover them, and bring to a boil. Reduce the heat to a simmer, cover, and cook for 10 minutes. Allow to cool slightly.

3 Tip away the water from the sesame seeds by draining them in a sieve.

4 Transfer the onions, cashews, and chilies to a blender along with the cooking liquid and the drained sesame seeds. Top with cold water if necessary, to just cover the ingredients (the cooking liquid may be enough), and blitz.

5 In a saucepan, warm the oil over high heat, and fry the Ginger–Garlic Paste until it develops an aroma, about 1 minute. Add the lamb and sauté for 4 to 5 minutes to sear but not brown it. Lower the heat if browning starts to happen.

6 Mix in the garam masala and cook for another minute. Pour in the masala sauce from the blender, rinse the blender out with 3 to 4 tablespoons of water, and add this water to the pan. Season with salt, cover, and bring to a boil. Lower the heat and simmer for 30 minutes; then raise the heat and pour in the coconut milk. Bring back to a boil, lower the heat, and simmer until the lamb is tender, for about 30 to 40 minutes.

7 Remove from the heat and stir in the cream.

TIP: Serve with Naan (Leavened Oven-Baked Bread; see Chapter 19) or Paratha (Layered Bread; see Chapter 19).

VARY IT! You can make this with chicken, too — thighs will work well. Use half a can of coconut milk (a full one may make it too runny with a shorter cooking time) and simmer for 30 minutes.

Malabar Beef Roast (Deep, Dark Beef with Spices)

PREP TIME: 20 MIN	COOK TIME: 1 HR 30 MIN	YIELD: 3–4 SERVINGS

INGREDIENTS

1.25 pounds beef shoulder on the bone (or boneless, if you prefer, cubed)

1 tablespoon Ginger-Garlic Paste (see Chapter 6)

3 green chilies, slit in half lengthwise (see Chapter 6)

Salt to taste

3 tablespoons coconut or vegetable oil

2 onions, sliced

10 fresh curry leaves or 2 big pinches dried curry leaves

½ teaspoon turmeric

2 teaspoons garam masala

1 teaspoon crushed black pepper

1 teaspoon crushed fennel seeds

2 tablespoons sliced unsweetened coconut

DIRECTIONS

1 In a pan, place the beef, Ginger-Garlic Paste, chilies, and salt. Add just enough water to cover, and bring to a boil. Reduce the heat, cover, and simmer until the meat is tender, about 1 hour. You shouldn't have too much liquid left in the pan.

2 In a heavy frying pan, heat the oil over high heat. Add the onions, and cook until they start to color, about 3 to 4 minutes. Then turn down the heat and sauté for 8 to 10 minutes, stirring from time to time, until golden and soft.

3 Add the curry leaves, turmeric, garam masala, pepper, and fennel seeds, and sauté over high heat until the spices begin to sizzle. Scrape them into the onions with a spatula, adding some of the stock created by the cooking of the beef. Let the stock evaporate and then repeat the process until the onions get dark.

4 Add the beef and the remaining liquid (along with the chilies) from the pan and sauté until the curry is quite dry, about 10 to 15 minutes.

5 Heat a small pan, and dry-toast the coconut without oil until it starts to turn golden, about 1 to 2 minutes. Remove from the heat and sprinkle over the beef.

TIP: Serve with Chapati or Roti (Flatbread; see Chapter 19) or Paratha (Layered Bread; see Chapter 19).

TIP: If you have a pressure cooker or Instant Pot, follow the manufacturer's instructions and Step 1 will be less time-consuming.

NOTE: In South India, where this recipe comes from, a roast is not an oven-cooked dish as you would assume in the West. Instead, it's made by a process of pan-frying and sautéing until you get a dry, spiced dish.

Chapter **11**

Scrumptious Poultry Dishes

RECIPES IN THIS CHAPTER

* Murgh Malaiwala (Chicken in a Creamy Cashew Nut and Saffron Curry)
* Murgh Makhani (Butter Chicken)
* Kombdi Batata (Chicken and Potato Curry)
* Karahi Murgh (Chicken Curry with Tomatoes)
* Chicken Tikka Masala (Chicken Curry with Spices)
* Sali Marghi (Chicken Curry with Apricots)
* Malvani Kombdi (Chicken and Coconut Curry)
* Chicken Madras (Chicken Curry with Fennel)
* Kerala Duck Mappas (Duck Curry with Coconut Milk and Pepper)
* Bengali Chicken Korma (Chicken Curry with Cream)
* Saag Murgh (Chicken Curry with Spinach)
* Chicken 65 (Indo Chinese Chicken)

Look at any average Indian restaurant menu and, chances are, most of the nonvegetarian dishes have chicken in them. Chicken is the most popular meat in India, where beef and pork are not widely eaten. Goat, the preferred red meat in India, is heavy and meaty, whereas chicken is seen as lighter and easier to cook.

Some people prefer boneless breast meat, but many Indian curries benefit from having meat on the bone — it contributes to the overall flavor and helps to keep the meat juicy, even through relatively long cooking times. Boneless chicken, because it's more expensive, is used in dishes considered to be special; these dishes often have other expensive ingredients, such as nuts and cream. This rule isn't carved in stone, though — home-cooked curries are a matter of preference. Buying a whole chicken, cutting it up, and using it in a curry is cost-effective, and you and your family or friends can have a choice of cut. (Turn to Chapter 5 for more on what a curry cut is.)

In Indian cooking, chicken is always used skinless. I prefer it this way — the slippery skin falling off into a curry is just gross. Leaving the skin on would also prevent the spices and aromatic flavors from permeating fully to the meat.

Murgh Malaiwala (Chicken in a Creamy Cashew Nut and Saffron Curry)

| PREP TIME: 15 MIN | COOK TIME: 45 MIN | YIELD: 3–4 SERVINGS |

INGREDIENTS

2 yellow onions, finely sliced

3 tablespoons unsalted cashew nuts

2 fresh green chilies, diced, with seeds

1¼ cups plus 2 tablespoons whole milk, divided

¼ teaspoon saffron strands

2 tablespoons vegetable oil

2 fresh or dried bay leaves

1.25 pounds chicken thighs or drumsticks, skinned

2 teaspoons Ginger-Garlic Paste (see Chapter 6)

2 teaspoons garam masala, plus extra for garnish

2 teaspoons ground coriander

Salt to taste

6 green cardamom, seeds finely crushed (husks discarded)

3 tablespoons heavy cream

DIRECTIONS

1   In a saucepan, place the onions, cashew nuts, chilies, and 1¼ cups of the milk. (The onions should be submerged in the milk; if they aren't, add enough milk to cover the onions.) Bring to a boil. Then reduce the heat and simmer, partially covered, until the onions are soft, about 10 minutes.

2   In the meantime, in a small pan, warm the remaining 2 tablespoons of milk over high heat for 30 seconds until warm. Remove from the heat and add the saffron strands. Set aside to steep.

3   Transfer the mixture to a blender, and blitz to a fine puree, adding more milk if needed to just about cover the mixture. Set aside in the blender.

4   In a heavy pan, warm the oil over high heat. Add the bay leaves, and fry for a few seconds, until they darken slightly. Add in the chicken, and turn to seal for a few minutes. Add the Ginger-Garlic Paste, mix well, and cook, stirring, until the raw aroma disappears, about 1 minute.

5   Sprinkle in the garam masala and coriander, and cook for another 1 minute.

6   Pour in the masala sauce from the blender. Rinse the blender with 2 tablespoons of water and add this water in as well. Season with salt.

7   Bring to a boil; then reduce the heat, cover, and simmer until the chicken is white all the way through when you cut a piece, about 30 minutes.

8   Fold in the saffron milk, cardamom, and cream.

9   Sprinkle with garam masala, and serve.

Murgh Makhani (Butter Chicken)

PREP TIME: 20 MIN	COOK TIME: 40 MIN	YIELD: 3–4 SERVINGS

INGREDIENTS

For the marinade

1 teaspoon Kashmiri red chile powder

2 teaspoons garam masala powder, divided

Salt to taste

1 tablespoon plus 1 teaspoon Ginger-Garlic Paste (see Chapter 6), divided

1.25 pounds chicken breast, chopped into 1-inch cubes

2 tablespoons vegetable oil plus a little more for drizzling

1 large onion, sliced

1 or 2 green chilies, finely chopped, with seeds

4 tablespoons tomato puree

2 tablespoons unsalted butter

1 teaspoon dried fenugreek leaves (kasuri methi)

1 teaspoon turmeric

3½ tablespoons single cream or coconut milk

2 tablespoons honey

DIRECTIONS

1 Preheat the oven to 425 degrees.

2 In a plastic container with a lid, combine the chile powder, 1 teaspoon of the garam masala, the salt, and 1 tablespoon of the Ginger-Garlic Paste. Add the chicken and mix well. Then drizzle with oil to seal the spices to the chicken. Refrigerate for 30 minutes.

3 Transfer the chicken to a baking dish and bake until cooked, about 10 to 15 minutes.

4 To make the sauce, in a frying pan, heat the 2 tablespoons of oil over high heat. Add the onion, and fry until slightly golden, about 3 to 4 minutes. Then reduce the heat and cook until very soft, about 7 to 8 minutes. Add the chilies and the remaining 1 teaspoon of Ginger-Garlic Paste, and fry for 30 seconds. Add the tomato puree, and cook for 1 minute. Transfer this mixture to a blender, add enough water to barely cover it, and blitz until pureed.

5 Wipe the saucepan, add the butter and a few drops of oil, and warm over high heat. Add the fenugreek, the remaining 1 teaspoon of garam masala, turmeric, and salt. Fry for a few seconds until the spices sizzle; then add ¼ cups of water. When the water evaporates, add the puree from the blender. Rinse out the blender with 2 to 3 tablespoons of water, and add this water to the pan. Return to a boil.

6 Season with salt. Add the cream or coconut milk and a splash of water to adjust the consistency to a pouring one. Stir in the honey.

7 Add the baked chicken and serve.

TIP: Serve hot with Naan (Leavened Oven-Baked Bread; see Chapter 19) or Kashmiri Pulao (Rice with Mushrooms, Dried Fruit, Nuts, and Spices; see Chapter 14).

Kombdi Batata (Chicken and Potato Curry)

PREP TIME: 20 MIN	COOK TIME: 40 MIN	YIELD: 3-4 SERVINGS

INGREDIENTS

3 dried red Kashmiri chilies

3 tablespoons vegetable oil, divided

10 black peppercorns

2 teaspoons coriander seeds

2 onions, finely sliced

2 tablespoons Ginger-Garlic Paste (see Chapter 6)

2 tablespoons desiccated unsweetened coconut

1.25 pounds skinless chicken thighs on the bone

2 medium waxy potatoes, peeled and quartered

½ teaspoon Kashmiri chile powder

1 teaspoon turmeric

2 teaspoons garam masala

Salt to taste

Juice of ½ lemon

2 tablespoons fresh cilantro, chopped, with the stalks

DIRECTIONS

1 In a small bowl, place the dried red chilies in enough boiling hot water to cover; steep for 15 minutes.

2 In a large frying pan, warm 1½ tablespoons of the oil. Add the peppercorns and coriander. When the oil gets hot and they begin to sizzle, add the onions and fry over high heat for 3 to 4 minutes. Then lower the heat and cook until very soft, about 7 to 8 minutes. Add the Ginger–Garlic Paste and cook for 1 minute.

3 Tip in the coconut. Lift the chilies from the water and add them to the pan. Cook until the coconut turns slightly golden, about 2 to 3 minutes. Transfer this mixture to a blender, add just enough cold water to cover it, and blitz to a puree. Set aside in the blender.

4 Wipe the pan and warm the remaining 1½ tablespoons of oil over high heat. Fry the chicken and potatoes until the chicken seals, about 3 to 4 minutes. Add the chile powder, turmeric, garam masala, and 4 tablespoons of water, and cook over high heat to evaporate some of the water and cook the spices.

5 Add the masala sauce from the blender, rinse out the blender with 4 tablespoons water, and add the water into the pan as well. Season with salt. Bring to a boil. Lower the heat, cover, and cook until the chicken is done all the way through, about 30 minutes.

6 Stir in the lemon juice, sprinkle with cilantro, and serve.

TIP: Serve hot with rice and a salad.

NOTE: This recipe is from the western state of Maharashtra — the coconut in the curry sauce is a giveaway.

Karahi Murgh (Chicken Curry with Tomatoes)

PREP TIME: 15 MIN	COOK TIME: 35 MIN	YIELD: 3-4 SERVINGS

INGREDIENTS

2 tablespoons vegetable oil

2 onions, finely diced

2 tablespoons Ginger-Garlic Paste (see Chapter 6)

1.25 pounds boneless chicken thighs, cut into cubes

1 teaspoon Kashmiri chile powder

1 teaspoon turmeric

1 teaspoon ground cumin

2 teaspoons garam masala powder

3 tomatoes, finely diced with the skins and seeds

1 tablespoon tomato paste

Salt to taste

Large pinch of caster sugar

2 tablespoons fresh cilantro, chopped with the stalks

DIRECTIONS

1 In a large frying pan, warm the oil over high heat. Add the onions, and cook over high heat for 3 to 4 minutes. Lower the heat and continue cooking until very soft, 7 to 8 minutes. Add the Ginger–Garlic Paste and cook for 1 minute.

2 Add the chicken and fry until it seals, about 3 to 4 minutes. Mix in the chile powder, turmeric, cumin, garam masala, and 4 tablespoons of water, and cook over high heat to evaporate some of the water off and cook the spices.

3 Add the tomatoes and tomato paste. Season with salt and add the sugar. Add ¼ cup of water and bring to a boil. Then lower the heat to medium, cover, and cook until the chicken is done all the way through and the curry is thick, about 30 minutes.

4 Sprinkle with cilantro and serve.

TIP: Serve hot with Chapati or Roti (Flatbread; see Chapter 19) and a vegetable side dish.

NOTE: Karahi is the wok-shaped pan used in Indian kitchens. It's wide at the top allowing for evaporation and, therefore, thickening of curries. A frying pan will do the same thing.

Chicken Tikka Masala (Chicken Curry with Spices)

PREP TIME: 15 MIN PLUS 30 MIN–OVERNIGHT FOR MARINATING	COOK TIME: 40 MIN	YIELD: 3–4 SERVINGS

INGREDIENTS

2 tablespoons Ginger-Garlic Paste (see Chapter 6), divided

1 teaspoon Kashmiri chile powder

1 teaspoon turmeric

1 teaspoon ground cumin

1 teaspoon ground coriander

1 teaspoon garam masala

3 pods of cardamom, seeds crushed, husks discarded

2 tablespoons plain full-fat Greek yogurt

Salt to taste

1.25 pounds chicken breast, cubed

3 tablespoons vegetable oil, divided

2 medium onions, sliced

2 tablespoons unsalted cashew nuts

2 tablespoons tomato puree

2 tablespoons half-and-half

Several stalks of fresh cilantro, chopped, for garnish

DIRECTIONS

1 In a plastic box with a lid, combine 1 tablespoon of the Ginger-Garlic Paste, chile powder, turmeric, cumin, coriander, garam masala, crushed cardamom seeds, yogurt, and salt. Taste to make sure it's powerful in flavor; add more salt if necessary. Place the chicken in this mixture, cover, and refrigerate overnight (or at least 30 minutes).

2 In a heavy frying pan, heat 2 tablespoons of the oil. Add the onions, and fry over high heat until they start to turn brown, about 3 to 4 minutes. Reduce the heat to medium, and continue cooking until they become very soft, about 7 to 8 minutes. Add the remaining 1 tablespoon of Ginger-Garlic Paste and the cashew nuts, and cook for 30 seconds. Stir in the tomato puree, and fry for 2 minutes.

3 Cool slightly. Transfer to a blender, add enough water to cover the mixture, and blend until smooth. Set aside this masala curry base in the blender.

4 In the frying pan, heat the remaining 1 tablespoon of oil and add the chicken. Fry over high heat until the chicken is sealed. Add 2 tablespoons cold water and boil the water away.

5 Add in the curry paste and rinse out the blender with ¼ cup of water. Add this water to the curry and season with salt. Bring to a boil, reduce the heat, cover, and cook over low heat until the chicken, when cut, is white all the way through, about 10 minutes.

6 Swirl in the half-and-half, top with the cilantro leaves, and serve.

TIP: Serve with Naan (Leavened Oven-Baked Bread; see Chapter 19).

Sali Marghi (Chicken Curry with Apricots)

PREP TIME: 15 MIN	COOK TIME: 40 MIN	YIELD: 3–4 SERVINGS

INGREDIENTS

2 tablespoons vegetable oil, plus more for deep frying

1 teaspoon cumin seeds

2 onions, diced finely

1 tablespoon Ginger-Garlic Paste (see Chapter 6)

1 teaspoon Kashmiri chile powder

1 teaspoon turmeric

1 teaspoon ground coriander

1 teaspoon garam masala

1.25 pounds skinned chicken thighs or drumsticks

2 large fresh tomatoes, diced with skin and seeds or 14 ounces canned chopped tomatoes

2 tablespoons white or brown vinegar (not balsamic)

1 tablespoon soft brown sugar

Salt to taste

½ cup dried whole apricots

Several stalks cilantro, chopped with the stalks

2 medium potatoes, peeled and cut into fine matchsticks

DIRECTIONS

1 In a frying pan, warm the 2 tablespoons of oil. Add the cumin seeds, and fry over high heat until they start to darken, about 1 minute. Add the onions, and cook over high heat for 3 to 4 minutes. Stir in the Ginger-Garlic Paste and cook for 1 minute.

2 Add the chile powder, turmeric, coriander, and garam masala. Cook for 1 minute, and then add a splash of water to cook the spices. Boil off the water.

3 Tip in the chicken, cook until sealed, and turn. Add the tomatoes, vinegar, sugar, and salt. Add ½ cup of water and cook until bubbling. Lower the heat, cover, and cook for 30 minutes.

4 Add the apricots and cilantro, and cook until the chicken is white all the way through, about 10 minutes.

5 In the meantime, heat enough oil in a frying pan to hold the potato sticks in a single layer. Fry them in batches until they're crisp and golden, about 12 to 14 minutes, turning them halfway through the cooking. Drain on paper towel and sprinkle with a pinch of salt. These are called *sali*.

6 Serve the curry hot, topped with the sali.

TIP: Serve with Sunhera Pulao (Golden Turmeric Rice; see Chapter 14).

TIP: Potato straws are available to buy in some Indian grocery shops. You can use these in place of the sali. To cut potatoes into matchsticks, peel and thinly slice the potatoes; then cut them into fine strips.

Malvani Kombdi (Chicken and Coconut Curry)

PREP TIME: 15 MIN	COOK TIME: 50 MIN	YIELD: 3–4 SERVINGS

INGREDIENTS

3 tablespoons vegetable oil, divided

2 teaspoons coriander seeds

1 teaspoon black peppercorns

½ teaspoon fenugreek seeds

3 cloves

2 onions, sliced finely

1 tablespoon Ginger-Garlic Paste (see Chapter 6)

3 tablespoons desiccated unsweetened coconut

4 or 5 stalks of cilantro, roughly chopped

1.25 pounds skinned chicken thighs or drumsticks

1 teaspoon Kashmiri chile powder

1 teaspoon turmeric

1 teaspoon garam masala

Salt to taste

Juice of ½ lemon

1 cup coconut milk

DIRECTIONS

1 In a frying pan, warm 1½ tablespoons of the oil over high heat. Fry the coriander seeds, peppercorns, fenugreek seeds, and cloves until they start to sizzle. Add the onions and cook over high heat for 3 to 4 minutes. Then lower the heat and cook until very soft, about 7 to 8 minutes. Stir in the Ginger-Garlic Paste and cook for 1 minute. Add the coconut, and brown it for 1 minute. Turn off the heat, and throw in the cilantro.

2 Transfer the mixture to a blender with enough cold water to just cover it, and blend to a puree.

3 In the frying pan, heat the remaining 1½ tablespoons of oil, add the chicken, cook until sealed, and turn. Add the chile powder, turmeric, and garam masala, and cook for 1 minute. Then add a splash of water to cook the spices, and boil off the water.

4 Tip in the masala sauce from the blender. Rinse the blender with 3 to 4 tablespoons of water, and add the water into the pan. Season with salt. Add ½ cup of water and cook until bubbling. Lower the heat, cover, and cook until the chicken is white all the way through, about 30 minutes.

5 Turn off the heat, stir in the lemon juice and coconut milk, and serve.

TIP: Serve hot with Chapati or Roti (Flatbread; see Chapter 19) or rice and a vegetable side dish.

Chicken Madras (Chicken Curry with Fennel)

PREP TIME: 15 MIN	COOK TIME: 45 MIN	YIELD: 3–4 SERVINGS

INGREDIENTS

4 dried red chilies, broken in half

½ teaspoon black peppercorns, crushed

2 teaspoons fennel seeds

4 cloves

6 green cardamom pods, seeds removed (discard husks)

1 teaspoon ground cinnamon

2 tablespoons plus 1 teaspoon vegetable oil, divided

10 fresh curry leaves or 3 pinches of dried curry leaves

2 onions, finely diced

2 teaspoons Ginger-Garlic Paste (see Chapter 6)

2 tomatoes, diced with the skin and seeds

Salt to taste

1 teaspoon turmeric

1 teaspoon Kashmiri chile powder

1.25 pounds chicken thighs, skinned

4 to 5 stalks of fresh cilantro leaves, chopped finely, for garnish

DIRECTIONS

1 Heat a small frying pan over high heat and dry-roast the chilies, peppercorns, fennel seeds, cloves, and cardamom seeds until they begin to darken and develop an aroma, about 2 minutes. Remove from the heat and crush to a powder in a mortar and pestle or spice mill. Then mix in the ground cinnamon; set aside.

2 In the frying pan, heat 2 tablespoons of the oil over high heat and tip in the curry and onions. Stir-fry for 3 to 4 minutes, reduce the heat, and continue stir-frying until the onions are soft, about 4 minutes. Then add in the Ginger-Garlic Paste and cook for 30 seconds.

3 Add the tomatoes and season with salt. Cook for 3 to 4 minutes until mushy.

4 Add the ground spices from Step 1, the turmeric, and the chile powder, and cook over high heat for a few seconds. Add ¼ cup of cold water, bring to a boil, and let the water evaporate, releasing the oil around the edges of the mixture.

5 Move the mixture to one side of the pan, add the remaining 1 teaspoon of oil, and place the chicken in the oil in the pan. Cook, turning, until sealed on all sides. Mix the chicken with the masala (onion mixture) in the pan.

6 Add a few tablespoons of water and cook, covered, until the chicken is white all the way through when you cut open a piece, about 15 minutes. Sprinkle with cilantro and serve.

TIP: Serve hot with rice and a side salad.

Kerala Duck Mappas (Duck Curry with Coconut Milk and Pepper)

PREP TIME: 15 MIN	COOK TIME: 1 HR	YIELD: 3–4 SERVINGS

INGREDIENTS

2 tablespoons vegetable or coconut oil

2 onions, finely sliced

2 teaspoons Ginger-Garlic Paste (see Chapter 6)

2 green chilies, finely chopped, with seeds

10 fresh curry leaves or 3 pinches of dried curry leaves

1 teaspoon turmeric

1 teaspoon finely crushed black pepper

1.3 pounds duck legs, halved at the joint

One 13-ounce can coconut milk, shaken well, divided

2 tablespoons white vinegar

Salt to taste

4 to 5 stalks fresh cilantro leaves, chopped finely, for garnish

DIRECTIONS

1 In a frying pan, heat the oil over high heat. Add the onions, and cook until they start to turn golden, about 3 to 4 minutes. Then lower the heat and cook for 3 to 4 minutes more. Add the Ginger-Garlic Paste, green chilies, and curry and cook for 1 minute.

2 Mix in the turmeric and pepper, cook for 1 minute, and then push the mixture to the side of the pan. Place the duck in the pan (skin side down if using skin on) and brown lightly on both sides.

3 Mix half the can of coconut milk with ½ cup of water and pour into the pan, reserving the remaining coconut milk to add at the end. Add the vinegar and season with salt. Bring to a boil and then reduce the heat to low and simmer, covered, until the meat is tender, about 45 minutes. Add a splash of water if the sauce dries out.

4 Add the remaining ½ can of coconut milk and bring back to boil. Turn off the heat, and sprinkle with cilantro and a dash of crushed pepper.

TIP: Serve with Paratha (Layered Bread; see Chapter 19) and a vegetable side dish.

Bengali Chicken Korma (Chicken Curry with Cream)

| PREP TIME: 15 MIN | COOK TIME: 45 MIN | YIELD: 3–4 SERVINGS |

INGREDIENTS

3 tablespoons vegetable oil, divided

1 large onion, sliced

2 fresh green chilies, chopped

3 tablespoons skinned almonds

1 tablespoon Ginger-Garlic Paste (see Chapter 6)

1.25 pounds chicken thighs, skinned

1 teaspoon ground coriander

1 teaspoon ground cumin

1 teaspoon garam masala

½ teaspoon turmeric

Salt to taste

Dash of single or double cream

3 or 4 stalks of cilantro, chopped

DIRECTIONS

1 In a saucepan, heat 1½ tablespoons of the oil. Add the onion, chilies, and almonds, and fry until the onion softens but not colors, about 3 to 4 minutes. Pour in enough water to just cover the ingredients, and bring to a boil. Lower the heat and simmer until the onion is soft, about 10 to 15 minutes. Transfer to a blender with the cooking liquid, and blitz to a paste. Set aside.

2 In a heavy frying pan, heat the remaining 1½ tablespoons of oil. When hot, add the Ginger–Garlic Paste, and cook for 30 seconds. Add the chicken to the pan, and fry until sealed on all sides.

3 Stir in the coriander, cumin, garam masala, turmeric, and salt. Add ¼ cup of water and cook for a few seconds to evaporate the water. Add the masala base sauce from the blender. Rinse the blender with 2 to 3 tablespoons of water, and add the water to the pan. Bring to a boil. Then reduce the heat to medium, cover, and simmer until the chicken is cooked through, about 30 minutes.

4 Remove from the heat and swirl with cream. Serve topped with the cilantro and a sprinkle of garam masala.

TIP: Serve with Naan (Leavened Oven-Baked Bread; see Chapter 19) or rice.

Saag Murgh (Chicken Curry with Spinach)

PREP TIME: 15 MIN	COOK TIME: 40 MIN	YIELD: 3–4 SERVINGS

INGREDIENTS

1.25 pounds chicken breast, cubed

1 teaspoon turmeric

1 teaspoon Kashmiri chile powder

2 teaspoons ground coriander

2 teaspoons garam masala powder

Salt to taste

1 teaspoon plus 3 tablespoons vegetable oil, divided

1 bunch spinach, washed, drained, and chopped, stems and all

2 medium onions, sliced

2 tablespoons Ginger-Garlic Paste (see Chapter 6)

2 tomatoes, diced with seeds and skin

1 tablespoon lemon juice

Small knob of ginger, skin scraped off and cut into fine matchsticks, for garnish

DIRECTIONS

1 In a bowl, mix the chicken, turmeric, chile powder, coriander, garam masala, and salt. Drizzle in 1 teaspoon of the vegetable oil. Set aside.

2 In a saucepan, add the spinach with 3 tablespoons of water, and bring to a boil. Cook until just wilted, about 2 to 3 minutes. Set aside in the pan.

3 In a frying pan, warm 1½ tablespoons of the vegetable oil over high heat. Add the onions and fry until they start to turn brown, about 3 to 4 minutes. Lower the heat and continue cooking until soft, about 6 to 7 minutes. Add the Ginger-Garlic Paste, and cook for 1 minute. Add the tomatoes, and fry until soft, about 2 minutes. Transfer this mixture to a blender. Add just enough water to cover it, and blitz to make a smooth masala base sauce. Set aside in the blender.

4 In the same frying pan, warm the remaining 1½ tablespoons of oil over high heat. Add the chicken, and fry to seal in the juices. Then add a splash of water to cook the spices. When the water has more or less evaporated, add in the masala sauce. Rinse out the blender with 2 to 3 tablespoons of water and add the water to the pan. (Hold onto the blender for the next step — no need to wash it!) Season with salt. (Remember you added some to the chicken.) Bring to a boil. Then lower the heat to medium, cover, and cook until the chicken is done, about 10 to 12 minutes.

5 In the meantime, blitz the wilted spinach to a fine puree in the blender, along with any cooking juices or a splash of water. When the chicken is cooked, fold in the spinach puree and lemon juice, and adjust the seasoning. Top with the ginger matchsticks and serve.

TIP: Serve with Chapati or Roti (Flatbread; see Chapter 19) and a side salad.

Chicken 65 (Indo Chinese Chicken)

PREP TIME: 15 MIN	COOK TIME: 40 MIN	YIELD: 3-4 SERVINGS

INGREDIENTS

1.25 pounds boneless chicken thighs, cut into bite-size chunks

2 teaspoons Ginger-Garlic Paste (see Chapter 6)

1 teaspoon Kashmiri chile powder

Salt to taste

2 teaspoons corn flour

1 teaspoon rice flour

Sunflower oil for frying

3 tablespoons ketchup

1 tablespoon hot chile sauce

3 teaspoons soy sauce

One 1-inch piece of ginger, scraped and finely chopped

10 cloves garlic, finely chopped

6 to 7 fresh curry leaves or 2 pinches of dried curry leaves

2 green chilies, sliced with the seeds left in

½ teaspoon crushed black pepper

4 to 5 stalks of cilantro, finely chopped

DIRECTIONS

1 In a bowl, rub the chicken with the Ginger-Garlic Paste, chile powder, and salt. Sprinkle in the corn flour and rice flour, mix gently, and set aside.

2 In a frying pan, heat enough oil to deep-fry the chicken. Fry it in batches until it's golden brown and slightly crisp, about 6 to 7 minutes, reducing the heat to medium halfway through the frying. (Cut open a piece to make sure it's white all the way through.) Drain on paper towel and set aside.

3 To make the sauce, in a medium bowl, combine the ketchup, hot chile sauce, and soy sauce. Set aside.

4 Into a bowl, pour all but 2 tablespoons of oil from the frying pan and fry the ginger and garlic. When the garlic begins to brown, add the curry leaves and green chilies. Fry for 1 minute; then add the pepper and the mixed sauces from Step 3.

5 Fold in the fried chicken. Sprinkle with cilantro and serve.

TIP: Serve with rice.

NOTE: Indo Chinese, a hybrid of the two cuisines, is the second most popular one in India and you can find it everywhere, from street stalls to posh restaurants. It's typically spicy but very delicious!

Chapter **12**

Delish Fish and Seafood Dishes

RECIPES IN THIS CHAPTER

* Tilapia Fry (Spicy Fried Fish)

* Kolmbichi Kadhi (Shrimp Curry with Coconut Milk)

* Khekda Masaledaar (Crab Curry with Pepper)

* Bangda Ghassi (Mackerel Curry with Tamarind)

* Kolmbi Fry (Fried Spiced Shrimp)

* Meen Moilee (Salmon Curry with Mustard Seeds)

* Goan Fish Curry (Fish Curry with Coriander Seeds and Coconut)

* Kube Sukke (Clams in a Coconut Crust)

* Jhinga Masala (North Indian Shrimp Curry)

* Prawn Patia (Sweet and Sour Shrimp Curry)

* Lobster Kalvan (Lobster Curry)

With a coastline more than 4,000 miles long and a superb fish and seafood cuisine to show for it, I've always been surprised that most Indian restaurants don't showcase more fish curries on their menus. That's probably why, sadly, this repertoire isn't as familiar to diners outside of India as chicken or vegetable dishes are.

If you look at the map of India, the whole of the south is surrounded by seas, and there are countless rivers teeming with river fish and shrimp. All along the coast is a cuisine rich in fish and seafood; the curries are sweet with coconut and sour with tamarind, both of which grow here.

In this chapter, I substitute local Indian fish with those that are easier to find in the West and have a similar taste and texture. You'll want firm, meaty fish that doesn't fall apart easily in curries. My preference is for fish with few bones, but sometimes I make an exception for mackerel, which, because it's an oily fish, is good for me. I skin my fish because I don't like the skin slipping off into the curry, and I always shell, devein, and butterfly shrimp (see Chapter 5).

I include a recipe for clams, too. Make sure to clean them well and then, after you've cooked them, discard any that haven't opened.

You may want to try a typical coastal meal: fish or shrimp curry with rice and a couple of pieces of fried fish on the side for texture. Add a colorful vegetable side and you'll have a feast!

Tilapia Fry (Spicy Fried Fish)

PREP TIME: ABOUT 10 MIN PLUS 30 MIN FOR MARINATING	COOK TIME: 10 MIN	YIELD: 4 SERVINGS

INGREDIENTS

4 fillets of tilapia (around ½ pound each)

Salt to taste

1 teaspoon ground turmeric

1 teaspoon Kashmiri chile powder

1 teaspoon ground coriander

1 tablespoon Ginger-Garlic Paste (see Chapter 6)

½ teaspoon freshly ground black pepper

2 to 3 stalks cilantro, very finely chopped

2 tablespoons white or brown vinegar (not balsamic)

Coconut or vegetable oil, for shallow-frying

3 tablespoons rice flour

DIRECTIONS

1 Rub the fish fillets with salt.

2 In a bowl, combine the turmeric, child powder, coriander, Ginger–Garlic Paste, pepper, cilantro, and vinegar. Put the fish in the bowl, and rub the marinade onto the fish with your fingers to coat it evenly. Cover and refrigerate for 30 minutes.

3 In a frying pan, add enough oil to lightly cover the base of the pan. Warm the oil over high heat. Dip each fillet in rice flour, making sure it's well coated, and shallow-fry for 3 to 4 minutes on each side, covering the pan and turning down the heat to medium after you flip the fish. Make sure it's cooked through (the flesh will go opaque and firm).

4 Drain on paper towel, and serve.

TIP: This dish goes well with onion rings.

VARY IT! You can use salmon instead of tilapia if you prefer. Just fry it for 3 minutes on one side and 8 minutes on the other side, covering the pan and turning down the heat to medium after you flip the fish.

Kolmbichi Kadhi (Shrimp Curry with Coconut Milk)

PREP TIME: ABOUT 15 MIN | COOK TIME: 30 MIN | YIELD: 3–4 SERVINGS

INGREDIENTS

2 tablespoons tamarind block (choose wet or soft tamarind)

3 tablespoons vegetable oil, divided

1 teaspoon cumin seeds

2 onions, sliced

8 cloves garlic, peeled and chopped

1 tablespoon tomato paste

1 cup coconut milk

1 teaspoon ground coriander

1 teaspoon turmeric

1 teaspoon Kashmiri chile powder

Salt to taste

1 pound raw shrimp, shelled, deveined and butterflied (see Chapter 5)

3 to 4 stalks cilantro, finely chopped

DIRECTIONS

1 In ½ cup of hot water, soak the tamarind.

2 In a saucepan, warm 1½ tablespoons of the oil, and fry the cumin seeds over high heat until they start to darken, about 1 minute. Add the onions and cook until they begin to turn golden, about 3 to 4 minutes. Lower the heat and continue cooking until very soft, about 6 to 7 minutes. Add the garlic and cook for 1 minute. Add the tomato paste. Transfer this mixture into a blender with the coconut milk and blend to a fine puree.

3 Mash the tamarind with your fingers until the water becomes thick and pulpy. Strain to extract the pulp (do 2 or 3 pressings with ¼ cup of water each time; see Chapter 6). Discard the seeds and fibers.

4 Wipe the pan, warm the remaining 1½ tablespoons of oil over high heat, and add the coriander, turmeric, and chile. When they sizzle, add ¼ cup of water and cook over high heat until the water has evaporated. Add the sieved tamarind pulp and cook for 2 minutes, turning the heat down when the mixture boils. Add 2 tablespoons of water if the mixture dries out.

5 Pour in the masala sauce from the blender and bring to a boil. Season with salt. Add the shrimp and cook until opaque, about 4 to 5 minutes.

6 Adjust the consistency (it should be thick but pourable) by adding a little more coconut milk if desired. Scatter with cilantro, and serve.

TIP: Serve with rice.

Khekda Masaledaar (Crab Curry with Pepper)

PREP TIME: ABOUT 15 MIN	COOK TIME: 45 MIN	YIELD: 3–4 SERVINGS

INGREDIENTS

3 tablespoons vegetable oil, divided

10 black peppercorns

6 cloves

One ½-inch stick cinnamon

2 onions, thinly sliced

3 green chilies, diced, seeds and all

1 tablespoon Ginger-Garlic Paste (see Chapter 6)

4 tablespoons desiccated coconut

4 to 5 stalks cilantro, chopped

1 teaspoon black mustard seeds

8 cooked crab claws, lightly cracked

1 teaspoon ground turmeric

Salt to taste

½ lemon, juiced

DIRECTIONS

1 In a large frying pan, warm 1½ tablespoons of the oil over high heat. Add the peppercorns, cloves, and cinnamon, and cook until they sizzle. Add the onions and fry until they start to turn golden, about 3 to 4 minutes. Reduce the heat to medium and cook until soft, about 7 to 8 minutes. Add the chilies and Ginger-Garlic Paste and cook for 2 minutes.

2 Stir in the coconut, and stir-fry until brown, about 4 minutes, taking care not to burn the mixture. Add the cilantro and turn off the heat. Transfer the mixture to a blender, add just enough cold water to cover it, and blend to a puree. Set aside.

3 Wipe the pan and warm the remaining 1½ tablespoons of oil over high heat. Add the mustard seeds. When they pop, add the crabs and the turmeric, and fry for 2 to 3 minutes.

4 Pour in the masala sauce from the blender, rinse the blender with 3 tablespoons of water, and add this to the pan as well. Bring to a boil and season with salt. Add a splash of water if the curry is too thick, reduce the heat to medium, cover, and simmer until you see specks of oil around the edges of the pan, about 10 minutes. Remove from the heat, stir in the lemon juice, and serve.

TIP: Serve with rice.

Bangda Ghassi (Mackerel Curry with Tamarind)

PREP TIME: ABOUT 15 MIN | COOK TIME: 30 MIN | YIELD: 3–4 SERVINGS

INGREDIENTS

2 tablespoons tamarind block (choose wet or soft tamarind)

4 fillets of mackerel (about ½ pound each) or 2 mackerel steaks, skinned or unskinned

1 teaspoon turmeric, divided

Salt to taste

3 tablespoons vegetable oil, divided

1 teaspoon black peppercorns

6 dried Kashmiri red chilies, broken into bits and deseeded

1 onion, sliced

¼ cup desiccated coconut

2 teaspoons Ginger-Garlic Paste (see Chapter 6)

1 teaspoon garam masala

1 cup coconut milk

DIRECTIONS

1 In ½ cup hot water, soak the tamarind. Rub the pieces of fish with ½ teaspoon of the turmeric and enough salt to season. Set aside.

2 In a frying pan, warm 1½ tablespoons of the oil. Add the peppercorns and dried chilies, and fry over high heat until they sizzle, about 2 minutes. Tip in the onion and cook over high heat until it begins to change color, about 3 to 4 minutes. Reduce the heat to medium and cook until soft, about 5 minutes. Add the coconut and continue to fry until light brown, about 3 minutes.

3 Remove from the heat, tip into a blender, add enough cold water to cover the mixture, and blend until smooth. Set aside.

4 Mash the tamarind with your fingers until the water becomes thick and pulpy. Strain to extract the pulp (do 2 to 3 pressings with ¼ cup of water each time; see Chapter 6). Discard the seeds and fibers.

5 Wipe out the frying pan, heat the remaining 1½ tablespoons of oil, and fry the Ginger–Garlic Paste over high heat for 1 minute. Add the remain ½ teaspoon of turmeric and the garam masala, and cook for 1 minute. Stir in the tamarind pulp and bring to a boil.

6 Pour in the masala sauce from the blender, rinse the blender with ¼ cup water, and add to the pan. Pour in the coconut milk. Season with salt. Bring to a boil.

7 Gently slip the fish fillets into the curry and cook over medium heat, covered, until the fish is cooked, about 6 to 7 minutes. Serve.

TIP: Serve with rice.

TIP: If you can't find mackerel in your area, you can use mahi-mahi instead.

Kolmbi Fry (Fried Spiced Shrimp)

PREP TIME: ABOUT 20 MIN PLUS 30 MIN TO OVER-NIGHT FOR MARINATING	COOK TIME: 15 MIN	YIELD: 4 SERVINGS

INGREDIENTS

1 pound raw shrimp, shelled, deveined, and butterflied (see Chapter 5)

1 teaspoon Kashmiri chile powder

1 teaspoon turmeric

1 teaspoon ground coriander

1 teaspoon Ginger–Garlic Paste (see Chapter 6)

Salt to taste

1 squeeze lemon

Vegetable oil for frying

4 tablespoons fine semolina

4 lemon wedges, for garnish

DIRECTIONS

1 In a large bowl, put the butterflied shrimp. Add the chile, turmeric, coriander, Ginger–Garlic Paste, and salt. Mix well and leave to marinate 30 minutes to overnight if you have the time. If you're tight for time, skip the marinating and go straight to Step 2.

2 Just before you're ready to fry the shrimp, squeeze in the lemon juice and mix well.

3 To a frying pan, add enough oil to make a thin layer. Warm over high heat. While the oil is heating, line a plate with paper towel and have it ready on the side. On a small side plate, put the semolina. To check that the oil is at the correct temperature, put a small pinch of semolina into the oil; it should sizzle.

4 Roll a few shrimp (enough to cook in a single layer in the pan) in the semolina to coat them evenly, and fry in batches, around 3 to 4 minutes on each side. Drain on the paper towel, and serve hot, garnished with wedges of lemon.

TIP: Try this with fish curry and rice!

TIP: Don't cook the shrimp too long or they'll go rubbery. The shrimp will continue cooking for a bit even after they've been taken off the heat, so factor that in.

Meen Moilee (Salmon Curry with Mustard Seeds)

PREP TIME: ABOUT 15 MIN	COOK TIME: 35 MIN	YIELD: 3–4 SERVINGS

INGREDIENTS

2 tablespoons vegetable or coconut oil

1 teaspoon black mustard seeds

2 medium onions, diced finely

2 teaspoons Ginger-Garlic Paste (see Chapter 6)

2 green chilies, finely diced, seeds and all

10 fresh curry leaves or 3 pinches dried curry leaves

2 tomatoes, finely chopped, with skin and seeds

1 teaspoon turmeric

½ teaspoon finely crushed black pepper

4 fillets of salmon, skinned (about ½ pound each)

1 cup coconut milk

Salt to taste

2 tablespoons lemon juice

DIRECTIONS

1 In a frying pan, warm the oil over high heat. Add the mustard seeds and wait until they pop, about 1 minute. Add the onions and cook until they begin to soften, about 3 to 4 minutes. Reduce the heat to medium and continue cooking, stirring from time to time, until they're very soft, about 7 to 8 minutes.

2 Add the Ginger-Garlic Paste and the chilies. Cook until the raw smell disappears, about 1 minute. Stir in the curry leaves and then the tomatoes and cook for 2 minutes.

3 Stir in the turmeric and pepper, and cook for 30 seconds.

4 Push the mixture to the side of the pan, add a drizzle of oil to the pan, place the salmon in, and fry 2 to 3 minutes. Turn down the heat to medium, flip the salmon, and fry another 2 to 3 minutes.

5 After both sides of the fish are well sealed, pour in the coconut milk. Raise the heat to high and season with salt. Mix well, taking care not to break the fish, and bring to a boil.

6 Cover, reduce the heat to medium, and simmer for 8 to 10 minutes. Remove from the heat and add the lemon juice. Serve.

TIP: Serve hot with rice and a vegetable side dish.

TIP: For extra flavor, top with 1 teaspoon coconut oil just before serving.

Goan Fish Curry (Fish Curry with Coriander Seeds and Coconut)

| PREP TIME: ABOUT 15 MIN | COOK TIME: 40 MIN | YIELD: 3–4 SERVINGS |

INGREDIENTS

1 tablespoon tamarind block (choose wet or soft tamarind)

3 tablespoons plus 1 teaspoon vegetable oil, divided

2 teaspoons coriander seeds

½ teaspoon fenugreek seeds

1 teaspoon black peppercorns

5 cloves

2 onions, finely diced

2 tablespoons cashew nuts

1 tablespoon Ginger-Garlic Paste (see Chapter 6)

8 dried Kashmiri chilies, deseeded and broken into bits

2 tablespoons tomato paste

1 teaspoon turmeric

1 teaspoon Kashmiri chile powder

¾ cup coconut milk

Salt to taste

4 fillets of firm white fish (such as monkfish, haddock, or halibut)

1 teaspoon black mustard seeds

10 fresh curry leaves or 3 pinches dried curry leaves

DIRECTIONS

1 In ½ cup hot water, soak the tamarind for 10 minutes.

2 In a saucepan, warm 1½ tablespoons of the oil over high heat. Add the coriander, fenugreek, peppercorns, and cloves, and fry until they start to sizzle, about 1 minute. Add the onions and cook until they begin to turn slightly golden, about 3 to 4 minutes. Lower the heat and continue cooking until very soft, about 6 to 7 minutes.

3 Raise the heat to high. Add the cashew nuts, Ginger-Garlic Paste, and dried chilies, and cook for 2 minutes. Add the tomato paste, and continue cooking for 1 minute. Transfer this mixture to a blender with just enough water to cover it and blend to a fine puree.

(continued)

4 Mash the tamarind with your fingers. Strain to extract the pulp (do 2 to 3 pressings with ¼ cup of water each time; see Chapter 6), and discard the seeds and fibers.

5 Wipe the pan, warm 1½ tablespoons oil over high heat and add the turmeric and chile. When they sizzle, add a splash of water and cook until the water has evaporated. Add the sieved tamarind pulp and cook for 2 minutes.

6 Pour in the masala sauce from the blender, add the coconut milk, and bring to a boil. Season with salt. Add the fish and cook for 5 to 6 minutes.

7 Warm the remaining 1 teaspoon of oil over high heat and fry the mustard seeds until they pop, about 1 minute. Add the curry leaves and fry for another minute. Then pour this oil and its contents over the curry. Serve.

TIP: Serve with rice.

Kube Sukke (Clams in a Coconut Crust)

| PREP TIME: 45 MIN | COOK TIME: 35 MIN | YIELD: 3-4 SERVINGS |

INGREDIENTS

1.25 pounds clams

3 tablespoons salt plus
1 teaspoon, divided

2 onions, diced roughly

¼ cup desiccated coconut

1 tablespoon Ginger-Garlic
Paste (see Chapter 6)

2 tablespoons vegetable oil

1 teaspoon black mustard
seeds

10 fresh curry leaves or
3 pinches dried curry leaves

1 teaspoon garam masala

1 teaspoon Kashmiri chile
powder

1 teaspoon turmeric

Salt to taste

1 squeeze lemon

DIRECTIONS

1   Discard any clams that are open or don't shut when you tap them. Fill a big bowl with cold water halfway; add about 3 tablespoons of salt (it should taste like seawater). Add the clams and leave for 30 minutes, so they can filter out any sand and grit. Then transfer them in a bowl of fresh cold water for 15 minutes. Brush the clams to remove any buildup from the sea.

2   Heat a frying pan and dry-roast the onion, stirring frequently, until it begins to change color, about 4 to 5 minutes. Tip in the coconut and continue frying until the coconut turns a light brown, about 2 to 3 minutes. Stir in the Ginger-Garlic Paste and cook for 1 minute.

3   Transfer this mixture to a blender along with ¼ cup water and blend to a coarse paste, using the pulse button to control the texture.

4   In a saucepan, warm the oil over high heat and add the mustard seeds. When they pop, add the curry leaves and the coarse masala from the blender. Rinse the blender with ¼ cup water, and add to the pan. Add the garam masala, chile, and turmeric. Bring to a bubble and add the clams. Season with salt.

5   Mix well, cover the pan, and cook the clams until the pot is steaming, about 5 to 10 minutes. Uncover and stir well. When the clams open, they're cooked. Discard any clams that remain stubbornly closed.

6   Drizzle with lemon juice, and serve.

TIP: Try this dish with rice and Palak Pappu (South Indian Spinach Dal; see Chapter 15).

Jhinga Masala (North Indian Shrimp Curry)

PREP TIME: ABOUT 20 MIN	COOK TIME: 35 MIN	YIELD: 3–4 SERVINGS

INGREDIENTS

2 tablespoons vegetable oil

1 teaspoon cumin seeds

2 onions, finely diced

1 tablespoon Ginger-Garlic Paste (see Chapter 6)

1 teaspoon turmeric

1 teaspoon Kashmiri chile powder

1 teaspoon ground coriander

1 teaspoon garam masala

1 small green pepper, deseeded and diced

2 small red, yellow, and/or orange bell peppers, deseeded and diced

One 15-ounce can diced tomatoes

¾ pound large raw shrimp, shelled, deveined, and butterflied (see Chapter 5)

Salt to taste

Pinch of caster sugar

4 to 5 stalks cilantro, finely chopped, for garnish

DIRECTIONS

1 In a heavy saucepan, warm the oil over high heat, and fry the cumin seeds until they go a shade darker, about 1 minute. Add the onions and fry until they start to turn golden, about 3 to 4 minutes. Turn the heat down to medium and continue cooking until very soft, about 6 to 7 minutes.

2 Add the Ginger-Garlic Paste and fry until the raw smell disappears, about 1 minute.

3 Add the turmeric, chile, coriander, and garam masala. When they sizzle, add a splash of cold water. Cook over high heat until the water evaporates and the oil begins to separate around the edges, about 3 minutes.

4 Add the mixed peppers, and cook for 3 to 4 minutes. Tip in the tomatoes, and cook until they soften, about 3 to 4 minutes. Add the shrimp, salt, and sugar. Bring to a boil, lower the heat, and simmer, covered, for 5 minutes.

5 Remove from the heat, garnish with cilantro, and serve.

VARY IT! Try adding other firm vegetables to make a different curry next time. How about zucchini, eggplant, or long green beans?

Prawn Patia (Sweet and Sour Shrimp Curry)

| PREP TIME: ABOUT 20 MIN | COOK TIME: 30 MIN | YIELD: 3–4 SERVINGS |

INGREDIENTS

¾ pound large raw shrimp, shelled, deveined, and butterflied (see Chapter 5)

1 teaspoon ground turmeric, divided

1 teaspoon Kashmiri chile powder, divided

Salt to taste

2 tablespoons vegetable oil

2 onions, finely diced

2 green chilies, finely diced

10 fresh curry leaves or 3 large dried curry leaves

2 tablespoons Ginger–Garlic Paste (see Chapter 6)

1 teaspoon ground coriander

1 teaspoon ground cumin

One 15-ounce can diced tomatoes

3 tablespoons white or brown vinegar (not balsamic)

2 tablespoons grated jaggery or soft brown sugar

4 to 5 stalks cilantro, chopped, for garnish

DIRECTIONS

1 In a bowl, add the shrimp, ½ teaspoon of the turmeric, ½ teaspoon of the chile powder, and salt. Toss the shrimp to season it.

2 In a frying pan, heat the oil over high heat. Add the onions, and fry until they begin to soften, about 3 to 4 minutes. Lower the heat to medium and cook until very soft and golden, about 7 to 8 minutes.

3 Tip in the chilies and curry leaves. Stir in the Ginger–Garlic Paste, and fry for 2 minutes.

4 Add the coriander, cumin, the remaining ½ teaspoon of turmeric, and the remaining ½ teaspoon of chile powder, and cook for 1 minute. Add a splash of water, and cook over high heat to let the water evaporate.

5 Add the tomatoes, and cook until the curry thickens, about 5 to 6 minutes. Mix in the vinegar and jaggery or sugar.

6 Add the shrimp, season the curry with salt (remember the shrimp have been salted), and cook until they're opaque, about 7 to 8 minutes. Sprinkle with the cilantro, and serve.

TIP: Serve with rice and Tarka Dal (Spiced Lentils; see Chapter 15).

NOTE: Jaggery is unrefined, solidified sugarcane juice and can be found in Indian grocery stores. It's quite delicious, so if you manage to buy it, you may find yourself nibbling at it while you cook!

Lobster Kalvan (Lobster Curry)

PREP TIME: ABOUT 20 MIN	COOK TIME: 30 MIN	YIELD: 3–4 SERVINGS

INGREDIENTS

2 teaspoons tamarind block (choose soft or wet tamarind)

3 tablespoons vegetable oil, divided

1 teaspoon black mustard seeds

2 onions, finely sliced

2 teaspoons Ginger-Garlic Paste (see Chapter 6)

1 or 2 green chilies, finely diced with the seeds

10 fresh curry leaves or 3 pinches of dried curry leaves

1 teaspoon turmeric

1 teaspoon Kashmiri chile powder

1 teaspoon ground coriander

1 teaspoon garam masala

1¼ cups coconut milk

1 pound lobster meat (tail and claw)

DIRECTIONS

1 In ½ cup of hot water, soak the tamarind.

2 In a frying pan, heat 2 tablespoons of the oil over high heat, and fry the mustard seeds until they pop. Add the onions and cook until they begin to turn golden, about 3 to 4 minutes. Lower the heat to medium and continue cooking until very soft, about 6 to 7 minutes.

3 While the onions are cooking, mash the tamarind with your fingers until the water becomes thick and pulpy. Strain to extract the pulp (repeat this process with ¼ cup of water each time; see Chapter 6). Discard the seeds and fibers. Set aside.

4 Add the Ginger-Garlic Paste, chilies, and curry leaves to the cooked onions, and fry for 1 minute.

5 Tip in the turmeric, chile powder, coriander, and garam masala. Cook for a few seconds; then add a splash of cold water. Bring to a boil and let the water evaporate. Pour in the tamarind, and cook for 2 minutes.

6 Add the coconut milk and salt, and bring to a boil. Lower the heat and simmer for 2 to 3 minutes.

7 While the curry is simmering, heat the remaining 1 tablespoon of oil in a frying pan and fry the lobster until it starts to turn slightly golden. Pour the lobster into the curry. Turn off the heat and serve.

TIP: Serve with rice and a side salad.

VARY IT! This curry can be made heartier by adding a handful of small shrimps to the sauce when the curry is simmering in Step 7.

TIP: You can use frozen, precooked lobster meat. Just Let it thaw in the refrigerator first.

IN THIS CHAPTER

» **Adding spices to your vegetables**

» **Creating delicious vegetarian main courses**

» **Experimenting with new vegetables**

» **Jazzing up your plate with color**

» **Learning to fire roast an eggplant**

Chapter **13**

Vegetables Cooked the Indian Way

RECIPES IN THIS CHAPTER

🍲 **Baingan ka Bharta (Fire-Roasted Eggplant with Spices)**

🍲 **Aloo Gobi (North Indian Potatoes with Cauliflower)**

🍲 **Kobichi Bhaji (Cabbage with Peas and Turmeric)**

🍲 **Baghara Baingan (Sweet-and-Sour Eggplant Curry)**

🍲 **Kerala Vegetable Curry (Mixed Vegetable Curry with Coconut Milk)**

🍲 **Paneer Makkai Simla Mirch (Paneer with Corn and Capsicum)**

🍲 **Palak Paneer (Spinach with Paneer)**

🍲 **Methi Shakarkand (Fresh Fenugreek with Sweet Potatoes)**

🍲 **Carrot Poriyal (Carrots Cooked with Mustard Seeds and Coconut)**

🍲 **Bharvan Bhindi (Okra Stuffed with Spices)**

🍲 **Fanshachi Bhaji (Curried Young Jackfruit)**

🍲 **Beans Upkari (French Green Beans with Chile and Coconut)**

🍲 **Kaddu ki Subzi (Sweet-and-Sour Pumpkin)**

🍲 **Shepuchi Bhaji (Dill with Mung Lentils)**

🍲 **Aloo Mutter (Pea and Potato Curry)**

I f you visit India, one stop you have to make is at a fresh vegetable market. Or you can find videos on YouTube and enjoy the colors, bustle, and activity that create the excitement of these places. As a bonus, you'll see plenty of vegetables of different shapes, sizes, and textures that you've never seen before. Tender jackfruit, okra and eggplants in jeweled colors, beans and gourds — all provide the basis for a huge repertoire of vegetarian dishes.

An Indian meal always has a vegetable dish as part of it. It can be a wet curry or a dry *subzi* or *subji* (in North India) or a *bhaji* (in western India). A bread such as Chapati or Roti (Flatbread; see Chapter 19), a dal, and *subzi* is comfort food to many people, and it's what Indians often eat for lunch.

TIP

Indian cooking requires vegetables to be cooked fully to improve their digestibility and so that they absorb the flavors of the spices as they cook. We don't like our vegetables al dente unless they're in a salad.

Baingan ka Bharta (Fire-Roasted Eggplant with Spices)

PREP TIME: ABOUT 15 MIN   COOK TIME: 30 MIN   YIELD: 3 TO 4 SERVINGS

INGREDIENTS

1 large dark purple, pear-shaped eggplant (at least 6 x 3 inches)

2 tablespoons vegetable oil

1 teaspoon cumin seeds

1 large onion, finely diced

2 teaspoons Ginger-Garlic Paste (see Chapter 6)

2 green chilies, diced with the seeds

1 teaspoon turmeric

1 teaspoon ground coriander

2 large, ripe tomatoes, diced with the seeds

¼ cup frozen peas

Salt to taste

Pepper to taste

4 to 5 stalks of fresh cilantro, chopped, for garnish

DIRECTIONS

1   Place the eggplant on its thickest side directly on a gas stovetop. Cook, turning from time to time with a pair of tongs, until it's evenly cooked, about 7 to 10 minutes. Test for doneness by inserting a knife through the thickest part; it should go through easily. (If you don't have a gas stove, see the Note.) Remove to a plate, allow the eggplant to cool, and peel off the crisp skin by pinching it off with your fingers. Cut off and discard the stalk and finely mash the flesh of the eggplant with a fork, until there are no stringy bits left. Set aside.

2   In a saucepan, warm the oil over high heat, add the cumin seeds, and fry until they go a couple of shades darker, about 1 minute. Add the onion and fry until it starts to soften, about 3 to 4 minutes. Then lower the heat to medium and continue cooking until it's very soft, about 3 to 4 minutes more.

3 Turn up the heat to high, add the Ginger-Garlic Paste and the green chilies, and fry for 1 minute. Add the turmeric and coriander, and cook for 1 minute. Add a splash of cold water, and let the water cook away.

4 Tip in the tomatoes and peas, season with salt and pepper, and cook until the mixture sizzles, about 3 to 4 minutes. Turn down the heat to low, and continue cooking until the tomatoes have broken down, about 4 to 5 minutes more. Add a few tablespoons of water if the mixture dries out.

5 Stir in the eggplant and adjust the seasoning. Sprinkle with cilantro, and serve hot.

NOTE: Because the smokiness of the eggplant makes this dish, it's important to cook it directly on an open flame. If you don't have a gas stove, brush the eggplant with oil and grill until the skin is crisp or cook on a barbecue. You can also broil the eggplant and turn it after 3 to 4 minutes; cook another 3 to 4 minutes on the other side.

TIP: This dish goes well with Chapati or Roti (Flatbread; see Chapter 19) or Paratha (Layered Bread; see Chapter 19).

Aloo Gobi (North Indian Potatoes with Cauliflower)

PREP TIME: ABOUT 15 MIN	COOK TIME: 40 MIN	YIELD: 3 TO 4 SERVINGS

INGREDIENTS

2 tablespoons vegetable oil

1 large onion, diced

2 teaspoons Ginger-Garlic Paste (see Chapter 6)

1 to 2 green chilies, diced with the seeds

2 large potatoes, peeled and chopped into ¾-inch cubes

1 teaspoon turmeric

1 teaspoon garam masala

1 teaspoon ground cumin

1 teaspoon ground coriander

½ head cauliflower, washed and cut into bite-size florets

Salt to taste

Half of 15-ounce can diced tomatoes

4 to 5 stalks cilantro, finely chopped, for garnish

DIRECTIONS

1 In a heavy-bottomed pan, heat the oil over high heat. Add the onion, and fry until it begins to soften, about 3 to 4 minutes. Add the Ginger-Garlic Paste and chilies, and fry for 1 minute.

2 Add the potatoes, and fry for 4 to 5 minutes, stirring frequently to prevent the mixture from sticking. Tip in the turmeric, garam masala, cumin, and coriander, and fry for 2 minutes. Add 4 to 5 tablespoons of cold water, and allow it to cook off.

3 Tip in the cauliflower and season with salt. Mix well to combine the cauliflower with the spices. Add the tomatoes and cook until everything gets very hot.

4 Reduce the heat to low, cover, and cook for 15 minutes, stirring from time to time to make sure it doesn't stick to the bottom of the pan. If it sticks, add 1 tablespoon of water and scrape the stuck bits back into the sauce. Check whether the potatoes are cooked by inserting the tip of a small knife. This is a dry dish, so you're not looking for lots of sauce.

5 Remove from the heat, sprinkle with cilantro, and serve.

TIP: Make sure to keep the vegetables bite sized so that they absorb the flavors of the spices as they cook. Cut too big, the spices don't permeate right through.

TIP: Try this dish with a Chapati or Roti (Flatbread; see Chapter 19) or Paratha (Layered Bread; see Chapter 19). It also goes well with rice and Tarka Dal (Spiced Lentils; see Chapter 15).

Kobichi Bhaji (Cabbage with Peas and Turmeric)

INGREDIENTS

2 tablespoons vegetable oil

1 teaspoon black mustard seeds

1 teaspoon cumin seeds

¼ teaspoon asafetida

2 green chilies, sliced lengthwise, stalks left on

1 teaspoon fresh grated ginger

1 teaspoon turmeric

½ head white cabbage, very finely shredded

⅓ cup fresh or frozen peas

Salt to taste

4 to 5 stalks of fresh cilantro, chopped, for garnish

DIRECTIONS

1   In a heavy frying pan, warm the oil over high heat. Add the mustard seeds. When they begin to pop, reduce the heat to low, add the cumin seeds and asafetida, and cook for 10 seconds.

2   Stir in the chilies and grated ginger. Sprinkle in the turmeric, and add the cabbage and peas. Turn up the heat to high, season with salt, and stir until the cabbage starts to turn translucent, about 4 to 5 minutes.

3   Cover the pan and cook over low heat for 20 minutes, stirring occasionally. The salt should draw out enough moisture from the cabbage to cook it. If it begins to stick, add 2 to 3 tablespoons water, and allow to cook off. The final dish should be dry.

4   Remove from the heat, scatter the cilantro on top, and serve.

TIP: Serve with Chapati or Roti (Flatbread; see Chapter 19) and a raita or as a side dish with any chicken or meat curry and rice.

Baghara Baingan (Sweet-and-Sour Eggplant Curry)

PREP TIME: ABOUT 25 MIN	COOK TIME: 40 MIN	YIELD: 3 TO 4 SERVINGS

INGREDIENTS

6 small eggplants

3 tablespoons vegetable oil, divided

2 dried red Kashmiri chilies, seeds shaken out, broken into bits

1 tablespoon coriander seeds

1 medium onion, sliced

2 teaspoons Ginger-Garlic Paste (see Chapter 6)

2 tablespoons fresh or frozen grated or desiccated coconut

1 tablespoon white sesame seeds

2 tablespoons roasted salted peanuts

1 teaspoon turmeric

1 teaspoon Kashmiri chile powder

4 teaspoons tamarind pulp (see Chapter 6)

2 tablespoons soft brown sugar

Salt to taste

4 to 5 stalks of fresh cilantro, chopped, for garnish

DIRECTIONS

1 Quarter the eggplants almost to the stalks but leave the stalks on. Set aside.

2 In a heavy saucepan, warm 1½ tablespoons of the oil over high heat. Add the chilies and coriander seeds and fry until they turn a couple of shades darker, about 2 minutes. Add the onion and cook until it begins to color, about 3 to 4 minutes. Then turn the heat to low and cook for another 6 to 7 minutes. Add the Ginger-Garlic Paste and cook for 1 minute. Add the coconut, sesame seeds, and peanuts. When the coconut turns golden brown, after about 2 minutes, remove the mixture from the heat and transfer to a blender. Add just enough cold water to cover the mixture, and blend to a fine puree. Transfer this masala base sauce into a big bowl.

3 Add the turmeric, chile powder, tamarind, brown sugar, and salt. Mix well. With a teaspoon, rub some of this mix into each eggplant, spreading the sections apart to get the mix right into the center.

4 In a heavy saucepan, heat the remaining 1½ tablespoons of oil over high heat. Fry the eggplants until they begin to change color evenly, about 3 to 4 minutes. Pour in the remaining masala sauce from the bowl.

5 Bring to a boil. Reduce the heat to low, cover, and simmer until the eggplants are cooked through, about 15 to 20 minutes. You can test for doneness by inserting the tip of a small knife into the thickest part.

6 Remove from the heat, sprinkle with cilantro, and serve.

TIP: Enjoy this with Chapati or Roti (Flatbread; see Chapter 19) or as a side to Chicken Biryani (Festive One-Pot Chicken and Rice; see Chapter 14).

Kerala Vegetable Curry (Mixed Vegetable Curry with Coconut Milk)

PREP TIME: ABOUT 15 MIN	COOK TIME: 45 MIN	YIELD: 3 TO 4 SERVINGS

INGREDIENTS

3 tablespoons vegetable or coconut oil, divided

One 1-inch stick cinnamon, broken up

1 large onion, sliced

2 green chilies, roughly chopped, with the seeds

2 large ripe tomatoes, diced

1 teaspoon black mustard seeds

15 fresh curry leaves or 3 pinches dried curry leaves

2 teaspoons Ginger-Garlic Paste (see Chapter 6)

2 carrots, peeled and diced into ¼-inch pieces

Handful of green beans, chopped into ¾-inch lengths

⅓ cup frozen green peas

¾ cup coconut milk

1 teaspoon turmeric

Salt to taste

Pepper to taste

2 tablespoons lemon juice

4 to 5 stalks fresh cilantro, chopped, for garnish

DIRECTIONS

1 In a heavy saucepan, warm 1½ tablespoons of the oil over high heat. Add the cinnamon, onion, and chilies and fry until the onion begins to turn golden, about 3 to 4 minutes. Add the tomatoes and ½ cup of water. Bring to a boil, and then lower the heat, cover, and simmer until everything is soft and the water has reduced, about 10 minutes.

2 While the onions and tomatoes are cooking, warm the remaining 1½ tablespoons of oil in a frying pan over high heat and add the mustard seeds. When they begin to pop, after about 1 minute, add the curry leaves and the Ginger-Garlic Paste. Fry for 1 minute, and then tip in the carrots, green beans, and peas and cook for 4 to 5 minutes. Turn off the heat.

3 Tip the cooked onions and tomatoes into a blender along with the coconut milk and blend to a fine puree.

4 Pour the masala from the blender into the vegetables. Season with salt and pepper.

5 Bring the curry to a boil over high heat. Lower the heat and simmer until the carrots are cooked, about 30 minutes.

6 Remove from the heat, stir in the lemon juice, scatter the cilantro over top, and serve.

VARY IT! Try other firm vegetables here — butternut squash, cauliflower, and potatoes work well. Adjust the cooking times as necessary, and remember to chop everything small.

TIP: Serve with rice and a popadam.

Paneer Makkai Simla Mirch (Paneer with Corn and Capsicum)

PREP TIME: ABOUT 15 MIN	COOK TIME: 30 MIN	YIELD: 3 TO 4 SERVINGS

INGREDIENTS

9 ounces store-bought paneer, cut into ½-inch cubes

3 tablespoons vegetable oil, divided

Salt to taste

Pepper to taste

1 large onion, finely diced

1 teaspoon Ginger-Garlic Paste (see Chapter 6)

2 green chilies, sliced in half, stalks left on

1 teaspoon ground cumin

1 teaspoon ground coriander

1 teaspoon turmeric

1 teaspoon garam masala

½ cup frozen or canned sweetcorn kernels

2 small red, yellow, or orange bell peppers, deseeded and diced into ½-inch pieces

4 to 5 stalks fresh cilantro, chopped, for garnish

DIRECTIONS

1 Preheat the oven to 350 degrees.

2 On a large baking tray, put the paneer. Drizzle 1½ tablespoons of the oil over it, season with salt and pepper, and mix. Spread out the paneer to make a single layer and bake until the edges are golden, about 10 minutes.

3 Meanwhile, heat the remaining 1½ tablespoons of oil in a heavy pan over a high heat. Add the onion and fry until it begins to soften, about 3 to 4 minutes. Add the Ginger–Garlic Paste and the chilies, and cook for about 1 minute. Then add the cumin, coriander, turmeric, and garam masala, and cook for a few seconds. Pour in 4 to 5 tablespoons of water, and cook off the water.

4 Add the corn and diced peppers, season with salt, and add a splash of water. Bring to a boil, reduce the heat, cover, and cook until the peppers are soft, about 8 to 10 minutes. Fold in the baked paneer. Check and adjust the seasoning. This dish has very little sauce.

5 Sprinkle with cilantro and serve hot.

TIP: Enjoy this dish with Chapati or Roti (Flatbread; see Chapter 19) or as side dish with curry and rice.

VARY IT! Use tofu for a vegan version of this recipe.

Palak Paneer (Spinach with Paneer)

PREP TIME: ABOUT 10 MIN	COOK TIME: 30 MIN	YIELD: 3 TO 4 SERVINGS

INGREDIENTS

1 pound fresh spinach, washed and drained

3 tablespoons vegetable oil

1 teaspoon cumin seeds

1 onion, chopped finely

1 tablespoon Ginger-Garlic Paste (see Chapter 6)

1 large tomato, finely chopped with the seeds

1 teaspoon Kashmiri chile powder

1 teaspoon garam masala

1 teaspoon ground coriander

Salt to taste

9 ounces store-bought paneer, cubed

1 big squeeze of lemon juice

1 teaspoon ghee or butter

A few juliennes of fresh ginger, for garnish

2 tablespoons of light cream (optional), for garnish

DIRECTIONS

1 In a heavy pan, put the spinach with 4 to 5 tablespoons of water and cook, uncovered, over high heat until the spinach is wilted, about 3 to 4 minutes. You may need to cook the spinach in batches, if your pan isn't large enough. Cool slightly. Then transfer to a blender along with the cooking water, and blend to a thick puree. Set aside.

2 In a heavy pan, warm the oil over high heat. Add the cumin seeds, and fry until they turn a couple of shades darker, about 1 minute. Add the onion and fry until it begins to soften, about 3 to 4 minutes. Lower the heat to medium and cook for 4 or 5 minutes more. Stir in the Ginger–Garlic Paste, and cook for 1 minute.

3 Add the tomato, and cook over high heat until soft, about 3 to 4 minutes. Sprinkle in the chile powder, garam masala, and coriander, and mix well. Add a splash of water, and let the water cook away.

4 Pour in the spinach puree, season with salt, and mix. Bring to a boil.

5 Reduce the heat to medium and gently add the cubed paneer. Simmer for 3 to 4 minutes and remove from the heat. The paneer will soften in the heat. Add the lemon juice and the ghee or butter. Garnish with ginger and a swirl of cream, and serve.

TIP: I love this dish with Chapati or Roti (Flatbread; see Chapter 19) or Paratha (Layered Bread; see Chapter 19).

Methi Shakarkand (Fresh Fenugreek with Sweet Potatoes)

PREP TIME: ABOUT 15 MIN	COOK TIME: 35 MIN	YIELD: 3 TO 4 SERVINGS

INGREDIENTS

2 tablespoons vegetable oil

1 teaspoon cumin seeds

1 onion, finely sliced

2 teaspoons Ginger-Garlic Paste (see Chapter 6)

2 green chilies, finely diced, seeds and all

2 large sweet potatoes, peeled and cut into ½-inch cubes

1 teaspoon turmeric

1 teaspoon ground coriander

2 handfuls fresh fenugreek (methi), leaves picked off the woody stalks, washed, and finely chopped, or 2 tablespoons dried fenugreek leaves (kasuri methi)

Salt to taste

DIRECTIONS

1 In a heavy pan, warm the oil over high heat. Add the cumin seeds and fry until they go a shade or two darker, about 1 minute. Add the onion, and cook for 2 to 3 minutes. Stir in the Ginger-Garlic Paste and chilies and cook for 1 minute.

2 Tip in the sweet potatoes and fry well until they start to brown, 3 or 4 minutes. Turn the heat to low and add the turmeric and coriander, and cook for a few seconds. Turn up the heat to high. Then stir in the fenugreek leaves and season with salt. Add a splash of water, and bring to a bubble (see the Tip for more info). Cover and cook over a low heat until the potatoes are tender and you can pierce them easily with a knife, about 25 minutes. Stir the potatoes from time to time to prevent them from sticking. If they dry out, add another splash of water, but not much. The final dish should be dry.

3 Remove from the heat and serve hot.

TIP: Fenugreek can bring a bitter flavor if it's boiled, so you'll want to make sure you don't add too much water to the pan. Try to cook it in the oil and just a splash of water. Add a little more oil if the pan dries out.

TIP: Serve with Chapati or Roti (Flatbread; see Chapter 19) or as a side dish.

Carrot Poriyal (Carrots Cooked with Mustard Seeds and Coconut)

PREP TIME: ABOUT 10 MIN	COOK TIME: 25 MIN	YIELD: 3 TO 4 SERVINGS

INGREDIENTS

2 tablespoons vegetable oil

1 teaspoon black mustard seeds

Small pinch of asafetida

1 teaspoon white urad lentils, washed and drained (optional)

10 fresh curry leaves or 3 pinches dried curry leaves

2 green chilies, finely diced, seeds and all

4 carrots, peeled and finely diced (about ¼ inch)

Salt to taste

1 teaspoon turmeric

2 tablespoons freshly grated frozen or desiccated coconut

3 to 4 stalks fresh cilantro, chopped, for garnish

DIRECTIONS

1 In a frying pan, warm the oil over high heat. Add the mustard seeds. When they begin to pop, after about 1 minute, add the asafetida and urad dal (if using). When the lentils begin to darken, after a few seconds, turn down the heat and add the curry leaves and green chilies; cook for a few seconds.

2 Add the carrots and salt. Mix in the turmeric. Pour in ⅔ cup of water and bring to a boil. Lower the heat to low, cover the pan, and simmer until the carrots are soft, about 20 minutes. Uncover, and if there's any cooking liquid, turn up the heat and let the liquid cook off.

3 Remove from the heat, stir in the coconut, sprinkle with cilantro, and serve hot.

TIP: You can use other firm vegetables such as French beans, green peas and cabbage instead of carrots. Remember to adjust the amount of water you add in Step 2 (carrots need more liquid than these vegetables) and the cooking time.

TIP: Serve with Chapati or Roti (Flatbread; see Chapter 19) or as a side dish with rice and dal or curry.

Bharvan Bhindi (Okra Stuffed with Spices)

PREP TIME: ABOUT 15 MIN PLUS 1 HR FOR DRYING	COOK TIME: 15 MIN	YIELD: 3 TO 4 SERVINGS

INGREDIENTS

1 pound okra

1 teaspoon Kashmiri chile powder

1 teaspoon turmeric

1 teaspoon ground coriander

1 teaspoon ground cumin

1 teaspoon amchur (dried mango powder)

1 large pinch of kasuri methi (dried fenugreek leaves) (optional)

1 pinch white sugar

Salt to taste

1 to 2 tablespoons vegetable oil

DIRECTIONS

1 Wash the okra, pat it dry, and lay it out on a clean kitchen towel to dry. It may take up to 1 hour. I usually do this the night before, so it's ready to cook when I am. Okra is a slimy vegetable, but you don't want that sliminess in Indian cooking. Water encourages the okra to become gloopy, so make sure it's absolutely dry before you begin.

2 Slice the okra lengthwise down the middle, leaving the tops intact so they hold it together.

3 On a dinner plate, mix the chile powder, turmeric, coriander, cumin, amchur, kasuri methi (if using), sugar, and salt. Stuff the mixture generously into each piece of okra.

4 In a frying pan, add enough oil to coat the base. Warm the oil over high heat. Lay the okra in a single layer. Cook the okra, turning it from time to time with a pair of tongs, until it has turned dark green and is soft enough to insert a knife into the tops, about 7 to 8 minutes. You may need to cook the okra in batches if it doesn't fit in the pan in a single layer.

5 Drain on paper towel and serve.

NOTE: Okra can go slimy, so never add water to the pan. Instead, regulate the heat so that if the okra starts to blacken too quickly, you can turn it down. Don't worry if there are some blackened areas on the okra — this is desirable and gives a lovely charred flavor.

TIP: Serve as a side dish with rice and curry or dal.

Fanshachi Bhaji (Curried Young Jackfruit)

PREP TIME: ABOUT 15 MIN	COOK TIME: 35 MIN	YIELD: 3 TO 4 SERVINGS

INGREDIENTS

Two 14-ounce cans young jackfruit in water

1 onion, sliced

2 teaspoons Ginger-Garlic Paste (see Chapter 6)

2 green chilies, diced, seeds left in

¼ cup desiccated coconut

1 teaspoon black mustard seeds

1 teaspoon turmeric

1 teaspoon garam masala

Salt to taste

4 to 5 stalks fresh cilantro, chopped, for garnish

DIRECTIONS

1 In a sieve, rinse the jackfruit and drain. Pat dry with paper towels. Cut it into 1-inch chunks.

2 In a frying pan, warm 1 tablespoon of the oil over high heat. Add the jackfruit and fry for 3 to 4 minutes, turning the heat down to medium if it begins to stick. Lift it out onto a plate.

3 Add 1 tablespoon of the oil to the pan and fry the onion until it starts to turn golden, about 3 to 4 minutes. Add the Ginger-Garlic Paste and chilies, reduce the heat to low and cook until the onions are soft, about 6 to 7 minutes. Stir in the coconut and cook until it turns golden, about 3 to 4 minutes. Transfer this mixture to a blender with enough water to cover and blend to a fine puree.

4 Warm the remaining 1 tablespoon of oil in the same pan over high heat and add the mustard seeds. When they begin to pop, after about 30 seconds, tip in the jackfruit. Sprinkle in the turmeric and garam masala and add the salt. Mix well and add 1 tablespoon of water to blend the spices.

5 Pour in the masala sauce from the blender, rinse the blender with 3 to 4 tablespoons of water, and add the water from the blender into the pan. Bring the curry to a boil, reduce the heat to medium, and cook, uncovered, for 3 to 4 minutes. The curry should have a thick sauce. Remove from the heat, sprinkle with cilantro, and serve.

NOTE: If the jackfruit is canned in brine, adjust the seasoning in the curry.

TIP: Serve with rice or Chapati or Roti (Flatbread; see Chapter 19) and store-bought mango pickle.

Beans Upkari (French Green Beans with Chile and Coconut)

PREP TIME: ABOUT 15 MIN	COOK TIME: 20 MIN	YIELD: 3 TO 4 SERVINGS

INGREDIENTS

2 tablespoons vegetable oil

1 teaspoon black mustard seeds

1 teaspoon cumin seeds

3 dried red Kashmiri chilies, left whole

1 pinch of asafetida

1½ cups fresh green beans, topped, tailed, and cut into ½-inch pieces

3 tablespoons whole cashew nuts (salted or unsalted)

Salt to taste

2 tablespoons fresh or frozen grated or desiccated unsweetened coconut

DIRECTIONS

1 In a frying pan, warm the oil over high heat. Add the mustard seeds and fry until they start to pop, about 1 minute. Add the cumin seeds and fry for a few seconds until they turn a shade darker.

2 Add the chilies and the asafetida. Press the chilies into the oil with the back of a ladle so they sizzle. Add the green beans and cashew nuts.

3 Season with salt, adjusting the quantity if you're using salted cashews. Mix well. Add 3 to 4 tablespoons of water and bring to a boil. Reduce the heat to low, cover, and simmer, stirring occasionally until the beans are cooked but still have a slight crunch, about 10 to 12 minutes.

4 Stir in the coconut, remove from the heat, and serve.

TIP: Serve as a side dish with rice or Chapati or Roti (Flatbread; see Chapter 19) and a curry such as Malvani Kombdi (Chicken and Coconut Curry; see Chapter 11).

Kaddu ki Subzi (Sweet-and-Sour Pumpkin)

PREP TIME: ABOUT 15 MIN	COOK TIME: 35 MIN	YIELD: 3 TO 4 SERVINGS

INGREDIENTS

2 tablespoons vegetable oil

1 teaspoon cumin seeds

1 onion, finely diced

1 teaspoon grated ginger

3 cups pumpkin or butternut squash, washed and cut into ¼-inch cubes (with the skin on if the pumpkin is finely skinned or if using butternut squash)

Salt to taste

1 teaspoon turmeric

1 teaspoon Kashmiri chile powder

1 teaspoon ground coriander

3 tablespoons tamarind pulp (see Chapter 6) or juice of ½ lemon

2 tablespoons jaggery or soft brown sugar

DIRECTIONS

1 In a frying pan, warm the oil over high heat. Add the cumin seeds and fry. When they go a couple of shades darker, after about 1 minute, add the onion and fry for 3 to 4 minutes. Add the ginger and fry for 1 minute.

2 Tip in the pumpkin or squash and add the salt. Mix well. Add the turmeric, chile, and coriander, and give it another stir.

3 If you're using tamarind, add it now. (If you're using lemon juice, add it in the next step). Sprinkle in the jaggery or brown sugar.

4 Add ¼ cup of water, give everything a good mix, and bring to a sizzle. Lower the heat, cover, and cook until the pumpkin is soft, about 20 minutes. Remove from the heat and if using lemon juice, add it now. Serve hot.

TIP: If you're using butternut squash, use a sharp knife to cut it in half, and scoop out the seeds with a spoon. No need to peel it — the skin cooks down with the squash. So easy!

TIP: Serve with a bread such as Chapati or Roti (Flatbread; see Chapter 19) or Thepla (Fenugreek Bread; see Chapter 19).

Shepuchi Bhaji (Dill with Mung Lentils)

PREP TIME: ABOUT 10 MIN PLUS 30 MIN FOR SOAKING	COOK TIME: 30 MIN	YIELD: 3 TO 4 SERVINGS

INGREDIENTS

3 tablespoons mung lentils (yellow mung dal)

2 tablespoons vegetable oil

1 teaspoon cumin seeds

2 onions, finely diced

1 or 2 green chilies, diced, seeds left in

1 teaspoon Ginger–Garlic Paste (see Chapter 6)

½ teaspoon turmeric

2 big handfuls baby spinach leaves, finely chopped

1 big handful dill, thick stalks removed and finely chopped

1 teaspoon ground coriander

Salt to taste

DIRECTIONS

1 Soak the mung lentils in boiling hot water for 30 minutes. You should be able to cut through a lentil easily with a knife. Drain and set aside.

2 In a frying pan, warm the oil over high heat. Add the cumin seeds. When they go a couple of shades darker, after about 1 minute, add the onion and fry for 3 to 4 minutes. Add the chilies and Ginger–Garlic Paste, and fry for 1 minute.

3 Tip in the mung lentils and the turmeric, and stir-fry for 1 minute. Then add ½ cup water, bring to a boil, reduce the heat to low, cover, and simmer for 6 to 7 minutes. The lentils should have softened but not turned to mush. Uncover the pan and stir them from time to time, adding a splash of water if they start to stick to the bottom of the pan.

4 Turn up the heat to high and add the spinach and dill. Add the coriander and salt. (Greens don't need too much salt, so go with less rather than more at this stage.) When everything is very hot, turn down the heat to low and cook until the juices from the greens have cooked off and they're completely wilted and dry, about 7 to 8 minutes.

5 Remove from the heat, adjust the seasoning if necessary, and serve.

TIP: Serve as a side dish with rice and curry.

Aloo Mutter (Pea and Potato Curry)

PREP TIME: ABOUT 10 MIN	COOK TIME: 30 MIN	YIELD: 3 TO 4 SERVINGS

INGREDIENTS

2 tablespoons vegetable oil

1 teaspoon cumin seeds

1 large pinch asafetida

2 green chilies, sliced lengthwise, leaving the stalks intact

3 large tomatoes, grated (see Chapter 6)

1 teaspoon turmeric

1 pinch white sugar

Salt to taste

3 potatoes, peeled and diced into ¼-inch cubes

¾ cup peas, fresh or frozen

4 or 5 stalks cilantro, chopped, divided

DIRECTIONS

1 In a saucepan, warm the oil over high heat. Add the cumin seeds. When they turn a couple of shades darker, after about 1 minute, add the asafetida and chilies and cook for a few seconds. Then stand back, reduce the heat to low, add the tomatoes, and cook for 3 to 4 minutes.

2 Stir in the turmeric, sugar, and salt; mix well. Add the potatoes, peas, half the cilantro, and enough water to just cover the potatoes (see the Tip). When the curry has come to a boil, reduce the heat to low, cover, and simmer until the potatoes are cooked through, about 20 minutes. Test for doneness by inserting the tip of a knife through a couple potatoes. (This curry can be made with some sauce or none — it depends on your preference. If you'd like it to be wetter, add some water when it starts to go dry.)

3 Sprinkle with the remaining cilantro and serve.

TIP: You don't want to add too much water in Step 2. It'll take too long to cook away and the potatoes may overcook. Or you'll have a really soupy curry.

TIP: Try this with Chapati or Roti (Flatbread; see Chapter 19) or Paratha (Layered Bread; see Chapter 19).

Chapter **14**

Rice with a Bit of Anything

RECIPES IN THIS CHAPTER

- Jeera Pulao (Cumin-Flavored Rice)
- Kashmiri Pulao (Rice with Mushrooms, Dried Fruit, Nuts, and Spices)
- * Chicken Biryani (Festive One-Pot Chicken and Rice)
- Paneer Pulao (Aromatic Rice with Indian Cottage Cheese)
- * Jhinga Pulao (Spiced Rice with Shrimp)
- Egg Biryani (South Indian Spiced Rice with Eggs)
- * Kheema Pulao (Spiced Rice with Ground Meat)
- Sunhera Pulao (Golden Turmeric Rice)
- Channa Pulao (Brown Rice with Chickpeas)
- Khichdi (Warming Rice and Lentil Stew)

It's eaten with lentils, curries and yogurt. It's flavored with spices, vegetables, meat, and seafood. And it's even made into snacks and desserts! India *loves* its rice, and few meals are complete without it. Rice is intrinsically linked to life. Religious ceremonies are incomplete without it. And it's the first solid food an Indian baby eats.

India grows a vast number of varieties of rice, but the one most available outside the country is *basmati*, a long grained, slender type of rice that should cook up fluffy and has a wonderful aroma. (*Basmati* loosely translates to "queen of fragrance.") Everyday rice is served plain, boiled, and drained, to provide a neutral contrast to the accompanying curry or dal (which would be considered the main course in the West). Unless it's a *khichdi* (a slightly soupy, sticky stew of rice, lentils, and spices), you'll want your rice to be fluffy with separate grains.

I'm often asked whether white or brown rice is better. In India, white rice is most popular. In some parts of India, people eat unprocessed red rice. But before you judge the cuisine for its love of white rice (brown often being considered healthier by Western nutritionists), look at what rice is served with. The vast repertoire of lentils, beans, fresh vegetables, fish, and lean meats, as well as dairy products like yogurt and paneer, provide balance and raise the nutritional bar of the meal.

In this chapter, I offer ideas for jazzing up your rice in a biryani and pulao, as well as show you how to make a pot of comforting khichdi. If it's plain rice you're after, go to my recipes in Chapter 6. For a simple meal of rice, curry, and a salad or vegetable side dish, I'd make ¼ cup of rice per person.

Jeera Pulao (Cumin-Flavored Rice)

PREP TIME: ABOUT 5 MIN	COOK TIME: 15 MIN	YIELD: 3-4 SERVINGS

INGREDIENTS

1 tablespoon vegetable oil

1 teaspoon cumin seeds

1 cup basmati rice, washed and drained in a sieve

Salt to taste

6 cups hot water

DIRECTIONS

1 In a heavy saucepan, warm the oil over high heat. Fry the cumin seeds until they turn a couple of shades darker, about 1 minute.

2 Tip in the rice, and season with salt. Stir very gently to blend. Fry until the rice looks shiny, about 2 to 3 minutes.

3 Add the water, stir, and return to a boil. Reduce the heat to low, and simmer until the rice is cooked, about 10 minutes. (Test for doneness by tasting a few grains or by mashing a couple of grains between your thumb and forefinger.) Drain in a colander in the sink and serve hot.

TIP: Don't stir the rice too much or too vigorously. Doing so can break the grains and make the final dish stodgy.

Kashmiri Pulao (Rice with Mushrooms, Dried Fruit, Nuts, and Spices)

PREP TIME: 10 MIN PLUS 15 MIN FOR SOAKING	COOK TIME: 25 MIN	YIELD: 3–4 SERVINGS

INGREDIENTS

8 to 10 morel or chestnut mushrooms (dried or fresh)

2 tablespoons vegetable oil or ghee

1 tablespoon raisins

1 tablespoon blanched almonds

2 black cardamom pods, seeds crushed and husks discarded

4 cloves

2 bay leaves

1 cup basmati rice, washed and drained

¼ teaspoon turmeric

Salt to taste

2 cups hot water

DIRECTIONS

1 If using dried mushrooms, wash them and soak them in warm water for 15 minutes, covered, or until they plump up; drain them and squeeze out the excess water. If using fresh mushrooms, wash them well and slice them.

2 In a saucepan, warm the oil or ghee over high heat. Add the raisins and almonds, and fry until the almonds start to turn golden, about 1 minute. Lift out the raisins and almonds and transfer them to a small bowl.

3 Reduce the heat to low; add the cardamom, cloves, and bay leaves; and fry for a few seconds. Turn up the heat to high, add the mushrooms, and cook about 3 to 4 minutes.

4 Add the rice and turmeric, and fry gently until shiny, about 2 to 3 minutes. Season with salt. Pour in the water and bring to a boil. Reduce the heat to low, cover the pan tightly, and simmer for 10 minutes without opening the lid. Turn off the heat and leave covered for 5 minutes.

5 Remove the lid, fluff with a fork, sprinkle with the fried raisins and almonds, and serve.

Chicken Biryani (Festive One-Pot Chicken and Rice)

PREP TIME: 20 MIN PLUS 2 HR FOR MARINATING	COOK TIME: 1 HR	YIELD: 3–4 SERVINGS

INGREDIENTS

3 tablespoons Ginger-Garlic Paste (see Chapter 6)

1 teaspoon Kashmiri chile powder

2 teaspoons turmeric

2 teaspoons garam masala

3 to 4 fresh green chilies, finely chopped, seeds and all

Juice of ½ lemon

½ cup plain Greek yogurt

Salt to taste

1 pound chicken on the bone or boneless, cut into small pieces

¼ cup ghee, melted, divided

3 large onions, thinly sliced

1 cup basmati rice, washed and drained in a sieve

1 small cinnamon stick

5 green cardamom pods, seeds crushed and husks discarded

5 cloves

8 to 10 stalks cilantro, chopped, divided

8 to 10 stalks mint, leaves chopped and stalks discarded, divided

2 pinches saffron dissolved in 1 tablespoon warm milk

DIRECTIONS

1 In a bowl, combine the Ginger-Garlic Paste, chile powder, turmeric, garam masala, chilies, lemon, yogurt, and salt. Taste before adding the chicken; it should be distinctly salty, sour, and hot. Add the chicken, mix to coat it in the marinade, and refrigerate, covered, for 2 to 3 hours.

2 In a frying pan, heat 1 tablespoon of the melted ghee over high heat. Add the onions and fry until they start to turn golden, about 4 to 5 minutes. Turn the heat to low and continue cooking, stirring frequently, until they're a rich, even golden brown, about 15 to 20 minutes. Lift them out onto a plate and set aside.

(continued)

3 In the meantime, in a saucepan, add the rice, cinnamon stick, cardamom, and cloves. Add 4 cups of water. Season well with salt and bring to a boil. Reduce the heat and simmer, uncovered, for 5 minutes (the rice will just be partially cooked). Drain in a colander. Pick out the whole spices if you like.

4 Start assembling the dish: Coat the base of a saucepan with 1 tablespoon of ghee. Next, put the chicken in along with all the marinade. Add another 1 tablespoon of ghee over it and around the edges. Sprinkle half of the chopped cilantro, half of the mint, and half of the fried onions over the top. Spread the rice over top.

5 Drizzle over the remaining 1 tablespoon of ghee and saffron along with the milk. Sprinkle the remaining cilantro, mint, and onions over the top.

6 Place a folded tea towel over the pan and place a lid on top to seal it tightly so that no steam escapes. Cook over a high heat for 6 to 8 minutes or until you can hear a sizzle from the pan. Then reduce the heat to low (as low as it will go) and cook for 15 to 20 minutes (20 minutes if you're using chicken on the bone).

7 Turn off the heat and leave the biryani to rest for 5 minutes. Then remove the lid, and mix gently with a fork to combine the rice, chicken, and spices. If you see a little liquid on the bottom, it's probably due to the variations in the fat content of the yogurt used. Just put the biryani back on a high heat for 3 to 4 minutes, uncovered, to cook off the liquid. Serve hot.

TIP: This dish goes well with Kheere Tamater ka Raita (Cucumber and Tomato Salad with Yogurt; see Chapter 20) and Kachumber (Onion, Cucumber, Tomato, and Carrot Salad; see Chapter 20).

TIP: In Step 1, the salty, sour, and hot flavors should taste slightly overwhelming, because they'll tone down when the chicken is added. If they taste just right at the start, the addition of the chicken will make the flavors underwhelming.

Paneer Pulao (Aromatic Rice with Indian Cottage Cheese)

PREP TIME: ABOUT 10 MIN	COOK TIME: 25 MIN	YIELD: 3–4 SERVINGS

INGREDIENTS

9 ounces paneer, cut into ¾-inch cubes

Salt to taste

Pepper to taste

1 tablespoon vegetable oil or ghee, plus extra oil for drizzling

5 cloves

One 1½-inch stick of cinnamon

1 onion, finely sliced

1 green bell pepper, diced (about ¾-inch)

1 teaspoon turmeric

1 cup basmati rice, washed and drained

2 cups hot water

3 to 4 stalks cilantro, chopped, for garnish

DIRECTIONS

1 Preheat the oven to 350 degrees.

2 On a baking sheet, place the paneer in a single layer. Season it with salt and pepper and drizzle with oil. Bake until it's golden around the edges, about 10 minutes.

3 In the meantime, in a saucepan, warm the oil or ghee over high heat. Add the cloves and cinnamon, and fry until they start to sizzle, about 1 minute. Add the onion, and fry until it starts to change color, about 3 to 4 minutes. Add the green pepper and fry for 1 minute. Add the turmeric and the rice, stir gently, and season with salt.

4 Pour in the water and bring to a boil. Reduce the heat to low (as low as it will go), cover tightly, and simmer for 10 minutes without lifting the lid. Turn off the heat and leave to rest, covered, for 5 minutes. Remove the lid, fluff up with a fork, fold in the paneer, scatter with the cilantro, and serve hot.

TIP: Enjoy this dish with a curry or dal, and a vegetable side dish.

Jhinga Pulao (Spiced Rice with Shrimp)

PREP TIME: ABOUT 15 MIN	COOK TIME: 35 MIN	YIELD: 3–4 SERVINGS

INGREDIENTS

2 tablespoons vegetable oil

1 teaspoon cumin seeds

1 large onion, finely chopped

2 teaspoons Ginger-Garlic Paste (see Chapter 6)

2 green chilies, finely chopped with the seeds

2 to 3 stalks mint, leaves chopped and stalks discarded

¼ pound raw or cooked shrimp (shelled and deveined if using raw; see Chapter 5)

1 cup basmati rice, washed and drained

1 teaspoon turmeric

1 teaspoon garam masala

1 tablespoon tomato paste

Salt to taste

4 to 5 stalks cilantro, chopped, divided

2 cups hot water

Juice of ½ lemon

DIRECTIONS

1 In a saucepan, warm the oil over high heat. Add the cumin seeds, and fry until they turn a couple of shades darker, about 1 minute. Add the onion and fry until it starts to change color, about 3 to 4 minutes. Lower the heat and fry until the onion is golden brown, about 7 to 8 minutes. Add the Ginger–Garlic Paste and chilies, and cook for a few seconds.

2 Stir in the mint and the shrimp. Add the rice, turmeric, and garam masala; stir gently. Stir in the tomato paste, salt, and half the cilantro.

3 Pour in the water and bring to a boil. Reduce the heat, cover the pan, and simmer for 12 to 14 minutes without removing the lid. Turn off the heat and leave the rice to rest, covered, for 5 minutes. Fluff up with a fork, sprinkle the remaining cilantro on top, drizzle the lemon juice on top, and serve hot.

TIP: All you need with this dish is some store-bought mango or lime pickle and Kachumber (Onion, Cucumber, Tomato, and Carrot Salad; see Chapter 20).

Egg Biryani (South Indian Spiced Rice with Eggs)

PREP TIME: ABOUT 15 MIN	COOK TIME: 45 MIN	YIELD: 3–4 SERVINGS

INGREDIENTS

4 hard-boiled eggs

2 tablespoons vegetable oil

5 green cardamom pods, seeds crushed and husks discarded

8 cloves

4 star anise

2 dried red Kashmiri chilies, seeds shaken out

1 large onion, finely chopped

2 teaspoons Ginger-Garlic Paste (see Chapter 6)

2 green chilies, finely chopped

10 fresh curry leaves or 3 pinches dried curry leaves

1 teaspoon ground coriander

1 teaspoon turmeric

1 teaspoon garam masala

2 tablespoons tomato paste

Salt to taste

Dash of pepper

4 to 5 stalks cilantro, chopped, divided

3 to 4 stalks mint, leaves chopped and stalks discarded, divided

1 cup basmati rice, washed and drained

2 cups plus 2 tablespoons hot water

Juice of ½ lemon

DIRECTIONS

1 Peel the eggs and make shallow gashes all over them with the tip of a small knife. Set aside.

2 In a saucepan, warm the oil over high heat. Add the crushed cardamom, cloves, star anise, and red chilies, and fry. As they sizzle, add the onion and soften for 2 minutes. Add the Ginger-Garlic Paste, green chilies, and curry leaves, and cook for a few seconds.

3 Stir in the coriander, turmeric, and garam masala. Add the tomato paste, salt, pepper, half the cilantro, and half the mint leaves. Gently fold in the rice. Add the eggs.

4 Pour in the water and bring to a boil. Reduce the heat to the lowest setting, cover the pan tightly, and simmer for 14 minutes without lifting the lid. Turn off the heat and rest the rice for 5 minutes without removing the lid. Fluff up with a fork. Sprinkle with the remaining cilantro and mint leaves. Remove the red chilies and drizzle the lemon juice over the top. Serve hot.

TIP: To find out how to boil eggs perfectly, turn to Chapter 16.

TIP: This dish pairs well with yogurt and store-bought mango or lime pickle.

Kheema Pulao (Spiced Rice with Ground Meat)

PREP TIME: ABOUT 15 MIN | COOK TIME: 30 MIN | YIELD: 3-4 SERVINGS

INGREDIENTS

2 tablespoons vegetable oil

6 green cardamom, seeds crushed and husks discarded

2 black cardamom, seeds crushed and husks discarded

5 cloves

1 teaspoon crushed black pepper

1 large onion, finely chopped

2 teaspoons Ginger-Garlic Paste (see Chapter 6)

2 green chilies, finely chopped

⅓ pound lean ground lamb or beef

1 teaspoon turmeric

1 teaspoon garam masala

2 tablespoons tomato paste

Salt to taste

4 to 5 stalks cilantro chopped, divided

1 teaspoon dried fenugreek leaves (optional)

1 cup basmati rice, washed and drained

2 cups hot water

Juice of ½ lemon

DIRECTIONS

1 In a saucepan, warm the oil over high heat. Add the green and black cardamom, cloves, and pepper. As they sizzle, add the onion and soften for 2 minutes. Add the Ginger-Garlic Paste and green chilies, and cook for a few seconds.

2 Add the ground meat and cook until evenly brown, 3 to 4 minutes. Drain off as much grease as you can. Tip in the turmeric and garam masala, and cook for another 1 minute.

3 Stir in the tomato paste, salt, half the cilantro, and the dried fenugreek leaves, if using.

4 Add the rice and gently mix. Pour in the water and bring to a boil. Reduce the heat to a minimum, cover with a tight-fitting lid, and simmer for 12 minutes without lifting the lid. Turn off the heat and leave to rest, covered, for 5 more minutes. Uncover, fluff with a fork, and drizzle with lemon juice, and scatter the remaining cilantro over the top. Serve hot.

TIP: This dish is lovely with plain Greek yogurt and Kachumber (Onion, Cucumber, Tomato, and Carrot Salad; see Chapter 20).

Sunhera Pulao (Golden Turmeric Rice)

PREP TIME: ABOUT 10 MIN	COOK TIME: 15 MIN	YIELD: 3–4 SERVINGS

INGREDIENTS

1 cup basmati rice, washed and drained

3½ cups boiling hot water

½ teaspoon turmeric

¼ teaspoon salt

DIRECTIONS

1 In a saucepan, add the rice, water, turmeric, and salt. Bring to a boil over high heat. Stir once, gently, then reduce the heat to a simmer and cook until the rice is done, about 8 to 10 minutes. (Test the rice for doneness by squashing a grain between your thumb and forefinger or simply by tasting it.)

2 Drain the rice through a colander in the sink. Fluff up with a fork, and serve.

TIP: This rice goes well with a curry and a vegetable side dish.

TIP: Try adding some frozen peas or sweetcorn along with the rice for a pop of color and some texture.

Channa Pulao (Brown Rice with Chickpeas)

PREP TIME: ABOUT 10 MIN	COOK TIME: 40 MIN	YIELD: 3–4 SERVINGS

INGREDIENTS

2 tablespoons vegetable oil or ghee

4 cloves

Two 1½-inch sticks of cinnamon

1 onion, sliced

1 teaspoon turmeric

1 teaspoon garam masala

Half of 15-ounce can of chickpeas, rinsed and drained

1 cup brown basmati rice, washed and drained

Salt to taste

2 cups hot water

2 tablespoons lemon juice

4 to 5 stalks cilantro, chopped

DIRECTIONS

1 In a saucepan, warm the oil over high heat. Add the cloves and cinnamon, and fry until they sizzle. Add the onion, and cook for 3 to 4 minutes to soften.

2 Add the turmeric, garam masala, and chickpeas. Mix well and tip in the rice. Stir gently, and season with salt.

3 Pour in the water and bring to a boil. Reduce the heat to a minimum, cover the pan, and cook for 25 minutes, without lifting the lid until the rice is cooked. Turn off the heat and leave the pan covered for another 5 minutes.

4 Uncover the rice, fluff it up, and if there is still a bit of moisture at the bottom, cook off over high heat. (The rice will still have a bite.)

5 Drizzle with lemon juice, sprinkle with cilantro, and serve.

TIP: Enjoy this rice with a meat, chicken, or vegetable curry, or on its own with some plain Greek yogurt.

Khichdi (Warming Rice and Lentil Stew)

PREP TIME: ABOUT 10 MIN	COOK TIME: 40 MIN	YIELD: 3–4 SERVINGS

INGREDIENTS

2 tablespoons ghee, divided

5 cloves

10 black peppercorns, crushed

2 bay leaves

1 teaspoon cumin seeds

Pinch of asafetida

1 teaspoon grated ginger

¼ cup yellow mung dal, washed and drained

½ teaspoon ground turmeric

⅔ cup short- or medium-grain rice, washed and drained

1 small carrot, peeled and grated

1 small handful dill or spinach, finely chopped

Salt to taste

DIRECTIONS

1 In a saucepan, heat 1 tablespoon of the ghee over high heat. Add the cloves, peppercorns, bay leaves, and cumin seeds, and fry until the spices sizzle, about 1 minute. Add the asafetida and ginger, and fry for a few seconds. Add the mung dal and fry until the grains look shiny, about 1 minute.

2 Add the turmeric, rice, carrot, dill or spinach, and 2½ cups hot water. Season with salt and bring back to a boil. Reduce the heat, and simmer for about 30 minutes, stirring and adding more hot water as necessary to keep the mixture covered, until the rice and lentils are creamy and very soft. This dish will be quite moist, like a risotto.

3 Drizzle with the remaining 1 tablespoon of ghee, and serve.

TIP: All this needs to be comfort in a bowl is some plain Greek yogurt and a bit of store-bought mango or lime pickle.

Chapter **15**

Can't-Be-Beat Lentils and Beans

RECIPES IN THIS CHAPTER

⏱ **Tarka Dal (Spiced Lentils)**

⏱ **Dal Makhani (Creamy Black Beans with Garlic)**

⏱ **Channa Masala (Chickpea Curry)**

⏱ **Rajma Masala (Red Bean Curry)**

⏱ **Sambhar (South Indian Lentil Stew)**

⏱ **Palak Pappu (South Indian Spinach Dal)**

⏱ **Dal Dhokli (Lentil Stew with Flour Dumplings)**

⏱ **Masoor Dal (Brown Lentils with Coconut Milk)**

⏱ **Kadhi (Chickpea Flour and Yogurt Curry)**

⏱ **Mung Usal (Sprouted Mung Beans with Turmeric)**

n India, the word *dal* is used to mean all lentils and legumes, both raw and cooked. It's such a common food that it's combined with the word *roti* (bread) as *dal roti*, meaning "one's bread and butter" or basic income. In a country with so many vegetarians, lentils, beans, and legumes form a part of every meal and provide a good source of protein. They're cheap, and a small amount cooked, fluffs up to feed many people.

There are many varieties of lentils, beans, and legumes (see Chapter 4). Lentils are cooked in an Indian home daily. Because there are so many to choose from, it never gets dull or boring.

I often get asked in my cooking classes whether to drain lentils after they've cooked. The texture and consistency are the two main considerations here. You want the lentils to collapse and become mushy so you don't see each one. (This doesn't apply to beans and whole pulses, just the hulled ones.) When you cook lentils, you want to add just the right amount of water so there's no need to drain them (more about how to cook lentils in Chapter 6). In most Indian cooking, water is your friend — it helps build a curry, stops ingredients from burning, and allows spices to cook properly — but with lentils, adding too much water will make it a foe, and you'll either need to drain it away (losing some of the vital nutrients) or have to cook it off (which means wasting resources).

REMEMBER

Don't salt lentils and beans at the start — they may take much longer to cook.

Tarka Dal (Spiced Lentils)

PREP TIME: ABOUT 15 MIN	COOK TIME: 40 MIN	YIELD: 3-4 SERVINGS

INGREDIENTS

1 cup yellow mung lentils or red lentils, washed and drained

2 tablespoons vegetable oil

1 teaspoon cumin seeds

1 large onion, finely diced

1 teaspoon Ginger-Garlic Paste (Chapter 6)

2 green chilies, slit with stalks left on

1 tomato, diced

1 teaspoon turmeric

1 teaspoon garam masala plus a pinch for garnish

Salt to taste

1 tablespoon ghee (see Tip)

2 cloves garlic, finely diced

4 to 5 stalks cilantro, chopped

DIRECTIONS

1 In a saucepan, add the lentils and 1¾ cups of water. Cook over high heat until the water comes to a boil. Reduce the heat to low, cover, and simmer until very soft, about 30 minutes, adding more water to just cover them each time they dry out. They should have a pouring consistency similar to a creamy soup.

2 In a frying pan, warm the oil over high heat. Add the cumin seeds. When they turn a couple of shades darker, after about 1 minute, add the onion and cook until it starts to turn golden, about 3 to 4 minutes. Reduce the heat to medium and cook until very soft, about 7 to 8 minutes.

3 Add the Ginger–Garlic paste and cook for 1 minute. Add the chilies and tomato and allow to soften, about 3 to 4 minutes.

4 Stir in the turmeric and garam masala. Add a splash of water and bring to a bubble. Increase the heat to high and cook for 2 minutes.

5 Carefully pour in the cooked lentils and season with salt. Remove from the heat.

6 In a small frying pan, warm the ghee over high heat and add the garlic. Fry until golden, about 2 minutes. Pour the ghee with the garlic into the dal and stir, garnish with cilantro and garam masala, and serve.

TIP: If you don't have ghee, you can use vegetable oil, but ghee tastes better.

TIP: Serve with rice and a curry or a vegetable side dish.

Dal Makhani (Creamy Black Beans with Garlic)

PREP TIME: ABOUT 15 MIN PLUS OVER-NIGHT FOR SOAKING	COOK TIME: 1 HR 15 MIN	YIELD: 3–4 SERVINGS

INGREDIENTS

1 large onion, finely diced

1 tablespoon Ginger-Garlic Paste (Chapter 6)

1 teaspoon turmeric

1 teaspoon Kashmiri chile powder

2½ teaspoons garam masala, divided

¾ cup whole black urad beans, soaked in 4 cups hot water overnight, rinsed and drained

Salt to taste

4 to 5 stalks cilantro, finely chopped

2 tablespoons ghee (see Tip)

2 garlic cloves, finely diced

2 large tomatoes, finely diced

2 tablespoons heavy cream

Juice of ½ lemon

DIRECTIONS

1   In a saucepan, add the onion, Ginger–Garlic Paste, turmeric, chile powder, 2 teaspoons of the garam masala, and the beans. Add enough water to cover the mixture by 1 inch, and bring to a boil over high heat.

2   Reduce the heat to low, cover, and simmer for at least 1 hour, until the beans are very soft, creamy, and almost dissolving. Add water as necessary, to keep the beans submerged. If there is still quite a bit of water, keep cooking the beans for another 10 to 15 minutes, stirring from time to time, until they start to break down.

3   Remove from the heat, and stir in the salt and cilantro (saving some for garnish).

4   In a frying pan, heat the ghee over high heat. Add the garlic, and fry until it starts to turn golden brown, about 1 minute. Add the tomatoes and fry until soft, about 3 or 4 minutes. Stir this mixture into the lentils. Continue cooking the dal, mashing a few beans, until it thickens. It should resemble oatmeal.

5   Stir in the cream and lemon juice, garnish with the remaining cilantro and the remaining ½ teaspoon of garam masala, and serve.

TIP: If you don't have ghee, you can use butter or vegetable oil instead. I prefer ghee, though.

TIP: You can cook the beans in a pressure cooker (for example, an Instant Pot) to speed up the process if you prefer.

TIP: Serve with rice or Chapati or Roti (Flatbread; see Chapter 19).

Channa Masala (Chickpea Curry)

PREP TIME: ABOUT 10 MIN	COOK TIME: 30 MIN	YIELD: 4 SERVINGS

INGREDIENTS

Two 15-ounce cans chickpeas, drained and rinsed

1 black tea bag

2 black cardamom, seeds crushed and husks discarded

1 teaspoon salt

2 tablespoons vegetable oil, divided

2 medium onions, sliced

1 tablespoon Ginger-Garlic Paste (Chapter 6)

1 tablespoon tomato paste mixed with 2 tablespoons water

1 teaspoon turmeric

1 teaspoon Kashmiri chile powder

1 teaspoon ground coriander

1 teaspoon garam masala

4 to 5 stalks cilantro, chopped, for garnish

DIRECTIONS

1 In a saucepan, put the chickpeas, tea bag, cardamom, and salt. Fill 1 of the empty cans with water and add to the saucepan. When the water boils, reduce the heat to medium and simmer for 5 minutes. Turn off the heat.

2 In a large frying pan, heat 1 tablespoon of the oil over high heat. Add the onions and fry until they start to turn golden, about 3 to 4 minutes. Reduce the heat to medium and cook until they're very soft, about 7 to 8 minutes.

3 Add the Ginger-Garlic Paste, and fry for 30 seconds. Add the tomato paste mixed with water, and fry for 1 minute.

4 Transfer this mixture to a blender, adding enough water to just cover it, and puree.

5 In the same saucepan, warm the remaining 1 tablespoon of oil over high heat. Add the turmeric, chile powder, coriander, and garam masala. Fry for a few seconds, until they sizzle. Then add a splash of cold water. When the water has evaporated, leaving the spices in oil, add the chickpeas with the cooking liquid (discard the tea bag).

6 Pour in the masala sauce. Rinse the blender with about ½ cup of water, and add this water in. Adjust the seasoning and bring to a boil. Reduce the heat, cover, and cook for about 4 to 5 minutes.

7 Remove from the heat, garnish with cilantro, and serve.

TIP: You can use dried chickpeas for this recipe. Soak overnight in plenty of water and cook the next day in a pressure cooker (for example, an Instant Pot), according to manufacturer's instructions, using fresh water.

TIP: Serve with rice or a bread.

Rajma Masala (Red Bean Curry)

PREP TIME: ABOUT 10 MIN	COOK TIME: 25 MIN	YIELD: 4 SERVINGS

INGREDIENTS

2 tablespoons vegetable oil, divided

1 teaspoon cumin seeds

2 onions, finely sliced

1 tablespoon Ginger-Garlic Paste (Chapter 6)

Half of 15-ounce can chopped tomatoes

1 teaspoon Kashmiri chile powder

1 teaspoon turmeric

2 teaspoons garam masala

Two 15-ounce cans dark red kidney beans, rinsed and drained

Salt to taste

1 teaspoon granulated sugar

4 to 5 stalks cilantro, chopped

DIRECTIONS

1 In a frying pan, warm 1 tablespoon of the oil over high heat. Add the cumin seeds and fry until they turn a couple of shades darker, about 1 minute. Add the onions and fry about 3 to 4 minutes. Turn down the heat to medium and fry until soft, 7 to 8 minutes.

2 Add the Ginger–Garlic Paste, and fry for 30 seconds. Add the tomatoes and ½ cup of water, and bring to a boil. Reduce the heat and simmer for 5 minutes. Allow the mixture to cool slightly.

3 Transfer this mixture to a blender and blend to a fine puree.

4 Wipe the pan, warm the remaining 1 tablespoon of oil over high heat, and add the chile, turmeric, and garam masala. When they sizzle and develop an aroma, add a splash of cold water, and allow it to cook away over high heat. Stir in the beans and cook over high heat for 2 minutes.

5 Pour in the masala curry sauce from the blender. Season with salt and add the sugar.

6 Bring to a boil. Then reduce the heat and simmer, covered, for 3 to 4 minutes. Garnish with cilantro and serve hot.

NOTE: Use dried red beans if you prefer, soaking them overnight and cooking them until very soft, in a pressure cooker (for example, an Instant Pot). Red beans contain a natural toxin that's destroyed by sufficient cooking.

TIP: Serve with rice or bread.

Sambhar (South Indian Lentil Stew)

PREP TIME: ABOUT 15 MIN	COOK TIME: 40 MIN	YIELD: 3-4 SERVINGS

INGREDIENTS

½ teaspoon fenugreek seeds

½ teaspoon cumin seeds

2 dried red Kashmiri chilies, stalks removed, deseeded, and chopped

½ teaspoon black peppercorns

1 teaspoon coriander seeds

2 teaspoons split black lentils (urad dal)

1 cup yellow mung lentils

1 large carrot, diced in ¾-inch pieces

2 tablespoons vegetable oil

1 teaspoon black mustard seeds

1 large pinch asafetida

12 fresh curry leaves or 3 pinches dried curry leaves

1 tablespoon tamarind block, made into pulp (see Chapter 6)

1 teaspoon turmeric

Salt to taste

4 to 5 stalks of cilantro, chopped

1 tablespoon ghee (optional)

DIRECTIONS

1 Heat a frying pan and dry-roast the fenugreek until it has turned a couple of shades darker. Transfer to a dry bowl. Repeat with the cumin, chilies, peppercorns, coriander, and split black lentils, each one separately.

2 Cool the mixture and blend to a powder in a spice mill or mortar and pestle. The resulting powder is called *sambhar powder*. You can store any leftovers for up to 3 months. You can also make a small batch of it for next time.

3 In a saucepan, add the yellow mung lentils and 2 cups water, and bring to a boil. Reduce the heat to low and simmer for 15 minutes, adding more water as necessary to keep the lentils just submerged. Add the carrot, and simmer another 15 minutes, adding more water as necessary each time the lentils dry out.

4 In a pan, warm the oil and add the mustard seeds. When they crackle, add the asafetida and curry leaves. Cook for 15 seconds and add the tamarind pulp. Cook over low heat for a few seconds.

5 Add 4 teaspoons of the sambhar powder (from Step 2), turmeric, and ¼ cup of water, and cook for 1 minute over high heat. Pour the lentils into the mixture and stir.

6 Garnish with the cilantro and serve with ghee if desired.

NOTE: Black lentils look creamy white. Turn to Chapter 4 for more on lentils.

TIP: Serve with rice.

Palak Pappu (South Indian Spinach Dal)

PREP TIME: ABOUT 15 MIN	COOK TIME: 40 MIN	YIELD: 3–4 SERVINGS

INGREDIENTS

1 cup yellow mung lentils or red lentils

2 tablespoons vegetable oil

1 teaspoon black mustard seeds

1 large pinch asafetida

1 onion, finely diced

12 fresh curry leaves or 3 pinches dried curry leaves

2 teaspoons Ginger-Garlic Paste (Chapter 6)

3 dried red Kashmiri chilies, kept whole

1 teaspoon turmeric

½ teaspoon Kashmiri chile powder

2 tomatoes, chopped

5 ounces baby spinach, chopped

Salt to taste

Pepper to taste

1 tablespoon lemon juice

DIRECTIONS

1 In a saucepan, put the lentils and 1¾ cups of water and cook over high heat until the water comes to a boil. Reduce the heat to low, cover, and simmer until very soft, about 30 minutes, adding more water to just cover them each time they dry out.

2 In the meantime, in a frying pan, warm the oil over high heat and fry the mustard seeds until they begin to pop. Add the asafetida and onion, and fry the onion until it begins to turn golden, about 3 to 4 minutes. Lower the heat to medium and fry until very soft, about 7 to 8 minutes.

3 Add the curry leaves, Ginger–Garlic Paste, and chilies, and fry for 1 minute. Tip in the turmeric and chile powder.

4 Stir in the tomatoes and spinach and cook until soft and blended, about 3 to 4 minutes.

5 Pour in the cooked lentils. Season with salt and pepper, and stir in the lemon juice.

TIP: Serve with rice and a curry or a vegetable side dish.

Dal Dhokli (Lentil Stew with Flour Dumplings)

PREP TIME: ABOUT 15 MIN PLUS 1 HR FOR SOAKING	COOK TIME: 1 HR	YIELD: 3–4 SERVINGS

INGREDIENTS

1 cup yellow lentils (toor dal), soaked in boiling hot water for 1 hour, then drained

¾ cup atta (see Chapter 4)

1½ teaspoons turmeric, divided

½ teaspoon ajowan (carom seeds) (optional)

½ teaspoon salt, plus more to taste

1 tablespoon vegetable oil

1 teaspoon black mustard seeds

½ teaspoon fenugreek seeds

4 cloves

10 fresh curry leaves or 3 pinches dried curry leaves

2 teaspoons grated ginger

2 green chilies, finely diced with the seeds

1 teaspoon ground cumin

1 tablespoon tamarind block made into pulp (see Chapter 6)

1 teaspoon jaggery or soft brown sugar

2 tablespoons peanuts (optional)

4 to 5 stalks of cilantro, chopped

DIRECTIONS

1 In a saucepan, put the lentils and 2 cups of water and cook over high heat until the water comes to a boil. Reduce the heat to low, cover, and simmer until very soft, about 40 minutes, adding more water to just cover them each time they absorb the liquid. The lentils should collapse and resemble a creamy soup (you shouldn't be able to see the water and lentils separate).

2 In the meantime, in a bowl, combine the atta, ½ teaspoon of the turmeric, the ajowan (if using), and salt to taste. Add a little water at a time to make a stiff dough. Place under a moist tea towel and set aside.

(continued)

3 In a frying pan, warm the oil over high heat. Add the mustard seeds and fenugreek. As soon as they pop and darken, add the cloves, curry leaves, ginger, and chilies and cook for 1 minute.

4 Tip in the turmeric, cumin, tamarind, and jaggery or sugar. Add a splash of water and bring to a boil. Reduce the heat to medium and simmer for 2 minutes.

5 Pour in the cooked lentils, peanuts, and cilantro. Season with ½ teaspoon salt and bring to a boil. Turn off the heat.

6 Roll out the dough as thinly as you can, and cut it into diamond shapes (about 1 inch long and ½ inch wide) with a sharp knife.

7 Just before serving (otherwise they'll go gloopy), add the wheat flour diamonds to the dal one at a time. Stir them in gently and cook over high heat until soft, about 3 to 4 minutes.

TIP: Serve with rice.

Masoor Dal (Brown Lentils with Coconut Milk)

PREP TIME: ABOUT 15 MIN PLUS1 HR FOR SOAKING	COOK TIME: 45 MIN	YIELD: 3–4 SERVINGS

INGREDIENTS

1 cup brown lentils, soaked in 3 cups boiling hot water for 1 hour and drained

2 tablespoons vegetable oil

1 teaspoon cumin seeds

1 large onion, finely sliced

2 teaspoons Ginger-Garlic Paste (see Chapter 6)

2 green chilies, chopped, seeds and all

2 tomatoes, finely chopped

1 teaspoon turmeric

1 teaspoon garam masala

¾ cup coconut milk

Salt to taste

4 to 5 stalks cilantro, chopped

1 tablespoon ghee, to serve (optional)

DIRECTIONS

1 In a saucepan, put the drained lentils with 1¾ cups of boiling water and cook over high heat until they come to a boil. Reduce the heat and simmer until very soft, about 35 minutes, adding more water to just cover them if they absorb all the liquid. Test the softness by tasting or squashing a few between your thumb and forefinger.

2 In a saucepan, warm the oil over high heat and add the cumin seeds. Fry them until they go a couple of shades darker, about 1 minute. Add the onions and fry until they begin to turn golden, about 3 to 4 minutes. Reduce the heat to low and cook until they're very soft, about 7 to 8 minutes.

3 Add the Ginger–Garlic Paste and chilies, and cook for 1 minute. Tip in the tomatoes, turmeric, garam masala, and a splash of water, and cook on a high heat until soft, about 4 to 5 minutes.

4 Stir in the cooked lentils. Pour in the coconut milk and season with salt. Bring to a boil.

5 Turn off the heat. Sprinkle with cilantro, drizzle with ghee (if using), and serve.

TIP: This dish is delicious with rice or bread.

Kadhi (Chickpea Flour and Yogurt Curry)

PREP TIME: ABOUT 15 MIN	COOK TIME: 40 MIN	YIELD: 3–4 SERVINGS

INGREDIENTS

1 cup plain full-fat Greek yogurt

½ cup gram flour

1 teaspoon salt, divided

2 tablespoons vegetable oil

1 teaspoon cumin seeds

½ teaspoon fenugreek seeds

6 cloves

1 large pinch asafetida

1 medium onion, finely diced

1 teaspoon Ginger-Garlic Paste (see Chapter 6)

2 green chilies, finely chopped

1 teaspoon turmeric

½ cup mixed vegetables (carrots, green beans, peas), finely diced

1 tablespoon ghee or oil

½ teaspoon Kashmiri chile powder

4 to 5 stalks of cilantro, chopped, for garnish

DIRECTIONS

1 In a bowl, whisk the yogurt with the gram flour, ½ teaspoon of the salt, and 1¼ cups cold water, making sure there are no lumps (pass through a sieve to be sure). Set aside.

2 In a saucepan, warm the oil over high heat. Add the cumin, fenugreek, cloves, and asafetida. When the seeds go a couple of shades darker, add the onion and cook until it starts to turn golden, about 3 to 4 minutes. Add the Ginger-Garlic Paste and chilies, and cook for 1 minute.

3 Tip in the turmeric and mixed vegetables, season with the remaining ½ teaspoon of salt, and pour in 1 cup of water. Bring to a boil. Then reduce the heat to low and simmer, covered, until the vegetables are soft, about 10 minutes.

4 Give the yogurt mixture from Step 1 a good stir, and pour it into the pan. Bring to a boil, reduce the heat, and cook for 8 to 10 minutes, stirring frequently, until it reaches the consistency of a thick batter and the raw flour aroma has gone. Remove from the heat and set aside.

5 In a small pan, heat the ghee or oil. Add the chile powder. As soon as it sizzles, pour it over the curry — don't stir it in. Garnish with cilantro and serve.

TIP: Serve with rice, store-bought mango or lime pickle, and a popadam.

Mung Usal (Sprouted Mung Beans with Turmeric)

PREP TIME: ABOUT 15 MINUTES PLUS 2 DAYS FOR SPROUTING	COOK TIME: 20 MIN	YIELD: 3–4 SERVINGS

INGREDIENTS

¾ cup mung beans

1 tablespoon vegetable oil

1 teaspoon cumin seeds

2 green chilies slit lengthways, seeds left in

1 medium onion, finely chopped

1 teaspoon turmeric

Salt to taste

2 tablespoons freshly grated coconut or desiccated coconut, for garnish

4 to 5 stalks cilantro, chopped, for garnish

1 tablespoon lemon juice

DIRECTIONS

1 In a bowl, soak the beans in hot water at room temperature for at least 4 hours. Drain them in a sieve. Then tie the drained beans in cheesecloth. Put the beans in a dark place to sprout. Rinse them every day (still in the cheesecloth), or a couple of times per day in very hot weather, and put them back in their draining position. In a couple of days, they'll begin to sprout. As soon as little white shoots appear, they're ready to be cooked. The shoots will grow longer with each day and poke through the cheesecloth. Cook them after no more than 4 days of sprouting (they can go moldy).

2 Refresh the sprouted beans in cold water and set aside.

(continued)

3 In a frying pan, warm the oil over high heat. Add the cumin seeds. When they go a couple of shades darker, add the chilies and onion, and fry until the onion starts to turn golden, about 3 to 4 minutes. Reduce the heat to medium and cook until soft, about 7 to 8 minutes.

4 Turn the heat to high, and add the sprouted beans, turmeric, and salt. Add about ¼ cup of water and bring to a boil. Reduce the heat to low, cover, and cook until the beans are soft but firm, about 10 minutes, adding more water if the pan dries out. The final dish should be dry. Sprinkle the coconut and cilantro on top and drizzle with lemon juice.

TIP: Serve with Chapati or Roti (Flatbread; see Chapter 19), store-bought mango or lime pickle, and some plain Greek yogurt.

NOTE: Beans take different amounts of time to sprout depending on a variety of factors, such as temperature, light, moisture, and the container used.

TIP: Try sprouting other legumes such as brown lentils and black chickpeas. You can swap them in this recipe, use them cooked in salads, or add them to curries to ramp up the nutritional value. To make the process a bit easier, you can buy a *sprouting jar* (a Mason jar with a sprouting lid that allows the shoots to grow through while keeping the beans drained).

Chapter **16**

Exotic Egg Dishes

RECIPES IN THIS CHAPTER

🍳 **Baida Masala (North Indian Egg Curry)**

🍳 **Egg Kurma (South Indian Egg Curry)**

🍳 **Bombay Anda Curry (Smooth Egg and Tomato Curry)**

🍳 **Kerala Egg Roast (Egg and Curry Leaf Curry)**

🍳 **Shahi Baida Korma (Egg Curry with Cashew Nuts and Fenugreek)**

🍳 **Papeta Par Eeda (Egg and Potato Fry)**

🍳 **Anda Mutter ki Hari Curry (Egg and Peas Green Curry)**

E gg curries are really popular in Indian homes, so I don't know why they don't often appear on restaurant menus. I include egg curries on the menu of some of my cookery classes, and people not of Indian origin are always surprised to see them.

TIP

You'll usually need to hard-boil eggs before adding them to curries. Even if you prefer your yolks runny, they would just look messy in a masala sauce. Place the eggs in enough boiling hot water to submerge them, and bring the water back to a boil. (Make sure that you don't crowd the pan, or they won't cook evenly.) Reduce the heat to a simmer, cover, and cook for 12 minutes. Turn off the heat, and plunge the eggs into very cold water to stop them from cooking further (and to prevent dark rings around the yolks). Let them steep for around 15 minutes, refreshing the water to keep it cold. (You'll be able to peel them more neatly if they're cold all the way through.) Crack the larger end first — this is where the air pocket is, so releasing that air pocket may help to peel away the shell more easily. I find them a bit easier to peel under a lightly running cold tap; it also gets rid of any small bits of shell that I don't want in my curry.

If you need to break eggs for a recipe like the Papeta Par Eeda, it's safer to break the eggs into a small bowl rather than directly into the pan. That way, if an egg isn't quite right, you won't end up having to throw away the entire dish.

Baida Masala (North Indian Egg Curry)

INGREDIENTS

3 tablespoons vegetable oil

2 dried or fresh bay leaves

5 green cardamom, seeds crushed (discard husks)

3 brown onions, diced finely

3 teaspoons Ginger-Garlic Paste (see Chapter 6)

1 teaspoon dried fenugreek leaves (kasuri methi), crumbled between your fingers

2 teaspoons garam masala

1 teaspoon turmeric

1 teaspoon Kashmiri chile powder

2 teaspoons ground coriander

Half of 15-ounce can tomatoes

Salt to taste

Pinch of caster sugar

8 hard-boiled eggs, peeled and halved lengthwise

Several stalks of fresh cilantro, chopped finely, for garnish

DIRECTIONS

1 In a frying pan, warm the oil over high heat. Add the bay leaves and cardamom; fry for a couple of minutes until an aroma develops. Add the onions, and fry until the onions turn light golden. Lower the heat to medium and cook, stirring intermittently, until the onions are very soft, about 8 to 10 minutes.

2 Turn up the heat, and add the Ginger-Garlic Paste. Fry for 30 seconds, and then tip in the fenugreek leaves, garam masala, turmeric, chile powder, and coriander; fry until an aroma develops. Add a splash of cold water to cool down the pan. Continue cooking over high heat until the water evaporates and the oil begins to separate at the edges.

3 Pour in the tomatoes, season with salt, add the sugar, and cook 3 to 4 minutes, lowering the heat when the mixture bubbles. Cook until the sauce is thick and well melded. Add a bit of water if you want more sauce, and heat through.

4 Gently fold the halved boiled eggs into the curry. Cook for 1 minute over high heat to warm up the eggs; then remove from the heat.

5 Sprinkle with fresh cilantro and serve.

TIP: Serve hot with rice or bread. Add a vegetable side dish to complete the meal.

Egg Kurma (South Indian Egg Curry)

PREP TIME: 15 MIN | COOK TIME: 40 MIN | YIELD: 3 TO 4 SERVINGS

INGREDIENTS

3 tablespoons vegetable oil, divided

1 teaspoon fennel seeds

One 1-inch stick of cinnamon, broken into small bits

2 yellow onions, sliced finely

2 teaspoons Ginger-Garlic Paste (see Chapter 6) or 5 cloves of garlic and a 2-inch piece of ginger, peeled and chopped

2 tablespoons desiccated coconut

2 teaspoons garam masala

1 teaspoon turmeric

1 teaspoon Kashmiri chile powder

2 teaspoons ground coriander

Salt to taste

8 hard-boiled eggs, peeled and halved lengthwise

3 or 4 sprigs of fresh mint, leaves only, for garnish

DIRECTIONS

1 In a frying pan, warm 1½ tablespoons of the oil over high heat. Add the fennel seeds and cinnamon, and fry for a couple of minutes, until the seeds begin to darken. Add the onions, and fry until the onions turn light golden. Lower the heat to medium and cook, stirring intermittently, until the onions are very soft, about 8 to 10 minutes.

2 Turn up the heat, add the Ginger–Garlic Paste, and fry for 30 seconds. Stir in the coconut, and cook over medium heat until golden. Transfer this mixture to a blender with enough cold water to cover, and blitz to a fine puree to make the masala base sauce.

3 Wipe the pan, and warm the remaining 1½ tablespoons of oil. Add the garam masala, turmeric, chile powder, and coriander; fry until an aroma develops. Add a splash of cold water to cool down the pan. Continue cooking over high heat until the water evaporates and the oil begins to separate along the edges.

4 Pour in the masala from the blender. Rinse the blender with 3 or 4 tablespoons of water, and pour this in as well. Season with salt, and cook for 4 or 5 minutes, lowering the heat when the mixture bubbles. Continue cooking until the sauce is thick, about 3 to 4 minutes. Add a bit of water if you want more sauce, and heat through.

5 Gently fold the halved boiled eggs into the curry.

6 Sprinkle with the fresh mint, and serve.

TIP: Serve hot with rice or bread.

VARY IT! Add a bit of coconut milk if you want a richer curry or some cooked vegetables if you want a heartier one.

Bombay Anda Curry (Smooth Egg and Tomato Curry)

PREP TIME: 15 MIN	COOK TIME: 30 MIN	YIELD: 3 TO 4 SERVINGS

INGREDIENTS

3 tablespoons vegetable oil, divided

1 teaspoon cumin seeds

2 yellow onions, sliced finely

2 teaspoons Ginger-Garlic Paste (see Chapter 6) or 5 cloves of garlic and a 1-inch piece of ginger, peeled and chopped

3 fresh tomatoes, chopped finely, seeds and all

3 or 4 sprigs of fresh cilantro, chopped

1 teaspoon garam masala

1 teaspoon turmeric

1 teaspoon Kashmiri chile powder

2 teaspoons ground coriander

2 tablespoons coconut milk, any cream or whole milk (optional)

Salt to taste

8 hard-boiled eggs, peeled and halved lengthwise

DIRECTIONS

1   In a frying pan, warm 1½ tablespoons of the oil over high heat. Fry the cumin seeds until they begin to darken; then add the onions. Fry until the onions turn light golden; then lower the heat to medium and cook, stirring intermittently, until very soft, about 8 to 10 minutes.

2   Turn up the heat, and add the Ginger–Garlic Paste. Fry for 30 seconds; then stir in the tomatoes. Cook until very soft, turning the heat down if they begin to stick. Turn off the heat, and fold in the cilantro, reserving a pinch for garnish.

3   Put this mixture in a blender with enough cold water to cover, and blitz to a fine puree to make the masala base sauce.

4   Wipe the pan and warm the remaining 1½ tablespoons of oil over high heat. Add the garam masala, turmeric, chile powder, and coriander. Fry until they sizzle and darken; then add a splash of cold water. Continue cooking over high heat until the water evaporates and the oil begins to separate along the edges.

5   Pour in the masala from the blender. Rinse the blender with 3 to 4 tablespoons of water, and add this to the pan as well. Season with the salt, and cook for 4 to 5 minutes, lowering the heat when the mixture bubbles. Fold in the coconut milk, cream, or milk, if using.

6   Gently fold the halved boiled eggs into the curry. Sprinkle with the reserved cilantro, and serve.

TIP: Serve hot with rice or bread.

Kerala Egg Roast (Egg and Curry Leaf Curry)

PREP TIME: 15 MIN	COOK TIME: 40 MIN	YIELD: 3 TO 4 SERVINGS

INGREDIENTS

2 tablespoons vegetable or coconut oil

1 teaspoon black mustard seeds

1 teaspoon fennel seeds

2 brown onions, diced finely

2 teaspoons Ginger-Garlic Paste (see Chapter 6)

15 fresh curry leaves or 3 large pinches of dried curry leaves

1 teaspoon turmeric

½ teaspoon crushed black pepper

1 teaspoon Kashmiri chile powder

2 teaspoons ground coriander

2 fresh large tomatoes, chopped finely, seeds included

3 or 4 sprigs of fresh cilantro, chopped

Salt to taste

9 hard-boiled eggs, 8 peeled and halved lengthwise, 1 peeled and chopped finely

DIRECTIONS

1 In a frying pan, warm the oil over high heat. Fry the mustard seeds until they pop. Reduce the heat to medium, add the fennel seeds, and fry until they sizzle. Add the onions, and fry over high heat until they turn light golden, about 3 to 4 minutes. Then lower the heat to medium and cook, stirring intermittently, until the onions are very soft, about 8 to 10 minutes.

2 Turn up the heat to high, add the Ginger–Garlic Paste and curry leaves, and fry for 30 seconds.

3 Add the turmeric, pepper, chile powder, and coriander, and cook for 1 minute. Pour in ¼ cup of cold water, mix, and allow the water to evaporate.

4 Stir in the tomatoes, and cook until very soft, about 3 to 4 minutes, stirring intermittently. Fold in the cilantro, reserving a pinch for garnish.

5 Fold the chopped egg into the curry, and then fold in the halved eggs. Sprinkle with the reserved cilantro and serve.

TIP: Serve hot with Chapati or Roti (Flatbread; see Chapter 19) or Paratha (Layered Bread; see Chapter 19).

Shahi Baida Korma (Egg Curry with Cashew Nuts and Fenugreek)

PREP TIME: 15 MIN	COOK TIME: 45 MIN	YIELD: 3 TO 4 SERVINGS

INGREDIENTS

2 green chilies, roughly chopped with the seeds, stalks discarded

2 yellow onions, diced finely

3 tablespoons cashew nuts

2 tablespoons vegetable oil or ghee, divided

2 teaspoons Ginger-Garlic Paste (see Chapter 6)

1 teaspoon garam masala

1 teaspoon ground cumin

1 teaspoon ground coriander

½ teaspoon dried fenugreek leaves (kasuri methi)

Salt to taste

2 tablespoons light or heavy cream or 4 tablespoons coconut milk

8 hard-boiled eggs, peeled and halved lengthwise

1 teaspoon mixed raisins

1 teaspoon pistachios

1 teaspoon cranberries

DIRECTIONS

1 In a saucepan, place the chilies, onions, and cashew nuts and cover with enough water to cover; bring to a boil. Reduce the heat and simmer, covered, for 15 minutes.

2 Cool the mixture slightly and puree in a blender along with the cooking liquid to make the masala base sauce.

3 In a frying pan, heat 1 tablespoon of the oil or ghee over high heat. Add the Ginger–Garlic Paste, and fry for 30 seconds. Stir in the garam masala, cumin, coriander, and fenugreek; fry until they sizzle and darken. Add a splash of cold water. Continue cooking over high heat until the water evaporates and the oil begins to separate along the edges.

4 Pour in the masala from the blender. Rinse the blender with 2 to 3 tablespoons of water, and add this to the pan as well. Season with salt, and cook for 4 or 5 minutes, lowering the heat when the mixture bubbles. Fold in the cream or coconut milk.

5 Gently fold the eggs into the curry.

6 Rinse the saucepan from Step 1. Add the remaining 1 tablespoon of oil or ghee to the saucepan and warm over high heat. Fry the raisins, pistachios, and cranberries until they're just sizzling; pour on top of the curry. Serve.

TIP: Serve with rice or bread and a colorful vegetable side dish like Kaddu ki Subzi (Sweet-and-Sour Pumpkin; see Chapter 13).

Papeta Par Eeda (Egg and Potato Fry)

PREP TIME: 15 MIN	COOK TIME: 35 MIN	YIELD: 2 SERVINGS

INGREDIENTS

2 tablespoons vegetable oil

1 teaspoon cumin seeds

2 yellow onions, diced finely

2 teaspoons Ginger-Garlic Paste (see Chapter 6)

2 green chilies, diced with the seeds

2 medium potatoes, peeled and chopped into ¾-inch cubes

2 teaspoons garam masala

1 teaspoon turmeric

1 teaspoon Kashmiri chile powder

2 teaspoons ground coriander

3 fresh large tomatoes, diced, seeds included

1 tablespoon tomato paste

Salt to taste

4 large eggs

Several stalks of fresh cilantro, chopped finely, for garnish

DIRECTIONS

1 In a frying pan that you can take to the table, warm the oil over high heat. Add the cumin seeds, and fry until they darken. Add the onions, and fry until they turn light golden. Then lower the heat to medium and cook, stirring intermittently, for 3 to 4 minutes.

2 Turn up the heat, add the Ginger-Garlic Paste and chilies, and fry for 30 seconds. Then tip in the potatoes, and fry until they begin to turn golden. Add the garam masala, turmeric, chile powder, and coriander.

3 Add 4 to 5 tablespoons cold water and bring to a boil. Add the tomatoes and tomato paste. Season with salt. Reduce the heat when the tomatoes start to break down and cook until the potatoes are cooked, about 10 minutes.

4 Break the eggs into a bowl and pour over the potatoes. Sprinkle salt over them. Cover the pan and cook over high heat until the eggs are set but the yolks are still a bit runny, about 3 to 4 minutes.

5 Sprinkle with fresh cilantro and serve.

TIP: Serve hot in the pan, with Paratha (Layered Bread; see Chapter 19).

NOTE: This recipe comes from the Parsi community who migrated to India hundreds of years ago from Iran, bringing with them, a distinct and delicious cuisine.

Anda Mutter ki Hari Curry (Egg and Peas Green Curry)

PREP TIME: 15 MIN	COOK TIME: 40 MIN	YIELD: 3–4 SERVINGS

INGREDIENTS

2 large handfuls of fresh cilantro leaves and stems, washed and chopped

2 large handfuls of fresh mint leaves, washed and chopped (no stems)

2 green chilies, roughly diced with the seeds, stalks discarded

3 tablespoons Ginger-Garlic Paste (see Chapter 6), divided

1 large onion, chopped into large chunks

One 13½-ounce can of coconut milk, divided

3 tablespoons vegetable oil

2 yellow onions, diced finely

2 teaspoons garam masala

1 teaspoon turmeric

2 teaspoons ground coriander

½ cup frozen peas

Salt to taste

8 hard-boiled eggs, peeled and left whole, with light gashes made all over them

Juice of ½ lemon

DIRECTIONS

1 In a blender, add the cilantro, mint, chilies, 2 tablespoons of the Ginger-Garlic Paste, onion, half of the can of coconut milk, and ¼ cup of water, and blitz until smooth. Reserve the remaining coconut milk for the curry.

2 In a frying pan, heat the oil over high heat. Add the onions, and fry until they turn light golden. Lower the heat to medium and cook, stirring intermittently, until the onions are very soft, about 8 to 10 minutes.

3 Turn up the heat to high, add the remaining 1 tablespoon of Ginger-Garlic Paste, and fry for 30 seconds. Stir in the garam masala, turmeric, and coriander, and fry until an aroma develops. Add 4 to 5 tablespoons cold water to cool down the pan. Continue cooking over high heat until the water evaporates and the oil begins to separate along the edges.

4 Pour in the herby masala from the blender. Rinse the blender with 2 to 3 tablespoons of water, and pour this in to the pan as well. Add the peas, season with salt, and cook for 4 to 5 minutes, lowering the heat when the mixture bubbles. Cook until the sauce is thick, adding more coconut milk as necessary.

5 Gently fold the eggs into the curry. Mix in the lemon juice, and serve.

TIP: Serve hot with rice or bread.

4

Whipping Up Breads, Chutneys, and Tasty Treats

Start your day with an Indian breakfast.

Plan the perfect party with easy appetizers and snacks.

Get out your rolling pin and learn the secret of Indian bread making.

Jazz up your Indian meal with colorful salads and tasty chutneys

Satisfy your sweet tooth with fresh desserts and drinks.

Chapter **17**

Dishes to Start the Day

RECIPES IN THIS CHAPTER

- Masala Omelet (Omelet with Spices)
- Upma (Savory Semolina Cake)
- Chile Toast (Cheese Toast with Spices)
- Baida Bhurji (Spicy Scrambled Eggs)
- Rava Utappam (Semolina Pancakes)
- Dosa (Fermented Rice and Lentil Crêpes)
- Poha (Spiced Flaked Rice)
- Batata Bhaji (Spiced Yellow Potatoes)
- Aam aur Kaju ki Smoothie (Mango and Cashew Smoothie)

In India, breakfast has always been an important meal. Breakfast foods vary from region to region, depending on what grows there. People generally wake early and always find time to eat a hearty meal before they leave home. The Indian kitchen begins with the making of tea or coffee. In larger cities, people leave for work after a breakfast of toast and eggs, but in smaller towns, you'll find a hot regional breakfast on the table. In the south, this could be fermented lentil and rice pancakes, called *dosa,* while in the west it could be easy-to-cook, spiced flaked rice called *poha.*

These dishes are served as teatime snacks as well, just as you might have a piece of toast for breakfast or as a midafternoon snack at the weekend. Don't be surprised that so many of the recipes have a good amount of spice (first thing in the morning!) — it just makes everything more delicious.

In this chapter, I show you how to jazz up your eggs with chilies and cilantro; make a soft, savory semolina cake with curry leaves; and ferment batter to make the lightest pancakes. You'll see how easy it is to add spices to your smoothies, too!

Masala Omelet (Omelet with Spices)

PREP TIME: ABOUT 10 MIN	COOK TIME: 12 MIN	YIELD: 1 SERVING

INGREDIENTS

2 large eggs

Salt to taste

Pepper to taste

½ teaspoon turmeric

1 tablespoon vegetable oil

½ teaspoon cumin seeds

1 small onion, diced finely

1 or 2 green chilies, (depending on how hot you want it to be), diced finely, seeds and all

1 tomato chopped with the seeds and skin

2 or 3 stalks cilantro, chopped finely

DIRECTIONS

1 In a bowl, place the eggs, salt, pepper, and turmeric. Beat together. Set aside.

2 In a frying pan, warm the oil over high heat and fry the cumin seeds. When they turn a couple of shades darker, add the onion and chilies. Cook until the onion begins to turn golden, about 2 to 3 minutes. Reduce the heat to medium and cook until soft, about 3 to 4 minutes.

3 Stir in the tomato and cook 2 to 3 minutes.

4 Pour in the beaten eggs and spread them to evenly coat the onion and tomato mixture in the pan. Sprinkle in the cilantro. Cook covered, over low heat, until the eggs set into an omelet, about 5 minutes. Serve.

TIP: Serve with toast, ketchup (a beloved condiment in India!), and Masala Chai (Spiced Tea; see Chapter 21).

NOTE: Omelets can be served flat or folded, depending on how heavy they become with the addition of onion and tomato and whether folding will break the omelet.

Upma (Savory Semolina Cake)

PREP TIME: ABOUT 15 MIN | COOK TIME: 10 MIN | YIELD: 3–4 SERVINGS

INGREDIENTS

2½ cups water

1 cup coarse semolina

2 tablespoons vegetable oil

1 teaspoon black mustard seeds

1 teaspoon cumin seeds

1 onion, diced finely

2 green chilies, slit lengthwise, leaving the stalks intact

10 fresh curry leaves or 3 pinches dried curry leaves

1 large pinch asafetida

1 tablespoon roasted, salted cashew nuts

4 tablespoons frozen green peas

1 tomato, diced

1 teaspoon sugar

Salt to taste

4 to 5 stalks cilantro, finely chopped

2 tablespoons lemon juice

3 tablespoons Chivda (Hot, Savory, and Sweet Mix of Grains, Seeds, and Nuts; see Chapter 18) or salted potato chips (optional)

DIRECTIONS

1 In a pot or kettle, bring the water to a boil.

2 In the meantime, dry-roast the semolina in a large frying pan over medium heat until it starts to turn slightly brown on the bottom, about 5 minutes. Keep stirring so that it goes a couple of shades darker evenly. Tip into a bowl and set aside.

3 Pour the oil into the same pan and add the mustard seeds. Turn the heat to high. As the oil heats, the seeds will pop. Add the cumin seeds, and fry for 10 seconds. Add the onion, chilies, curry leaves, and asafetida. Cook until the onion starts to soften, about 3 to 4 minutes. Add the cashew nuts and cook for 2 to 3 minutes more.

4 Add the peas and tomato, and cook over high heat, until the tomato softens, about 2 minutes. Add the semolina, sugar, and salt. Standing away from the pan, stir in the hot water. (This will make the semolina bubble out of the pan, so be careful!)

5 Reduce the heat to low and simmer until all the water has been absorbed and the semolina gets a dough-like texture, about 3 to 4 minutes.

6 Loosen with a fork and serve hot, sprinkled with cilantro, lemon juice, and the Chivda or potato chips if using.

Chile Toast (Cheese Toast with Spices)

INGREDIENTS

½ cup grated mature cheddar cheese or similar

2 scallions, diced finely

2 green chilies, diced finely

Salt to taste

Pepper to taste

4 slices white or wheat bread

Butter to spread

1 clove garlic, grated (optional)

Ketchup, to serve

DIRECTIONS

1 In a bowl, mix the cheese, scallions, and chilies. Season with a big pinch of salt and plenty of pepper.

2 Toast the slices of bread lightly in a toaster. Spread one side with butter and some grated garlic if using.

3 Divide the cheese mixture into four parts, and spread each part evenly over the buttered side of the bread. Place under a broiler on high until bubbly and golden, about 3 to 4 minutes. Serve with ketchup.

Baida Bhurji (Spicy Scrambled Eggs)

PREP TIME: ABOUT 10 MIN | COOK TIME: 10 MIN | YIELD: 2 SERVINGS

INGREDIENTS

4 large eggs

Salt to taste

Pepper to taste

1 tablespoon vegetable oil

½ teaspoon cumin seeds

1 large onion, finely diced

1 teaspoon Ginger-Garlic Paste (see Chapter 6)

1 or 2 green chilies, finely diced (depending on how hot you want it)

2 tomatoes, diced finely

½ teaspoon turmeric

½ teaspoon ground coriander

½ teaspoon garam masala

4 to 5 stalks of cilantro, chopped, divided

DIRECTIONS

1 In a bowl, beat the eggs and season with salt and pepper. Set aside.

2 In a frying pan, heat the oil over high heat and add the cumin seeds. Fry the seeds until they go a couple of shades darker, about 1 minute. Add the onion and fry until it starts to soften, about 3 to 4 minutes. Then turn the heat down to low and cook until very soft, about 7 to 8 minutes.

3 Stir in the Ginger–Garlic Paste and chilies, turn the heat up to high, and cook for 1 minute. Tip in the tomatoes, turmeric, coriander, and garam masala, and cook for 1 minute. Add a splash of water and cook this off.

4 Lower the heat to medium, add in half the cilantro and pour in the eggs. Scramble the eggs quickly before they set completely. Cook until you get the consistency you desire (I prefer to keep mine quite soft and runny).

5 Turn off the heat and tip the eggs onto a plate. Garnish with the remaining cilantro and serve.

TIP: Serve with bread or Chapati or Roti (Flatbread; see Chapter 19).

Rava Utappam (Semolina Pancakes)

PREP TIME: ABOUT 15 MIN PLUS 15 MIN FOR SOAKING	COOK TIME: 15 MIN	YIELD: 3–4 SERVINGS

INGREDIENTS

1 cup coarse semolina

2 tablespoons all-purpose flour

¼ cup plain full-fat Greek yogurt, plus more to serve

¼ teaspoon turmeric

Salt to taste, divided

1 tablespoon vegetable oil, plus extra for shallow-frying

2 onions, diced finely

2 green chilies, diced finely

1 tomato, diced

3 to 4 stalks cilantro, chopped

1 pinch white sugar

2 tablespoons lemon juice

DIRECTIONS

1 In a mixing bowl, combine the semolina, flour, yogurt, turmeric, and salt. Pour in enough cold water to make a batter of pouring consistency, almost like thick cream. Leave for 15 minutes to allow the semolina to soften.

2 In the meantime, make the topping. In a frying pan, heat the 1 tablespoon of oil and fry the onions until they begin to soften, about 3 to 4 minutes. Lower the heat and cook until very soft, another 7 to 8 minutes. Add the chilies; wait a few seconds, and add the tomato and cilantro. Add the salt, sugar, and lemon juice, and cook until soft, about 3 to 4 minutes. Set aside.

3 Check the semolina mixture. If it has thickened, add about 2 tablespoons water to loosen the mixture back to a loose, dough–like consistency.

4 Heat a nonstick frying pan. Lower the heat to medium, pour in 1 tablespoon of batter, and pat it gently with the back of a spoon to flatten it into a thin disc, about 2 inches in diameter. Turn up the heat and drizzle the edges with oil. Cover the pan and allow the pancake to cook in its steam. Depending on the size of your pan, you can cook 2 to 3 pancakes at a time.

5 Flip the pancake over when the underside has turned golden and spotty. Cook the other side by dotting the edges with some oil and covering the pan. Take off the heat and keep warm while you cook the rest of the pancakes.

6 Pile some of the topping on each pancake and serve with yogurt.

Dosa (Fermented Rice and Lentil Crêpes)

PREP TIME: ABOUT 10 MIN PLUS 5 HR SOAKING TIME PLUS 12–18 HR FERMENTING TIME	COOK TIME: 15 MIN	YIELD: 3–4 SERVINGS

INGREDIENTS

1 cup basmati rice, washed and drained

½ teaspoon fenugreek seeds

½ cup split skinless black lentils, washed and drained

3 tablespoons Indian flaked rice (poha)

Salt to taste

Vegetable oil to drizzle

DIRECTIONS

1 In a bowl, soak the rice, fenugreek seeds, and lentils in 4½ cups of water. Leave for a minimum of 5 hours, but overnight if you can.

2 After the rice and lentils have finished soaking, in a separate bowl soak the flaked rice for 30 minutes in 1 cup of cold water. Drain away the water from the rice, lentils, fenugreek seeds, and flaked rice and put them all into a blender. Add enough cold water to just cover the mixture, and blitz to the consistency of a thick, pouring cream.

3 Pour the batter into a glass bowl, and stir. Cover and leave to ferment in a warm place for 12 hours. When the batter becomes a bit bubbly, add 4 to 5 pinches of salt to season.

4 In a nonstick frying pan, warm 1 teaspoon of oil over high heat. Turn the heat to low and pour a ladleful of the batter into the center of the pan. Spread the mixture quickly but gently with the back of the ladle, making a thin disc.

(continued)

5 Turn up the heat to high to make the edges crisp. When the pancake starts to brown on the underside, reduce the heat to low and cook for a few seconds. Turn over the pancake with a spatula, and cook the other side for a few seconds.

6 Continue for the rest of the pancakes. Serve immediately.

TIP: Choose the cheapest rice (see Chapter 4), because it'll just be blended into a batter.

NOTE: Stir the batter in Step 3 using a clean hand to stir rather than a ladle, if you can. This process is said to promote fermentation.

TIP: If the crêpe tears while spreading, either the batter is too thick or the pan is too hot.

TIP: Serve with Sambhar (South Indian Lentil Stew; see Chapter 15), Thengai Chutney (Coconut and Tender Mango Chutney; see Chapter 20), and Batata Bhaji (Spiced Yellow Potatoes; later in this chapter) if desired.

Poha (Spiced Flaked Rice)

PREP TIME: ABOUT 10 MIN PLUS 5 MIN FOR REHYDRATING	COOK TIME: 15 MIN	YIELD: 3–4 SERVINGS

INGREDIENTS

1 cup Indian flaked rice (poha)

1 teaspoon turmeric

1 teaspoon sugar

2 tablespoons vegetable oil

½ teaspoon cumin seeds

1 large pinch asafetida

2 green chilies, slit down the middle

1 onion, diced finely

1 large potato, peeled and cut into ½-inch cubes

1 tomato, diced

2 tablespoons roasted peanuts (optional)

Salt to taste

2 teaspoons lemon juice

4 to 5 stalks cilantro, chopped, for garnish

DIRECTIONS

1 Put the flaked rice in a sieve, and wash under a running tap for 30 seconds. Leave to rehydrate for 5 minutes so it can absorb any residual water and soften.

2 Sprinkle the rehydrated rice with turmeric and sugar while still in the sieve.

3 In a frying pan, warm the oil over high heat and add the cumin seeds. When they turn a couple of shades darker, add the asafetida and chilies.

4 When the chilies sizzle, add the onion and fry for 2 to 3 minutes. Add the potato, and fry for 1 minute. Then stir in the tomato and peanuts (if using). Season with salt, add a splash of water, and cook for 2 minutes. Turn the heat down to medium, cover, and cook until the potatoes are soft, about 6 to 7 minutes. Mix in the flaked rice, and turn the heat up to high. Add about ¼ cup water and cook 3 to 4 minutes, stirring regularly so that the flakes don't stick to the bottom of the pan. Drizzle in the lemon juice.

5 Garnish with the cilantro and serve hot.

TIP: See Chapter 4 for more on the type of rice to buy.

Batata Bhaji (Spiced Yellow Potatoes)

PREP TIME: ABOUT 10 MIN	COOK TIME: 45 MIN	YIELD: 3–4 SERVINGS

INGREDIENTS

2 large potatoes, boiled, peeled, and roughly chopped

2 tablespoons vegetable oil

1 teaspoon black mustard seeds

1 teaspoon cumin seeds

1 large pinch asafetida

1 onion, finely diced

2 to 3 green chilies, finely diced

1 teaspoon turmeric

4 to 5 stalks cilantro, chopped, divided

Salt to taste

DIRECTIONS

1 In a large pan, place the potatoes; add enough hot water to completely cover them. Bring to a boil over high heat. Turn down the heat to medium, cover the pan, and cook until they're cooked and a knife pierced into them goes through easily, about 30 minutes.

2 In a frying pan, warm the oil over high heat and add the mustard seeds. When they crackle, add the cumin seeds and the asafetida. Cook for a few seconds until the seeds go a couple shades darker. Then tip in the onion and fry until it begins to soften, about 3 to 4 minutes. Turn down the heat to medium and cook until very soft, about 6 to 7 minutes. Add the chilies, and fry for a few seconds. Sprinkle in the turmeric, and cook for 10 seconds.

3 Add the potatoes, half the cilantro, and the salt. Cook for 2 minutes, mashing some of the potatoes as you go. Remove from the heat, sprinkle with the remaining cilantro, and serve.

TIP: Folding these potatoes into Dosa (Fermented Rice and Lentil Crêpes; earlier in this chapter) will make it a Masala Dosa. Enjoy these also with fried bread called Poori (Festive Fried Bread; see Chapter 19) or in a grilled sandwich.

Aam aur Kaju ki Smoothie (Mango and Cashew Smoothie)

PREP TIME: ABOUT 10 MIN	COOK TIME: NONE	YIELD: 3–4 SERVINGS

INGREDIENTS

2 cups chopped mango (fresh or frozen chunks)

1 cup cashew milk

3 green cardamom, seeds crushed, husks discarded

½ teaspoon ground cinnamon

2 tablespoons rolled oats

Honey to taste

1 teaspoon crushed pistachios, for garnish

DIRECTIONS

1 In a blender, put the mango, cashew milk, cardamom, cinnamon, and oats, and blend to a fine puree.

2 Sweeten with honey and pour into 3 or 4 cups. Garnish with the pistachios, and serve cold.

TIP: If using fresh mangoes, choose ripe, fragrant ones.

VARY IT! You can throw in other fruit, too; try bananas or berries. Thicken up your smoothie with a couple tablespoons of Greek yogurt or cashew yogurt, if you like a thicker consistency.

Chapter **18**

Tasty Snacks and Appetizers

RECIPES IN THIS CHAPTER

- Onion Bhajia (Savory Onion Fritters)
- Pakora (Savory Mixed Vegetable Fritters)
- Chicken Tikka (Spicy Chicken Bites)
- Gosht ke Kebab (Mini Lamb or Beef Skewers with Mint)
- Vegetable Samosas (Vegetable and Pastry Parcels)
- Shankarpali (Crisp, Sweet Pastry Diamonds)
- Chivda (Hot, Savory, and Sweet Mix of Grains, Seeds, and Nuts)
- Dahi Vada (Lentil Fritters in Yogurt)
- Pav Bhaji (Crushed Vegetable Curry with Bread Rolls)
- Bombay Sandwich (Sandwich with Chutney, Vegetables, and Cheese)
- Macchi ke Cutlet (Spiced Fishcakes)
- Shakarkand Chaat (Sweet Potatoes with Nuts and Yogurt)
- Amritsari Fish (Spiced Fish Fingers in a Gram-Flour Crust)

Although serving appetizers before a meal is more of a restaurant thing, you can make plenty at home and serve at parties or when you just want a snack. The distinction between a nibble, a snack, and an appetizer is blurry. Many Indian homes serve these up to guests who arrive at any time of the day (feeding a guest is seen as honoring them).

In this chapter, I show you how to make the prefect homestyle Onion Bhajia (Savory Onion Fritters) that's light and crisp. You'll make Pakora (Savory Mixed Vegetable Fritters), Chicken Tikka (Spicy Chicken Bites), and Gosht ke Kebab (Mini Lamb or Beef Skewers with Mint) — any of these can work as a light lunch. And you'll never have to buy a samosa again because the Vegetable Samosas (Vegetable and Pastry Parcels) in this chapter are so good!

TIP

Many Indian snacks are sprinkled with chaat masala, a store-bought blend of aromatic spices, so you may want to consider buying some to try (see Chapter 4) or make your own (see Chapter 7). Some snacks have a long shelf life and can be stored for weeks.

Onion Bhajia (Savory Onion Fritters)

PREP TIME: ABOUT 10 MIN | COOK TIME: 15 MIN | YIELD: 3–4 SERVINGS

INGREDIENTS

½ teaspoon Kashmiri chile powder

½ teaspoon turmeric

Salt to taste

Pinch ajowan (carom seeds) or cumin seeds

⅓ cup gram flour

2 medium onions, sliced very finely

Vegetable oil for frying

Chaat Masala (Finishing Mix for Sprinkling over Snacks; see Chapter 7) (optional)

DIRECTIONS

1 In a mixing bowl, combine the chile powder, turmeric, salt, ajowan or cumin seeds, and gram flour. Pour in a little water at a time to make a thick batter (you're aiming for the consistency of heavy cream). Mix with a whisk for 1 minute to make sure there are no lumps of flour.

2 In a frying pan, heat enough oil to come up about ½ inch in height. Test the temperature by immersing 1 slice of onion into it; if the onion sizzles, the oil is ready.

3 Mix a few spoons of the onions into the gram-flour mixture, evenly coating the onion with the batter.

4 Take a tablespoon of the mixture, press it on the side of the bowl to remove the excess batter, and place it gently in the oil. Add as many spoonsful as will fit in the pan. When the fritters begin to turn golden, after about 2 to 3 minutes, lower the heat to medium, flip them over, and cook them on the other side until evenly golden, about 4 to 5 minutes. Drain and lift onto a plate lined with paper towel. Fry the rest of the fritters in the same way over medium heat.

5 Sprinkle with Chaat Masala if using, and serve.

TIP: Don't add the onions to the batter all at once — the salt will draw out the juices from the onions, making the batter watery. Add handfuls of the onions as you go. If you find that the bhajia doesn't hold together when you fry it, either the oil is too cold (so heat it up) or the batter is too loose (so add another spoon of gram flour). Reuse the oil for stir-frying onions — it's already onion-flavored!

TIP: Serve with Hari Chutney (Cilantro and Peanut Chutney; see Chapter 20) or Khajur Imli ki Chutney (Sweet-and-Sour Date and Tamarind Chutney; see Chapter 20) as dips.

Pakora (Savory Mixed Vegetable Fritters)

PREP TIME: ABOUT 15 MIN	COOK TIME: 15 MIN	YIELD: 3–4 SERVINGS

INGREDIENTS

½ teaspoon Kashmiri chile powder

1 teaspoon ground coriander

1 teaspoon ground cumin

1 teaspoon Ginger-Garlic Paste (see Chapter 6)

Salt to taste

6 tablespoons gram flour

Vegetable oil for frying

Handful of spinach, chopped

3 to 4 stalks cilantro, chopped

3 tablespoons grated cabbage or cauliflower (or a mix of both)

1 carrot grated

Chaat Masala (Finishing Mix for Sprinkling over Snacks; see Chapter 7) (optional)

DIRECTIONS

1 In a mixing bowl, combine the chile powder, coriander, cumin, Ginger-Garlic Paste, salt, and gram flour. Whisk in a little water at a time to make a thick, lump-free batter (you're aiming for the consistency of thick cream).

2 In a frying pan, add enough oil to come up about ½ inch in height. Warm over high heat. Test the temperature by immersing a piece of vegetable into it; if it sizzles, the oil is ready.

3 In a bowl, combine the spinach, cilantro, cabbage or cauliflower, and carrot. Add a few spoons of the vegetable mixture to the gram-flour mixture.

4 Gather 1 tablespoon of the mixture, press it on the side of the bowl to remove the excess batter, and place it gently in the oil. Add as many fritters as will fit in the pan. When they begin to turn golden, after about 2 to 3 minutes, lower the heat to medium, flip them over, and cook them on the other side until evenly golden, about 4 to 5 minutes. Drain and lift onto a plate lined with paper towel. Fry the rest of the fritters the same way.

5 Sprinkle with Chaat Masala if desired, and serve.

TIP: Add in only a few tablespoons of the vegetable mix to the batter at a time to prevent the batter from becoming runny.

TIP: Serve with Hari Chutney (Cilantro and Peanut Chutney; see Chapter 20) or Khajur Imli ki Chutney (Sweet-and-Sour Date and Tamarind Chutney; see Chapter 20) as dips.

Chicken Tikka (Spicy Chicken Bites)

PREP TIME: ABOUT 15 MIN PLUS 3½ HR OR OVER-NIGHT FOR MARINATING	COOK TIME: 15 MIN	YIELD: 3–4 SERVINGS

INGREDIENTS

1½ teaspoons Kashmiri chile powder, divided

3 teaspoons Ginger-Garlic Paste (see Chapter 6)

2 tablespoons lemon juice

½ teaspoon salt plus more to taste, divided

1 pound chicken breast cut into 1-inch cubes

1 teaspoon ground cumin

1 teaspoon garam masala

2 tablespoons plain full-fat Greek yogurt

2 tablespoons gram flour

2 tablespoons mustard oil or 1 teaspoon yellow mustard mixed with 1 tablespoon vegetable oil

Vegetable oil for drizzling

Chaat Masala (Finishing Mix for Sprinkling over Snacks; see Chapter 7) (optional)

DIRECTIONS

1 Soak 3 bamboo skewers in a bowl of water.

2 In a mixing bowl, combine 1 teaspoon of the chile powder, the Ginger-Garlic Paste, the lemon juice, and ½ teaspoon of the salt. Add the chicken and mix well, rubbing the spices into it. Cover and refrigerate for 30 minutes.

3 In a second mixing bowl, combine the remaining ½ teaspoon chile powder, the cumin, the garam masala, the yogurt, the gram flour, the mustard oil, and salt to taste. Taste the marinade and adjust the seasoning if it's too bland.

4 Take the chicken out of the fridge, and mix in the second marinade. Cover and refrigerate at least 3 hours but overnight if you can.

5 Preheat the oven to 400 degrees. Thread the chicken onto the skewers, making sure to leave gaps between the cubes. Place on the rack of a roasting pan and drizzle with vegetable oil. Bake until they appear a bit charred, about 12 minutes. If they're not charred, broil them under a hot grill for 2 to 3 minutes. Cut open a tikka to make sure it's cooked all the way through.

6 Remove from the skewers, sprinkle with Chaat Masala if desired, and serve.

TIP: Use metal skewers instead of bamboo skewers if those are what you have. (You don't need to soak metal skewers, though.)

TIP: Serve with Pudine aur Pyaz ki Chutney (Mint and Onion Chutney; see Chapter 20).

VARY IT! Grill the chicken if you prefer. Preheat the grill to a high heat and cook the tikka for 3 to 4 minutes on each side. If the chicken sticks when you try to flip it, give it a few more seconds.

Gosht ke Kebab (Mini Lamb or Beef Skewers with Mint)

PREP TIME: ABOUT 20 MIN PLUS 1 HR FOR MARINATING	COOK TIME: 15 MIN	YIELD: 3-4 SERVINGS

INGREDIENTS

1 pound ground lamb or beef (at least 20 percent fat)

1 onion, grated and juice squeezed out

2 teaspoons Ginger-Garlic Paste (see Chapter 6)

3 green chilies, very finely diced

4 to 5 stalks mint, leaves very finely chopped and stalks discarded

1 teaspoon garam masala

½ teaspoon finely crushed pepper

Salt to taste

2 tablespoons vegetable oil

Wedges of lemon to serve

DIRECTIONS

1   In a food processor, put the meat, onion, Ginger-Garlic Paste, chilies, and mint; process until very fine. (The finer you can make it at this stage, the softer the kabobs will be.)

2   Tip the mixture into a bowl. Add the garam masala, pepper, and salt to season. Mix well with clean hands. The warmth of your hands will help to blend the fat and meat with the spices.

3   Place a bowl of cold water on the counter. Lightly dip your hand into the water, and scoop up a lime-size ball of meat. Press the meat onto a skewer in a sausage shape. Press the meat to the skewer to secure it. Each kabob should be 2 inches long and stuck closely to the skewer.

4   Heat the oven to 400 degrees and bake the kabobs on the rack of a roasting pan for 13 to 15 minutes until they're cooked through.

5   In a frying pan, heat the oil over high heat. Remove the kabobs from the skewers gently and pan-fry them for 3 to 4 minutes to brown them a bit. Serve.

TIP: Using a thicker, possibly square, skewer can help the kabob to not fall off while you're forming and cooking it.

TIP: Serve hot with Pudine aur Pyaz ki Chutney (Mint and Onion Chutney; see Chapter 20) and lemon.

Vegetable Samosas (Vegetable and Pastry Parcels)

PREP TIME: ABOUT 20 MIN	COOK TIME: 1 HR	YIELD: 4–5 SERVINGS

INGREDIENTS

2 large potatoes

1¾ cups all-purpose flour, plus extra for dusting

½ teaspoon salt, plus extra to taste

½ teaspoon ajowan (carom seeds) (optional)

3 tablespoons ghee

2 tablespoons vegetable oil, plus extra for deep-frying

1 teaspoon cumin seeds

2 green chilies, finely diced with the seeds

1 teaspoon turmeric

2 tablespoons frozen green peas

2 teaspoons amchur (dried mango powder)

Pepper to taste

DIRECTIONS

1 Put the potatoes to cook in a large saucepan with enough water to cover them on a high heat. When the water boils, reduce the heat to medium and simmer for 40 minutes until they are very soft and cooked through. Drain in a colander and when cool enough to handle, peel and mash them in a bowl.

2 While the potatoes are cooking, make the pastry. In a bowl, combine the flour, salt, and ajowan. In a small saucepan, melt the ghee over high heat and pour into the bowl with the flour. Carefully rub the ghee into the flour with your fingers until you get a breadcrumb texture. Pour in 2 tablespoons of cold water and bring the dough together. Add 1 or 2 tablespoons more if necessary. The dough should be firm and springy to touch. Knead for 3 to 4 minutes; then set aside to rest while you make the filling.

3 In a frying pan, warm 2 tablespoons of the oil over high heat. Add the cumin seeds. When they go a couple of shades darker, add the chilies and turmeric and cook for a few seconds. Add the peas and 2 tablespoons of water and cook for 1 minute over high heat. When the water cooks away, turn off the heat and tip in the potato and amchur. Season with salt and pepper. Divide into 14 equal parts.

4 Divide the dough into 7 equal parts and form into balls. Flatten one of the balls and roll out on a floured surface into a flat disc about 6 inches in diameter. Cut the disc in half. Moisten the side that's a straight line with water. Making sure that the line is closest to you, lift the left edge up to the center of the top arch and press lightly to seal. Then lift the right edge to touch the upper-left edge so that it overlaps the first fold and creates a pocket. Lift the cone up to hold it in one hand and seal the edges, keeping the top of the pocket open. Fill the pocket with one part of the potato mixture. Fold over the open edge and press together to seal. Make 14 samosas similarly (1 round disc will make 2 samosas). Figure 18-1 illustrates this process.

5 In a deep frying pan, heat enough oil to completely submerge the samosas, without letting them sit on the bottom of the pan. Test the temperature of the oil by putting in a pea-size ball of dough. It should rise to the surface in about 5 to 10 seconds. Turn the heat to medium and deep-fry the samosas, a few at a time, for 5 to 6 minutes. Flip halfway through cooking, to fry evenly, until they turn golden brown. Remove with a slotted spoon and transfer to a plate lined with paper towels to drain. Serve.

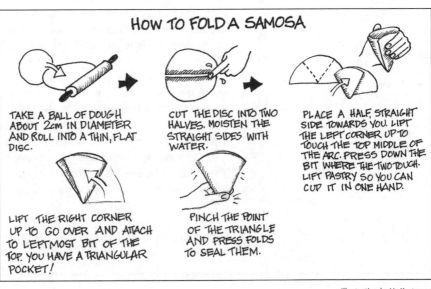

HOW TO FOLD A SAMOSA

TAKE A BALL OF DOUGH ABOUT 2cm IN DIAMETER AND ROLL INTO A THIN, FLAT DISC.

CUT THE DISC INTO TWO HALVES. MOISTEN THE STRAIGHT SIDES WITH WATER.

PLACE A HALF, STRAIGHT SIDE TOWARDS YOU. LIFT THE LEFT CORNER UP TO TOUCH THE TOP MIDDLE OF THE ARC. PRESS DOWN THE BIT WHERE THE TWO TOUCH. LIFT PASTRY SO YOU CAN CUP IT IN ONE HAND.

LIFT THE RIGHT CORNER UP TO GO OVER AND ATTACH TO LEFTMOST BIT OF THE TOP. YOU HAVE A TRIANGULAR POCKET!

PINCH THE POINT OF THE TRIANGLE AND PRESS FOLDS TO SEAL THEM.

FIGURE 18-1: How to fold a samosa.

Illustration by Liz Kurtzman

Shankarpali (Crisp, Sweet Pastry Diamonds)

PREP TIME: ABOUT 20 MIN PLUS 10 MIN FOR RESTING	COOK TIME: 15–20 MIN	YIELD: 5–6 SERVINGS

INGREDIENTS

¼ cup caster sugar

2 tablespoons ghee

¼ cup water

3 green cardamom, seeds crushed and husks discarded

1 cup all-purpose flour

1 tablespoon fine semolina

Pinch of salt

Vegetable oil for deep-frying

DIRECTIONS

1 In a saucepan, mix the sugar, ghee, water, and cardamom and cook over high heat until the sugar dissolves. Let cool until it's just warm.

2 In a mixing bowl, put the flour, semolina, and salt, and gradually pour in the sugar syrup. Knead into a firm, springy dough. Cover and let rest for 10 minutes.

3 Divide the dough into 4 portions. Roll out each portion into a circle about 6 inches in diameter. It should neither be too thin (because it will make the diamonds too hard) nor too thick (because they won't cook through). Run a pizza cutter or knife around the circumference of the circle to neaten the edges for prettier-looking diamonds. Next, run the cutter across the circle horizontally, leaving a gap of about ¾ inch between each line to make long strips. Cut diagonal lines to intersect the strips to make diamond shapes. Lift these onto a plate and proceed similarly with the remaining 3 portions of dough.

4 In a deep frying pan, add enough oil to come up to ½ inch; warm over medium heat. Line a plate with paper towel and have ready. Test the temperature by frying a small piece of the dough; it should sizzle and rise to the top in a few seconds. Fry a few of the diamonds around 2 minutes — make sure they don't brown too quickly before cooking all the way through. They should be golden in color. Lift them out onto the plate with a slotted spoon. Fry the remaining diamonds similarly, in batches.

5 Cool completely and store in an airtight container for up to 3 weeks.

Chivda (Hot, Savory, and Sweet Mix of Grains, Seeds, and Nuts)

PREP TIME: ABOUT 15 MIN	COOK TIME: 10 MIN	YIELD: 5–6 SERVINGS

INGREDIENTS

1 tablespoon vegetable oil

1 teaspoon black mustard seeds

10 fresh curry leaves, finely chopped, or 3 pinches dried curry leaves, crumbled

2 green chilies, diced in ¼-inch pieces with the seeds

½ teaspoon turmeric

2 tablespoons roasted cashew nuts, broken up

2 tablespoons roasted peanuts

2 tablespoons black or green raisins

2 tablespoons sunflower or pumpkin seeds, or a mix of both

2 cups cornflakes

Salt to taste

Pepper to taste

DIRECTIONS

1 In a large frying pan, warm the oil over high heat. Add the mustard seeds. When they begin to pop, add the curry leaves and chilies. Cook for 10 seconds; then stir in the turmeric.

2 Reduce the heat to medium, and add the cashews, peanuts, raisins, and seeds. Fry for 3 to 4 minutes.

3 Add the cornflakes, and season with salt and pepper. Mix well and cook for 2 minutes to combine the flavors. Remove from the heat, cool completely, and store in an airtight container. If stored properly, it should stay crisp for around 2 weeks.

VARY IT! You can add a mix of your favorite nuts and fruit. Try hazelnuts and Brazil nuts with dried cranberries or blueberries.

Dahi Vada (Lentil Fritters in Yogurt)

PREP TIME: ABOUT 15 MIN PLUS 2 HR FOR SOAKING	COOK TIME: 15 MIN	YIELD: 3–4 SERVINGS

INGREDIENTS

½ cup urad lentils (see Chapter 4)

2 green chilies, finely diced with the seeds

Salt to taste

Pepper to taste

Vegetable oil for deep-frying

1 cup plain full-fat Greek yogurt

2 teaspoons caster sugar

1 teaspoon cumin seeds, dry roasted and crushed to a powder (see Chapter 7)

½ teaspoon Kashmiri chile powder

Chaat Masala (Finishing Mix for Sprinkling over Snacks; see Chapter 7) (optional)

Khajur Imli ki Chutney (Sweet-and-Sour Date and Tamarind Chutney; see Chapter 20) (optional)

Hari Chutney (Cilantro and Peanut Chutney; see Chapter 20) (optional)

4 to 5 stalks cilantro, finely chopped

DIRECTIONS

1 Wash the lentils and soak them in 1½ cups of water for at least 2 hours. Drain off the water and blend the lentils in a blender with 4 to 5 tablespoons of fresh water. The result should be a smooth paste with no grains in it. The consistency should be such that the batter drops off a spoon rather than pours off it. (If the batter gets too runny, thicken it with a bit of all-purpose flour.) Scoop into a bowl, add the chilies, and season with salt and pepper.

2 Line a plate with paper towel.

3 In a deep frying pan, add enough oil to come up ½ an inch. Warm over high heat. Test the temperature by putting in a drop of the batter; it should rise to the surface in 4 to 5 seconds. Reduce the heat and gently drop a few tablespoons of batter into the oil. Don't overcrowd the pan. Cook until they set, about 2 to 3 minutes; then flip them over and cook them 4 to 5 minutes on the other side.

4 When the fritters are evenly golden, remove them on a slotted spoon and drain on the plate. Cook the remaining fritters the same way.

5 If you want the fritters to be soft, dip them in a bowl of warm water for 2 to 3 minutes; squeeze them gently to remove the excess moisture. If you prefer a crisp texture, don't soak them.

6 In a separate bowl, mix the yogurt, salt, pepper, sugar, and 4 to 5 tablespoons of cold water. Add the fritters and let them steep for 5 minutes.

7 Dust the top of the yogurt with the cumin, chile powder, and Chaat Masala if desired. Drizzle the chutneys on top if desired. Scatter cilantro over the top and serve cold. Store in the fridge for up to 1 day.

Pav Bhaji (Crushed Vegetable Curry with Bread Rolls)

PREP TIME: ABOUT 20 MIN	COOK TIME: 40 MIN	YIELD: 3–4 SERVINGS

INGREDIENTS

2 tablespoons vegetable oil

1 onion, finely diced

2 teaspoons Ginger–Garlic Paste (see Chapter 6)

2 green chilies, finely diced with the seeds

1 teaspoon turmeric

1 teaspoon ground coriander

1 teaspoon garam masala

3 large tomatoes, finely diced

1 cup mixed raw vegetables, such as carrots and beans (both finely diced) and peas

Salt to taste

½ lemon, squeezed

6 to 8 small dinner rolls, to serve

3 tablespoons salted butter, to serve

Chaat Masala (Finishing Mix for Sprinkling over Snacks; see Chapter 7) (optional)

4 to 5 stalks cilantro, finely chopped

DIRECTIONS

1 In a frying pan, heat the oil over high heat. Add the onion, and fry until it starts to turn golden, about 3 to 4 minutes. Add the Ginger–Garlic Paste and chilies, and fry for 30 seconds.

2 Reduce the heat to medium, and add the turmeric, coriander, and garam masala; cook for 1 minute.

3 Turn up the heat to high, and add ¼ cup water. Let the water cook off. Stir in the tomatoes, and fry for 2 to 3 minutes.

4 Add the mixed vegetables, and season with salt. Add enough water to just cover the vegetables and bring to a boil. Reduce the heat to medium, cover, and cook until the vegetables are very soft, about 25 to 30 minutes. (You can use a pressure cooker or Instant Pot for this if you like; you really want the vegetables to go to a mush.) Sprinkle in the lemon juice. Roughly mash the mixture with a potato masher. Stir in the cilantro, keeping some for garnish.

5 Cut the rolls in half, and spread with butter. Place the buttered side down on a hot frying pan. Fry for until golden, about 1 minute. Put a generous pat of butter on the hot curry, sprinkle the Chaat Masala if using, garnish with the remaining cilantro, and serve with the warm rolls and butter.

TIP: You can sprinkle 1 teaspoon of finely diced onion on top if you want some crunch. And don't skimp on the butter — it's what makes this so delicious!

Bombay Sandwich (Sandwich with Chutney, Vegetables, and Cheese)

| PREP TIME: ABOUT 20 MIN | COOK TIME: NONE | YIELD: 1 SERVING |

INGREDIENTS

2 slices white bread

Salted butter to spread

Hari Chutney (Cilantro and Peanut Chutney; see Chapter 20) or Pudine aur Pyaz ki Chutney (Mint and Onion Chutney; see Chapter 20) to spread

4 to 5 slices peeled cucumber

4 to 5 slices tomato, deseeded

2 to 3 slices beets, peeled (optional)

Ketchup to drizzle

Salt to taste

Pepper to taste

4 pinches Chaat Masala (Finishing Mix for Sprinkling over Snacks; see Chapter 7) (optional)

1 slice mature cheddar cheese

DIRECTIONS

1 Butter one side of each slice of bread.

2 Spread a layer of the cilantro or mint chutney over the butter. Arrange the slices of cucumber, tomato, and beets on top of one slice of bread. Season with salt and pepper.

3 Place the cheese over the vegetables, and sprinkle with Chaat Masala if desired. Drizzle with ketchup.

4 Place the second slice of bread over top to make a sandwich, and toast it in a sandwich toaster or grill pan until the cheese melts, about 2 to 3 minutes. Serve.

Macchi ke Cutlet (Spiced Fishcakes)

PREP TIME: ABOUT 15 MIN | COOK TIME: 20 MIN | YIELD: 4 SERVINGS

INGREDIENTS

Two 5-ounce cans no-salt-added tuna, drained

1 large potato, boiled, peeled, and mashed

Juice of 1 lemon

½ onion, very finely diced

2 teaspoons Ginger-Garlic Paste (see Chapter 6)

1 tablespoon tomato paste

2 green chilies, minced with the seeds

½ teaspoon garam masala

4 to 5 stalks cilantro, finely chopped

½ teaspoon cumin seeds

Salt to taste

Pepper to taste

Vegetable oil, for shallow-frying

2 tablespoons plain flour

DIRECTIONS

1 Squeeze out all the water from the tuna. In a mixing bowl, add the tuna, mashed potato, lemon juice, onion, Ginger-Garlic Paste, tomato paste, chilies, garam masala, and cilantro.

2 Warm a small frying pan over high heat, add the cumin seeds, and dry-toast without oil until they go a couple shades darker. Tip them into a mortar and pestle or spice mill and crush or blend to a fine powder. Add to the bowl and season the mixture with salt and pepper.

3 Shape the mixture into 8 equal-size balls, and flatten. Heat enough oil over high heat to liberally coat the base of a frying pan. Dip each fish cake in the flour, shake off the excess, and shallow-fry 4 to 5 minutes on each side until golden brown, reducing the heat to medium if the cakes brown too quickly.

4 Drain on paper towel and serve.

TIP: Add the salt and pepper just before you're ready to fry the fishcakes, or else the mixture may become too loose to hold together while frying.

TIP: Serve warm with Pudine aur Pyaz ki Chutney (Mint and Onion Chutney; see Chapter 20).

Shakarkand Chaat (Sweet Potatoes with Nuts and Yogurt)

PREP TIME: ABOUT 15 MIN	COOK TIME: 30 MIN	YIELD: 3-4 SERVINGS

INGREDIENTS

2 cups sweet potatoes, peeled and cut into ¾-inch squares

Salt to taste

2 tablespoons vegetable oil

2 cloves garlic, finely grated

2 green chilies, finely diced with the seeds

2 tablespoons roasted, salted peanuts, roughly crushed

½ teaspoon turmeric

4 to 5 stalks cilantro, chopped

½ teaspoon crushed pepper

¼ cup plain full-fat Greek yogurt

Chaat Masala (Finishing Mix for Sprinkling over Snacks; see Chapter 7) (optional)

DIRECTIONS

1   In a saucepan, put the sweet potatoes, cover with water, season with salt, and set to cook over high heat. When the water boils, reduce the heat, cover, and simmer for 15 to 20 minutes until they're just cooked, which means that each cube is cooked through but still holds its shape. Drain and reserve.

2   In a frying pan, add the oil and warm over high heat. Add the garlic and fry until it begins to turn golden, about 2 minutes. Add the chilies and cook for a few seconds. Turn down the heat to medium and add the peanuts and turmeric; cook for 30 seconds, stirring frequently.

3   Add the cooked sweet potato, cilantro (saving a bit for the garnish), and pepper. Mix well and adjust the seasoning as needed.

4   Drizzle with yogurt and sprinkle the remaining cilantro and the Chaat Masala, if desired, over the top. Serve.

Amritsari Fish (Spiced Fish Fingers in a Gram-Flour Crust)

PREP TIME: ABOUT 15 MIN PLUS 20 MIN FOR MARINATING	COOK TIME: 20 MIN	YIELD: 3-4 SERVINGS

INGREDIENTS

12 ounces any white fish cut into fingers or bite-size chunks

2 teaspoons Ginger-Garlic Paste (see Chapter 6)

2 tablespoons lemon juice

Salt to taste

3 tablespoons gram flour

½ teaspoon ajowan (carom seeds), roughly crushed in a mortar and pestle

1 teaspoon Kashmiri chile powder

½ teaspoon turmeric

¼ teaspoon crushed black pepper

Vegetable oil for deep-frying

Chaat Masala (Finishing Mix for Sprinkling over Snacks; see Chapter 7) (optional)

DIRECTIONS

1 In a bowl, combine the fish, Ginger-Garlic Paste, lemon juice, and salt. Marinate the fish for 20 minutes, covered, in the refrigerator.

2 In the meantime, make a thick batter by whisking the gram flour, ajowan, chile powder, turmeric, and enough water to make the consistency resemble a thick cream. Season with salt and pepper.

3 Line a plate with paper towel and have ready.

4 In a frying pan, heat the oil over high heat. Test the temperature by dropping a little batter in; it should sizzle in 3 to 4 seconds. Turn down the heat to medium. Dip a few pieces of fish in the batter and fry until crisp, about 4-5 minutes, stirring them from time to time to make them evenly golden. Drain with a slotted spoon onto the lined plate. Cook the rest of the fish in similar batches, raising the heat before adding a new batch, to maintain the temperature of the oil.

5 Sprinkle with Chaat Masala if desired and serve.

TIP: Serve with Hari Chutney (Cilantro and Peanut Chutney; see Chapter 20) as a dip.

Chapter 19

No-Bake Breads

RECIPES IN THIS CHAPTER

- Chapati or Roti (Flatbread)
- Naan (Leavened Oven-Baked Bread)
- Paratha (Layered Bread)
- Poori (Festive Fried Bread)
- Gobi Paratha (Cauliflower-Stuffed Bread)
- Thepla (Fenugreek Bread)
- Neer Dosa (South Indian Rice Crêpes)
- Chilla (Gram-Flour Pancakes)

The first time a North Indian person asked me if I'd had my "roti," I replied that, on that day, I'd eaten rice. My friend patiently explained that, in the North, that question means "Have you eaten?" Roti or chapati (both refer to the same flatbread) is the most common kind of bread eaten all over India. The North, being the main wheat-growing region, eats more bread, and the South, more rice. Leavened breads, such as naan, are cooked commercially for several reasons: They're traditionally cooked in a tandoor, which you don't see in a home, and Indian kitchens don't have Western-style ovens to make baked versions.

There are plenty of stove-top breads to choose from, and they're eaten as part of a main meal, for breakfast, as teatime snacks, and even as picnic foods. In this chapter, I show you how to make rotis in under 30 minutes, how to make homemade naans, and how to cook a layered bread called paratha.

I also show you how to make one of India's most festive breads, poori, which can be eaten as an indulgent breakfast with Batata Bhaji (Spiced Yellow Potatoes; see Chapter 17), as part of a thali meal (see Chapter 1), or even with a curry when you're feeling like a treat. I explain how to make flavored breads like thepla and stuffed parathas, which keep so well that you can bring them to work or school. Finally, I explain how to make a quick vegan bread, too, with just a few ingredients and packed with lots of flavor!

Chapati or Roti (Flatbread)

PREP TIME: ABOUT 10 MIN PLUS 10 MIN FOR RESTING	COOK TIME: 20 MIN	YIELD: 4–5 SERVINGS

INGREDIENTS

2 cups atta (see Chapter 4), plus 3 tablespoons for dusting

½ teaspoon salt

¾ cup warm water

2 tablespoons vegetable oil or ghee

DIRECTIONS

1 In a mixing bowl, put the flour and salt. Pour in about ¼ cup water. Using your fingers, mix until the flour resembles breadcrumbs. Add the rest of the water, 2 tablespoons at a time until a dough begins to form. (You may need a little less or more water, depending on the brand of atta you're using.) Be careful not to bring it together too forcefully because this will result in a dry dough. Knead for 5 minutes, stretching and pulling the dough until it looks smooth and is springy to the touch. Place under a moist tea towel, and allow to rest 10 minutes.

2 Divide the dough into 8 to 10 portions, each the size of a lime. Coat lightly with the flour, shape into a ball in your palm, and flatten slightly.

3 Roll out into flat discs, about 4 inches in diameter, flouring the surface lightly, if necessary.

4 Heat a heavy frying pan over medium heat. Roast the roti until the surface appears bubbly. Flip over and press the edges down with a spatula to cook evenly. As soon as brown spots appear on both sides, the roti is done. Make sure that the roti is cooked evenly all over. Each roti should take 2 to 3 minutes to cook. Flipping it over too many times will make it dry and parched. Remove and brush with oil or ghee.

5 Cook all the rotis the same way, keeping them warm by wrapping in foil or a tea towel.

TIP: Cooked rotis will last 2 days in an airtight box. Make sure they're completely cool before storing. The dough will last for 2 days in the fridge in an airtight box.

Naan (Leavened Oven–Baked Bread)

PREP TIME: ABOUT 15 MIN PLUS 2 HR FOR PROVING	COOK TIME: 10 MIN	YIELD: 4 SERVINGS

INGREDIENTS

¾ cup warm water, divided

1½ teaspoons active dry yeast

1 teaspoon sugar

2½ cups all-purpose flour

5 teaspoons baking powder

½ teaspoon salt

2 tablespoons vegetable oil, divided

1 tablespoon plain full-fat Greek yogurt

DIRECTIONS

1 In a bowl, whisk 5 tablespoons of the water, the yeast, and the sugar until the yeast has dissolved. Let stand for 10 minutes to activate the yeast. You should see a slight foam and little bubbles on the surface of the liquid.

2 In a separate bowl, sift the flour and baking powder. Add the yeast, salt, 1 tablespoon of the oil, and the yogurt. Mix together with your fingers until you get a breadcrumb texture, about 1 to 2 minutes. Add the remaining water, a little at a time, until a soft dough forms. Knead the dough on a floured surface until the dough is smooth, about 5 minutes.

3 Place the dough in a greased bowl, cover, and let stand in a warm place for 2 hours or until the dough rises.

4 Preheat the oven to 425 degrees. Punch the dough down and knead well. Divide into 12 balls and, using a rolling pin, roll into ovals 2 to 4 inches long and 2 inches wide.

5 Place the naans on a lined baking tray. Bake in batches until brown spots appear and the naans fluff up, about 6 to 7 minutes. Drizzle with oil and serve.

VARY IT! To make garlic naans, finely dice a couple of cloves of garlic, mix with oil, and brush onto the naans before baking them.

Paratha (Layered Bread)

PREP TIME: ABOUT 15 MIN PLUS 10 MIN FOR RESTING	COOK TIME: 25 MIN	YIELD: 4 SERVINGS

INGREDIENTS

2 cups atta (see Chapter 4), plus extra for dusting

½ teaspoon salt

1 cup tepid water, as needed, divided

2 tablespoons vegetable oil or melted ghee, plus extra for brushing and shallow-frying

DIRECTIONS

1 In a mixing bowl, put the flour and salt. Pour in about ¼ cup water, and using your fingers, mix until the flour resembles breadcrumbs. Add the remaining water, 2 tablespoons at a time, until a dough begins to form. (You may need a little less or more water, depending on the brand of atta you're using.) Knead for 5 minutes, stretching and pulling the dough until it looks smooth and is springy to the touch. Place the dough under a moist tea towel, and allow to rest for 10 minutes.

2 Divide the dough into 8 equal portions. Coat lightly with atta, shape into a ball in your palm, and flatten slightly.

3 Roll out into flat discs, about 4 inches in diameter, flouring the surface lightly, if necessary.

4 Brush some oil or ghee over the entire surface; then fold the disc in half. Brush more ghee on the top surface, and fold it once more to make a triangle.

5 Dust with flour and roll out thinly, about the thickness of a nickel, into a triangle shape.

6 Heat a frying pan over high heat and place the paratha in it. Wait until bubbles appear on the surface; then drizzle some oil on top and flip the paratha. Press down lightly. Drizzle a few drops of oil or ghee around the edges and on the surface and cook for 30 seconds or so. Flip it a few times until it's evenly cooked with brown spots all over it. Pressing it down helps the layers to separate.

7 Cook all the parathas the same way, keeping them warm by wrapping in foil or a tea towel.

VARY IT! You can flavor the parathas by adding a large pinch of dried fenugreek leaves (kasuri methi), ajowan (carom seeds), turmeric, or cumin seeds while kneading the dough.

Poori (Festive Fried Bread)

PREP TIME: ABOUT 15 MIN PLUS 10 MIN FOR RESTING	COOK TIME: 25 MIN	YIELD: 5 SERVINGS

INGREDIENTS

2 cups atta (see Chapter 4), plus extra for dusting

½ teaspoon salt

1 tablespoon warm vegetable oil or melted ghee

Tepid water, as needed

Vegetable oil for deep-frying

DIRECTIONS

1 In a mixing bowl, combine the flour, salt, and oil or ghee. Mix well. Pour in about ¼ cup water and, using your fingers, mix until the flour resembles breadcrumbs. Add more water, a couple of tablespoons at a time to make a stiff but springy dough. Place the dough under a moist tea towel, and allow to rest for 10 minutes.

2 Break off bits of the dough, each the size of a large cherry, and roll into tiny discs about 2½ inches in diameter. Place these on a floured surface.

3 Heat enough oil for deep-frying in a pan over high heat. Test if it's hot enough by putting in a pea-size ball of dough. It should sink at first but then rise to the surface in 2 to 3 seconds. Fry one poori at a time: Gently slip it into the oil, and after the initial sizzle, press it gently back into the oil (this helps to puff it). After it has puffed, drain it and transfer to a plate lined with paper towel. If the poori darkens in color too quickly, reduce the heat to medium.

4 Cook all the poories similarly. They're best served right away, because they collapse if you store them. They still taste very good, though, even if they've collapsed!

Gobi Paratha (Cauliflower-Stuffed Bread)

PREP TIME: ABOUT 15 MIN PLUS 10 MIN FOR RESTING	COOK TIME: 25 MIN	YIELD: 4 SERVINGS

INGREDIENTS

2 cups atta (see Chapter 4), plus extra for dusting

½ teaspoon salt

Tepid water, as needed

3 tablespoons warm vegetable oil or melted ghee, divided, plus extra for brushing and shallow-frying

2 cups finely grated cauliflower (chop any large bits that fall into the bowl)

1 teaspoon amchur (dried mango powder)

½ teaspoon cumin seeds, crushed

½ teaspoon Kashmiri chile powder

1 teaspoon ground coriander

3 to 4 stalks cilantro, leaves chopped finely and talks discarded

Salt to taste

DIRECTIONS

1 In a mixing bowl, put the flour and salt. Pour in about ¼ cup water and 2 tablespoons of the oil or ghee. Using your fingers, mix until the flour resembles breadcrumbs. Add more water, a couple of tablespoons at a time, until a dough begins to form. Knead for 5 minutes, stretching and pulling the dough until it looks smooth and is springy to the touch. Place the dough under a moist tea towel, and allow to rest for 10 minutes.

2 To make the filling, in a bowl, combine the cauliflower, amchur, cumin seeds, chile powder, ground coriander, and cilantro. Mix well with your hands. Add salt to season only when you're ready to start rolling the parathas; otherwise, the filling will become soggy as the salt draws the juices out of the cauliflower.

3 Divide the dough into 8 equal balls. Dust each ball with flour and roll out to a thick disc about 2 inches in diameter. Place a heaping tablespoon of the filling in the center. Gently lift the edges and gather them up to make a tight pouch. Twist the top to seal and pinch off excess dough, if any. Flatten the pouch with your fingers. Place it on a floured surface, and pat it with your fingers to stretch it into a small circle; spread the filling evenly inside it. Using a rolling pin, roll it out very gently, to a disc about 4 inches in diameter. Figure 19-1 illustrates how to roll and fold a stuffed paratha.

4 Heat a frying pan over high heat and place the paratha on it. In a few seconds, flip it over and brush liberally with oil or ghee (preferred). Flip it again and brush with more oil or ghee. Press down gently on the paratha as it shallow-fries. The paratha is done when you see brown spots on both sides and the whole thing turns golden.

5 Cook all the parathas similarly, keeping warm in foil.

TIP: If the filling becomes soggy, add a large pinch of atta to it, and it'll become crumbly again.

TIP: Serve with plain full-fat Greek yogurt and store-bought mango pickle.

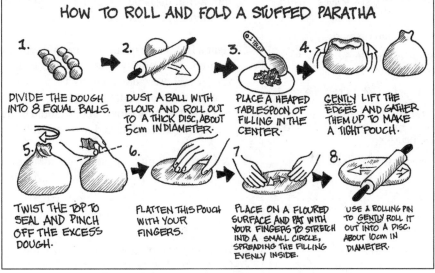

FIGURE 19-1:
How to roll and fold a stuffed paratha.

Illustration by Liz Kurtzman

Thepla (Fenugreek Bread)

PREP TIME: ABOUT 15 MIN PLUS 10 MIN FOR RESTING	COOK TIME: 25 MIN	YIELD: 5 SERVINGS

INGREDIENTS

2 cups atta (see Chapter 4), plus extra for dusting

2 tablespoons gram flour (see Chapter 8)

½ teaspoon salt

6 to 8 stalks fresh fenugreek leaves (leaves chopped and stalks discarded) or 1 teaspoon dried fenugreek leaves (kasuri methi)

½ teaspoon turmeric

½ teaspoon Ginger-Garlic Paste (see Chapter 6)

1 teaspoon white sesame seeds

1 tablespoon warm vegetable oil or melted ghee, plus more for brushing

Tepid water, as needed

DIRECTIONS

1 In a mixing bowl, put both the atta, gram flour, salt, fenugreek, turmeric, Ginger-Garlic Paste, sesame seeds, and oil or ghee. Pour in about ¼ cup water and begin mixing a dough. Add more water, a tablespoonful at a time, until you get a firm, springy dough. Place the dough under a moist tea towel, and leave to rest for 10 minutes.

2 Divide the dough into 10 equal parts. Dust with atta and roll into a thin disc about 4 inches in diameter, flouring the surface lightly, as necessary.

3 Heat a frying pan over high heat. When very hot, place the disc in it and wait until you see bubbles form on the surface. Flip it over and press down gently for a few seconds. Flip it again to cook the other side. Brush both sides with oil or ghee and flip a couple more times. There should be brown spots all over, and it should have firmed up but still be pliable.

4 Transfer to a plate, brush with more oil or ghee, and keep warm enclosed in foil. Make all the theplas similarly.

TIP: Serve with store-bought mango chutney or Aam ki Launji (Sweet-and-Sour Mango Chutney; see Chapter 20).

TIP: Don't flip the theplas (or any other stove-top breads) too many times. Overcooking will make them hard and crusty. Regulate the heat, turning it down to medium if the pan gets too hot and smoky.

Neer Dosa (South Indian Rice Crêpes)

PREP TIME: ABOUT 15 MIN PLUS OVERNIGHT SOAKING	COOK TIME: 15 MIN	YIELD: 4 SERVINGS

INGREDIENTS

1 cup white rice, washed and drained

2 cups cold water, divided

½ teaspoon salt

Vegetable oil, for the pan

½ onion

DIRECTIONS

1 Soak the rice overnight in the water. Drain the rice when you're ready to blend the batter.

2 In a blender, put the drained rice and 1 cup of the water. Blend to a very fine batter. You shouldn't see any rice grains in it. Pour the batter into a bowl, season with salt, and add the remaining 1 cup of water. You want a thin, watery batter (*neer dosa* translates as "water dosa").

3 Warm a 6-inch nonstick frying pan or crêpe pan over high heat. Drizzle a few drops of oil in the pan. Pierce the round side of the onion half with a fork, and smear the oil around the pan with the flat side. When the pan is hot, remove it from the heat and pour in a ladle of batter into the center, moving the pan to spread the batter thinly until it reaches the sides of the pan. It should appear lacy. Fill any large gaps with more batter if required, but make sure to keep the dosa really thin.

4 Turn the heat to medium, cover the pan, and cook the dosa until the edges come away from the pan, about 45 to 60 seconds. Uncover the pan, lift one side, and fold into a semicircle. Fold again into a triangle and lift off the pan. Repeat the onion and oil technique before you cook each dosa.

TIP: Serve as soon as you can. These dosas are fine in texture and go well with curries.

TIP: These make a great gluten-free alternative to the more common Indian breads.

Chilla (Gram–Flour Pancakes)

PREP TIME: ABOUT 15 MIN | COOK TIME: 20 MIN | YIELD: 3–4 SERVINGS

INGREDIENTS

2 cups gram flour (see Chapter 8)

½ teaspoon turmeric

1 teaspoon ground cumin

1 teaspoon salt

Cold water

1 onion, finely diced

2 green chilies, finely diced with the seeds

4 to 5 stalks cilantro, finely chopped

Vegetable oil, for brushing

DIRECTIONS

1 In a bowl, put the flour, turmeric, cumin, and salt. Add enough cold water, a little at a time, to make a smooth, thick batter the consistency of heavy pouring cream. Whisk to remove any lumps.

2 In a small bowl, mix the onion, chilies, and cilantro.

3 Heat a nonstick frying pan over high heat and pour about half of the batter into the center. Using the back of a ladle, spread the batter into a thin disc about 4 inches in diameter. Sprinkle a teaspoonful of the onion mixture over it and press down lightly with the back of the ladle. The onions should stick to the pancake. Drizzle a few drops of oil on the top and around the edges of the pancake.

4 When the underside has turned golden brown (check by lifting one corner), flip the pancake over. Drizzle a bit more oil and cook for about 45 seconds.

5 Cook all the pancakes similarly, keeping them warm by wrapping in foil. Turn the heat down to medium when the pan becomes hot and smoky, turning the heat up when adding a new batch of batter.

TIP: Serve as a gluten-free alternative to bread, with curries or on their own with plain full-fat Greek yogurt.

Chapter **20**

Chutneys and Salads

RECIPES IN THIS CHAPTER

- Khajur Imli ki Chutney (Sweet-and-Sour Date and Tamarind Chutney)
- Pudine aur Pyaz ki Chutney (Mint and Onion Chutney)
- Thengai Chutney (Coconut and Tender Mango Chutney)
- Hari Chutney (Cilantro and Peanut Chutney)
- Aam ki Launji (Sweet-and-Sour Mango Chutney)
- Kheere Tamater ka Raita (Cucumber and Tomato Salad with Yogurt)
- Kachumber (Onion, Cucumber, Tomato, and Carrot Salad)
- Gujarati Sambharo (Cabbage and Carrot Salad)

When you think of an Indian meal, curry probably comes to mind, not salad. And you'd be right to think of curry, given what most Indian restaurants offer in this department. But a simple salad is almost always served to accompany a meal to provide crunch and color. A huge variety of these salads, which are never seen on restaurant menus, showcase the best of the fresh local produce in the region where they're eaten. However, unlike in the West, Indian salads are not stand-alone dishes, so you'll never hear anyone in India say that they had a salad for lunch.

Indian chutneys can be wet or dry, but they're always highly flavored and, therefore, eaten in small quantities. Their main role is to personalize your plate, making your meal a bit hotter, sweeter, or tangier, depending on your preference.

In this chapter, I show you how to make some of India's best-loved chutneys — a powerfully sweet-and-sour tamarind one, a North Indian mint one, a velvety coconut one, and my favorite, a cilantro and nut chutney that works with anything from a sandwich (try spreading a cheese sandwich with this!) to samosas. I show you how to make a really easy mango chutney, a fragrant raita (a salad with yogurt), and kachumber, which goes with vegetarian and meat curries. I also show you a neat way of combining the humble cabbage and carrots in a super-delicious spicy Gujarati salad.

TIP Don't add too much water while blitzing ingredients for a chutney, or it will become too runny. Try adding just a few tablespoons at a time until the blades turn easily and you get a smooth, thick puree.

Khajur Imli ki Chutney (Sweet-and-Sour Date and Tamarind Chutney)

PREP TIME: ABOUT 15 MIN | COOK TIME: 15 MIN | YIELD: ABOUT 1 CUP

INGREDIENTS

1 teaspoon cumin seeds

1 teaspoon fennel seeds

½ cup grated jaggery or soft brown sugar

4 tablespoons tamarind block

6 dates, stoned and chopped

¼ teaspoon Kashmiri chile powder

Salt to taste

Pinch of Chaat Masala (optional; see Chapter 7)

DIRECTIONS

1 Put the cumin and fennel seeds in a small frying pan with no oil and start to cook over high heat. As the seeds heat up, they'll start to change color and go a couple of shades darker. Tip them into a mortar and pestle, and crush to a fine powder. Set aside.

2 In a saucepan, put the jaggery or sugar, tamarind, and dates. Pour in 1 cup of hot water. Bring to a boil. Reduce the heat, add the chile powder, and simmer until the dates are soft, about 7 to 8 minutes. (If you prefer, you can cook this in a pressure cooker or an Instant Pot for 8 to 9 minutes on the Pressure Cooker setting.)

3 Mash this mixture with a masher, and add ½ cup cold water. Or add the water first and use a hand blender. Strain it through a sieve back into the pan, adding a bit more water to the pan if the mixture is too thick. Do a second pressing by putting what's in the sieve back in the pan, adding 3 to 4 tablespoons of water, and passing it through the sieve again.

4 Season with salt and mix in the toasted ground cumin, fennel seeds and Chaat Masala if using. The consistency should be like ketchup.

TIP: This chutney will keep in the fridge for up to 1 month. Serve it with snacks such as Vegetable Samosas (Vegetable and Pastry Parcels; see Chapter 18) and Onion Bhajia (Savory Onion Fritters; see Chapter 18), or drizzle it on top of plain Greek yogurt or Kheere Tamater ka Raita (Cucumber and Tomato Salad with Yogurt; later in this chapter).

Pudine aur Pyaz ki Chutney (Mint and Onion Chutney)

PREP TIME: ABOUT 15 MIN	COOK TIME: 1 MIN	YIELD: ABOUT 1 CUP

INGREDIENTS

½ onion, grated

1 cup fresh mint leaves

3 cloves garlic, peeled and diced

¾-inch knob of ginger, peeled and diced

1 or 2 green chilies, diced with the seeds

4 tablespoons plain full-fat Greek yogurt

Salt to taste

1 teaspoon caster sugar

1 tablespoon lemon juice

1 teaspoon cumin seeds

DIRECTIONS

1 Put the onion, mint, garlic, ginger, and chilies in a blender along with ¼ cup of water, and blitz to a fine puree. Make sure that there are no bits. If there are, add another table-spoon or so of water and blitz until smooth.

2 Put the yogurt in a bowl, and fold in the onion and mint puree. Season with salt, and add the sugar and lemon juice.

3 Put the cumin seeds in a small frying pan with no oil, and start to cook over high heat. As they heat up, they'll start to change color and go a couple of shades darker. Tip them into a mortar and pestle, crush to a fine powder, and add to the chutney.

Thengai Chutney (Coconut and Tender Mango Chutney)

PREP TIME: ABOUT 15 MIN	COOK TIME: 1 MIN	YIELD: ABOUT 1 CUP

INGREDIENTS

½ cup fresh or frozen grated coconut or desiccated unsweetened coconut

3 to 4 slices ginger, peeled and chopped

2 green chilies, diced with the seeds

½ tender green mango, peeled and diced (see Figure 20-1)

Salt to taste

1 tablespoon lemon juice

1 tablespoon coconut or vegetable oil

1 teaspoon black mustard seeds

½ teaspoon white urad dal (optional)

Pinch of asafetida

10 fresh curry leaves or 3 pinches dried curry leaves

DIRECTIONS

1 In a frying pan without any oil, dry-roast the coconut over medium heat for 3 to 4 minutes. You don't want it to turn golden, so take it off the heat before that happens, and pour it into a bowl to stop it from cooking further.

2 Put the coconut, ginger, chilies, and mango in a blender along with enough cold water to just cover the mixture, and blitz to a fine puree. Pour into a bowl, season with salt, and stir in the lemon juice.

(continued)

3 In a small frying pan, warm the oil and add the mustard seeds. They'll pop as they heat up. Then add the urad dal and cook for a few seconds, until it starts to turn golden. Sprinkle in the asafetida and curry leaves. Pour this mixture along with the oil on top of the chutney.

NOTE: The toasting of the coconut helps prevent it from releasing fat when it's blitzed in the blender.

TIP: Serve cold as a side with Dosa (Fermented Rice and Lentil Crêpes; see Chapter 17), Neer Dosa (South Indian Rice Crêpes; see Chapter 19), or Upma (Savory Semolina Cake; see Chapter 17).

VARY IT! If you can't find mango or just want a change, you can use ½ sour cooking apple in place of the tender green mango.

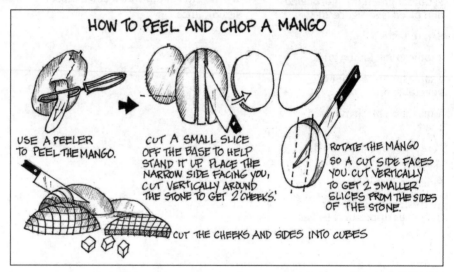

HOW TO PEEL AND CHOP A MANGO

USE A PEELER TO PEEL THE MANGO.

CUT A SMALL SLICE OFF THE BASE TO HELP STAND IT UP. PLACE THE NARROW SIDE FACING YOU, CUT VERTICALLY AROUND THE STONE TO GET 2 'CHEEKS'.

ROTATE THE MANGO SO A CUT SIDE FACES YOU. CUT VERTICALLY TO GET 2 SMALLER SLICES FROM THE SIDES OF THE STONE.

CUT THE CHEEKS AND SIDES INTO CUBES

FIGURE 20-1:
How to peel and chop a mango.

Illustration by Liz Kurtzman

Hari Chutney (Cilantro and Peanut Chutney)

PREP TIME: 10 MIN | COOK TIME: NONE | YIELD: ABOUT 1 CUP

INGREDIENTS

2 tablespoons roasted, salted peanuts

1 cup cilantro leaves and stalks, roughly chopped

4 to 5 slices of ginger, peeled and chopped

3 cloves of garlic, peeled and diced

2 green chilies, diced with the seeds

½ teaspoon cumin seeds

Salt to taste

2 tablespoons lemon juice

2 tablespoons plain full-fat Greek yogurt (optional)

DIRECTIONS

1 Soak the peanuts in 3 tablespoons of boiling hot water while you prepare the other ingredients.

2 Put the cilantro, ginger, garlic, chilies, cumin seeds, and peanuts along with the water in a blender and add ¼ cup cold water. Blitz to a fine, thick puree, adding a little more water if necessary.

3 Pour into a bowl, season with salt, and add the lemon juice and yogurt.

TIP: Serve cold as a dip with Onion Bhajia (Savory Onion Fritters; see Chapter 18), Vegetable Samosas (Vegetable and Pastry Parcels; see Chapter 18), and Bombay Sandwich (Sandwich with Chutney, Vegetables, and Cheese; see Chapter 18).

Aam ki Launji (Sweet-and-Sour Mango Chutney)

PREP TIME: 15 MIN	COOK TIME: 15 MIN	YIELD: ABOUT 2 CUPS

INGREDIENTS

1 tablespoon vegetable oil

1 teaspoon fennel seeds

½ teaspoon fenugreek seeds

1 teaspoon cumin seeds

1 cup tender green mango cubes (½-inch cubes)

½ teaspoon turmeric

1 teaspoon Kashmiri chile powder

½ cup grated jaggery or soft brown sugar

Salt to taste

DIRECTIONS

1 In a large frying pan, warm the oil over high heat. Add the fennel, fenugreek, and cumin seeds. When they heat up and go a couple of shades darker, stir in the cubed mango.

2 Sprinkle in the turmeric and chile powder and mix well. Add ½ cup hot water, and cook over high heat until the water begins to boil, about 3 to 4 minutes. Pierce a cube of mango with a knife to check if it's cooked. The knife should go in easily. If there is still some resistance, cook for a few more minutes.

3 Add the jaggery or sugar, season with salt, and cook over medium heat until the jaggery or sugar has melted, about 3 to 4 minutes. Cool completely, put into a clean jar, and store for up to 1 month in the fridge.

Kheere Tamater ka Raita (Cucumber and Tomato Salad with Yogurt)

PREP TIME: 10 MIN | COOK TIME: 1 MIN | YIELD: 3-4 SERVINGS

INGREDIENTS

½ large cucumber, diced finely along with the seeds and skin

1 tomato, diced finely with the seeds and skin

1 green chile, diced finely

3 to 4 stalks cilantro, chopped

6 tablespoons plain full-fat Greek yogurt

Salt to taste

Pepper to taste

1 teaspoon caster sugar

½ teaspoon cumin seeds

DIRECTIONS

1 Put the cucumber, tomato, chile, and cilantro (set aside a little for garnish) in a large bowl. Stir in the yogurt, salt, pepper, and sugar.

2 Warm a small frying pan, and start to cook the cumin seeds on a high heat with no oil. As they heat up, they'll start to change color and go a couple of shades darker. Tip them into a mortar and pestle, and crush to a fine powder. Stir this into the raita, saving a pinch to sprinkle on top as a garnish along with the reserved cilantro.

TIP: You can replace the cucumber and tomato with your favorite salad vegetable or fruit. Some cooked vegetables are also suitable. Here are some ideas: cooked beetroot; mint, lettuce, and cucumber; cooked or raw zucchini; wilted spinach and dill; onion and cilantro; cooked potatoes; or banana and peach, apple, or pear.

Kachumber (Onion, Cucumber, Tomato, and Carrot Salad)

PREP TIME: 10 MIN	COOK TIME: NONE	YIELD: 3–4 SERVINGS

INGREDIENTS

1 onion, diced finely

¼ large cucumber, diced finely with the seeds and skin

1 tomato, diced finely with the seeds and skin

1 small carrot, peeled and grated

1 green chile, diced finely, with the seeds

3 to 4 stalks cilantro, chopped

2 tablespoons lemon juice or white vinegar

Salt to taste

Pepper to taste

½ teaspoon caster sugar

Pinch of Chaat Masala (optional; see Chapter 7)

DIRECTIONS

1 In a large bowl, mix the onion, cucumber, tomato, carrot, chile, and cilantro (setting aside a little for garnish).

2 Just before serving, stir in the lemon juice or vinegar, season with salt and pepper, and add the sugar. Sprinkle with Chaat Masala if using.

TIP: Serve with any curry and rice.

Gujarati Sambharo (Cabbage and Carrot Salad)

PREP TIME: 15 MIN	COOK TIME: 10 MIN	YIELD: 3–4 SERVINGS

INGREDIENTS

1 tablespoon vegetable oil

1 teaspoon black mustard seeds

1 teaspoon white sesame seeds

10 fresh curry leaves or
3 pinches dried curry leaves

1 teaspoon turmeric

1 cup shredded white cabbage

2 carrots, peeled and grated

Salt to taste

Pepper to taste

1 teaspoon caster sugar

2 tablespoons lemon juice

4 to 5 stalks cilantro, chopped

DIRECTIONS

1 In a large frying pan, warm the oil over high heat. Add the mustard seeds. When the seeds begin to pop, add the sesame seeds, curry leaves, and turmeric. Cook for 30 seconds. Add the cabbage and carrot. Season with salt and pepper.

2 Continue to cook over high heat, stirring occasionally, until the vegetables have softened slightly but still retain a crunch, about 5 to 6 minutes.

3 Remove from the heat and tip into a bowl to stop the vegetables from cooking further. Stir in the sugar, lemon juice, and cilantro.

TIP: Serve with any curry and rice or bread.

Chapter **21**

Desserts and Drinks

RECIPES IN THIS CHAPTER

- Chaval aur Narial ki Kheer (Rice and Coconut Pudding)
- Kesar Kulfi (Rich Saffron Ice Cream)
- Sooji ka Halva (Warm Semolina and Raisin Pudding)
- Aam ka Custard (Mango Custard with Tropical Fruit)
- Chibuda Hashale (Melon and Coconut Milk Pudding)
- Badam ke Laddoo (Almond Fudge)
- Aam ki Lassi (Mango and Yogurt Drink)
- Masala Chai (Spiced Tea)
- Nimbu Pani (Spiced Fresh Lemonade)
- Elaichi Kapi (Pulled Coffee with Cardamom and Brown Sugar)

When you read the title of this chapter, you may have thought of those overly sweet, syrupy desserts commonly found in Indian restaurants. Before you skip this chapter, have a go at making one of these recipes in your own kitchen. Homemade Indian desserts are a far cry from commercial ones (which have to be very sugary to increase their shelf life, just like a box of chocolates does). I absolutely *love* Indian desserts made at home because they're not too sweet and they're beautifully scented with cardamom and saffron, two of the world's most expensive and aromatic spices. I always crush my cardamom seeds and throw away the woody husks, and I soak saffron in some warm milk or water to extract its lovely color and aroma.

In this chapter, I show you how to make Chaval aur Narial ki Kheer (Rice and Coconut Pudding) and Kesar Kulfi (Rich Saffron Ice Cream). If you enjoy warm desserts, you'll love Sooji Ka Halva (Warm Semolina and Raisin Pudding). For fruit lovers, there's Aam Ka Custard (Mango Custard with Tropical Fruit) or Chibuda Hashale (Melon and Coconut Milk Pudding). My children loved making Badam ke Laddoo (Almond Fudge) with me when they were little — it's so easy! Indian drinks are full of spice and flavor, so you'll want to try Aam ki Lassi (Mango and Yogurt Drink); Masala Chai (Spiced Tea); Nimbu Pani (Spiced Fresh Lemonade), served on carts in many cities; and Elaichi Kapi (Pulled Coffee with Cardamom and Brown Sugar), popular in South India.

Chaval aur Narial ki Kheer (Rice and Coconut Pudding)

PREP TIME: ABOUT 10 MIN PLUS 30 MIN FOR SOAKING	COOK TIME: 45 MIN	YIELD: 3–4 SERVINGS

INGREDIENTS

½ cup basmati rice

1 tablespoon ghee

1 cup water

3 cups coconut milk, divided

2 tablespoons desiccated coconut

½ cup caster sugar

4 green cardamom, seeds crushed and husks discarded

Pinch of saffron

1 tablespoon raisins

1 tablespoon chopped unsalted pistachios or cashew nuts

DIRECTIONS

1 Soak the rice in enough boiling hot water to cover; leave for 30 minutes, and then drain in a sieve.

2 In a frying pan, warm the ghee over high heat; add the drained rice. Stir-fry for 3 to 4 minutes. Then add the water and 1½ cups of the coconut milk. Bring the mixture to a boil. Reduce the heat, cover, and simmer for about 30 minutes, stirring occasionally to make sure it doesn't stick to the bottom of the pan.

3 When the rice is very soft, stir in the desiccated coconut, sugar, cardamom, saffron, and nuts (saving a bit for the garnish). Pour in the remaining 1½ cups of coconut milk and bring to a boil. Reduce the heat, simmer for 2 to 3 minutes, and remove from the heat. Stir in the raisins.

4 Serve warm or cold, sprinkled with the reserved nuts.

TIP: Choose a nonaged, cheaper rice (see Chapter 4).

Kesar Kulfi (Rich Saffron Ice Cream)

PREP TIME: ABOUT 10 MIN PLUS 30 MIN FOR SOAKING PLUS OVERNIGHT FREEZING	COOK TIME: 5 MIN	YIELD: 10–12 SERVINGS

INGREDIENTS

2 cups heavy cream, divided

½ teaspoon saffron strands

4 green cardamom pods, seeds finely crushed and husks discarded

One 14-ounce can sweetened condensed milk

3 tablespoons crushed unsalted pistachios

DIRECTIONS

1 In a saucepan, heat ½ cup of the cream, the saffron, and the cardamom over medium heat, stirring frequently. When the cream is very hot (but not yet boiling) and the saffron has started to release its color, remove the pan from the heat.

2 Pour the spiced cream into a large bowl and leave to cool, covered, for 30 minutes in the refrigerator.

3 Remove from the refrigerator and add the remaining 1½ cups cream and the condensed milk to the bowl. Using a whisk or an electric hand blender, beat the mixture until it's thick and drops off a spoon.

4 Crumble the nuts at the bottom of individual popsicle molds or a lidded freezer container. Spoon the mixture on top of the nuts and freeze overnight. These will last up to 4 weeks in the freezer.

VARY IT! You can flavor this ice cream with a fruit puree such as mango or strawberry — just add a couple of tablespoons to the mixture before whisking it.

Sooji ka Halva (Warm Semolina and Raisin Pudding)

PREP TIME: ABOUT 10 MIN	COOK TIME: 10 MIN	YIELD: 3–4 SERVINGS

INGREDIENTS

3 tablespoons ghee or salted butter

1 tablespoon unsalted cashew nuts

1 tablespoon green or black raisins

1 cup coarse semolina

1 cup caster sugar (or a bit less for a less sweet pudding)

Pinch of salt (if using ghee instead of butter)

2½ cups hot water

4 green cardamom, seeds crushed and husks discarded

DIRECTIONS

1 In a saucepan, melt the ghee or butter over high heat. Add the nuts and raisins, and fry for 1 minute. Then add the semolina, and fry for 2 to 3 minutes, stirring frequently.

2 Reduce heat to low, add the sugar and salt (if using), and cook for 1 minute.

3 Stand back, and slowly pour in the water (it will sputter). Cook for 4 to 5 minutes, stirring frequently, until it forms a soft dough. Turn off the heat, stir in the cardamom, and serve warm.

VARY IT! You can add fruit to the semolina mixture in Step 2 if you want. Try mashed banana, finely chopped mango, orange segments, or blueberries.

Aam ka Custard (Mango Custard with Tropical Fruit)

PREP TIME: ABOUT 15 MIN	COOK TIME: 10 MIN	YIELD: 3-4 SERVINGS

INGREDIENTS

2 cups whole milk, divided

3 tablespoons cornstarch or custard powder

6 tablespoons caster sugar, or to taste

1 cup canned or fresh mango puree

1½ cups chopped tropical fruit (banana, pineapple, oranges, or grapes)

2 tablespoons chopped mixed nuts, for garnish

DIRECTIONS

1 In a small bowl, combine ¼ cup of the milk with the cornstarch or custard powder. Mix well to remove any lumps. Set aside.

2 In a saucepan, heat the remaining 1¾ cups of milk with the sugar over high heat. When the mixture is almost boiling (the edges should be simmering), turn down the heat to low and add the cornstarch mixture. Stir as you pour, so that no lumps form. Continue stirring and cook until the mixture thickens enough to coat the back of the ladle, about 3 to 4 minutes. Remove from the heat, pour into a bowl, cover, and cool in the refrigerator.

3 When the custard has cooled down, stir in the mango puree and then fruit.

4 Serve topped with the nuts.

TIP: If a film layer develops on top of the custard as it's chilled, you can either scrape it off and discard it before adding the fruit, or just stir it back into the custard.

Chibuda Hashale (Melon and Coconut Milk Pudding)

PREP TIME: ABOUT 15 MIN	COOK TIME: NONE	YIELD: 3–4 SERVINGS

INGREDIENTS

2 or 3 tablespoons jaggery, grated, or soft brown sugar

One 13.5-ounce can coconut milk

4 green cardamom, seeds finely crushed and husks discarded

2 cups any sweet melon (such as cantaloupe or canary), peeled, deseeded, and diced into ½-inch pieces

2 tablespoons pomegranate seeds, for garnish

DIRECTIONS

1 In a medium bowl, mix the jaggery or brown sugar into the coconut milk until it dissolves. Stir in the crushed cardamom.

2 In a serving bowl, place the melon and pour the coconut milk over it.

3 Garnish with the pomegranate seeds and serve cold.

VARY IT! Try other fruits in this recipe. I love mango, mixed berries, and papaya!

Badam ke Laddoo (Almond Fudge)

PREP TIME: ABOUT 15 MIN	COOK TIME: 15 MIN	YIELD: 10–15 SERVINGS

INGREDIENTS

2 cups almond flour or ground almonds

½ cup water

¾ cup caster sugar

4 green cardamom, seeds finely crushed and husks discarded

¼ teaspoon saffron strands

2 teaspoons ghee

2 teaspoons almonds, roughly crushed

DIRECTIONS

1. Pass the almond flour through a fine sieve and discard any bits left in the sieve. Set aside.

2. In a saucepan, heat the water, sugar, cardamom, and saffron over high heat and cook until the sugar has melted, about 5 to 6 minutes.

3. Reduce the heat to low and add the almond flour. Stir continuously until the mixture thickens and forms a dough that leaves the sides of the pan. Stir in the ghee and cook for another minute.

4. Remove from the heat and transfer to a plate. After it has cooled enough to be handled (but is still slightly warm), break off a large cherry-size ball and roll between your palms to make a sphere. Repeat with the remainder of the dough.

5. Roll each ball in the crushed almonds and serve cold. Store in an airtight container for 4 to 5 days at room temperature.

Aam ki Lassi (Mango and Yogurt Drink)

PREP TIME: ABOUT 10 MIN	COOK TIME: NONE	YIELD: 3–4 SERVINGS

INGREDIENTS

1 cup canned or fresh mango puree

2 cups plain full-fat Greek yogurt

½ to 1½ cups cold water (see Tip)

3 green cardamom, seeds crushed and husks discarded

Caster sugar to taste

DIRECTIONS

In a large bowl, place all the ingredients. Whisk for 1 minute to blend everything. Serve chilled.

TIP: I like to make this recipe as thick as cream, so I add less water. If you prefer a thinner drink, add more water.

TIP: Drink on a hot day or serve as dessert. Contrary to what Indian restaurants may suggest, lassi is not a drink we have with a meal!

Masala Chai (Spiced Tea)

PREP TIME: ABOUT 10 MIN	COOK TIME: 5 MIN	YIELD: 3–4 SERVINGS

INGREDIENTS

¾-inch knob of fresh root ginger

3 green cardamom

1 clove

1 cup water

1 cup whole or low-fat milk

3 black tea bags

Caster sugar to taste

DIRECTIONS

1 In a mortar and pestle, roughly crush the ginger, cardamom, and clove in a mortar and pestle.

2 Add to a saucepan with the water, milk, and tea bags, and bring to a boil. Reduce the heat and simmer for a couple of minutes. Strain through a sieve and serve hot, with sugar if desired.

NOTE: In India, *chai* means "tea," so saying "chai tea" is redundant. When black tea is combined with spices, it's called masala chai.

Nimbu Pani (Spiced Fresh Lemonade)

PREP TIME: ABOUT 10 MIN	COOK TIME: NONE	YIELD: 3–4 SERVINGS

INGREDIENTS

Juice of 2 lemons (or more for a tangy taste)

2 cups cold water

½ teaspoon salt, or to taste

3 to 4 teaspoons caster sugar, or to taste

3 or 4 stalks of mint, leaves finely chopped and stalks discarded

Pinch of freshly ground black pepper

¼ teaspoon Chaat Masala (see Chapter 7; optional)

DIRECTIONS

In a jug, combine all the ingredients. Let steep for 10 minutes. Strain through a sieve, and serve cold, with ice, if desired.

Elaichi Kapi (Pulled Coffee with Cardamom and Brown Sugar)

PREP TIME: ABOUT 5 MIN	COOK TIME: 5 MIN	YIELD: 3–4 SERVINGS

INGREDIENTS

1 cup whole or low-fat milk

3 green cardamom, seeds crushed and husks discarded

4 teaspoons soft brown sugar

4 tablespoons instant coffee granules

1 cup boiling hot water

DIRECTIONS

1 In a saucepan, add the milk, cardamom, and sugar. Bring to a boil over high heat. Turn off the heat.

2 In another pan, mix the coffee granules and boiling hot water. Add the spiced milk to the coffee. Carefully pour the mixture from one pan to the other from a height, to create froth. Do this 3 or 4 times, taking care not to cool it down. Then serve the frothy coffee.

5

The Part of Tens

IN THIS PART . . .

Get practical tips on how to be more efficient in the kitchen.

Check out the myths that surround Indian food and learn the truth.

Master the rules of Indian table etiquette that will make you a better guest.

» **Batch cooking to save time**

» **Freezing curry masala bases**

» **Using a pressure cooker or Instant Pot**

Chapter **22**

Ten Time-Saving Tips for the Kitchen

Cooking is fun, but you don't want to spend hours in the kitchen every day, preparing your average dinner (I know I don't). You may do that occasionally, when you're cooking for a party or spending an afternoon making snacks to store, but if you're like me, cooking on a Wednesday night, after work, has to be quick.

In this chapter, I share ten tips that I've learned over the years while juggling a full-time food business and bringing up the kids. Some of these tips were handed to me as a throwaway remark in the middle of a conversation about something completely different, but I filed them away and they changed my life, helping with time management and putting healthy food on the table.

You can apply these tips to all cuisines, but Indian cooking has an unfair reputation for being time-consuming, so I enjoy demolishing that stereotype. In this chapter, I tell how to create an efficient spice storage system and make batches of your favorite curries, why every home in India has a pressure cooker, how choosing the right size pan can cut down cooking time, and why covering the pan will speed things up even more.

Prepare Your Ingredients Ahead of Time

This stellar advice was given to me when my children were quite little and I was constantly chasing time to get things done. Start your prep when you have time, and don't wait for when you begin cooking. So, for me, this means chopping vegetables while having my morning tea or prepping an onion in the morning for a curry I'll cook that evening. Put the prepped food into a storage container in the fridge, and pop it in the pan in the evening.

This trick is especially helpful during the week. You'll have decided what to cook for dinner (everyone's greatest dilemma) and done some of the prep, so motivating yourself to get into the kitchen will be easier. Plus, getting dinner on the table will be quicker.

Store Your Spices Efficiently

Spices can make or break your Indian cooking. To avoid that frantic scramble to assemble them as you cook, start by storing those spices for convenience:

>> **Limit the number of spices you keep on hand.** Buy spices to cover your go-to recipes. You may have a few extra spices for those adventurous times, but keeping your collection small will make your life easier.

>> **Keep whole spices together and ground ones separate.** They'll be easier to find this way.

>> **Pour the spices from their packaging into labeled jars.** Store the jars inside a dark cupboard, away from direct light. Better still, head to your local Indian store or the Internet and buy a *masala dabba* (spice tin); the typical masala dabba has seven compartments that you can fill with your favorite spices.

Storing your spices this way will prevent you from throwing in the wrong one and ending up with a dish from the other side of India.

Cook in Batches

Batch cooking is a well-known tip for saving time cooking. Here are some items specific to Indian cooking that are especially good for batch cooking:

- >> **Spice blends:** If you love the magic of creating your own spice blends but find it too time-consuming, make a batch to have at the ready whenever you need it. Spice blends store well for up to three months in airtight containers. You'll feel like a star using one of your very own!

- >> **Fresh chutney:** You can use this as a dip or a condiment, spread it on toast, or use it as a quick curry base sauce.

- >> **Ginger garlic paste:** It goes into most savory dishes, and it's a fiddle to make some every time you cook. But it freezes beautifully and loses none of its power in the process.

- >> **Roti or other bread dough:** You'll have some for the next day, and life will be good.

- >> **Meat curries:** Cooking these can take a bit of time, so batch cooking makes sense. Be sure to freeze curries in smaller portions so that you don't have to thaw the whole batch at once.

Chop Ingredients Evenly

Evenly sized pieces cook evenly. If you want something to break down into a sauce, such as tomatoes, dice them finely as well. I don't use too many gadgets for chopping — no food processor for me — because I find the time I've saved in the prep is all spent in washing up.

TIP

Buy a sharp knife and look after it so that chopping becomes a joy and doesn't take forever. If you're always in a hurry, consider frozen vegetables that have already been diced for you. Or make your freezer work for you even harder: Chop your own fresh ingredients and freeze them for later.

Freeze Basic Curry Sauces

Cooking onions for a curry takes time and patience, and it's sometimes what puts me off from cooking when I'm tired. Curry sauces freeze well, so make a batch on a day when you're not working, portion it out, and freeze for up to three months. You'll spend a *bit* more time (not a lot) making a double portion, but you'll save time later by not having to cook your next curry from scratch.

REMEMBER

Be sure to label and date each container — it's easy to mistake pasta sauce for a red masala. Now that's fusion cuisine!

TIP

Some masala base sauces can get a bit watery in the freezer, but this moisture will cook off when you add the next ingredient and carry on to the next step. Remember not to add too much water to the curry base in the first place. Having to boil it off will just waste energy.

Why not have a curry-base-making party with friends? Or delegate some of the work to a friend or family member? (I've found that teenagers are the prefect candidates for this task, willing or otherwise.) Cooking together is fun, and it makes light of the most time-consuming tasks.

Figure Out the Proper Prep Order

All recipes work in a specific sequence. Read the recipe, understand the sequence, and do your prep, in the order in which the ingredients appear. After you've turned on the heat, the recipe will flow like clockwork and save you time and energy.

Also, have your appliances ready. You'll need a blender for some curries and perhaps a peeler, grater, or mortar and pestle or spice mill. Place all the utensils you'll need by the stove, too. A recipe stand also helps — in my classes, I have a paper-clip-hook attached to the wall, close enough to be able to read from but not so close to pose a fire hazard.

As you gain more confidence, you'll be able to prep some things as you go along. So, if your onions are in the pan and will take 10 minutes to cook, you could be chopping tomatoes in that time. If you're a novice Indian cook, though, you'll be more relaxed if you have everything ready before you begin.

Reduce Food Waste

Wash fruits and vegetables thoroughly so you don't need to peel away edible skins. The additional step of peeling takes time, and reducing food waste means you're also helping the environment. If you eat the skins, you'll get a lot more fiber in your diet. Plus, they'll add texture (though they soften down in the cooking time that many curries take). I try not to peel potatoes, carrots, pumpkins, cucumbers, tomatoes, and squash; I eat pretty much all fruit skins, too.

How about zesting up or finely grating the outer skins of those lemons, limes, and oranges to scatter over rice dishes and salads? They have aromatic oils that will add a citrusy perfume to your food.

I've heard of people peeling eggplant and zucchini. These tender-skinned vegetables don't need it, though. You'll hardly notice the skin after it's cooked, and it'll also help to hold the flesh together.

Keep Your Compost Pail Nearby

Moving around the kitchen for every little task is a waste of time. I always keep a big plastic bowl nearby when I'm chopping ingredients so that I'm not messing up my kitchen counter and chopping board. It keeps chopped ingredients skin-free, too! With one swoop, I can move the waste into the compost pail and carry it out to the yard. I sometimes line the bowl with a recyclable food bag, so all I need to do at the end of cooking, is tie up the bag and throw it away.

If your compost pail is manageable in size, you can have it open nearby when you're prepping.

Another mantra I follow is to clean up as I go along. I start washing up when the onions go into the pan and wipe down counters when the curry is cooking. I don't like working in a messy kitchen, and multitasking helps me get done quicker. Some utensils may need a bit of a soak — get them into hot soapy water as soon as you've finished using them.

Use a Pressure Cooker or Instant Pot

It's India's biggest cooking secret and now you know it: Everyone uses a pressure cooker to get those beans, lentils, and meats done in minutes rather than hours. Walk into a residential area around 11 a.m., and you'll hear pressure cooker whistles going off.

It's really worth investing in a pressure cooker or Instant Pot if you want to cook healthy, delicious foods quickly. Follow the manufacturer's instructions, and take baby steps if you're new to it. Check out *Instant Pot Cookbook For Dummies*, by Wendy Jo Peterson and Elizabeth Shaw (Wiley), for more on working with an Instant Pot.

Both of these appliances work by sealing in the steam and creating pressure that cooks the food faster. They reach a temperature of above boiling very quickly and can save a massive amount of energy. I can get a lamb curry cooked in 20 minutes after pressure has built up, as opposed to an hour and a half in a pot. It really takes the pressure off cooking Indian!

Choose the Right Size Pan and Use a Lid

If the pan is too small, you'll have to move the curry into a bigger one each time you add a bulky ingredient. If the pan is too big, food may catch because there's too little of it on the bottom. Find that Goldilocks pan in your kitchen, and make sure it also has a lid. (If your pan doesn't have a lid, use another pan of the same size, inverted as a "lid," or just use some aluminum foil. Then go out and buy a lid!)

TIP

Lids help to lock in the steam when you're boiling or simmering something. Leave the top off if you're reducing a liquid, but sealing it will help cook meat, vegetables, rice, and more — efficiently. For some dishes that tend to boil over very quickly, try partially covering the pan. When boiling lentils, put a long wooden spoon over the top of the pan horizontally and then place the lid on top. The spoon helps to break up the bubbles as they rise and pushes everything down, back into the pan.

Chapter **23**
Ten Myths about Indian Food

Y ou've heard the old idiom "Variety is the spice of life." It was probably first said to describe Indian cooking. In a country of billions of people, with so many geographical variations and climatic differences, it's no wonder that Indian food is varied and distinct from one place to another. India has more than 25 states, each with its own cuisine.

Not all Indian food is hot, but almost all Indian food does have spice. India is the world's largest producer and consumer of spices. Many other cuisines of the world — such as Thai, Mexican, and Jamaican — use spices, too, but India's sheer size means that spices are used in countless different ways all over the country.

If you've enjoyed dinner at a good French restaurant, you know that cream and butter are what make the food so rich. With Indian food, instead of cream and butter, it's *ghee* (clarified butter); ghee is used to cook special dishes, but it's not what you use for cooking your average weeknight dinner. Many Indian dietitians consider ghee to be healthy when it's eaten in moderation (as long as you don't have any health issues that prohibit you from eating fats).

If you've heard contrasting versions of what Indian food is all about, this chapter is for you. Here, I bust some myths about Indian food so you have the facts.

All Indian Food Is Extremely Hot

If you've shied away from Indian food because you thought it was all hot, just think about all the lovely breads, rice dishes, side dishes, salads, and desserts you've missed out on. Knowing whether a curry on a restaurant menu will be hot or not can be difficult, I grant you that, but a great selection of other dishes will definitely *not* be blazing on your palate. Indian food is definitely spiced, but a lot of it isn't even *mildly* hot.

REMEMBER

The words *spicy* and *hot* have come to mean the same thing, but they're not. Not all spicy foods are hot — they may just be flavorful, and what's to complain about there?

TIP

A great way to eat only as much heat as you can handle is to cook your Indian food at home. Restaurant cooking varies from chef to chef, so you can never be sure of heat levels. Home cooking typically is more subtle and nuanced, so the only way you'll make something too hot is if you accidentally spice it twice. (I did that once, or so my children tell me, and I traumatized them in the process.) When cooking your curry, go easy on the masala and try to *woo* those flavors out of core ingredients with technique.

Popadams and Dips Are Eaten at the Start of a Meal

A balanced Indian meal has color, texture, and flavor, all on one plate (see Chapter 9). Popadams are always served *with* a meal to provide texture; they're never served at the start. Eating popadams at the start of the meal would just ruin your appetite. Serving popadams this way is a restaurant practice. My guess is that they sneakily want you to order more beer and keep you busy while they prepare your food. Many restaurants charge for these popadams, so they're being cheeky about it as well!

TIP

If you want to be seen as a *true* Indian food connoisseur, ask for your popadams *with* the meal.

And those dips — mango chutney, mint raita, and so on — are actually condiments designed to personalize your meal. They aren't meant to saturate your palate with flavor before you've even begun. If dips are being eaten and there's no dinner nearby, odds are, there's a glass of beer or whisky around. In India, popadams, sometimes scattered with diced onions and chilies, are served as bar snacks.

I always buy ready-made popadams. (Homemade ones are sun-dried on flat roofs during Indian summers.) There are plenty of flavors — such as garlic, black pepper, and chile — to choose from.

All Indian Food Is Curry

That's like saying all American food is burgers. Only the uninitiated think that. Visit an Indian home for dinner, and you'll find lots of bowls on the table, with some curries, rice, bread, dry dishes, salads, and more.

Curry has become an oversimplified term for every Indian food that has spice in it. When the British first tasted curry in India, hundreds of years ago, they surely thought, "Whoa, that's different!" But they probably didn't realize that each curry had a specific name, so they called everything "curry." The word migrated to Britain, and soon, all over the world. Indians refer to very few dishes as "curry," and even then, only in big towns and cities where English is spoken. When Indians use the term *curry*, they're usually referring to a dish that has sauce in it (and that sauce is called *gravy*).

It's wonderful that Indian food has traveled all over the world and that people everywhere are curious about it! But don't make the mistake of referring to all Indian recipes as "curry." Indian people everywhere will thank you for it.

Indian Food Is Unhealthy

Indian restaurant food *can* be unhealthy, but the same is true of all types of restaurant food. Homestyle cooking is far healthier and more subtle. Restaurants want to give you a unique eating experience, so they add too much spice, salt, and oil. Of course, it tastes good. But it's similar to eating a bag of salted potato chips — lovely, but not great for you.

Calorie-rich curries are the forte of many Indian restaurants. The telltale sign: the oil that floats on top. That oil grosses me out and makes me feel heavy and thirsty (you can probably tell, I'm not a fan of restaurant food).

Home cooking is based on the principles of *Ayurveda* (a form of holistic healing), so everything that goes into the pan has a purpose and is cooked in a way that will help it contribute to well-being.

All Indian Bread Is Naan

Naan is a yeast-leavened bread, cooked in a *tandoor* (a clay oven fired up to over 800 degrees, by burning coals at its base). Naan takes a bit of time to make (and that's not counting the time it takes to get the tandoor to the right temperature), because the dough is left to rise for hours in order to become fluffy. Firing up a tandoor to cook bread for a family of four every day is a bit fiddly.

Tandoori cooking is mainly a Punjabi thing. In fact, many Punjabi villages have a communal tandoor where families take their dough to be turned into *rotis* (unleavened bread that can be prepared in minutes) rather than naans.

I believe there's another reason for this preference of roti over naan. All over the country, Indians prefer whole, unrefined foods. Rotis made with whole-wheat flour are a healthier, lighter everyday bread than naans made with refined white flour. Naans are more an occasional treat at restaurants, brushed amply with butter or ghee and sprinkled liberally with herbs, garlic, and magic.

Outside of India, most people not of Indian origin have eaten Indian food at restaurants that have tandoors and offer Punjabi-style food, which has led to this notion that all Indian bread is naan.

REMEMBER

All naans are Indian breads, but not all Indian breads are naans.

Adding Curry Powder Makes a Dish Indian

If I were you, I wouldn't mention curry powder to an Indian chef. That would be like opening a jar of Ragu in front of an Italian chef. Curry powder is seen as an insult to the skill of creating a fine balance of spice and technique in order to conjure up dishes that are appealingly complex and beautiful. Although curry powder has the spices that are used in curry making, the proportions can change, making each dish unique. Just as you can't add Worcestershire sauce to a curry in order to make it an English stew, you can't add curry powder to a stew to make it a curry.

Besides, adding curry powder to everything makes it all taste the same, and then you're missing the joy of Indian cooking!

Eating with Your Fingers Is Unhygienic

Not long ago, I went to an exhibition in London about flavor and taste. Their research showed that the best way to taste food was by eating with your fingers so that there was no interruption by another sensation such as metal or wood. (The only element that replicated the purity of hand eating was gold!)

Perhaps this is one reason why people eat with their fingers. Fingers can also gauge the temperature of the food before it goes into the mouth. Indian people wash their hands before and after a meal, and all Indians will say that eating Indian food in this way makes it taste better. Of course, they've learned since they were small children to maneuver those tiny grains of rice and sloppy curries from plate to mouth in an elegant fashion, a skill that takes time and practice.

Don't try to eat with your fingers for the first time in public — especially not on a date!

Indians Eat Food off Leaves and Not Plates

In some rural parts of India and at many south Indian weddings, food is served on banana leaves. This practice is considered environmentally friendly (the used leaves are fed to cattle). Plus, there's no washing up (saving time, effort, and water), and food looks prettier on a fresh leaf.

Wedding feasts in India are sumptuous meals with many dishes. You'd need a large banana leaf (cut into a manageable size) to hold all that food!

Most city folk, not having access to banana trees in the same way, look forward to a banana leaf meal because it's always associated with something special. But normally, Indian people eat off plates or metal dishes called *thalis.*

All Indian Food Is Cooked in Ghee

Ghee, like butter, is an indulgence. Everyday home-cooked food doesn't all need to be prepared using ghee. But it does taste rich and wonderful when poured over a dal or rice, brushed onto rotis and swirled into desserts.

Some recipes benefit from flavored oils such as coconut and mustard, whereas other recipes will become heavenly with a spoon of ghee. Cooks choose when to add ghee and when not to add it.

Indian Food Is Mainly Vegetarian

Roughly one-third of Indians are vegetarian, and meat eaters don't eat it every day. There's a huge repertoire of Indian dishes, but it's hard to generalize about the cuisine and say that it's mainly anything. Indian feasts would be much less fun without those platters of meat, fish, and chicken kabobs and biryanis.

A huge number of vegetables, legumes, lentils, beans, nuts, and dairy products are available to cook with, so being vegetarian in India is easy and common, but it's not mandatory.

Chapter **24**

Ten Tips on Indian Table Etiquette

One of the top ways your Indian friend will show you love is by cooking for you. Being invited home is a huge compliment and shows that your host wants to pamper you and make you want to fall in love with their country, through food. Always accept such an invitation — you'll have the time of your life! Such culinary joys are not to be found in restaurants, and you'll offend your host by turning down the invite.

Now that you've said yes, what are the do's and don'ts? What time should you arrive and what should you bring? When Indian people give you a time as part of the invite, take my word for it: They expect you to be late. Everyone in India arrives late. If you ring the doorbell precisely on time, you'll very like see the cook in a fluster and the rest of the family in their casual clothes. Arriving half an hour late is quite acceptable.

In this chapter, I tell you what to expect at the table, how to serve yourself, and which hand to use for eating and serving. I explain why *double-dipping* (immersing a spoon you've just tasted from back into the curry) is a big no-no and why finishing what's on your plate is such a compliment to the chef. And should you ask for alcohol with your meal? Read on to find out more.

Save Room for Seconds and Thirds

Indian meals are served as sharing plates, unless you're having a thali (see Chapter 9), where everything arrives pre-plated. You'll be expected to help yourself to a bit of everything, so don't overload your plate on the first go. You will always — I repeat, *always* — be offered seconds, so it's more polite to have another helping than it is to pile food on your plate the first time. Loading up your plate with food on the first helping is seen as disrespectful of the other diners who may feel that there's not enough to go around. (There will always be plenty of food.) This goes for the main course as well.

You'll be offered a third and perhaps a fourth helping, too — this is your host's way of showing you hospitality. You'll find Indian hosts coaxing you to eat more and offering you all the various plates of food over and over again. They're never offended if you help yourself over and over again, too. Just keep the helpings small. And if they think you're shy, they'll serve you themselves!

Eat with Your Right Hand

Eating with the right hand is the norm and is considered clean. The left hand is reserved for personal cleansing and, therefore, unclean. Eat with your right hand as much as you can. Use your left hand to lift your drinking vessel, to pass dishes around, and to serve yourself.

It is considered very rude and unclean to use your eating hand (your right hand) to serve yourself with. If you're eating with your fingers or if some of the foods on your plate are finger foods, you shouldn't touch ladles that everyone else will also need to touch with sullied hands. Your host will be too embarrassed to bring a new ladle to the table, and you may find that the host stops eating because they can't help themselves to more food with the ladle you mucked up. Although this may seem like a good idea (you get more food if the host stops eating), you'll never be invited back.

Don't Double-Dip

Personal hygiene rules mean that Indians don't eat from the same plate or drink from the same cup as other people, even their friends. The exception to this rule is sometimes made for a person's closest family members, but even that isn't always the case. When friends pass around a bottle, you'll see them *sky-drink* from it, which means that the bottle never touches their lips. If a stranger offers you a drink, be sure to sky-drink; otherwise, they won't be able to have any of it themselves.

While cooking, a cook will have a tasting spoon. Using the same spoon twice in a curry made for the family or for guests means that no one else will touch it. Some cooks pour a little drop of sauce on their palms to taste it and then always wash their hands after.

Similarly, don't use your spoon or fork to serve yourself from sharing plates. Always use the ladle provided, and make sure that it doesn't touch your plate. I've seen people help themselves, tap the ladle on their plate (from which they've already eaten), and then return the ladle to the curry. Indians consider that practice unhygienic. Keeping your dinnerware separate from everyone else's is seen as thoughtful.

Show Appreciation to Your Host

An old Sanskrit saying "Athithi Devo Bhava" means that a guest is equal to God. This is truly what many Indians believe. So, if you're invited around to a home, even for work, you may find yourself being asked to stay for dinner — and your host may insist on it. Expect to be honored with plenty of food. The ingredients won't be expensive, but there will be many dishes. If it's an impromptu invitation, they'll offer you everything they would have eaten themselves.

Always compliment your host on the time and effort they've put in and show appreciation for the food they've cooked. They'll feel honored if you accept their invitation to stay for a meal and will expect you to eat well. They'll also want to make you feel at home, so they'll make compromises for the fact that you may not know all their customs. You may be offered cutlery even if the hosts are eating with their fingers, for example, and your host may talk you through what goes with what on your plate.

After dinner, wait a while before you leave. It's not seen as polite to simply eat and run. On the other hand, don't hang around until everyone is falling asleep. Balance is key.

Wash Your Hands

Indian dining can require some use of the hands (for eating and for serving your-self or others), so it's thoughtful to wash your hands before you come to the dinner table. Ask the host where you can do this, and you'll be politely shown a sink and given your own napkin to use. (Washing your hands before any meal is a good idea, Indian or not — it helps stop the transfer of germs between diners and keeps your own food relatively free of bacteria.)

REMEMBER

Wash your hands after the meal as well. If you've used your hands to eat or to serve, your hosts don't want you touching other things in their home without first washing your hands. If you're eating with your fingers, this step is, of course, more essential than ever.

If your hosts are eating with their fingers and you've been offered cutlery, do whatever you're comfortable with. The most important thing is that you're all getting to enjoy the meal together.

WARNING

If you're at a traditional South Indian feast (lucky you!) served on a banana leaf, you won't want to use cutlery — it'll tear through the leaf and you'll make a mess. Very embarrassing. Better to practice eating with your fingers before you go.

Don't Lick Your Fingers

If you decide to eat with your fingers, there's table etiquette involved. First, you'll use your right hand to eat (see the earlier section, "Eat with Your Right Hand"). You'll also need to practice eating gracefully and delicately. Imagine having to mix curry and rice, gather a single mouthful and bring it up to your mouth in one move — all without letting a single grain of rice fall. Or think of using just one hand to tear a bit of roti off, scoop up curry sauce, and eat it without spilling any. Now you know why Indian children are taught to eat with their hands from the moment they're weaned. (Apparently, this helps develop motor skills and improves their handwriting, too!)

Throughout most of India, using just your fingertips when eating is polite. If you get food all over your hands, it's seen as sloppy and ill-mannered. Licking your fingers to clean them is also a no-no. When you pop food into your mouth, it's accompanied by the lips scooping everything off the fingers so that you don't have to clean them individually afterward by licking them.

Even traditional Indian people use spoons for things like yogurt or milky desserts.

REMEMBER

Don't stop yourself from asking for cutlery — no one will be offended. If you're planning on being invited often, practice eating with your hands at home (preferably when you're alone!).

Mix Your Food Intentionally

When you help yourself, the main grain will be in the middle of your plate and everything else will be served around it. I've seen people not used to Indian food pile ladles of food, one on top of the other, and eat it with a knife and fork as you would a pie. I've watched as naans have been placed on a plate, followed by rice on top of it, curry on top of that, and a salad to crown it all. The entire effort it took the cook to create nuance, harmony, and variety was lost in that one moment.

REMEMBER

An Indian plate is designed for variety. Mix your rice or roti with different side dishes with each bite. Add a dot of pickle or salad so that each mouthful is a new surprise.

Clean Your Plate

Try to finish everything on your plate. If there are leftovers, your host will take it to mean that you didn't enjoy the food, which will be disrespectful. That's another reason to help yourself to small portions at the start and take seconds only of the dishes you particularly enjoyed — that way, you won't be tempted to waste food.

Your hosts will most likely be gracious about your wasting food, but it's seen as thoughtless and extravagant in a country where food is deeply respected and so many go without.

Try to keep pace with your host. If you eat too quickly, they'll feel obligated to hurry up, too, and if you eat too slowly, they may take it as a sign that you don't like the food.

When you're sure you've eaten enough, compliment your host and tell them how delicious you thought the meal was.

Bring Flowers instead of Food for Your Host

The Muslim population in India doesn't eat pork, and the Hindus and Sikhs don't eat beef. If you bring something for your host, make sure it doesn't contain either. Almost a third of India is vegetarian for religious reasons, so you may find yourself sitting down to a meat-free dinner.

TIP

Your best bet is not to even bring up pork, beef, or other meats in homes where they're not consumed. Vegetarians in India don't even eat eggs so a gift-wrapped cake won't go down well. Best to bring flowers, really.

Don't Drink Alcohol with Your Dinner Unless You're Offered It

The best drink with an Indian meal is water, and this is probably what you'll be served in an Indian home. Alcohol is not served as an accompaniment to an Indian meal, but it can be served before the meal as a predinner drink or cocktail. Many Indians think of drinking as taboo and won't do so in front of their elders. In a restaurant, you'll probably be offered beer, and it has become common practice now to pair beer with curry.

If you're a woman, it's even more complicated: You may or may not be offered alcohol, depending on what customs your host follows. (The rules slacken a bit for non-Indian women.)

Appendix

Metric Conversion Guide

Note: The recipes in this book weren't developed or tested using metric measurements. There may be some variation in quality when converting to metric units.

Common Abbreviations

Abbreviation(s)	What It Stands For
cm	Centimeter
C., c.	Cup
G, g	Gram
kg	Kilogram
L, l	Liter
lb.	Pound
mL, ml	Milliliter
oz.	Ounce
pt.	Pint
t., tsp.	Teaspoon
T., Tb., Tbsp.	Tablespoon

Volume

U.S. Units	Canadian Metric	Australian Metric
¼ teaspoon	1 milliliter	1 milliliter
½ teaspoon	2 milliliters	2 milliliters
1 teaspoon	5 milliliters	5 milliliters
1 tablespoon	15 milliliters	20 milliliters
¼ cup	50 milliliters	60 milliliters
⅓ cup	75 milliliters	80 milliliters
½ cup	125 milliliters	125 milliliters
⅔ cup	150 milliliters	170 milliliters
¾ cup	175 milliliters	190 milliliters
1 cup	250 milliliters	250 milliliters
1 quart	1 liter	1 liter
1½ quarts	1.5 liters	1.5 liters
2 quarts	2 liters	2 liters
2½ quarts	2.5 liters	2.5 liters
3 quarts	3 liters	3 liters
4 quarts (1 gallon)	4 liters	4 liters

Weight

U.S. Units	Canadian Metric	Australian Metric
1 ounce	30 grams	30 grams
2 ounces	55 grams	60 grams
3 ounces	85 grams	90 grams
4 ounces (¼ pound)	115 grams	125 grams
8 ounces (½ pound)	225 grams	225 grams
16 ounces (1 pound)	455 grams	500 grams (½ kilogram)

Length

Inches	Centimeters
0.5	1.5
1	2.5
2	5.0
3	7.5
4	10.0
5	12.5
6	15.0
7	17.5
8	20.5
9	23.0
10	25.5
11	28.0
12	30.5

Temperature (Degrees)

Fahrenheit	Celsius
32	0
212	100
250	120
275	140
300	150
325	160
350	180
375	190
400	200
425	220

Fahrenheit	Celsius
450	230
475	240
500	260

Index

A

Aam aur Kaju ki Smoothie (Mango and Cashew Smoothie) recipe, 283

Aam ka Custard (Mango Custard with Tropical Fruit) recipe, 327

Aam ki Lassi (Mango and Yogurt Drink) recipe, 330

Aam ki Launji (Sweet-and-Sour Mango Chutney) recipe, 318

achaar, defined, 161

acidic ingredients, adding to curries, 136

ajwain spice, shopping for, 47

alcohol, taboo nature of, 354

almonds
  adding texture and thickness to dishes with, 49, 149
  Badam ke Laddoo (Almond Fudge) recipe, 329

Aloo Gobi (North Indian Potatoes with Cauliflower) recipe, 219–220

Aloo Mutter (Pea and Potato Curry) recipe, 233

amchur spice, shopping for, 47

Amritsari Fish (Spiced Fish Fingers in a Gram-Flour Crust) recipe, 300

Anda Mutter ki Hari Curry (Egg and Peas Green Curry) recipe, 270

anti-meat sentiment, 24

appetizers
  Amritsari Fish (Spiced Fish Fingers in a Gram-Flour Crust) recipe, 300
  Bombay Sandwich (Sandwich with Chutney, Vegetables, and Cheese) recipe, 297
  Chicken Tikka (Spicy Chicken Bites) recipe, 288
  Chivda (Hot, Savory, and Sweet Mix of Grains, Seeds, and Nuts) recipe, 293
  Dahi Vada (Lentil Fritters in Yogurt) recipe, 294–295
  Gosht ke Kebab (Mini Lamb or Beef Skewers with Mint) recipe, 289
  Macchi ke Cutlet (Spiced Fishcakes) recipe, 298
  Onion Bhajia (Savory Onion Fritters) recipe, 286

  overview, 285
  Pakora (Savory Mixed Vegetable Fritters) recipe, 287
  Pav Bhaji (Crushed Vegetable Curry with Bread Rolls) recipe, 296
  Shakarkand Chaat (Sweet Potatoes with Nuts and Yogurt) recipe, 299
  Shankarpali (Crisp, Sweet Pastry Diamonds) recipe, 292
  Vegetable Samosas (Vegetable and Pastry Parcels) recipe, 290–291

appreciation, showing to hosts, 351

aromatics
  adding to curries, 136
  Paneer Pulao (Aromatic Rice with Indian Cottage Cheese) recipe, 241
  shopping for, 58–59

asafetida spice, shopping for, 47

astringent taste, description of, 30

atta grain, shopping for, 48

Ayurveda, 26–27, 345

Ayurvedic diet
  identifying rasa, 29–31
  rules of, 27–29
  seasonal eating, 31–32

B

Badam ke Laddoo (Almond Fudge) recipe, 329

Baghara Baingan (Sweet-and-Sour Eggplant Curry) recipe, 222

Baida Bhurji (Spicy Scrambled Eggs) recipe, 277

Baida Masala (North Indian Egg Curry) recipes, 264

Baingan ka Bharta (Fire-Roasted Eggplant with Spices) recipe, 218–219

banana leaves, 151–152, 347

Bangda Ghassi (Mackerel Curry with Tamarind) recipe, 208

basmati rice
cooking properly, 86–87
foreign influences on, 13
shopping for, 48
Batata Bhaji (Spiced Yellow Potatoes) recipe, 282
batch cooking, saving time by, 338–339
beans
Channa Masala (Chickpea Curry) recipe, 253
Dal Makhani (Creamy Black Beans with Garlic), 252
Kadhi (Chickpea Flour and Yogurt Curry) recipe, 260
Mung Usal (Sprouted Mung Beans with Turmeric), 261–262
Mung Usal (Sprouted Mung Beans with Turmeric) recipe, 261–262
Rajma Masala (Red Bean Curry) recipe, 254
shopping for, 50–51, 53–54
Beans Upkari (French Green Beans with Chile and Coconut) recipe, 230
beef
recipes containing
Beef Vindaloo (Sour Hot Goan Curry), 183
Kofta Curry (Lamb or Beef Meatball Curry), 182
Malabar Beef Roast (Deep, Dark Beef with Spices), 187
overview, 173–174
Safed Gosht (Lamb in a Coconut and Cashew Nut Curry), 186
shopping for, 62
Beef Vindaloo (Sour Hot Goan Curry) recipe, 183
Bengali Chicken Korma (Chicken Curry with Cream) recipe, 199
Bengali sweets, foreign influences on, 16
besan grain, shopping for, 48
Bharvan Bhindi (Okra Stuffed with Spices) recipe, 228
Bhuna Gosht (Brown Lamb Curry) recipe, 180
bhuna technique, 79–80
biryani cut meat, 70
bitter taste
balancing in meals, 167
compensating for, 141
description of, 29–30

black gram, 51
bland flavor, compensating for, 140
blender, types to buy, 42
blooming technique. See tarka technique
boiled eggs, garnishing curries with, 150
Boiled Rice (Chaval), Absorption Method, 88
Boiled Rice (Chaval), Draining Method, 89
Bombay Anda Curry (Smooth Egg and Tomato Curry) recipes, 266
Bombay Sandwich (Sandwich with Chutney, Vegetables, and Cheese) recipe, 297
boti meat, 70
breads
Chapati or Roti (Flatbread) recipe, 302
Chilla (Gram Flour Pancakes) recipe, 310
Gobi Paratha (Cauliflower-Stuffed Bread) recipe, 306–307
Naan (Leavened Oven-Baked Bread) recipe, 303
Neer Dosa (South Indian Rice Crêpes) recipe, 309
overview, 301
Paratha (Layered Bread) recipe, 304
Poori (Festive Fried Bread) recipe, 305
Thepla (Fenugreek Bread) recipe, 308
types of, 346
breakfast dishes
Aam aur Kaju ki Smoothie (Mango and Cashew Smoothie) recipe, 283
Baida Bhurji (Spicy Scrambled Eggs) recipe, 277
Batata Bhaji (Spiced Yellow Potatoes) recipe, 282
Chile Toast (Cheese Toast with Spices) recipe, 276
Dosa (Fermented Rice and Lentil Crêpes) recipe, 279–280
Masala Omelet (Omelet with Spices) recipe, 274
overview, 273
Poha (Spiced Flaked Rice) recipe, 281
Rava Utappam (Semolina Pancakes) recipe, 278
Upma (Savory Semolina Cake) recipe, 275
brown masala sauce, 143
burned spices, 113
butter, garnishing curries with, 150–151
butterflying shrimp, 72

C

canned goods, shopping for, 52

canned tomatoes, cooking with, 52, 96–97

canola oil, 57

capsaicin, defined, 11

cardamom spice
  Elaichi Kapi (Pulled Coffee with Cardamom and Brown Sugar) recipe, 333
  seeds versus husk, 117
  Seyal Teevan (Lamb Chop Curry with Cardamom) recipe, 184
  shopping for, 47

Carrot Poriyal (Carrots Cooked with Mustard Seeds and Coconut) recipe, 227

cashews
  adding texture and thickness to dishes with, 49
  Murgh Malaiwala (Chicken in a Creamy Cashew Nut and Saffron Curry) recipe, 190
  Safed Gosht (Lamb in a Coconut and Cashew Nut Curry) recipe, 186
  Shahi Baida Korma (Egg Curry with Cashew Nuts and Fenugreek) recipe, 268

Chaat Masala (Finishing Mix for Sprinkling over Snacks) recipe, 121

chaat masala spice, shopping for, 47

chaats. See popadams

chai, 52

Channa Masala (Chickpea Curry) recipe, 253

Channa Pulao (Brown Rice with Chickpeas) recipe, 246

Chapati or Roti (Flatbread) recipe, 302

Chaval aur Narial ki Kheer (Rice and Coconut Pudding) recipe, 324

chef's knife, 34

Chibuda Hashale (Melon and Coconut Milk Pudding) recipe, 328

chicken. See poultry

Chicken 65 (Indo Chinese Chicken) recipe, 201

Chicken Biryani (Festive One-Pot Chicken and Rice) recipe, 239–240

Chicken Madras (Chicken Curry with Fennel) recipe, 197

Chicken Tikka Masala (Chicken Curry with Spices) recipe, 194

Chicken Tikka (Spicy Chicken Bites) recipe, 288

chiffonade, defined, 69

children, introducing to Indian cuisine, 30

chile flowers, 149

chile powder spice, shopping for, 47

Chile Toast (Cheese Toast with Spices) recipe, 276

chile-free curry, 31

chilies
  cooking with, 103–105
  garnishing curries with, 149
  increasing heat levels in curries with, 131, 138
  recipes containing
    Beans Upkari (French Green Beans with Chile and Coconut), 230
    Chile Toast (Cheese Toast with Spices), 276
    Haldi Gajar Mirchi ka Achaar (Fresh Carrot, Turmeric, Ginger, and Chile Pickle), 162
    Lasnechi Chutney (Dry Hot, Sour, Sweet Garlic, Chile, and Coconut Chutney), 163
  shopping for, 48
  trying varieties of, 58, 117

Chilla (Gram Flour Pancakes) recipe, 310

Chinese eggplant, shopping for, 60

chips, adding texture to meals with, 159

Chivda (Hot, Savory, and Sweet Mix of Grains, Seeds, and Nuts) recipe, 293

chopping, cooking techniques for, 68–69

chownk technique. See tarka technique

Christianity, influence on cooking, 18

chutney
  batch cooking, 339
  cooling hot meals by adding, 160
  overview, 311–312
  recipes containing
    Aam ki Launji (Sweet-and-Sour Mango Chutney), 318
    Bombay Sandwich (Sandwich with Chutney, Vegetables, and Cheese), 297
    Hari Chutney (Cilantro and Peanut Chutney), 317
    Khajur Imli ki Chutney (Sweet-and-Sour Date and Tamarind Chutney), 313
    Lasnechi Chutney (Dry Hot, Sour, Sweet Garlic, Chile, and Coconut Chutney), 163
    Pudine aur Pyaz ki Chutney (Mint and Onion Chutney), 314
    Thengai Chutney (Coconut and Tender Mango Chutney), 315–316

cilantro
  chopping, 68
  garnishing curries with, 148
  Hari Chutney (Cilantro and Peanut Chutney) recipe, 317
  storing, 58–59
cinnamon spice, shopping for, 47
climate, influence on Indian cuisine, 11
coconut
  cooking with, 106–107
  processing, 106–107
  recipes containing
    Chaval aur Narial ki Kheer (Rice and Coconut Pudding), 324
    Chibuda Hashale (Melon and Coconut Milk Pudding), 328
    Goan Fish Curry (Fish Curry with Coriander Seeds and Coconut), 211–212
    Kerala Duck Mappas (Duck Curry with Coconut Milk and Pepper), 198
    Kolmbichi Kadhi (Shrimp Curry with Coconut Milk), 206
    Konkani Mutton (Lamb Curry with Cloves, Pepper, and Coconut), 181
    Kube Sukke (Clams in a Coconut Crust), 213
    Lasnechi Chutney (Dry Hot, Sour, Sweet Garlic, Chile, and Coconut Chutney), 163
    Malvani Kombdi (Chicken and Coconut Curry), 196
    Masoor Dal (Brown Lentils with Coconut Milk), 259
    Safed Gosht (Lamb in a Coconut and Cashew Nut Curry), 186
    Thengai Chutney (Coconut and Tender Mango Chutney), 315–316
coconut milk, 53, 107
coconut oil, 25, 57
coconut powder, shopping for, 53
colander, types to buy, 37
color, adding to meals, 156–157
compost pails, throwing waste into, 125, 341
conquest, influence on Indian cuisine, 12
contrasting flavors, in meals, 164
cooked foods, for easier digestion, 28
cooking techniques

bhuna, 79–80
chopping, mincing, and dicing, 68–69
cleaning and deveining shrimp, 71–72
dhungar, 81–82
dum, 76–77
marinating, 72–76
overview, 67–68, 76–77
peeling, 69
slicing, 69–71
talna, 80–81
tarka, 77–79
cookware
  overview, 33
  pots, pans, and griddles, 37–40
  utensils, 33–37
Coorgi-Style Pandi Curry (Pork Curry with Vinegar) recipe, 178
coriander spice
  Goan Fish Curry (Fish Curry with Coriander Seeds and Coconut) recipe, 211–212
  shopping for, 47
corn oil, 57
cream
  Bengali Chicken Korma (Chicken Curry with Cream) recipe, 199
  garnishing curries with, 150–151
  light versus heavy, 55
  shopping for, 55
cubed paneer, 55
cumin spice
  Jeera Pulao (Cumin-Flavored Rice) recipe, 237
  shopping for, 47
curries
  Anda Mutter ki Hari Curry (Egg and Peas Green Curry) recipe, 270
  Baghara Baingan (Sweet-and-Sour Eggplant Curry) recipe, 222
  Baida Masala (North Indian Egg Curry) recipes, 264
  balancing flavors in, 139–141
  Bangda Ghassi (Mackerel Curry with Tamarind) recipe, 208
  batch cooking, 339

Beef Vindaloo (Sour Hot Goan Curry) recipe, 183

Bengali Chicken Korma (Chicken Curry with Cream) recipe, 199

Bhuna Gosht (Brown Lamb Curry) recipe, 180

Bombay Anda Curry (Smooth Egg and Tomato Curry) recipes, 266

Channa Masala (Chickpea Curry) recipe, 253

Chicken Madras (Chicken Curry with Fennel) recipe, 197

Chicken Tikka Masala (Chicken Curry with Spices) recipe, 194

choosing oils to cook with, 126–127

choosing pans to cook with, 126

color of, 141–143

consistency of, 144–147

Coorgi-Style Pandi Curry (Pork Curry with Vinegar) recipe, 178

Egg Kurma (South Indian Egg Curry) recipes, 265

garnishes for, 147–152

Goan Fish Curry (Fish Curry with Coriander Seeds and Coconut) recipe, 211–212

Gosht ka Dalcha (Lamb and Lentil Curry) recipe, 177

Hara Gosht (Lamb in a Green Herby Curry) recipe, 185

heat levels in, 137–139

Jhinga Masala (North Indian Shrimp Curry) recipe, 214

Kadhi (Chickpea Flour and Yogurt Curry) recipe, 260

Karahi Murgh (Chicken Curry with Tomatoes) recipe, 193

Kerala Duck Mappas (Duck Curry with Coconut Milk and Pepper) recipe, 198

Kerala Egg Roast (Egg and Curry Leaf Curry) recipe, 267

Khekda Masaledaar (Crab Curry with Pepper) recipe, 207

Kofta Curry (Lamb or Beef Meatball Curry) recipe, 182

Kolmbichi Kadhi (Shrimp Curry with Coconut Milk) recipe, 206

Kombdi Batata (Chicken and Potato Curry) recipe, 192

Konkani Mutton (Lamb Curry with Cloves, Pepper, and Coconut) recipe, 181

Lobster Kalvan (Lobster Curry) recipe, 216

Malvani Kombdi (Chicken and Coconut Curry) recipe, 196

Masala Gosht (North Indian Lamb Curry) recipe, 175–176

meat for, 70

Meen Moilee (Salmon Curry with Mustard Seeds) recipe, 210

misconception of, 124–126

Murgh Malaiwala (Chicken in a Creamy Cashew Nut and Saffron Curry) recipe, 190

order in which ingredients are added

North Indian, 128–135

overview, 127–128

South Indian, 135–137

overview, 123–124

Pav Bhaji (Crushed Vegetable Curry with Bread Rolls) recipe, 296

Prawn Patia (Sweet and Sour Shrimp Curry) recipe, 215

Rajma Masala (Red Bean Curry) recipe, 254

Saag Murgh (Chicken Curry with Spinach) recipe, 200

Safed Gosht (Lamb in a Coconut and Cashew Nut Curry) recipe, 186

Sali Marghi (Chicken Curry with Apricots) recipe, 195

sauce of, 124

Seyal Teevan (Lamb Chop Curry with Cardamom) recipe, 184

Shahi Baida Korma (Egg Curry with Cashew Nuts and Fenugreek) recipe, 268

thickening and thinning, 144–145

without chilies, 31

curry leaves

chopping, 69

description of, 125–126

Kerala Egg Roast (Egg and Curry Leaf Curry) recipe, 267

storing, 59

curry powder, misconceptions about, 10–11, 124–125

curry sauce, saving time by freezing, 339–340

customizing food, 154

cutting boards, 34

D

Dahi Vada (Lentil Fritters in Yogurt) recipe, 294–295

Dal Dhokli (Lentil Stew with Flour Dumplings) recipe, 257–258

Dal Makhani (Creamy Black Beans with Garlic) recipe, 252

dal roti, 249

desserts
  Aam ka Custard (Mango Custard with Tropical Fruit) recipe, 327
  Aam ki Lassi (Mango and Yogurt Drink) recipe, 330
  Badam ke Laddoo (Almond Fudge) recipe, 329
  Chaval aur Narial ki Kheer (Rice and Coconut Pudding) recipe, 324
  Chibuda Hashale (Melon and Coconut Milk Pudding) recipe, 328
  eating with meals, 169–170
  Kesar Kulfi (Rich Saffron Ice Cream) recipe, 325
  overview, 323
  Sooji ka Halva (Warm Semolina and Raisin Pudding) recipe, 326

dessicated coconuts, processing, 107

Dhabe ka Kheema (Spicy Ground Lamb or Beef) recipe, 179

dhungar technique, 81–82

diced meat, marinating time for, 73

Dosa (Fermented Rice and Lentil Crêpes) recipe, 279–280

dosa pan, 38–39

doshas, 27

double-dipping, 349, 350–351

dried fruit
  adding color and texture to meals with, 52, 150
  garnishing curries with, 149–150
  Kashmiri Pulao (Rice with Mushrooms, Dried Fruit, Nuts, and Spices) recipe, 238

dried herbs, garnishing curries with, 150

drinks
  Elaichi Kapi (Pulled Coffee with Cardamom and Brown Sugar) recipe, 333
  Masala Chai (Spiced Tea) recipe, 331
  Nimbu Pani (Spiced Fresh Lemonade) recipe, 332

overview, 323

dry goods, shopping for, 45–52

dum technique, 76–77

E

Egg Biryani (South Indian Spiced Rice with Eggs) recipe, 243

Egg Kurma (South Indian Egg Curry) recipes, 265

eggplants
  Baghara Baingan (Sweet-and-Sour Eggplant Curry) recipe, 222
  Baingan ka Bharta (Fire-Roasted Eggplant with Spices) recipe, 218–219
  shopping for, 59–60

eggs
  recipes containing
    Anda Mutter ki Hari Curry (Egg and Peas Green Curry) recipe, 270
    Baida Bhurji (Spicy Scrambled Eggs) recipe, 277
    Baida Masala (North Indian Egg Curry) recipes, 264
    Bombay Anda Curry (Smooth Egg and Tomato Curry) recipes, 266
    Egg Biryani (South Indian Spiced Rice with Eggs) recipe, 243
    Egg Kurma (South Indian Egg Curry) recipes, 265
    Kerala Egg Roast (Egg and Curry Leaf Curry) recipe, 267
    Masala Omelet (Omelet with Spices) recipe, 274
    overview, 263
    Papeta Par Eeda (Egg and Potato Fry) recipe, 269
    Shahi Baida Korma (Egg Curry with Cashew Nuts and Fenugreek) recipe, 268
  shopping for, 56

Elaichi Kapi (Pulled Coffee with Cardamom and Brown Sugar) recipe, 333

exportation, of spices, 10–11

F

Fanshachi Bhaji (Curried Young Jackfruit) recipe, 229

fats. *See* oils

fenugreek spice
  Shahi Baida Korma (Egg Curry with Cashew Nuts and Fenugreek) recipe, 268
  shopping for, 47
  storing, 59
  Thepla (Fenugreek Bread) recipe, 308
fillet knife, 34
fingers
  avoiding licking, 352–353
  benefit of eating with, 347
  practicing eating with, 352–353
finishing spice, adding to curries, 134–135
flavor
  adding to meals, 164–167
  balancing in curries, 139–141
  combinations of, 167
  taste versus, 164
flavorings, 49–50
floury potatoes, 60
food waste, reducing, 340–341
fruit
  adding color and texture to meals with, 52
  garnishing curries with, 149–150
  recipes containing
    Aam ka Custard (Mango Custard with Tropical Fruit), 327
    Fanshachi Bhaji (Curried Young Jackfruit), 229
    Kashmiri Pulao (Rice with Mushrooms, Dried Fruit, Nuts, and Spices), 238
frying, 112–113, 158

G

Garam Masala (North Indian Spice Blend) recipe, 118
garam masala spice, shopping for, 47
garlic
  adding to curries, 130
  Dal Makhani (Creamy Black Beans with Garlic) recipe, 252
  Ginger-Garlic Paste (Adrak Lahsun), 92
  storing, 59

garlic crusher, types to buy, 36
garnishes, adding to curries, 135, 147–152
geography, influence on Indian cuisine, 11
ghee
  adding nutrition to vegetarian meals with, 25
  butter versus vegetable, 56
  misconception about, 347–348
  shopping for, 56–57
ginger
  adding to curries, 130
  garnishing curries with, 149
  Ginger-Garlic Paste (Adrak Lahsun), 92
  ginger-garlic paste, batch cooking, 90–92, 339
  Haldi Gajar Mirchi ka Achaar (Fresh Carrot, Turmeric, Ginger, and Chile Pickle) recipe, 162
  storing, 59
Ginger-Garlic Paste (Adrak Lahsun), 92
Goan Fish Curry (Fish Curry with Coriander Seeds and Coconut) recipe, 211–212
Gobi Paratha (Cauliflower-Stuffed Bread) recipe, 306–307
Gosht ka Dalcha (Lamb and Lentil Curry) recipe, 177
Gosht ke Kebab (Mini Lamb or Beef Skewers with Mint) recipe, 289
graffiti eggplant, shopping for, 60
grains
  adding nutrition to vegan and vegetarian meals with, 25
  Chivda (Hot, Savory, and Sweet Mix of Grains, Seeds, and Nuts) recipe, 293
  shopping for, 48
Gram Flour Roux recipe, 146
grater, types to buy, 36
Greek yogurt, 54, 76
green masala sauce, 142
griddles, 37–40
ground meat, marinating time for, 73
ground spices, 114–117, 131, 136
Gujarat, influences on Indian cuisine from, 20–21
Gujarati Sambharo (Cabbage and Carrot Salad) recipe, 321

H

halal meat, 70, 176

Haldi Gajar Mirchi ka Achaar (Fresh Carrot, Turmeric, Ginger, and Chile Pickle) recipe, 162

hands, washing before and after meals, 352

Hara Gosht (Lamb in a Green Herby Curry) recipe, 185

Hari Chutney (Cilantro and Peanut Chutney) recipe, 317

heat
  adding to meals, 160–161
  balancing in meals, 166
  classifying foods with, 154
  compensating for, 140–141
  in curries, 137–139

heavy cream, description of, 55

heavy foods, combining light foods with, 27

herbs
  garnishing curries with, 150
  Hara Gosht (Lamb in a Green Herby Curry) recipe, 185
  shopping for, 58–59

home cooking, restaurant food versus, 154–156

I

improvising, tips for, 146–147

Indian cuisine
  climate, influence on, 11
  conquest, influence on, 12
  creating meals
    adding color, 156–157
    adding flavor, 164–167
    adding heat, 160–161
    adding texture, 157–159
    making menus for, 168–169
    overview, 156
    thali, 169–170
    varying temperatures, 159–160

foreign influences on
  from Eastern India, 15–16
  from Northern India, 12–15
  from Southern India, 17–19
  from Western India, 19–20
geography, influence on, 11
migration, influence on, 12
myths about, 343–348
overview, 9
religious beliefs, influence on, 11–12, 17, 176
from restaurants versus home cooking, 154–156
sacredness of food in, 17
spices used in, 10–12
trade, influence on, 12

Indian eggplant, shopping for, 60

ingredients
  chopping evenly, 339
  cooking with
    chilies, 103–105
    coconuts, 106–107
    ginger-garlic paste, 90–92
    lentils, 97–99
    measuring, 85
    onions, 100–103
    overview, 83–84
    paneer, 108–109
    rice, 86–89
    tamarind, 93–95
    tomatoes, 95–97
  of food from restaurants versus home cooking, 155–156
  measuring, 85
  order in which to add to curries
    North Indian, 128–135
    overview, 127–128
    South Indian, 135–137
  preparing, 125, 338
  shopping for
    canned goods, 52
    dairy, 54–55

dry goods, 45–52

eggs, 56

meat, 62–63

oils, 56–58

overview, 45

produce, 57–58

simplifying, 151–152

standardizing recipes with, 84

washing prior to cooking with, 125

Instant Pots, saving time with, 340–341

instinct, cooking with, 83–84

intuitive eating, 28, 29

Islam, influences on Indian cuisine from, 12–13

J

jaggery, 50, 136

Japanese eggplant, shopping for, 60

Jeera Pulao (Cumin-Flavored Rice) recipe, 237

Jhinga Masala (North Indian Shrimp Curry) recipe, 214

Jhinga Pulao (Spiced Rice with Shrimp) recipe, 242

Judaism, influence on Indian cuisine, 18

K

kachumber, 159

Kachumber (Onion, Cucumber, Tomato, and Carrot Salad) recipe, 320

Kaddu ki Subzi (Sweet-and-Sour Pumpkin) recipe, 231

Kadhi (Chickpea Flour and Yogurt Curry) recipe, 260

Kapha, 27

karahi meat, 70

Karahi Murgh (Chicken Curry with Tomatoes) recipe, 193

karahis, 37–38, 80

karimeen, 18

Kashmir, influences on Indian cuisine from, 14–15

Kashmiri Pulao (Rice with Mushrooms, Dried Fruit, Nuts, and Spices) recipe, 238

kasuri methi, 134, 150

Kenyan eggplant, shopping for, 60

Kerala, influences on Indian cuisine from, 18

Kerala Duck Mappas (Duck Curry with Coconut Milk and Pepper) recipe, 198

Kerala Egg Roast (Egg and Curry Leaf Curry) recipe, 267

Kerala Vegetable Curry (Mixed Vegetable Curry with Coconut Milk) recipe, 223

Kesar Kulfi (Rich Saffron Ice Cream) recipe, 325

Khajur Imli ki Chutney (Sweet-and-Sour Date and Tamarind Chutney) recipe, 313

Kheema Pulao (Spiced Rice with Ground Meat) recipe, 244

Kheere Tamater ka Raita (Cucumber and Tomato Salad with Yogurt) recipe, 319

Khekda Masaledaar (Crab Curry with Pepper) recipe, 207

Khichdi (Warming Rice and Lentil Stew) recipe, 247

knives, types to buy, 34, 35

Kobichi Bhaji (Cabbage with Peas and Turmeric) recipe, 221

Kofta Curry (Lamb or Beef Meatball Curry) recipe, 182

kokum. *See* tamarind

Kolkata sweets, foreign influences on, 16

Kolmbi Fry (Fried Spiced Shrimp) recipe, 209

Kolmbichi Kadhi (Shrimp Curry with Coconut Milk) recipe, 206

Kombdi Batata (Chicken and Potato Curry) recipe, 192

Konkan, influences on Indian cuisine from, 20

Konkani Mutton (Lamb Curry with Cloves, Pepper, and Coconut) recipe, 181

koshimbir, 159

Kube Sukke (Clams in a Coconut Crust) recipe, 213

L

ladles, types to buy, 36

lamb

overview, 173–174

recipes containing

lamb *(continued)*
  Bhuna Gosht (Brown Lamb Curry), 180
  Dhabe ka Kheema (Spicy Ground Lamb or
      Beef), 179
  Gosht ka Dalcha (Lamb and Lentil Curry), 177
  Hara Gosht (Lamb in a Green Herby Curry), 185
  Kofta Curry (Lamb or Beef Meatball Curry), 182
  Konkani Mutton (Lamb Curry with Cloves,
      Pepper, and Coconut), 181
  Masala Gosht (North Indian Lamb Curry),
      175–176
  Safed Gosht (Lamb in a Coconut and Cashew
      Nut Curry), 186
  Seyal Teevan (Lamb Chop Curry with
      Cardamom), 184
  shopping for, 62
Lasnechi Chutney (Dry Hot, Sour, Sweet Garlic,
    Chile, and Coconut Chutney) recipe, 163
legumes. *See also* beans; lentils
  adding nutrition to vegan and vegetarian meals
      with, 25
  recipes containing
    Channa Masala (Chickpea Curry), 253
    Dal Dhokli (Lentil Stew with Flour Dumplings),
        257–258
    Dal Makhani (Creamy Black Beans with
        Garlic), 252
    Kadhi (Chickpea Flour and Yogurt Curry), 260
    Masoor Dal (Brown Lentils with Coconut
        Milk), 259
    Mung Usal (Sprouted Mung Beans with
        Turmeric), 261–262
    overview, 249–250
    Palak Pappu (South Indian Spinach Dal), 256
    Rajma Masala (Red Bean Curry), 254
    Sambhar (South Indian Lentil Stew), 255
    Tarka Dal (Spiced lentils), 251
  sprouting with sprouting jars, 262
lemons
  garnishing curries with, 148–149
  Nimbu Pani (Spiced Fresh Lemonade) recipe, 332
lentils
  recipes containing
    cooking, 98–99
    Dahi Vada (Lentil Fritters in Yogurt), 294–295
    Dal Dhokli (Lentil Stew with Flour Dumplings),
        257–258
    Dosa (Fermented Rice and Lentil Crêpes),
        279–280
    Gosht ka Dalcha (Lamb and Lentil Curry), 177
    Khichdi (Warming Rice and Lentil Stew), 247
    Masoor Dal (Brown Lentils with Coconut
        Milk), 259
    overview, 97–98
    Palak Pappu (South Indian Spinach Dal), 256
    Sambhar (South Indian Lentil Stew), 255
    Tarka Dal (Spiced lentils), 251
  texture and consistency of, 99
light cream, description of, 55
light foods, combining heavy foods with, 27
limes, garnishing curries with, 148–149
liquid, adding to curries, 133, 137
Lobster Kalvan (Lobster Curry) recipe, 216
low-fat yogurt, 55
lumpy curry, 145

M

Macchi ke Cutlet (Spiced Fishcakes) recipe, 298
Malabar Beef Roast (Deep, Dark Beef with Spices)
    recipe, 187
Malvani Kombdi (Chicken and Coconut Curry)
    recipe, 196
mango puree, shopping for, 54
mangoes
  recipes containing
    Aam aur Kaju ki Smoothie (Mango and Cashew
        Smoothie), 283
    Aam ka Custard (Mango Custard with Tropical
        Fruit), 327
    Aam ki Lassi (Mango and Yogurt Drink), 330
    Aam ki Launji (Sweet-and-Sour Mango
        Chutney), 318
    Thengai Chutney (Coconut and Tender Mango
        Chutney), 315–316
  shopping for, 61
marinating, techniques for, 72–76
masala, defined, 117
Masala Chai (Spiced Tea) recipe, 331
masala dabba. *See* spice tins

Masala Gosht (North Indian Lamb Curry) recipe, 175–176

Masala Omelet (Omelet with Spices) recipe, 274

masala sauce, varying base of, 141–143, 156

Masoor Dal (Brown Lentils with Coconut Milk) recipe, 259

meals

  contrasting flavors in, 164

  cooling, 160

  creating

    adding color, 156–157

    adding flavor, 164–167

    adding heat, 160–161

    adding texture, 157–159

    making menus for, 168–169

    overview, 156

    thali, 169–170

    varying temperatures, 159–160

    for weeknight dinners, 168

  eating desserts with, 169–170

  vegan and vegetarian, adding nutrition to, 25–26

measuring ingredients, 85

meat

  curries, batch cooking, 339

  overview, 173–174

  recipes containing

    Beef Vindaloo (Sour Hot Goan Curry), 183

    Bengali Chicken Korma (Chicken Curry with Cream), 199

    Bhuna Gosht (Brown Lamb Curry), 180

    Chicken 65 (Indo Chinese Chicken), 201

    Chicken Madras (Chicken Curry with Fennel), 197

    Chicken Tikka Masala (Chicken Curry with Spices), 194

    Coorgi-Style Pandi Curry (Pork Curry with Vinegar), 178

    Dhabe ka Kheema (Spicy Ground Lamb or Beef), 179

    Gosht ka Dalcha (Lamb and Lentil Curry), 177

    Hara Gosht (Lamb in a Green Herby Curry), 185

    Karahi Murgh (Chicken Curry with Tomatoes), 193

    Kerala Duck Mappas (Duck Curry with Coconut Milk and Pepper), 198

    Kheema Pulao (Spiced Rice with Ground Meat), 244

    Kofta Curry (Lamb or Beef Meatball Curry), 182

    Kombdi Batata (Chicken and Potato Curry), 192

    Konkani Mutton (Lamb Curry with Cloves, Pepper, and Coconut), 181

    Malabar Beef Roast (Deep, Dark Beef with Spices), 187

    Malvani Kombdi (Chicken and Coconut Curry), 196

    Masala Gosht (North Indian Lamb Curry), 175–176

    Murgh Makhani (Butter Chicken), 191

    Murgh Malaiwala (Chicken in a Creamy Cashew Nut and Saffron Curry), 190

    overview, 189

    Saag Murgh (Chicken Curry with Spinach), 200

    Safed Gosht (Lamb in a Coconut and Cashew Nut Curry), 186

    Sali Marghi (Chicken Curry with Apricots), 195

    Seyal Teevan (Lamb Chop Curry with Cardamom), 184

  shopping for, 62–63

meditation, as part of Ayurveda, 28

Meen Moilee (Salmon Curry with Mustard Seeds) recipe, 210

Methi Shakarkand (Fresh Fenugreek with Sweet Potatoes) recipe, 226

metric conversion guide, 355–358

migration, influence on Indian cuisine, 12

mint

  chopping, 69

  garnishing curries with, 148

  Gosht ke Kebab (Mini Lamb or Beef Skewers with Mint) recipe, 289

  Pudine aur Pyaz ki Chutney (Mint and Onion Chutney) recipe, 314

  storing, 58–59

mortar, pestle and, 43

Mughal, influences on Indian cuisine from, 12–13

Mumbai, influences on Indian cuisine from, 19–20

Mung Usal (Sprouted Mung Beans with Turmeric) recipe, 261–262

Murgh Makhani (Butter Chicken) recipe, 191

Murgh Malaiwala (Chicken in a Creamy Cashew Nut and Saffron Curry) recipe, 190

Muslim influence on cuisine, 18

mustard oil, marinating with, 76

mustard seeds

Carrot Poriyal (Carrots Cooked with Mustard Seeds and Coconut) recipe, 227

increasing heat levels in curries with, 139

Meen Moilee (Salmon Curry with Mustard Seeds) recipe, 210

shopping for, 48

mutton, 176

N

Naan (Leavened Oven-Baked Bread) recipe, 303

Neer Dosa (South Indian Rice Crêpes) recipe, 309

Nimbu Pani (Spiced Fresh Lemonade) recipe, 332

North Indian curry, order of ingredients in, 128–135

nuts

adding nutrition to vegan and vegetarian meals with, 25

garnishing curries with, 149–150

recipes containing

Chivda (Hot, Savory, and Sweet Mix of Grains, Seeds, and Nuts), 293

Hari Chutney (Cilantro and Peanut Chutney), 317

Kashmiri Pulao (Rice with Mushrooms, Dried Fruit, Nuts, and Spices), 238

Murgh Malaiwala (Chicken in a Creamy Cashew Nut and Saffron Curry), 190

Safed Gosht (Lamb in a Coconut and Cashew Nut Curry), 186

Shahi Baida Korma (Egg Curry with Cashew Nuts and Fenugreek), 268

shopping for, 49

O

Odisha, influences on Indian cuisine from, 16

oils

amounts to use when cooking, 127

with high smoke points, 126–127

shopping for, 56–58

used in food from restaurants versus home cooking, 176

Onion Bhajia (Savory Onion Fritters) recipe, 286

onions

adding to curries, 129–130, 136

carmelizing, 103

garnishing curries with, 148

Kachumber (Onion, Cucumber, Tomato, and Carrot Salad) recipe, 320

overview, 100

Pudine aur Pyaz ki Chutney (Mint and Onion Chutney) recipe, 314

slicing and dicing, 100–102

orange masala sauce, 142–143

P

Pakora (Savory Mixed Vegetable Fritters) recipe, 287

Palak Paneer (Spinach with Paneer) recipe, 225

Palak Pappu (South Indian Spinach Dal) recipe, 256

paneer

cooking instructions, 108–109

marinating time for, 74

recipes containing

Palak Paneer (Spinach with Paneer) recipe, 225

Paneer Makkai Simla Mirch (Paneer with Corn and Capsicum) recipe, 224

Paneer Pulao (Aromatic Rice with Indian Cottage Cheese) recipe, 241

shopping for, 55

Paneer Makkai Simla Mirch (Paneer with Corn and Capsicum) recipe, 224

Paneer Pulao (Aromatic Rice with Indian Cottage Cheese) recipe, 241

pans, 37–40, 342

papads. *See* popadams

Papeta Par Eeda (Egg and Potato Fry) recipe, 269

Paratha (Layered Bread) recipe, 304

paring, 69

Parsis, influences on Indian cuisine from, 19–20

passata, 53, 97

Pav Bhaji (Crushed Vegetable Curry with Bread Rolls) recipe, 296

peanuts
  adding texture and thickness to dishes with, 49, 150
  Hari Chutney (Cilantro and Peanut Chutney) recipe, 317
pearlspot, 18
peeler, types to buy, 36
peeling, techniques for, 69
pepper spice
  increasing heat levels in curries with, 138–139
  Konkani Mutton (Lamb Curry with Cloves, Pepper, and Coconut) recipe, 181
  shopping for, 48
  value of, 10
peppermills, types to buy, 43
pestle, mortar and, 43
pickles, shopping for, 51
pistachios, adding color and texture to meals with, 49, 149
Pitta, 27
plastic cutting boards, 34
Poha (Spiced Flaked Rice) recipe, 281
poha grain, shopping for, 48
Poori (Festive Fried Bread) recipe, 305
popadams, adding texture to meals with, 52, 157–159
pork, Coorgi-Style Pandi Curry (Pork Curry with Vinegar), 178
portions, 353
Portugual, influences on Indian cuisine from, 17–18
potatoes
  recipes containing
    Aloo Gobi (North Indian Potatoes with Cauliflower), 219–220
    Aloo Mutter (Pea and Potato Curry), 233
    Batata Bhaji (Spiced Yellow Potatoes), 282
    Kombdi Batata (Chicken and Potato Curry), 192
    Methi Shakarkand (Fresh Fenugreek with Sweet Potatoes), 226
    Papeta Par Eeda (Egg and Potato Fry), 269

    Shakarkand Chaat (Sweet Potatoes with Nuts and Yogurt), 299
  shopping for, 60–61
pots, 37–40
poultry
  marinating time for, 73
  overview, 189
  recipes containing
    Bengali Chicken Korma (Chicken Curry with Cream), 199
    Chicken 65 (Indo Chinese Chicken), 201
    Chicken Biryani (Festive One-Pot Chicken and Rice), 239–240
    Chicken Madras (Chicken Curry with Fennel), 197
    Chicken Tikka Masala (Chicken Curry with Spices), 194
    Chicken Tikka (Spicy Chicken Bites) recipe, 288
    Karahi Murgh (Chicken Curry with Tomatoes), 193
    Kerala Duck Mappas (Duck Curry with Coconut Milk and Pepper), 198
    Kombdi Batata (Chicken and Potato Curry), 192
    Malvani Kombdi (Chicken and Coconut Curry), 196
    Murgh Makhani (Butter Chicken), 191
    Murgh Malaiwala (Chicken in a Creamy Cashew Nut and Saffron Curry), 190
    Saag Murgh (Chicken Curry with Spinach), 200
    Sali Marghi (Chicken Curry with Apricots), 195
  shopping for, 62–63
Prawn Patia (Sweet and Sour Shrimp Curry) recipe, 215
predominant flavors, balancing in meals, 165–167
pressure cookers, saving time with, 38, 40, 340–341
produce, shopping for, 57–58
Pudine aur Pyaz ki Chutney (Mint and Onion Chutney) recipe, 314
Pune, influences on Indian cuisine from, 20
pungent taste, description of, 29
Punjab, influences on Indian cuisine from, 13–14

R

raisins, adding color and texture to meals with, 52, 150

raita, cooling hot meals by adding, 160

Rajma Masala (Red Bean Curry) recipe, 254

Rava Utappam (Semolina Pancakes) recipe, 278

raw foods, cooking for easier digestion, 28

recipes, standardizing, 84

red masala sauce, 142–143

religious beliefs, influence on Indian cuisine, 11–12, 17, 176

restaurant food, home cooking versus, 154–156

rice

  cooking properly, 86–89

  recipes containing

    Channa Pulao (Brown Rice with Chickpeas), 246

    Chicken Biryani (Festive One-Pot Chicken and Rice), 239–240

    Egg Biryani (South Indian Spiced Rice with Eggs), 243

    Jeera Pulao (Cumin-Flavored Rice), 237

    Jhinga Pulao (Spiced Rice with Shrimp), 242

    Kashmiri Pulao (Rice with Mushrooms, Dried Fruit, Nuts, and Spices), 238

    Kheema Pulao (Spiced Rice with Ground Meat), 244

    Khichdi (Warming Rice and Lentil Stew), 247

    overview, 235–236

    Paneer Pulao (Aromatic Rice with Indian Cottage Cheese), 241

    Sunhera Pulao (Golden Turmeric Rice), 245

  washing, 86–87

richness, compensating for, 140

right hand, eating solely with, 350

ritucharya, defined, 31

rolling pin, types to buy, 35–36

rotis

  Chapati or Roti (Flatbread) recipe, 302

  defined, 346

S

Saag Murgh (Chicken Curry with Spinach) recipe, 200

Safed Gosht (Lamb in a Coconut and Cashew Nut Curry) recipe, 186

saffron

  batch cooking, 339

  Kesar Kulfi (Rich Saffron Ice Cream) recipe, 325

  shopping for, 48

salads

  adding texture to meals with, 159

  cooling hot meals by adding, 160

  Gujarati Sambharo (Cabbage and Carrot Salad) recipe, 321

  Kachumber (Onion, Cucumber, Tomato, and Carrot Salad) recipe, 320

  Kheere Tamater ka Raita (Cucumber and Tomato Salad with Yogurt) recipe, 319

  overview, 311

Sali Marghi (Chicken Curry with Apricots) recipe, 195

salt

  adding to curries, 133–134

  balancing in meals, 166–167

  description of, 29

  in food from restaurants versus home cooking, 155

Sambhar (South Indian Lentil Stew) recipe, 255

Sambhar Powder (South Indian Spice Blend) recipe, 119

samosas

  folding, 291

  Vegetable Samosas (Vegetable and Pastry Parcels), 290–291

sauce, for curries, 124

seafood

  marinating time for, 74

  recipes containing

    Amritsari Fish (Spiced Fish Fingers in a Gram-Flour Crust), 300

    Bangda Ghassi (Mackerel Curry with Tamarind), 208

Goan Fish Curry (Fish Curry with Coriander Seeds and Coconut), 211–212

Jhinga Masala (North Indian Shrimp Curry), 214

Khekda Masaledaar (Crab Curry with Pepper), 207

Kolmbi Fry (Fried Spiced Shrimp), 209

Kolmbichi Kadhi (Shrimp Curry with Coconut Milk), 206

Kube Sukke (Clams in a Coconut Crust), 213

Lobster Kalvan (Lobster Curry), 216

Macchi ke Cutlet (Spiced Fishcakes) recipe, 298

Meen Moilee (Salmon Curry with Mustard Seeds), 210

overview, 203–204

Prawn Patia (Sweet and Sour Shrimp Curry), 215

Tilapia Fry (Spicy Fried Fish), 205

searing, 132

seasonal eating, 28

seeds

  adding nutrition to vegan and vegetarian meals with, 25

  Chivda (Hot, Savory, and Sweet Mix of Grains, Seeds, and Nuts) recipe, 293

  frying, 112–113

  Goan Fish Curry (Fish Curry with Coriander Seeds and Coconut) recipe, 211–212

  ground, cooking with, 136

  mustard

    Carrot Poriyal (Carrots Cooked with Mustard Seeds and Coconut) recipe, 227

    increasing heat levels in curries with, 139

    Meen Moilee (Salmon Curry with Mustard Seeds) recipe, 210

    shopping for, 48

  spices, 112–114, 128–129, 136

  toasting, 113–114

semolina

  Rava Utappam (Semolina Pancakes) recipe, 278

  shopping for, 48

  Sooji ka Halva (Warm Semolina and Raisin Pudding) recipe, 326

  Upma (Savory Semolina Cake) recipe, 275

serrated knives, 34

Seyal Teevan (Lamb Chop Curry with Cardamom) recipe, 184

Shahi Baida Korma (Egg Curry with Cashew Nuts and Fenugreek) recipe, 268

Shakarkand Chaat (Sweet Potatoes with Nuts and Yogurt) recipe, 299

Shankarpali (Crisp, Sweet Pastry Diamonds) recipe, 292

Shepuchi Bhaji (Dill with Mung Lentils) recipe, 232

shrimp

  cleaning and deveining techniques, 71–72

  recipes containing

    Jhinga Masala (North Indian Shrimp Curry), 214

    Jhinga Pulao (Spiced Rice with Shrimp), 242

    Kolmbi Fry (Fried Spiced Shrimp), 209

    Kolmbichi Kadhi (Shrimp Curry with Coconut Milk), 206

    Prawn Patia (Sweet and Sour Shrimp Curry), 215

side dishes, adding nutrition to vegan and vegetarian meals with, 26

sieve, types to buy, 37

Sindhis, influences on Indian cuisine from, 20

sky-drinking, 351

slicing, techniques for, 69–71

smoke points, 126–127

snacks

  Amritsari Fish (Spiced Fish Fingers in a Gram-Flour Crust) recipe, 300

  Bombay Sandwich (Sandwich with Chutney, Vegetables, and Cheese) recipe, 297

  Chicken Tikka (Spicy Chicken Bites) recipe, 288

  Chivda (Hot, Savory, and Sweet Mix of Grains, Seeds, and Nuts) recipe, 293

  cooling hot meals by adding, 160

  Dahi Vada (Lentil Fritters in Yogurt) recipe, 294–295

  Gosht ke Kebab (Mini Lamb or Beef Skewers with Mint) recipe, 289

  Macchi ke Cutlet (Spiced Fishcakes) recipe, 298

  Onion Bhajia (Savory Onion Fritters) recipe, 286

  overview, 285

snacks *(continued)*

    Pakora (Savory Mixed Vegetable Fritters) recipe, 287

    Pav Bhaji (Crushed Vegetable Curry with Bread Rolls) recipe, 296

    Shakarkand Chaat (Sweet Potatoes with Nuts and Yogurt) recipe, 299

    Shankarpali (Crisp, Sweet Pastry Diamonds) recipe, 292

    Vegetable Samosas (Vegetable and Pastry Parcels) recipe, 290–291

Sooji ka Halva (Warm Semolina and Raisin Pudding) recipe, 326

sour taste

    balancing in meals, 166

    compensating for, 141

    description of, 29

    recipes with

        Baghara Baingan (Sweet-and-Sour Eggplant Curry), 222

        Beef Vindaloo (Sour Hot Goan Curry), 183

        Khajur Imli ki Chutney (Sweet-and-Sour Date and Tamarind Chutney), 313

        Lasnechi Chutney (Dry Hot, Sour, Sweet Garlic, Chile, and Coconut Chutney), 163

        Prawn Patia (Sweet and Sour Shrimp Curry), 215

South Indian curry, order of ingredients in, 135–137

spice grinder, types to buy, 43

spice mill, types to buy, 42

spice seeds, adding to curries, 128–129, 136

spice tins, storing spices in, 41–42

spices

    adding to curries, 134–135

    Amritsari Fish (Spiced Fish Fingers in a Gram-Flour Crust) recipe, 300

    Baingan ka Bharta (Fire-Roasted Eggplant with Spices) recipe, 218–219

    Batata Bhaji (Spiced Yellow Potatoes) recipe, 282

    blends of

        batch cooking, 339

        Chaat Masala (Finishing Mix for Sprinkling over Snacks), 121

        Garam Masala (North Indian Spice Blend), 118

        overview, 117

        Sambhar Powder (South Indian Spice Blend), 119

        Tandoori Masala (Rub for Grilled Foods), 120

    burning, 113

    Chicken Tikka Masala (Chicken Curry with Spices) recipe, 194

    Chile Toast (Cheese Toast with Spices) recipe, 276

    Egg Biryani (South Indian Spiced Rice with Eggs) recipe, 243

    exportation of, 10–11

    foreign influences on, 11–12

    garnishing curries with, 150

    Goan Fish Curry (Fish Curry with Coriander Seeds and Coconut) recipe, 211–212

    ground, cooking with, 114–117, 131

    improving quality of, 116–117

    Jeera Pulao (Cumin-Flavored Rice) recipe, 237

    Jhinga Pulao (Spiced Rice with Shrimp) recipe, 242

    Kashmiri Pulao (Rice with Mushrooms, Dried Fruit, Nuts, and Spices) recipe, 238

    Kheema Pulao (Spiced Rice with Ground Meat) recipe, 244

    Kobichi Bhaji (Cabbage with Peas and Turmeric) recipe, 221

    Kolmbi Fry (Fried Spiced Shrimp) recipe, 209

    Konkani Mutton (Lamb Curry with Cloves, Pepper, and Coconut) recipe, 181

    Macchi ke Cutlet (Spiced Fishcakes) recipe, 298

    Malabar Beef Roast (Deep, Dark Beef with Spices) recipe, 187

    Masala Chai (Spiced Tea) recipe, 331

    measuring, 85

    Mung Usal (Sprouted Mung Beans with Turmeric) recipe, 261–262

    Nimbu Pani (Spiced Fresh Lemonade) recipe, 332

    overview, 40, 111

    Poha (Spiced Flaked Rice) recipe, 281

    Sambhar Powder (South Indian Spice Blend) recipe, 119

    seeds of, 112–114

shopping for, 46–48

storing, 41–42, 338

Sunhera Pulao (Golden Turmeric Rice) recipe, 245

Tarka Dal (Spiced lentils) recipe, 251

tools for blending and crushing, 42–43

spiciness. *See* heat

sprouting jars, sprouting legumes with, 262

stable oils, shopping for, 57–58

stirring intermittently, 68, 77

stuffed paratha, rolling and folding, 307

sultanas, adding color and texture to meals with, 52, 150

sunflower oil, 57

Sunhera Pulao (Golden Turmeric Rice) recipe, 245

sweet ingredients, adding to curries, 136–137

sweet pickles, 51

sweet taste

  balancing in meals, 165

  compensating for, 141

  description of, 29

T

table etiquette, 349–354

tadka technique. *See* tarka technique

talna technique, 80–81

tamarind

  Bangda Ghassi (Mackerel Curry with Tamarind) recipe, 208

  cooking with, 93–95

  description of, 50

  Khajur Imli ki Chutney (Sweet-and-Sour Date and Tamarind Chutney) recipe, 313

  pulp, extracting, 94

tandoori

  restaurant-style, 75–76

  Tandoori Masala (Rub for Grilled Foods) recipe, 120

Tandoori Masala (Rub for Grilled Foods) recipe, 120

tandoors, 13–14

Tarka Dal (Spiced lentils) recipe, 251

tarka technique, 77–79

taste, flavor versus, 164

taste-testing, 135

tasting spoons, 351

tava, 38–39

tea

  foreign influences on, 15

  Masala Chai (Spiced Tea) recipe, 331

tea infuser, types to buy, 36

temperatures, varying in meals, 159–160

tempering technique. *See* tarka technique

temple foods, influences on Indian cuisine from, 19

texture, adding to meals, 157–159

textured vegetable protein, adding nutrition to vegan and vegetarian meals with, 25

thali, 169–170

Thengai Chutney (Coconut and Tender Mango Chutney) recipe, 315–316

Thepla (Fenugreek Bread) recipe, 308

thick curry, thinning, 144–145

tikka meat, 70

Tilapia Fry (Spicy Fried Fish) recipe, 205

time-saving tips, 337–342

toasting popadams, 158

toasting spice seeds, 113–114

tofu, substituting for paneer, 55

tomatoes

  adding to curries, 132

  Bombay Anda Curry (Smooth Egg and Tomato Curry) recipes, 266

  cooking with, 95–97

  grating, 95–96

  Kachumber (Onion, Cucumber, Tomato, and Carrot Salad) recipe, 320

  shopping for, 52–53

tomato paste, 53, 97

turmeric

  recipes containing

    Haldi Gajar Mirchi ka Achaar (Fresh Carrot, Turmeric, Ginger, and Chile Pickle), 162

    Kobichi Bhaji (Cabbage with Peas and Turmeric), 221

    Mung Usal (Sprouted Mung Beans with Turmeric), 261–262

    Sunhera Pulao (Golden Turmeric Rice), 245

  shopping for, 48

U

Upma (Savory Semolina Cake) recipe, 275

utensils, 33–37

V

vegan dishes

  Aloo Gobi (North Indian Potatoes with Cauliflower) recipe, 219–220

  Aloo Mutter (Pea and Potato Curry) recipe, 233

  Baghara Baingan (Sweet-and-Sour Eggplant Curry) recipe, 222

  Baingan ka Bharta (Fire-Roasted Eggplant with Spices) recipe, 218–219

  Beans Upkari (French Green Beans with Chile and Coconut) recipe, 230

  Bharvan Bhindi (Okra Stuffed with Spices) recipe, 228

  Carrot Poriyal (Carrots Cooked with Mustard Seeds and Coconut) recipe, 227

  Channa Masala (Chickpea Curry) recipe, 253

  Dal Dhokli (Lentil Stew with Flour Dumplings) recipe, 257–258

  Dal Makhani (Creamy Black Beans with Garlic) recipe, 252

  Fanshachi Bhaji (Curried Young Jackfruit) recipe, 229

  Kaddu ki Subzi (Sweet-and-Sour Pumpkin) recipe, 231

  Kadhi (Chickpea Flour and Yogurt Curry) recipe, 260

  Kerala Vegetable Curry (Mixed Vegetable Curry with Coconut Milk) recipe, 223

  Kobichi Bhaji (Cabbage with Peas and Turmeric) recipe, 221

  Masoor Dal (Brown Lentils with Coconut Milk) recipe, 259

  Methi Shakarkand (Fresh Fenugreek with Sweet Potatoes) recipe, 226

  Mung Usal (Sprouted Mung Beans with Turmeric) recipe, 261–262

  overview, 217, 249–250

  Palak Paneer (Spinach with Paneer) recipe, 225

  Palak Pappu (South Indian Spinach Dal) recipe, 256

  Paneer Makkai Simla Mirch (Paneer with Corn and Capsicum) recipe, 224

  Rajma Masala (Red Bean Curry) recipe, 254

  Sambhar (South Indian Lentil Stew) recipe, 255

  Shepuchi Bhaji (Dill with Mung Lentils) recipe, 232

  Tarka Dal (Spiced lentils) recipe, 251

veganism

  creating meals, 24–26

  determining nutritional requirements, 25

  incorporating Ayurveda in

    identifying rasa, 29–31

    overview, 26–27

    rules of Ayurvedic diet, 27–29

    seasonal eating, 31–32

  origins of, 24

  overview, 23

vegetable ghee, 56

Vegetable Samosas (Vegetable and Pastry Parcels) recipe, 290–291

vegetables. *See also vegetables by name*

  garnishing curries with, 149

  marinating time for, 74

  recipes containing

    Bombay Sandwich (Sandwich with Chutney, Vegetables, and Cheese), 297

    Kachumber (Onion, Cucumber, Tomato, and Carrot Salad), 320

Kerala Vegetable Curry (Mixed Vegetable Curry with Coconut Milk), 223

Pakora (Savory Mixed Vegetable Fritters), 287

Pav Bhaji (Crushed Vegetable Curry with Bread Rolls), 296

Vegetable Samosas (Vegetable and Pastry Parcels), 290–291

vegetarian dishes

Aloo Gobi (North Indian Potatoes with Cauliflower) recipe, 219–220

Aloo Mutter (Pea and Potato Curry) recipe, 233

Baghara Baingan (Sweet-and-Sour Eggplant Curry) recipe, 222

Baingan ka Bharta (Fire-Roasted Eggplant with Spices) recipe, 218–219

Beans Upkari (French Green Beans with Chile and Coconut) recipe, 230

Bharvan Bhindi (Okra Stuffed with Spices) recipe, 228

Carrot Poriyal (Carrots Cooked with Mustard Seeds and Coconut) recipe, 227

Channa Masala (Chickpea Curry) recipe, 253

Dal Dhokli (Lentil Stew with Flour Dumplings) recipe, 257–258

Dal Makhani (Creamy Black Beans with Garlic) recipe, 252

Fanshachi Bhaji (Curried Young Jackfruit) recipe, 229

Kaddu ki Subzi (Sweet-and-Sour Pumpkin) recipe, 231

Kadhi (Chickpea Flour and Yogurt Curry) recipe, 260

Kerala Vegetable Curry (Mixed Vegetable Curry with Coconut Milk) recipe, 223

Kobichi Bhaji (Cabbage with Peas and Turmeric) recipe, 221

Masoor Dal (Brown Lentils with Coconut Milk) recipe, 259

Methi Shakarkand (Fresh Fenugreek with Sweet Potatoes) recipe, 226

Mung Usal (Sprouted Mung Beans with Turmeric) recipe, 261–262

overview, 217, 249–250

Palak Paneer (Spinach with Paneer) recipe, 225

Palak Pappu (South Indian Spinach Dal) recipe, 256

Paneer Makkai Simla Mirch (Paneer with Corn and Capsicum) recipe, 224

Rajma Masala (Red Bean Curry) recipe, 254

Sambhar (South Indian Lentil Stew) recipe, 255

Shepuchi Bhaji (Dill with Mung Lentils) recipe, 232

Tarka Dal (Spiced lentils) recipe, 251

vegetarianism

creating meals, 24–26

determining nutritional requirements, 25

incorporating Ayurveda in

identifying rasa, 29–31

overview, 26–27

rules of Ayurvedic diet, 27–29

seasonal eating, 31–32

origins of, 24

overview, 23

W

walnuts, adding texture and thickness to dishes with, 49

watery curry, thickening, 144–145

waxy potatoes, 60–61

weeknight dinners, creating meals for, 168

white masala sauce, 141–142

whole-milk yogurt, 55

wooden cutting boards, 34

Y

yellow masala sauce, 142

yoga, as part of Ayurveda, 28

yogurt

Aam ki Lassi (Mango and Yogurt Drink) recipe, 330

cooling hot meals by adding, 160

Dahi Vada (Lentil Fritters in Yogurt) recipe, 294–295

feeding children, 31

garnishing curries with, 150–151

Kadhi (Chickpea Flour and Yogurt Curry) recipe, 260

Kheere Tamater ka Raita (Cucumber and Tomato Salad with Yogurt) recipe, 319

shopping for, 54–55

About the Author

Monisha Bharadwaj is an award-winning author, chef, and food historian based in London. She has written 16 books and received numerous awards including a writing award from the Guild of Food Writers and most recently from the Gourmand World Cookbook Awards for the Best Indian Cookbook of 2020. She is often invited to be a guest on TV and radio both in Europe and in the United States and has been a judge on *Iron Chef America*. She regularly speaks on BBC Radio 4's *The Food Programme* and was a part of their show on turmeric, which won the Fortnum & Mason Award 2018.

Monisha is a qualified chef from the prestigious Institute of Hotel Management in Mumbai. She runs one of the UK's top Indian cooking schools, Cooking With Monisha, where she has been teaching her brand of simple, healthy cooking since 2006. She has curated and run Indian courses at some of the UK's best cooking schools and has been a guest chef at numerous venues including a Michelin-starred restaurant in London and at a luncheon for the vice president of India. She also holds a BA in Indian history and has been invited to present talks on topics such as Indian vegetarianism, the six tastes of Ayurveda, and how the British fell in love with curry for institutions such as SOAS University of London, the British Council, and the CIA at Copia.

Dedication

For my children, Arrush and India, in celebration of all the fabulous food journeys we've taken and in anticipation of those that are yet to come.

Author's Acknowledgments

This book was written during the lockdown in the UK when COVID-19 changed the way we worked and communicated.

A big thank-you to my acquisitions editor, Tracy Boggier, for making working across continents seamless and for being there at all times. I appreciate the guidance given by Vicki Adang in getting the first steps right, as they're so crucial in the process. Elizabeth Kuball, my editor, brought experience and detail, making the book flow more easily. Thank you for bringing it together so beautifully. Recipe testing was done meticulously by Rachel Nix — I am thankful for her contribution and I hope it was fun! A tip of the hat to the photographers Wendy Jo Peterson and Geri Goodale and to the illustrator Elizabeth Kurtzman — I love their work! Writing a book is a team effort, so I'm sending a million thanks across the pond to the team at Wiley who made this book what it is.

A special thank-you to my son Arrush Bharadwaj for reading through the first draft and adding his unique wit and humor. Big thanks to my daughter, India Bharadwaj, for creating the first draft of the artwork for me. With my limited drawing skills, I wouldn't trust myself to get across what I wanted to say. Many thanks to Bob, for helping me find balance between work and family time and for being supportive when the former took precedence.

Publisher's Acknowledgments

Senior Acquisitions Editor: Tracy Boggier

Project Editor: Elizabeth Kuball

Copy Editor: Elizabeth Kuball

Recipe Tester: Rachel Nix

Production Editor: Mohammed Zafar Ali

Photographers: Wendy Jo Peterson and Geri Goodale

Cover Image: © Wendy Jo Peterson and Geri Goodale

Illustrated by: Liz Kurtzman

Leverage the power

Dummies is the global leader in the reference category and one of the most trusted and highly regarded brands in the world. No longer just focused on books, customers now have access to the dummies content they need in the format they want. Together we'll craft a solution that engages your customers, stands out from the competition, and helps you meet your goals.

Advertising & Sponsorships

Connect with an engaged audience on a powerful multimedia site, and position your message alongside expert how-to content. Dummies.com is a one-stop shop for free, online information and know-how curated by a team of experts.

- Targeted ads
- Video
- Email Marketing
- Microsites
- Sweepstakes sponsorship

20 MILLION PAGE VIEWS EVERY SINGLE MONTH

15 MILLION UNIQUE VISITORS PER MONTH

43% OF ALL VISITORS ACCESS THE SITE VIA THEIR MOBILE DEVICES

700,000 NEWSLETTER SUBSCRIPTIONS TO THE INBOXES OF *300,000* UNIQUE INDIVIDUALS EVERY WEEK

# of dummies

Custom Publishing

Reach a global audience in any language by creating a solution that will differentiate you from competitors, amplify your message, and encourage customers to make a buying decision.

- Apps
- Books
- eBooks
- Video
- Audio
- Webinars

Brand Licensing & Content

Leverage the strength of the world's most popular reference brand to reach new audiences and channels of distribution.

For more information, visit **dummies.com/biz**

PERSONAL ENRICHMENT

Staying Sharp
9781119187790
USA $26.00
CAN $31.99
UK £19.99

Facebook
Carolyn Abram
9781119179030
USA $21.99
CAN $25.99
UK £16.99

Guitar
Mark Phillips
Jon Chappell
9781119293354
USA $24.99
CAN $29.99
UK £17.99

Investing
Eric Tyson, MBA
9781119293347
USA $22.99
CAN $27.99
UK £16.99

Beekeeping
Howland Blackiston
9781119310068
USA $22.99
CAN $27.99
UK £16.99

Digital Photography
Julie Adair King
9781119235606
USA $24.99
CAN $29.99
UK £17.99

Meditation
Stephan Bodian
9781119251163
USA $24.99
CAN $29.99
UK £17.99

Pregnancy
ALL-IN-ONE
6 Books in one
9781119235491
USA $26.99
CAN $31.99
UK £19.99

Samsung Galaxy S7
Bill Hughes
9781119279952
USA $24.99
CAN $29.99
UK £17.99

iPhone
Edward C. Baig
Bob "Dr. Mac" LeVitus
9781119283133
USA $24.99
CAN $29.99
UK £17.99

Crocheting
Karen Manthey
Susan Brittain
9781119287117
USA $24.99
CAN $29.99
UK £16.99

Nutrition
Carol Ann Rinzler
9781119130246
USA $22.99
CAN $27.99
UK £16.99

PROFESSIONAL DEVELOPMENT

Windows 10
Andy Rathbone
9781119311041
USA $24.99
CAN $29.99
UK £17.99

AutoCAD
Bill Fane
9781119255796
USA $39.99
CAN $47.99
UK £27.99

Excel 2016
Greg Harvey, PhD
9781119293439
USA $26.99
CAN $31.99
UK £19.99

QuickBooks 2017
Stephen L. Nelson, MBA, CPA, MS in Taxation
9781119281467
USA $26.99
CAN $31.99
UK £19.99

macOS Sierra
Bob "Dr. Mac" LeVitus
9781119280651
USA $29.99
CAN $35.99
UK £21.99

LinkedIn
Joel Elad, MBAs
9781119251132
USA $24.99
CAN $29.99
UK £17.99

Windows 10
ALL-IN-ONE
10 Books
Woody Leonhard
9781119310563
USA $34.00
CAN $41.99
UK £24.99

SharePoint 2016
Rosemarie Withee
Ken Withee
9781119181705
USA $29.99
CAN $35.99
UK £21.99

Fundamental Analysis
Matt Krantz
9781119263593
USA $26.99
CAN $31.99
UK £19.99

Networking
Doug Lowe
9781119257769
USA $29.99
CAN $35.99
UK £21.99

Office 2016
Wallace Wang
9781119293477
USA $26.99
CAN $31.99
UK £19.99

Office 365
Rosemarie Withee
Ken Withee
Jennifer Reed
9781119265313
USA $24.99
CAN $29.99
UK £17.99

Salesforce.com
Liz Kao
Jon Paz
9781119239314
USA $29.99
CAN $35.99
UK £21.99

Coding
Nikhil Abraham
9781119293323
USA $29.99
CAN $35.99
UK £21.99